K

DESCARTES'S THEORY OF ACTION

BRILL'S STUDIES
IN
INTELLECTUAL HISTORY

VOLUME 142

DESCARTES'S THEORY OF ACTION

BY

ANNE ASHLEY DAVENPORT

BRILL

LEIDEN · BOSTON

2006

Cover illustration: Saint Jeanne de Chantal in Meditation, by Elvire Jan (School of Manessier), 1975. Ink on wood. Private collection. Photo Leon Golub.

This book is printed on acid-free paper.

Library of Congress Cataloging-in-Publication Data

Davenport, Anne Ashley.
    Descartes's theory of action / by Anne Davenport.
        p. cm. — (Brill's studies in intellectual history, ISSN 0920-8607 ; v. 142)
    Includes bibliographical references and index.
    ISBN-13: 978-90-04-15205-2 (hardback : alk. paper)
    ISBN-10: 90-04-15205-9 (hardback : alk. paper)
        1. Descartes, René, 1596-1650. 2. Act (Philosophy) I. Title. II. Series.

    B1878.A27D38 2006
    128'.4092—dc22

                                                            2006043935

ISSN   0920-8607
ISBN-13: 978-90-04-15205-2
ISBN-10: 90-04-15205-9

PRINTED IN THE NETHERLANDS

Cust/Add: 158330000/04   POKC-N   OKANAGAN COLLEGE LIBRARY

Cust PO No.   2073   **Cust Ord Date:**   22-Aug-2006

BBS Order No: E614140   Ln:1   Del: 1   **BBS Ord Date:**   22-Aug-2006

9004152059-27353373   **Sales Qty:** 1   **#Vols:** 001

(9789004152052)

Descartes's theory of action

Subtitle: Stmt of Resp: by Anne Ashley Davenport.

HARDBACK   **Pub Year:** 2006   **Vol No.:**   Edition:

Davenport, Anne Ashley.   **Ser. Title:**

Brill Academic Publishers

Acc Mat:

Tech Services Charges:

Barcode Label   Spine Label Protector US

Base Charge Processing   Spine Label BBS US

Property Stamp US

Security Device US

Cust Fund Code: HSP   **Cust Location:** Acquisitions

Stock Category: **Cust Dept:**

Order Line Notes

Notes to Vendor

Blackwell's Book Services

To Leon, *sidereus nuncius*

CONTENTS

PREFACE

The present book has one, simple goal: to argue that Descartes's most fundamental discovery is not the discovery of the epistemologic subject, but the discovery of the underlying free agent without whom no epistemologic subject is possible. The Cartesian *cogito*, the leverage point that sets the world in motion, is not primarily the perception that "I perceive" but the perception that "I act." Action and the perception of acting, Descartes says, form a single mental event or *cogitatio*. The idea by means of which the agent is aware of acting does not differ from the action itself.[1] Put simply, in the first-person as Descartes would put it, I cannot act deliberately without knowing that I am the sole cause and origin of my action. Action reveals me to myself and reveals that my faculty of free will is *nota per se*, not derived or derivable from anything prior to it.[2]

1. *Philosophical aspects*

What are the philosophical implications of interpreting the Cartesian *cogito* to mean "I *act*, therefore I am"? First, the focus is shifted from epistemology to moral philosophy—from the question "how do I *know* things"? to the question: "why and for what purpose do I *cause* things"? The thesis of the present book is that Descartes's *cogito* is best compared, not to Kant's apperception, but to John Searle's notion of "intention in action," which is, simply, the experience of acting.[3] Citing Wittgenstein's

---

[1] Letter to Mersenne, January 28, in Oeuvres de Descartes, C. Adam et P. Tannery eds., Paris 1891–1912 [henceforth AT] III, 295: 1641, AT III, 295: "Nous ne sçaurions rien vouloir, sans sçavoir que nous le voulons, ny le sçavoir que par une idée; mais ie ne mets point que cette idée soit differente de l'action mesme."

[2] To Mersenne, December, 1640, AT III, 259: "Vous avez raison de dire que nous sommes aussi assurez de nostre libre Arbitre que d'aucune autre notion premiere; car c'en est veritablement une."

[3] John Searle, *Intentionality* (Cambridge, UK: Cambridge U. Press, 1983), 91: "The action, for example, of raising one's arm, contains two components, the experience of acting (which has a form of Intentionality that is both representational and causal), and

famous question, Searle argues that the agent's "intention in action" defines "what is left over if, when I raise my arm, I subtract the fact that my arm goes up."[4]

The differences between Searle and Descartes are as revealing as the similarities. Unlike Searle, Descartes draws a sharp distinction between deliberate actions that depend immediately on the rational will and habits that reflect empirically conditioned instincts. Descartes is a rationalist with regard to human actions precisely because he is a behaviorist with regard to animal motions. Not all human actions, moreover, are deliberate: according to Descartes, when we walk around or eat, we rarely think about what we are doing.[5] Thus while Searle applies the notion of "intention in action" equally to animals and human beings,[6] Descartes jealously restricts agency to human beings. Descartes's favorite example of distinctly human actions are speech acts. Animals may be trained to respond to stimuli with sounds, but only human beings, in Descartes's view, have the faculty of uttering inexhaustibly meaningful sound-sequences that are neither determined by stimuli nor random.[7] While we may scratch an itch as a matter of habit, without thinking, we cannot refrain from it, or suspend our judgment, or initiate a series of contingent events, except through a deliberate mobilization of agency that we ourselves and we alone bring about.

A second philosophical aspect of Descartes's theory of action concerns the central importance of inner action. To Descartes, the critical class of human actions is the subset of actions in which nothing physical intervenes or occurs. Searle's analysis, once again, helps to clarify the importance of this point. Like Descartes, Searle admits purely mental actions. The two examples that Searle cites, among others, to establish that mental actions count as *bona fide* actions, turn out to play a vital role in Descartes's theory. Searle cites, first, the action of refraining from physical action:

---

the event of one's arm going up. The Intentional content of the intention in action and the experience of acting are identical."

[4] Ludwig Wittengenstein, *Philosophical Investigations* (Oxford: Basil Blackwell, 1953), I, paragraph 621; cited and discussed by Searle in *Intentionality*, 16.

[5] To Newcastle, November 23, 1646, AT IV, 573, Descartes writes of "actions qui ne sont pas conduite par nostre pensée; car il arrive souvent que nous marchons et que nous mangeons, sans penser en aucune façon à ce que nous faisons."

[6] Searle, *Intentionality*, 101.

[7] Citing Noam Chomsky, *Language and Thought* (Wakefield, Rhode Island, and London: Moyer Bell, 1993), 36–37.

"It is easy to extend the account to actions where there is no bodily
movement or where only a mental act is performed. If, for example, I
am told to hold still and I comply, the relevant content of my intention
in action will be 'that this intention in action causes it to be the case that
there is no bodily movement'."[8]

Searle's analysis bolsters Descartes's claim that the paradigmatic case
of refraining from acting is witholding assent.[9] In the Cartesian case, a
mental action inhibits a second mental action rather than a physical
action. Descartes, in effect, argues that the relevant content of my
intention in action when I withold assent is "that this intention in action
causes it to be the case that my assent not be given."

Searle's second example describes what Descartes would call "guided
imagination"—a technique abundantly used in the Ignatian Exercises
practiced at *La Flèche*, where Descartes was schooled:

"If, for example, I am asked to form a mental image of the Eiffel tower
and I comply, the relevant portion of the intention in action will be (that
this intention in action causes me to have a mental image of the Eiffel
tower)."[10]

Thought experiments, such as supposing that I am the victim of a malicious deceiver, are deliberately conducted, not incurred. They result
from mental actions and imply an agent. Both of Searle's examples of
mental actions imply an immediate awareness of inner effort, or at least
an awareness of interrupting a passive chain of events by a deliberate
interference. Descartes will appeal to the experience of inner effort to
argue that thought-experiments and the voluntary suspension of judgment imply an immaterial principle in human being, radically distinct
from material principles.

Finally, a chief claim of the present book is that interpreting the
Cartesian *cogito* to mean "I *act*, therefore I am" solves the chronic problem of how to extract the concept of a first-person *ego* from the awareness of "thought." As Bertrand Russell, following a long line of critics,
points out, the most Descartes has the right to claim is that 'there is
thought,' not that *I* think.[11] More recently, the problem has been vig-
orously outlined by Peter Markie[12] and treated with great ingenuity by

---

[8] Searle, *Intentionality*, 102.
[9] Cf. Interview with Berman, AT V, 159: "Jam autem nos intime conscii sumus
nostrae libertatis, et nos ita posse cohibere assensum, cum volumus."
[10] Searle, *Intentionality*, 103.
[11] Russell, *History of Western Philosophy* (New York: Simon and Schuster, 1945), 567.
[12] "The Cogito and its Importance," in John Cottingham, ed., *The Cambridge Compan-*

Thomas Vinci, who proposes a model of the *cogito*, the "intuitive cogito," which includes the assumption of the two-level property "*actual-
ized thinking belonging to me*".[13] The present book argues that interpreting
Descartes's *cogito* correctly as "I *act*, therefore I am" makes the problem
disappear. We will see that the experience of acting is inherently the
experience of acting "in the first-person."

2. *Historical context*

Quite apart from the goal of revising current interpretations of the
Cartesian *cogito*, the present book hopes to place Descartes's theory of
action in a new historical context. To date, a fair amount of scholarship
has been devoted to Descartes's scholastic roots.[14] Descartes's doctrine
of *générosité* has been successfully tied to Stoic and Peripatetic ideals of
the good life.[15] Even the possibility of Neoplatonic roots has recently
been defended with regard to Descartes's notion of God as *causa sui*.[16]
But apart from Amélie Rorty's seminal essay on "The Structure of
Descartes's *Meditations*," comparatively little effort has been spent on
connecting Descartes to the most immediate and pressing context of
his generation, namely to the Catholic Reformation.

The present book argues that Descartes's theory of action belongs,
historically, to the wave of interest in lay orthopraxy that marks the
first quarter of the XVIIth century generally and the "French School"
in particular. Partly to co-opt some of the legitimate initiatives of the
Protestant Reform, the "French School" of spirituality placed new emphasis on the voluntary mental actions through which devout per-

---

ion to Descartes (Cambridge, UK: Cambridge U. Press), 162; "What is it about Descartes's
self-awareness when he clearly and distinctly perceives that he thinks that makes his
awareness an awareness of *him*?"

[13] Thomas Vinci, *Cartesian Truth* (Oxford: Oxford U. Press, 1998), 42.

[14] See, to name a few notable examples, Etienne Gilson, *Etudes sur le rôle de la pensée
médiévale dans la formation du suystème cartésien*, 4th ed. (Paris: Vrin, 1975); Roger Ariew,
"Descartes and scholasticism: the intellectual background to Descartes's thought," in
The Cambridge Companion to Descartes, ed. John Cottingham, 58–90; John Carriero, "The
Second Meditation and the Essence of Mind," and Calvin Normore, "Meaning and
Objective being; Descartes and His Sources," both in *Essays on Descartes's Meditations*, ed.
Amélie Rorty (Berkeley: U. of California Press, 1986), 199–222, and 223–242.

[15] See, in particular, Laurence Renault, *Descartes ou la félicité volontaire* (Paris: PUF,
2000).

[16] See Thierry Gonthier, *Descartes et la Causa Sui* (Paris: Vrin, 2005).

sons freely cooperate with grace. Descartes's *Method* was hardly unique in its aim of "raising human nature to its highest perfection." The new emphasis put by Descartes on orthopraxy—on *conducting* one-self rightly—ties his project of science to a wider devotional context. Rooted in the Ignatian ideal of "distinguished service to God" and imbued with Salesian "inwardness," Cartesian orthopraxy aims at re-forming science by first reforming human being through asserting the primacy of free agency over intellect. Cartesian orthopraxy—"Method"—is an integral part of the devotional current developed by Francis of Sales, Bennet of Canfield, Pierre de Bérulle and, last but not least, Arnauld's director, the charismatic abbé de Saint-Cyran. Like his religious counterparts, Descartes championed a new kind of men-tal orthopraxy, inspired, at least in part, by the urge to revitalize the contested Roman Catholic doctrine of salvation by works. Descartes's most innovative claim is that science is a matter, first and foremost, of reasoning *conscientiously*. Disciplining the mind is a moral work that lies within human power. Its fruits are open-ended benefits to humankind. The project of science is a double project of charitable works—to the self, by reforming it and making it effective for charity, and to others, through new technologies and medicine. In this regard, Catholic stu-dents of Descartes, most notably Maurice Blondel at the turn of the XIXth century and Jean-Luc Marion at the turn of the XXth century, have perhaps found riches in Descartes that remain concealed to those who cannot commune sympathetically with a Descartes who claimed to be, and perhaps genuinely was, *croyant et pratiquant*.

3. *Methods*

Over and beyond standard historiographic methods, the present book follows Descartes's own instructions to "assimilate" past philosophy through a distinctive sort of exegesis. In a letter inviting Elizabeth to read Seneca's *De vita beata*, Descartes explains that one of the most useful means to acquire wisdom

> "is to examine what the ancients have written on the subject, and try to improve upon them by adding something to their precepts; one thus makes these precepts one's very own and disposes oneself to put them into practice."[17]

---

[17] Descartes to Elizabeth, July 21, 1645, AT IV, 252: "L'un de ces moyens, qui me

Descartes's approach to philosophical texts is modelled, not on *lectio*, but on *meditatio*, which is interactive and digs for discoveries. Descartes's method of reading past philosophers is guided by personal responsibility. The goal is not erudition or expository mastery, but the emergence, through exercise, of an autonomous intelligence "in the first person." The purpose of examining ancient texts is to assimilate them through a fourfold agenda that nurtures a distinctive personalism. The student of philosophy is an apprentice who freely *cooperates* with the light of reason: the student of philosophy first identifies valid precepts, then assents to them by endorsing them, then extends their scope by drawing new consequences and, finally, tests them pragmatically through concrete implementation. Philosophy, the love of wisdom, consists in actively cultivating a personal moral conscience—an inner capacity to form judgments and therefore, to stand behind truths individually and personally—the way one stands personally and individually behind a promise, an oath, a contract or a charter.

Politically and religiously, Descartes's age, whatever else it was, was the age of *consent*—the age of voluntary association, of a promise-based theory of contract, of modern natural law and of civil society. In Francis of Sales, in Bérulle, in Grotius, in Selden, in Hobbes, in the "covenanting" of Puritan groups, in Locke, in the rise of commercial liability, the notion of personal consent, based on the individual conscience, emerged in the XVIIth century as the cornerstone of creative initiatives. The present book suggests that Descartes's theory of action is, above all, *a theory of conscientious consent*, and makes, as such, a hitherto undiagnosed contribution to political and legal theory. Chapters 9 and 10, in particular examine the connection between the *ego* of the Cartesian *cogito* and the moral *ego* that is required more broadly for a new range of promissory acts and initiatives. As we know, one of the shortcomings of Locke's empiricist theory of the first person is the difficulty of defining a legal self for the purposes of long-term liability. What place, if any, does Descartes's theory of agency occupy in the rise of "possessive individualism" and the advent of new civil societies?[18]

---

semble des plus utiles, est d'examiner ce que les anciens en ont escrit, et tascher a rencherir par dessus eux, en adioutant quelque chose a leurs preceptes; car ainsy on peut rendre ces preceptes parfaitement siens, et se disposer a les metre en pratique."

[18] Three books form the background of my discussion: C.B. Macpherson, *The Political Theory of Possessive Individualism* (Oxford: Oxford U. Press, 1962); Patrick Atiyah, *The Rise and Fall of Freedom of Contract* (Oxford: Oxford U. Press, 1979); and Charles Fried, *Contract as Promise* (Cambridge, MA: Harvard U. Press, 1981).

More expressly, how does Descartes's personalist approach to assimilating past philosophical texts color his own way of advancing philosophy and his choice of the meditational format?

4. *New perspectives*

Descartes warned that his writings are deceptively simple. Although it is possible to read the Meditations in just a few hours, they require, Descartes insists, "weeks, if not months" to be properly assimilated. Time is required to meditate seriously with Descartes—to separate the mind effectively from the senses and to let the contemplation of truth restore spiritual health and inspire new mental habits. The reader who communes with Descartes's writings in the personal spirit that he himself advocates, with patience and with the purpose of assimilating his precepts and testing them in practice, is rewarded by three new perspectives. First, there is a remarkable aesthetic evolution in Descartes towards simplicity. A youthful, enthusiastic but baroque Descartes gradually transforms into a sober and serene Descartes who speaks with the voice of French classicism. Descartes's early style, typified by the *Polybii cosmopolitani thesaurus mathematicus*,[19] reflects the cocky confusion of the late Renaissance, full of flashes of insight and ornate digressions. In contrast, Descartes's last writings, most especially the letter to Chanut on intellectual love, have the passionate simplicity of Racine. The present book argues that the gradual discovery of the primacy of action explains, in large part, Descartes's evolution from baroque concealment ("*larvatus prodeo*") to the open freedom of *le grand chemin*.[20]

Descartes's second evolution is political, also critically tied to his philosophy of action. Raised by the Jesuits at *La Flèche*, Descartes started with a strong commitment to the civil authority of the Church, combined with a predilection for glory. As he lost hope of being endorsed by Jesuit educators and as Calvinist factions, both in Holland and in England, grew repressive and belligerent, Descartes became increasingly secularist and irenicist. Whatever else Descartes's theory of action implies, it implies a sharp distinction, for penal purposes, between the natural law, which pertains to all rational human beings, and God's positive law, which pertains only to human beings who have been

---

[19] AT X, 214.
[20] Letter to Elizabeth, January 1646, AT IV, 357.

elected by God's grace to belong to an ecclesiastic community. Much like Grotius, Descartes came to champion peaceful coexistence and tolerance. The greatest achievement of a ruler is peace, the defense of religious minorities against persecution, and the decriminalization of offenses against God's positive law, such as fornication and usury.[21] Descartes's discovery of free agency and concern for orthopraxy led him, in effect, to champion freedom of conscience.

Descartes's third evolution, the present book argues, involves a subtle updating of the Stoic concept of wisdom. Descartes over time shifted the focus from controlling the passions to harnessing the passions for the purpose of experimental design and scientific progress. The ancient Stoic idea of wisdom was largely based on cultivating human dignity for its own sake—which is to say that it was based on preserving the Stoic sage from *shame*. Through rational self-control, the Stoic sage put himself above the demeaning vicissitudes of Fortune and lived in noble isolation from both fame and infamy. The new Cartesian idea of wisdom, in contrast, struggles more overtly with *guilt*. Since rational self-discipline is intimately tied to advancing science, the problem of a guilty conscience supersedes the problem of reputation. The torments of conscience suddenly emerge to inhibit initiatives and paralyse progress. Is technological innovation legitimate? Are animal dissections allowed? Does human being transgress the natural order with every new scientific advance, or does God call human being to take the initiative and cultivate his garden in new, experimental ways? Is the agenda of becoming "the masters and possessors of nature" compatible with piety? This book documents Descartes's struggle with his own conscience and argues that Descartes's theory of action belongs, in the final analysis, to the elusive but important story of the rise of the individual moral conscience in early modern Europe.

Finally, because Descartes's theory of action draws on a diversity of roots and carries a variety of implications, this book crosses a number of disciplinary boundaries. The hope is to promote new discussion through "hybrid vigor," not confusion. Had I not benefited from the generous help of colleagues from many disciplines, the project would not have borne fruit. My first debt is to John Murdoch, who taught

---

[21] For Grotius, see G.H.M. Posthumus Meyjes, "Hugo Grotius as an irenicist," in *The World of Hugo Grotius*, Proceedings of the International Colloquium organized by the Grotius Committee, Rotterdam, 6–9 April 1983 (Amsterdam and Maarssen: Holland U. Press, 1984), 43–63.

me to walk cautiously, probing every obstacle at every turn. My second debt is to the Boston College Bradley Center for Medieval Philosophy and to Steve Brown for commitment to the *philosophia perennis*. The Cartesian and early-modern scholars who have corrected me and inspired me at each step of the way are far too numerous to mention. At a very bare minimum, I must thank Noam Chomsky, Bashi Sabra, Jean-Luc Marion, Edith Sylla, Dennis Deschesnes, Matt Jones, Norman Wells, Laurence Renault, Robert Minor, Stephen Gaukroger, Jean-Luc Solère, Bo Blanchette, Richard Cobb-Stevens, Tom Vinci, Jason Taylor and Nathan Smith. Finally, the present book would not exist without the *générosité* of my trusted mentor, Leon Golub, to whom it is dedicated.

CHAPTER ONE

SPIRITUAL DIRECTORS AND SPIRITUAL ACTION

We start with the famous meeting that took place at the Paris home
of the papal nuncio in the late 1620's, recalled by Descartes in a 1631
letter to his friend Étienne de Villebrissieu. Descartes, invited to hear
the alchemist Chandoux propose new philosophical ideas, brilliantly
upstaged the speaker by presenting his own "beautiful rule or natural method."[1] The entire audience (*"toute la troupe"*) was converted.[2]
Among those who acclaimed Descartes's new principles and urged
him to publish them was Cardinal Pierre de Bérulle, leader of the
new "French School" of spirituality and founder of the French Ora-
tory. What, exactly, appealed to Bérulle about Descartes's method and
prompted him to invite Descartes to a private meeting for further discussion?[3] What impact, in turn, did the encounter with Bérulle have on
Descartes?

Scholars have long debated the precise nature and outcome of Descartes's interaction with Bérulle. According to Baillet, Bérulle was impressed by the utilitarian promise of improving medicine and the mechanical arts, and "used his authority" to enjoin Descartes to pursue
his scientific work as a moral duty—in gratitude to God for the special
gifts of intelligence he had received.[4] Baillet implies that Descartes,
in turn, took Bérulle as his spiritual director.[5] Based in large part on

[1] Letter to Villebrissieu, 1631, AT I, 213. The date of the event is uncertain. To
name just two scholars, Stephen Gaukroger accepts Baillet's date for this event of
December 1628 (*Descartes: an Intellectual Biography* [Oxford: Clarendon Press, 1995], 183)
while Geneviève Rodis-Lewis favors November 1627 (*Descartes* [Paris: Calmann-Lévy,
1995], 101).

[2] AT I, 213: "vous en restâtes convaincu, comme tous ceux qui prirent la peine de
me conjurer de les écrire et de les enseigner au public…"

[3] As reported by Baillet, *La Vie de Monsieur Descartes* (Paris, 1691), I, 164–165.

[4] Adrien Baillet, *Vie de Monsieur Descartes*, Livre Second; cited from the abridged
edition (Paris: La Table Ronde, 1946), 73–74: "Le cardinal … employa l'autorité qu'il
avait sur son esprit pour le porter à entreprendre ce grand ouvrage. Il lui en fit même
une obligation de conscience. Il lui fit entendre qu'ayant reçu de Dieu une pénétration
d'esprit avec des lumières sur cela qu'il n'avait pas accordées à d'autres, il lui rendrait
un compte exact de l'emploi de ses talents."

[5] A. Baillet, *Vie de Monsieur Descartes*, Livre Troisième, 83: "A son retour de Frise,

Baillet's account, Étienne Gilson argued that Oratorian ideas played a central role in the genesis of Cartesian philosophy.[6] Henri Brémond, reacting against Gilson's claim, stressed the vast gulf that separates Bérulle's metaphysics, which are "wholly Christian and mystical," from Descartes's metaphysics, which are instead "conspicuously secular and rationalistic."[7]

More recently, Geneviève Rodis-Lewis, revising Baillet's account, has argued that what the devout Oratorian saluted and encouraged in Descartes was not the humanitarian hope of a scientific medicine and reform of mechanics but the metaphysical project of rooting scientific certainty in God.[8] Citing the fact that Descartes started a treatise "on the divinity" shortly after his meeting with Bérulle (which she persuasively places in November 1627 rather than December 1628) as well as Descartes's arrangement in Paris to have his metaphysical treatise corrected by Bérulle's fellow Oratorian Gibieuf,[9] Rodis-Lewis argues that Bérulle mainly urged Descartes to develop the theocentric basis of his new epistemology. Stephen Gaukroger, in turn, speculates that Bérulle was impressed by the doctrine of the certainty of clear and distinct ideas. Since, for Bérulle "natural philosophy was charged with theological and metaphysical questions," the exchange resulted in Descartes's new concern for the metaphysical underpinnings of his scientific project and in the decision to work on a "beginning of metaphysics" as soon as he arrived in the Netherlands.[10] Both Gaukroger and Rodis-Lewis thus admit a limited Berullian influence on the genesis of Cartesian philosophy, restricted to either encouraging, or actually inspiring, Descartes's move to embed his mechanistic principles in a theistic framework.

If, however, we turn to Jean-Luc Marion's analysis, the hypothesis of a Berullian influence on Cartesian metaphysics stumbles against a major difficulty. Marion points out that Descartes's 1630 doctrine of the creation of eternal truths, far from bearing Bérulle's mark, contradicts

---

il (Descartes) perdit un excellent directeur et un ami très sincère en la personne du cardinal de Bérulle, mort subitement à Paris le II jour d'octobre." (1629)

[6] E. Gilson, *La liberté chez Descartes* (Paris: Félix Alcan, 1913), 161–163.

[7] H. Brémond, *Histoire Littéraire du sentiment religieux en France* (Paris: Bloud et Gay, 1921), 3, La Conquête Mystique, I, 40.

[8] G. Rodis-Lewis, *Descartes*, 102–103.

[9] See Descartes's letter to Gibieuf of July 18, 1629, AT I, 17.

[10] S. Gaukroger, *Descartes: an Intellectual Biography*, 184–185.

Bérulle's position "absolutely."[11] As a corollary, Marion also points out that, since the gathering at the nuncio's home took place in November 1627,[12] the immediate outcome of Descartes's interaction with Bérulle is not the "beginning of metaphysics," but, in fact, the *Regulae*. In Marion's view, Descartes received from Bérulle nothing more than psychological support, a sort of "intimate push" to accomplish without further delay the scientific task to which he had already dedicated himself.[13] As for Baillet's report that Descartes chose Bérulle as his spiritual director, Marion concedes that this might well be true, but so what? Personal direction, as such, implies no transmission of theological concepts. On the contrary, Marion suggests, spiritual direction *took the place* of serious theological discussion.[14] Had Bérulle indeed bothered to influence Descartes theologically, the philosopher would not have resorted to the idea of the creation of eternal truths for the purpose of restoring a lost framework of analogy.[15] Marion concludes without hesitation: "Bérulle and Descartes met, so to speak, only *not* to influence one another."

In light of Marion's argument that Descartes's 1630 thesis on eternal truths actually *contradicts* Bérulle's theology, is it fruitful to explore once again Bérulle's possible impact on Descartes? Descartes's continued relationship with Gibieuf after Bérulle's death in 1629 and his agreement with Gibieuf with regard to free will[16] suggest a deeper affinity with Oratorian spirituality than Marion seems to allow.[17] Rather than look for a transmission of doctrine or for evidence that Bérulle steered Descartes towards apologetics, I propose that we focus on the very idea of spiritual direction. Bérulle was not just a spiritual director, but one of the leading spiritual directors of his generation. Convinced that guiding souls was a veritable science—the "science of the saints"—Bérulle took a methodical approach to religious psychology and devised intricate principles to guide inner action and perfect the inner life. As we

---

[11] J.–L. Marion, *La théologie blanche de Descartes* (Paris: PUF, 1981), 140.

[12] See *La théologie blanche*, 157, ftn. 25.

[13] J.–L. Marion, *La théologie blanche*, 158: "Descartes ne reçoit de Bérulle qu'une assurance psychologique, un encouragement moral, bref une impulsion intime, qui le décident à entreprendre une tâche que, depuis 1619, il savait déjà être sienne."

[14] Marion, *La théologie blanche*, 158–159: "Entre Bérulle et Descartes, la direction spirituelle a pallié la défaillance d'un dialogue de pensée."

[15] Marion, *La théologie blanche*, 159.

[16] Letter to Mersenne, May 27, 1630, AT I, 153.

[17] See Descartes's letters to Gibieuf, AT I, 16 (1629); AT III, 236 (1640) and 472 (1642); also, Baillet's account, *Vie de Monsieur Descartes*, I, 139.

know, ten years after receiving Bérulle's encouragement, Descartes will consider publishing his method under the title "Project of a universal science capable of raising our nature to its highest degree of perfection."[18] The question is, does Bérulle's impact on Descartes appear in a new light if we shift the inquiry from orthodoxy to orthopraxy—from theological doctrine to practical rules of spiritual direction?

Whatever else they are, Descartes's *Rules for directing the intelligence* are just that: rules for disciplining cognitive activity, for guiding the intelligence step by step so as to improve it—*Regulae ad directionem ingenii*.[19] Descartes's underlying claim is that "method and exercise" make the intelligence (*ingenium*) more "apt," whereas haphazard guesses, no matter how lucky, only weaken it.[20] The explicit goal of the *Regulae* is to fortify the intelligence—to correct its sluggishness (*ingenii tarditas*) and increase its capacity.[21] Descartes's aim is to improve how the intelligence *conducts* itself. The goal is to foster a special attentiveness to each step that is taken—what religionists describe as "mindfulness." Better that the epistemologic subject apply his intellect consistently and methodically than stumble on truths at random. The dignity of human intelligence consists in deliberately *discovering* and *embracing* truth, not in poaching it from others and leaving it blindly to the whims of fortune.

As the episode with Chandoux reveals, and as the *Regulae* attests, Descartes's "beautiful natural method" empowers the mind with a new level of confidence precisely by cultivating a new spirit of humility. Better to reach "the intimate truth" of the most ordinary things than to indulge in exotic speculations that remain bereft of genuine understanding. Knowledge that is achieved through disciplined effort is less flamboyant, but also more luminous and more certain, than previous philosophies ever claimed or realized.[22] In a similar vein, Bérulle and other theorists of the inner life, most notably Francis of Sales, will

---

[18] Letter to Mersenne, AT I, 338–340.

[19] See AT X, 351, for the description of the abandoned treatise in the 1650 inventory of Descartes's papers: "Traité des Regles utiles et claires pour la direction de l'esprit en la recherche de la vérité…"

[20] Descartes, *Regulae*, Rule IX, AT X, 402: "… sed arte etiam et exercitio ingenia ad hoc reddi possunt longe aptiora" and Rule X, 405: "Et maxime cavendum est, ne in similibus casu et sine arte divinandis tempus teramus; nam etiamsi illa saepe inveniri possunt sine arte, et a felicius interdum celerius fortasse, quam per methodum, hebetarent tamen ingenii lumen."

[21] *Regulae*, Rule XI, AT X, 409: "… ingenii tarditatem emendari nemo non videt, et illius etiam amplificari capacitatem."

[22] See e.g. *Regulae*, Rule X, in AT X, 403–406.

emphasize the dignity of simple inner practices like mental prayer and fasting, which can be performed by anyone, in the most mundane settings. Better advance in the project of self-reform through modest and real steps than to fantasize vainly about heroic sacrifice and supernatural experiences. In both the Cartesian *Regulae* and in the new French School of spirituality, a conscious turn away from exotic dreams to what can be accomplished here and now, through human dedication, within the limitations of human ability, marks the mature blossom of Christian humanism and the irreversible historic shift from baroque exuberance to classicism.

The question of Bérulle's impact on Descartes may thus be reformulated as follows: to what extent did Bérulle's principles of spiritual direction, aimed at training the soul to acquire Christian virtues, help to shape Descartes's rules of intellectual direction, aimed at training the mind to acquire truth? In both cases, not only does othopraxy replace orthodoxy as the central focus of concern, but orthopraxy itself is approached innovatively. Physical, external orthopraxy is downplayed in favor of mental orthopraxy and "spiritual" actions. In both cases, the subject is encouraged to *think* better: to become conscious of inner reflective movements and take intentional control of these movements, fostering inner discipline and exercise.

A clear example of the shift that marks the new spirituality is found in a short but influential treatise, the *Spiritual Combat* written by the Italian Theatine Lorenzo Scupoli, first published in 1589.[23] The opening chapter of Scupoli's treatise condemns those who "ignorantly place their devotion in external acts" and "utterly neglect to watch the inner movements of their hearts."[24] The spiritual importance of acting inwardly, of watching, and then guiding, the "inner movements of the heart," calls in turn for new frameworks in which to relate action, intention, volition and "disposition." Scupoli, here again, is representative. Arguing that external good works are not, as such, conducive to holiness, but are instead the "precious fruits" of inner dispositions to holiness, he establishes that inner discipline is more fundamental to true piety than outer discipline.[25] Devotion does not consist in external practices but in the inner discipline that leads to "knowing

---

[23] See Benedict Groeschel's preface to Lorenzo Scupoli's *Spiritual Combat*, revised translation by William Lester and Robert Mohan (New York: Paulist Press, 1978), v.

[24] Lorenzo Scupoli, *Spiritual Combat*, Chapter I, 3.

[25] See L. Scupoli, *Spiritual Combat*, Chapter I, 2.

the infinite greatness and goodness of God together with our own
weakness."[26] Scupoli insists, in particular, that devotion includes the
"right use of our faculties." We must, he says, "control our minds
and not permit them to wander aimlessly about."[27] We will see that
a direct line of transmission, passing through Francis of Sales and
Bérulle, connects Scupoli's "right use of our faculties" to Descartes's
Regulae. Descartes's preoccupation with the importance of raising our
nature to its highest perfection suggests that, just as Bérulle and other
leading theorists of the Catholic Reform were inclined to appropriate
astronomy and optics for theological ends,[28] Descartes, in turn, appropriated features of the new orthopraxy to develop his own "beautiful
and natural method." Spiritual direction indeed calls attention to the
mind's self-conduct and requires just the sort of analysis that is developed in Descartes's *Regulae*. Philosophically, the shift from bodily action
to mental action provokes a number of questions. How are mental
actions apprehended, judged, classified? When do they count as *bona
fide* actions and by what criteria? What role does Intentionality play? Is
the inner experience of autonomy pivotal? Does including various types
of mental actions in a unified theory give rise to a new philosophy of
action?

We begin by examining the notion of inner action in two leading
XVIIth century spiritual directors, Bérulle himself and his older con-
temporary and personal friend Francis of Sales, both of whom prominently shaped the Parisian *milieu* of the Catholic Reform to which
Descartes was so intimately exposed between 1626 and 1628. Francis
of Sales, who met Bérulle in Paris in 1602 through the circle of Barbe
Acarie, published his widely successful *Introduction à la vie dévote*, based
on his experience as a spiritual director, in 1609. Bérulle, his junior by
roughly a decade, published an early *Brief Discourse on Inner Abnegation* in
Paris in 1597, and his famous *Discours de l'estat et des Grandeurs de Jésus* in

---

[26] L. Scupoli, *Spiritual Combat*, Chapter I, 5.

[27] Scupoli, *Spiritual Combat*, Chapter IX, 23.

[28] See, e.g., Bérulle's *Discours de l'estat et des Grandeurs de Jésus*, published in Paris
in 1623; Mersenne's *La Vérité des sciences contre les sceptiques et pyrrhoniens*, published in
Paris in 1625; a more obscure and controversial work, also published in Paris in 1625,
namely *Dissertatio contra aequivocationes, auctore Johanne Barnesio*, translated the same year
into French as *Traicté et dispute contre les équivoques*. Maurice Nédoncelle records his
"emotion" at what he feels are proto-Cartesian positions that invoke geometric optics
and the *camera oscura*. See Nédoncelle, *Trois Aspects du problème anglo-catholique au XVIIe
siècle* (Strasbourg: Bloud et Gay, 1951), 29.

1623, followed by a sequel in 1629.[29] Both were educated, like Descartes, at a Jesuit College (in their case, Clermont rather than La Flèche) and were intimately familiar with the Ignatian Exercises. Francis of Sales speaks of Ignatius of Loyola as the "divine Ignatius."[30] Bérulle underwent a special Ignatian retreat "of election" in 1600 after joining the priesthood.[31] A first question about the sources of Salesian and Berullian direction thus suggests itself: to what extent do the Ignatian *Exercices* identify and cultivate mental actions? What implicit theory of action do they promote?

1.1. *Mental Action in the Ignatian Exercises*

Scholars generally agree that the success of Ignatian retreats in the late XVIth century played a major role in the emergence of a "golden age of spiritual direction."[32] In addition to supervising Ignatian retreats, Jesuits took steps to disseminate key Ignatian methods and principles by composing books for lay audiences. A good example is Louis Richeome's *Pélerin de Lorette* (1602), which was probably known to Descartes, and which graphically juxtaposes mental and physical action.[33] A second example is the *First Book of Christian Exercises Appertaining to Resolution*, published by the English Jesuit Robert Persons in 1584, and focused on transmitting the content of the First Week, concerned with the resolution to undertake self-reform.[34] A third example is *Intérieure occupation d'une âme dévote* (1608) by Richeome's friend, the worldly Pierre Coton, who befriended and protected Bérulle.[35] These vernacular

---

[29] Following Jean Dagens, *Bérulle et les origines de la restauration catholique (1575–1611)* (Desclée de Brouwer, 1952), 139 and 389.

[30] *Traité de l'Amour de Dieu*, Livre I, chap. XIV, in *Oeuvres Complètes*, 394.

[31] See *Retraite* faite par le Cardinal de Bérulle à Verdun (August 1600); published in Habert de Cérisy, *La vie du Cardinal de Bérulle*, Paris, 1646.

[32] See Michel Olphe-Gaillard, "Direction Spirituelle en Occident; au 16ème siècle," and Gabriel de Sainte-Marie-Madeleine, "Direction Spirituelle en Occident; du 17ème siècle à nos jours," in *Dictionnaire de la Spiritualité* (Paris: Beauchesne, 1957), vol. III, cols. 1108–1119 and 1119–1194 respectively.

[33] H. Brémond is convinced that Richeome's work is a direct source of Francis of Sales: see *Histoire Littérarire du Sentiment Religieux en France*, I, L'Humanisme Dévot (Paris: Bloud et Gay, 1916), 31–32. For Descartes's possible familiarity with Richeome's *Pélerin*, see G. Rodis-Lewis, *Descartes*, 70–71.

[34] See Robert Persons, S.J., *The Christian Directory (1582)*, ed. Victor Houliston (Leiden: Brill, 1998).

[35] See Jean Dagens, *Bérulle et les origines*, 178–179.

guides emphasize that all Christians, whatever their worldly circumstances, and at whatever level, are called to inner reform.[36] As Brémond suggests, the Jesuits, who from the start supported the traditions
of Christian humanism "tirelessly and brilliantly," found themselves in
a unique position to reach out to worldlings and teach them the value
and method of inner action.[37] Francis of Sales, revealingly, will characterize the essence of the Jesuit Rule as fostering union with God
through "action, taken spiritually."[38]

At the start of the *annotaciones* that introduce the *Spiritual Exercises*,
Ignatius draws a parallel between spiritual and physical exercise: spiritual exercises are actions that "dispose the soul to free itself of inordinate attachments," just as running is an action that disposes the
body to better athletic performance.[39] Three inner actions, in particular, are required of the Ignatian exercitant: silence, constant observance
of the movements of the soul, and frequent petitioning for grace.[40] Are
these *bona fide* actions? Silence obviously satisfies philosophical criteria for mental acts, since *refraining* from a bodily movement is structurally isomorphic to executing a bodily movement.[41] By the same
token, inner petition is structurally isomorphic to voiced petition and
must be counted as a mental act. Inner vigilance also qualifies: to
keep one's attention focused on inner movements is to apply it, control
it, focus it. The technique of guided imagination, through which the
exercitant is asked to form various mental images,[42] calls attention to
the mind's power to override sensory impressions by acting mentally.[43]

---

[36] Respectively, Robert Persons S.J., *The Christian Directory*, ed. Victor Houliston, and
Pierre Coton S.J., *Intérieure occupation d'une âme dévote*, Paris, 1609.

[37] Brémond, *Histoire littéraire*, I, L'Humanisme Dévot, 15.

[38] Francis of Sales, *Introduction à la vie dévote*, in *Oeuvres*, ed. Pléiade (Paris: Gallimard,
1969), 1091.

[39] *The Spiritual Exercises of Saint Ignatius* (New York: Doubleday, 1964), 37.

[40] Citing Robert Gleason S.J., in *The Spiritual Exercises of Saint Ignatius*, 22.

[41] See John Searle, *Intentionality* (Cambridge, UK: Cambridge U. Press, 1983), 102–
103: "The absence of bodily movement may be as much a part of the conditions of
satisfaction of a causally self-referential intention in action as a bodily movement ...
Mental acts are formally isomorphic to the cases of physical acts we have considered."

[42] See e.g., *The Spiritual Exercises of Saint Ignatius*, Week I, Exercise V, First point, 59:
"To see in imagination the great fires, and the souls enveloped, as it were, in bodies of
fire."

[43] See John Searle, *Intentionality*, 103: "The only difference is that in place of a bodily
movement as a condition of satisfaction we have a purely mental event. If, for example,
I am asked to form a mental image of the Eiffel Tower and I comply, the relevant
portion of the intention in action will be: (that this intention in action causes me to
have a mental image of the Eiffel Tower)."

Finally, the cornerstone of the Ignatian Exercices is the technique of *agere contra*, or "acting against." The purpose is to liberate the exercitant from "inordinate attachments" by asking that he not only resist cravings and urges but intentionally do the opposite.[44] Thus if the exercitant has the impulse to abrogate the hour allocated to meditation, he must deliberately prolong it instead.[45] To the extent that the soul strenghtens itself by keeping silence, forming deliberate images and "acting against" spontaneous wishes, the Ignatian retreat is a prolonged experiment in inner action.[46] Inner action, in the Ignatian Exercises, is closely identified with effort. The Ignatian ethos of inner effort is not without paradox, since "the effectiveness of the Exercises depends wholly on personal effort and wholly on divine grace."[47] Put in less paradoxical form, the underlying doctrine is that original sin does not deprive human being either of the desire to act spiritually (love God) or of the power to *begin* to act spiritually, even though the strength required to act perfectly (love God perfectly) is beyond natural reach.[48] Francis of Sales thus points out that natural reason is sufficient to awaken the soul's desire to act spiritually (love God) and that the least effort in this direction receives immediate and unfailing divine assistance.[49] Similarly, Robert Persons, whose treatise popularizes the content of the First Week of Ignatian Exercises, stresses not only that "doing" is more central to the Christian life than "knowing," but that God has left it in our power "to ask for his ayde" and to "joyne our endevour with the same."[50]

---

[44] See *The Spiritual Exercises of Saint Ignatius*, "Notes Concerning Scruples," section 5, 138: "The soul that desires to advance in the spiritual life must always take a course contrary to that of the enemy."

[45] See Annotation XIII, in *The Spiritual Exercises of Saint Ignatius*, 40. See also W.W. Meissner, S.J., "Spiritual Exercises," in *Psyche and Spirit* (Lanham, MD: U. Press of America, 2003), 139–140.

[46] As Father Meissner points out (*Psyche and Spirit*, 139): "The emphasis on action is a recurrent theme in the *Exercises*."

[47] Citing Father Meissner, *Psyche and Spirit*, 121.

[48] See François de Sales, *Traité de l'Amour de Dieu*, Livre I, chaps. XVI and XVII, in *Oeuvres Complètes*, 400, 401–402.

[49] *Traité de l'Amour de Dieu*, Livre I, chap. XVI, in *Oeuvres Complètes*, 399: "et n'est pas possible qu'un homme pensant attentivement en Dieu, voire par le seul discours naturel, ne ressente un certain élan d'amour que la secrète inclination de notre nature suscite au fond su coeur"; and Livre I, chap. XVII, 404: "C'est une chose certaine qu'à celui qui est *fidèle en peu de chose* et qui fait ce qui est en son pouvoir, la bénignité divine ne dénie jamais son assistance pour l'avancer de plus en plus."

[50] *The First Booke of the Christian Exercise, Appertaynyng to Resolution*, ed. Victor Houliston, 8 (5–10), 3 (20–25), and 12 (32–33).

Postlapsarian man is not deprived of the power to *seek* guiding rules for inner action or to *cooperate* with higher injunctions. Note, in particular, that "personal reflection and reasoning" are regarded by Ignatius to be valuable spiritual actions, which means that they involve effort and initiate the appeal to higher assistance.[51] Although the Ignatian emphasis on human effort, which includes the effort to reflect and reason, was denounced by some as Pelagian or semi-Pelagian, its chief effect is to foster reverence for the human soul. Francis of Sales speaks of the "nobility and excellence" of the soul, in particular its free will, which "is able to love God and cannot, as such, hate God."[52] The key is that human nature, despite the Fall, is created in God's image.[53] Man has a natural capacity to cooperate with reason and act spiritually. Bérulle emphasizes that postlapsarian man, "no less than Adam," remains tied to God "inseparably, through the highest part of the soul," which is "made in God's image and semblance."[54] Francis of Sales speaks of the highest part of the soul as "our superior will," which is the inner compass that keeps the soul directed to God.[55] Ignatius, in turn, speaks of synderesis—the same term invoked by Descartes (at least according to Baillet) to explain moral conscience and the phenomenon of remorse.[56]

The purpose of spiritual direction is first to awaken, then to mobilize, the soul's innate power to act intentionally, "with effort," rather than impulsively gratify bodily appetites. Pierre Coton, throughout his treatise, aims explicitly at replacing inner idleness with activity (*occupa-*

---

[51] See, e.g., the second of Ignatius's famous *Annotaciones*, in *The Spiritual Exercises of Saint Ignatius of Loyola*, Eng. trans. by Anthony Mottola (New York: Doubleday, 1964), 37.

[52] François de Sales, *Introduction à la vie dévote*, Part V, chap. X, 307.

[53] *Traité de l'Amour de Dieu*, Livre I, chap. XV, in *Oeuvres Complètes*, 396: "Nous sommes créés à l'image et la semblance de Dieu; qu'est-ce à dire cela, sinon que nous avons une extrême convenance avec sa divine majesté? ... Notre âme est spirituelle, indivisible, immortelle, entend, veut et veut librement; est capable de juger, discourir, savoir, et avoir des vertus; en quoi elle ressemble à Dieu."

[54] Bérulle, "Oeuvres de Piété," CLXXXI, in *Oeuvres Complètes du Cardinal de Bérulle*, reproduction de l'édition princeps (Montsoult: Maison d'Institution de l'Oratoire, 1960), vol. II, p. 1071, col. 1237: "Le fonds de vostre Esprit est à Dieu: car il l'a créé à son image et semblance"; elaborating on Genesis, p. 1072, col. 1238: "... c'est une force de consecration primitive, comme essentielle, comme naturelle à nostre Estre ... par laquelle nostre Estre comme emanant de Dieu, et formé de la main de Dieu mesme, appartient à Dieu d'un droit si fort que rien ne le peut violer; et d'une propriété si intrinseque et inseparable, que le Diable et le peché ne la peuvent ravir ni oster."

[55] François de Sales, *Introduction à la vie dévote*, Part IV, chap. XII, 277.

[56] For Descartes, see AT X, 186: "L'épouvante dont il fut frappé dans le second songe, marquoit, à son sens, sa syndérèse, c'est-à-dire, les remords de sa conscience touchant les péchez qu'il pouvoit avoir commis pendant le cours de sa vie jusqu'alors."

tion).[57] By definition, spiritual actions cooperate with rules and deliberate planning, since the first action is to *resist* bodily impulses and resolve to *act otherwise*. Spiritual effort and human agency are so intimately joined that motivation increases with practice: the loftier the soul's inner intentions, the more vivacious, substantial and permanent are its actions.[58] Robert Persons defines devotion as a state in which the soul is "endewed with a joyful promptnes to the diligent execution of all things that appartayne to the honor of God."[59]

1.2. *Francis of Sales*

Francis of Sales also defines devotion as a special facility to execute spiritual actions: the devout soul acts "promptly and consistently" to serve God, unlike the beginner who acts sluggishly, or the unreformed person, who basically never acts spiritually at all.[60] Significantly, he steers the soul, "Philothée," away from seeking to experience the more mystic states of the Flemish School on the grounds that *actions* are what the devout properly should seek, not *passions*.[61] The actions that Francis has in mind are not the "material" actions that the "vulgar" prefer, but, quite specifically, spiritual actions, "mortifications of the heart," which are far more "excellent."[62] Actions performed spiritually within the heart, no matter how humble, are of greater value for spiritual progress than delights received, no matter how abundant. Francis urges

---

[57] *Intérieure occupation d'une âme dévote.* "Intérieure occupation" has the meaning of "inner doings" rather than "occupation," as in: "Je suis occupée"—"I am busy, I am doing something."

[58] François de Sales, *Traité de l'Amour de Dieu*, Livre I, chap. X, in *Oeuvres Complètes*, 385.

[59] *Christian directorie*, ed. Houliston, 5.

[60] Francis of Sales, *Introduction à la vie dévote*, Chap. 1, in *Oeuvres Complètes*, ed. Pléiade, 32.

[61] *Introduction à la vie dévote*, Part III, chap. 2, in *Oeuvres Complètes* ed. Pléiade, 131–132: "Il y a certaines choses que plusieurs estiment vertus et qui ne le sont aucunement… ce sont les extases ou ravissements, les insensibilités, impassibilités, unions déifiques … Il ne faut pas prétendre à telles grâces, puisqu'elles ne sont nullement nécessaires pour bien servir et aimer Dieu… ce sont plutôt des passions que des actions, lesquelles nous pouvons recevoir, mais non pas faire en nous." See also Antoine Daniels, S.J., *Les Rapports entre Saint François de Sales et les Pays Bas, 1500–1700* (Nijmegen: Centrale Drukkerj N.V., 1932), 44–69.

[62] Francis of Sales, *Introduction à la vie dévote*, Part III, chap.1, in *Oeuvres*, ed. Pléiade, 127.

Philothée to focus on "what we can accomplish within ourselves" ("*ce que nous pouvons faire en nous*"). The purpose of spiritual direction is not to *receive more* but to *act better*.

A special case of inner action is the attentive study of devotional books. Francis urged his spiritual sons and daughters to "make use of both the living and the dead."[63] "Making use of the dead" meant selecting a favorite author from the past to be kept close at hand (upon approval) and repeatedly read. His disciple Jean-Pierre Camus, for example, chose as his favorite book the *Method for serving God* by the Spanish Franciscan Alonso of Madrid.[64] Francis's own personal choice, as he confided to Jeanne de Chantal, was Lorenzo Scupoli's *Spiritual Combat*, which he carried around in his pocket and "never read without great profit."[65] Another deceased director recommended by Francis was Louis of Granada, whose entire *opus* should be regarded, he wrote, as a "second Breviary," because it "trains the mind to love true devotion" by providing "all necessary spiritual exercises."[66] Each one of Louis of Granada's books, Francis urged, should be "weighed and cherished, ruminated chapter after chapter, with a carefully attentive mind."[67]

Private reading not only furthered instruction in inner othopraxy but served as a form of orthopraxy in its own right. The key principle is to cultivate mindfulness—which is to say, that "nothing be done automatically, but always by election and application of the will."[68] Reading subordinates gesture to its inner source, harmonizing mental and physical action together into a single devotional undertaking. The

---

[63] Letter to Antoine de Revol, June 3, 1603, in *Oeuvres*, vol. XIII, 188. Cf. Bérulle, "Oeuvres de Piété," CLXXIX, in *Oeuvres*, II, 1068, col. 1233: "Pour estre bien regis nous avons besoin de regle et d'esprit, c'est à dire, et de loy vive et animée et animante, et de loi morte et escrite. La première est escrite en nos coeurs, la seconde est escrite sur le papier."

[64] See J.–P. Camus, *L'Esprit du B. François de Sales*, vol. V, 390–391.

[65] Letter of January 24, 1608, in *Oeuvres de Saint François de Sales*, Édition complète publiée par les soins des Religieuses de la Visitation du 1er monastère d'Annecy (Annecy, 1892–1932), vol. XIII, 358.

[66] Letter to Antoine de Revol, June 3, 1603, in *Oeuvres*, vol. XIII, 189.

[67] Letter to Antoine de Revol, June 3, 1608, in *Oeuvres*, vol. XIII, 190: "Il faut le lire avec reverence et devotion, comme un livre qui contient les plus utiles inspirations que l'ame peut recevoir d'en haut; et par la, reformer toutes les puissances de l'ame, les purgeant par detestation de toutes leurs mauvaises inclinations, et les addressant a leur vraye fin par des fermes et grandes resolutions." See on the subject Jean Leclerq, *Initiations aux auteurs monastiques du Moyen Âge: L'Amour des lettres et le désir de Dieu* (Paris: Cerf, 1963), 21.

[68] *Entretien Spirituel* I, in *Oeuvres*, 1005.

"external is born from the internal, and the internal is nourished from the external."[69] The reader disciplines himself to "know something perfectly by taking the time to learn it well."[70] Reading with the correct level of attention, moreover, cultivates "inner modesty," which consists most especially in bringing the understanding under control (*assujetir l'entendement*).[71]

As part of privileging mental actions over passions, Francis of Sales generally prefers "clear" authors who advance steadily in "lowly valleys" to "obscure" authors who venture out "on high mountain peaks."[72] Scupoli's *Spiritual Combat* exemplifies the sort of clear prescription and orderly succession of steps favored by Francis. Scupoli specifies, for example, that consideration of one's own weakness must precede consideration of the divine power, and both, in turn, must precede all undertakings.[73] Since the faculties must be correctly employed, the understanding must first be free of ignorance. Scupoli's remedy against ignorance is "exercise," which "makes the understanding lucid and brightens it."[74] Exercise helps the mind "clearly discern" how to purge the soul of irregular attachments.[75] One way to overcome ignorance is to apply oneself with persistence to the "serious and diligent examination of every object," so that a judgment can be formed that accords with Truth rather than "external appearances and the testimony of the senses."[76] The devout intellect is thus a lucid, exercised intellect, an intellect that proceeds step by step, one object at a time, in order to override sensory perception in favor of a rational judgment. Scupoli devotes two more chapters to methods of forming correct judgments: he warns, in particular, against rashness, against biases (which allow

---

[69] *Entretien Spirituel*, I, 1006.

[70] *Entretien Spirituel* VI, in *Oeuvres*, 1048.

[71] *Entretien Spirituel* VI, in *Oeuvres*, 1048.

[72] See Antoine L. Daniels S.J., *Les Rapports entre Saint François de Sales et les Pays-Bas, 1550–1700* (Nijmegen: Centrale Drukkerij, 1932), 50–52.

[73] Lorenzo Scupoli, *Spiritual Combat*, Chapter 3, p. 13.

[74] Lorenzo Scupoli, *Spiritual Combat*, Chapter 7, p. 19.

[75] *Ibid.*

[76] L. Scupoli, *Spiritual Combat*, Chapter 7, 20. If we replace Scupoli's "good and evil" with "clear and confused" and "comfortable to the Holy Ghost" with "comfortable with Truth," we obtain a nearly Cartesian statement: "The second [means] is a persistent application to the serious and diligent examination of every object in order to distinguish the good from the evil (i.e. the clear from the confused). A judgment is formed which is not in accord with external appearances, the testimony of the senses, or the standards of the corrupt world, but which is comfortable to the judgment of the Holy Spirit (i.e. to Truth)."

"incorrect ideas" to be imprinted on the mind) and against wanton
curiosity for exotic phenomena over solid knowledge of basic truths.[77]
Conceptually, Scupoli thus specifically presents correct judgment as
emerging from *orthopraxy*. Correct judgment is achieved through right
use of the intellect, which is to say through *acting* correctly, rather than
through rote learning of doctrine or memorizing facts. Scupoli's move
to integrate intellectual activity into general rules of orthopraxy bring
us to two key aspects of Salesian orthopraxy: its radicalism and its rationalism. First, transforming the Scriptural metaphor of discarding the
"old man" into an architectural image, Francis argues that the devout
soul must "resolve to tear down the old building that occupies the place
where the new one is to be raised."[78] Scupoli's idea that the exercised
and lucid intellect plays a pivotal role in purging the soul of all irregular
attachments is thus appropriated to bring about a radical and deliberate destruction of old attachements, until a *tabula rasa* is achieved upon
which correct judgments will erect a new edifice.

Secondly, Francis argues that a firm allegiance to reason is a chief
requirement of inner orthopraxy. Rationalism, in his view, is a means
to cultivate mental *modesty*, mental *patience* and mental *obedience*.[79] The
devout mind must be "just and reasonable."[80] Rationalism is a form of
mortification that destroys self-centered partiality. By inviting us to proceed step by step in the proper order, rationalism provides an opportunity to practice humility and discipline.[81] Rational action, moreover, is
broadly interpreted. Fasting, for example, is meritorious mainly because
it "subjects the body to the mind's law," which is to say that it replaces
bodily appetite with rational planning.[82] Gambling, conversely, is forbidden on the grounds that it looks to fortune for gain rather than
to human industry and therefore "offends reason."[83] Most importantly,

---

[77] L. Scupoli, *Combat Spirituel*, Chapter VIII ("An Obstacle to Forming a Correct
Judgment. An Aid to the Formation of a Correct Judgment"), 21–22; and Chapter IX
("Another Method to Prevent Deception of the Understanding.").

[78] *Entretien Spirituel*, XIII, in *Oeuvres*, 1174: "Il faut qu'il se résolve de faire ruiner le
vieil bâtiment qui est en la place de celui qu'il veut édifier de nouveau."

[79] Chiefly, *Entretien Spirituels* VI, 1048 and IX, 1093.

[80] *Introduction à la vie dévote*, Part III, Chap. 36, in *Oeuvres*, 228.

[81] *Introduction à la vie dévote*, Part III, chaps. 9 and 10, especially p. 160: "Tâchez de les
faire par ordre."

[82] *Introduction à la vie dévote*, Part III, Chap. 23, in *Oeuvres*, 195.

[83] *Introduction à la vie dévote*, Part III, Chap. 32, in *Oeuvres*, 221: "Le gain ne se fait pas
en ces jeux selon la raison, mais selon le sort, qui tombe bien souvent à celui qui part
habitude et industrie ne méritait rien: la raison est donc offensée en cela."

Francis calls on Philothée to cultivate the intellect with which she has been endowed rather than wish for a keener mind or a better judgment: such desires, he explains, are frivolous and maliciously take the place of the resolve each one of us should have to cultivate his mind to the best of his ability.[84] Intellectual improvement, in short, comes from devoutly disciplining a limited intellect, not from disguising or resenting its finitude. Rationalism is a key pillar of the devout life because it is a matter of orthopraxy: it requires right practice, which is always rooted in humility.

1.3. *Pierre de Bérulle*

If Lorenzo Scupoli occupies a special place among the dead spiritual directors recommended by Francis of Sales, Bérulle occupies a prominent position among the living. Francis praised Bérulle as "a man to whom God has given much and whom it is impossible to approach without much profit; he is as I would like myself to be."[85] By the time he interacted with Descartes over twenty years later, Bérulle had accumulated considerable experience in directing souls through supervising the Carmelite nuns whom he had himself brought to Paris from Spain and from whom he learned Teresian methods.[86] The chief difference between Bérulle and Francis of Sales is perhaps Bérulle's greater affinity for Flemish mysticism, to which he was exposed not only through Benet of Canfield and Barbe Acarie, but also through his own spiritual director Dom Richard Beaucousin, who translated the work of an anonymous XVth century mystic from Brabant, *La Perle Évangélique*, in 1602.[87] For our purpose, a noteworthy aspect of the *Pearl* is not that it scales great spiritual heights but that it starts with the modest project of

---

[84] *Introduction à la vie dévote*, Part III, Chap. 37, 231: "Je ne voudrais même pas que l'on désirât d'avoir meilleur esprit ni meilleur jugement, car ces désirs sont frivoles et tiennent la place de celui que chacun doit avoir de cultiver le sien tel qu'il est."

[85] Letter to Antoine de Revol, June 3, 1603, in *Oeuvres*, vol. XII, 188–189.

[86] See Jean Dagens, *Bérulle et les Origines de la Restauration Catholique*, 110–118 and 213–223.

[87] See Jean Dagens, *Bérulle et la Restauration Catholique*, 115. See also Dom J. Huyben, *Vie spirituelle*, XXVI (1931), 21–46; and L.J. Daniel's account in *Les Rapports de Saint François de Sales et les Pays Bas*, 44–48. As Jos Daniels remarks, Books II and III of the *Pearl* develop the sort of mystical Christocentrism that will become the hallmark of Bérulle's new "French School." See L.J. Daniels, *Les Rapports entre Saint François de Sales et les Pays Bas*, 46–47.

"teaching to know God and ourselves," in order to "restore the spoiled forces of our soul to their original justice," and to "unite with God, our origin, who is present inside of us."[88] Bérulle may have adopted the implicit layering of the spiritual life by distinct levels, including a preliminary level of rational self-reform. Bérulle's "wholly mystical" metaphysics and Descartes's rational metaphysics may turn out to be, not incompatible, so much as radically distinct levels of inner progress and action—what Bérulle terms "states" (*états*). Bérulle's Christocentric premiss indeed supports rather than contradicts the Cartesian project to discipline the mind rationally, since it serves to emphasize the developmental character of human psychology. Bérulle interpreted the Incarnation to imply that every human state, starting with infancy, holds a special dignity, derived from Christ's condescension to espouse it and live through it.

Bérulle's first treatise, *Bref Discours de l'abnégation intérieure*, illustrates the principle of developmental psychology. Largely drawn from the Milanese mystic Isabella Bellingzaga,[89] the *Discours* explains that only those who have already made "notable progress in self-hatred" will benefit from reading it, since it presupposes a firm resolve for self-conquest, based on previously understanding the cunning efficiency of self-love.[90] A preliminary state is thus implied, in which the soul presumably identifes the effects of self-love and becomes "persuaded" to free itself. The *Brief Discourse* thus builds on a lower level of transformation to outline practices aimed at uprooting self-love by degrees. As Dagens remarks, Bérulle's *Brief Discourse*, like Scupoli's *Spiritual Combat*, not only privileges inner orthopraxy over outer orthopraxy but defends inner orthopraxy as a more useful and "certain" means of spiritual reform than illumination of the intellect.[91] While Bérulle's position most explicitly agrees with Benet of Canfield's *Rule of Perfection* (1593), it also concurs with the Salesian doctrine that we must focus on mental actions rather than on what we receive passively. Useful as they may be, the consolations and illuminations we receive do not, as such, increase our merit, any more than the temptations we suffer decrease it. Action

---

[88] Cited in *ibid.*

[89] See J. Dagens, *Bérulle et les origines de la restauration Catholique*, 137–139.

[90] P. de Bérulle, Advertissement de l'autheur, preceding *Bref Discours de l'Abnégation Interieure*; in *Oeuvres Complètes*, Reproduction de l'édition Princeps (Montsoult: Maison d'Institution de l'Oratoire, 1960), II, p. 644 (875).

[91] See Jean Dagens, *Bérulle et les origines*, 147.

alone—for example, *resisting* temptation—properly originates with us and unites our will to God.

A few years before witnessing Descartes's intervention against Chandoux, Bérulle wrote a summary outlining the basic principles of spiritual direction. The first three axioms establish (1) that the soul has a unique dignity; (2) that the soul must strive for orderly self-conduct; and (3) that orderly action stems from pure love, not from self-interest. Bérulle reminds Oratorians that they must privilege directing souls over all other duties and tasks, since "God did not make the physical world for its own sake, but for the sake of the souls it contains." A single soul weighs more, in God's view, "than the whole universe."[92] Bérulle next emphasizes that the soul's vocation is a call for stable, orderly action. The heavens, Bérulle explains, "which proclaim God's glory, inform us of our duty and tell us how to conduct ourselves."[93] Like the stars, Oratorians must have motions that are ruled, not by passions, but by "angelic dispositions."[94] And just as the stars ceaselessly radiate their stabilizing influence everywhere, so must Oratorians by their example continuously influence souls to reform and to seek perfection.[95] Bérulle's third general axiom indeed specifies that spiritual direction starts with personal example and stems from a sort of spiritual overflow, a plenitude of grace.[96] The Oratorian director thus bears direct witness to the directee that the soul is immaterial, rational and ecstatic—called to immortality, truth and beatitude.

If we accept Baillet's report that Descartes put himself under Bérulle's direction, this means that three closely interrelated spiritual premisses would have been emphasized to him, namely: (1) metaphysical dualism; (2) the identification of spiritual perfection with constant inner action characterized by order; and (3) that the duty to pursue inner perfection is not vainglorious, but benefits others through personal example and instruction. This last premiss, characteristic as well of Salesian spirituality, explains the *form* of Bérulle's encouragement

---

[92] See Bérulle, *Memorial de quelques points servans la direction des superieurs en la Congregation de l'Oratoire de Jesus*, in *Oeuvres Complètes*, II, 617–618.

[93] Bérulle, *Memorial*, Chap. VIII, in *Oeuvres Complètes*, I, 622: "... les Cieux donc qui nous annoncent la gloire de Dieu, nous annoncent aussi nostre devoir, et nous apprennent quelle doit estre nostre conduite, nostre pureté, nostre élevation; et quel encore doit estre nostre soin et nostre industrie."

[94] *Ibid.*: "Les movements des Superieurs doivent estre reglez non par leurs passions, mais par des dispositions Angeliques."

[95] Bérulle, *Memorial*, chap. VIII, in *Oeuvres Complètes*, I, 621.

[96] Bérulle, *Memorial*, chap. XXI, in *Oeuvres Complètes*, II, 631.

to Descartes. As Baillet reports, Bérulle made publication a matter of
moral duty: *Il lui en fit même une obligation de conscience*.[97] The psychological *finesse* of Bérulle's encouragement derived from the director-
directee relationship. The gift of special intelligence, Bérulle stressed
to Descartes, is a gift from God, implying an absolute responsibility
"before the Sovereign Judge of Men" to pursue it and share its fruits
with others.[98] Bérulle used his authority over Descartes's conscience to
overcome the negative stigma attached to ambition and replace it with
a model of achievement based on *obedience*.[99]

As axiom (2) stipulates, orthopraxy most centrally involves the deliberate shaping of inner actions. Bérulle outlines four principles that
help the soul to replace disordered cravings with spiritual dispositions:
humility of mind, purity of heart, self-abnegation and adherence to
God. While Bérulle's four virtues are aimed at supernatural perfection,
they are not without relevance for the pursuit of natural perfection.
Bérulle indeed points out, elsewhere, that since God names Himself as
scientiarum Dominus, those who study to learn the sciences must cultivate
spiritual virtues, namely

> "humility of mind rather than presumption; submission of mind (i.e. to
> truth) rather than license and liberty that the mind gives itself; modesty
> of mind rather than arrogance and recklessness; stability of mind rather
> than the bad impulse to take pleasure only in contradiction."[100]

Bérulle regards scientific learning explicitly as an opportunity to reform
the soul by practicing a valuable first level of orthopraxy. The soul has
the natural power to curb presumption, submit to truth and resist pee-
vish gratification. The student who makes an effort to reason cautiously
rather than rashly, with impartiality rather than with bias, in good faith
rather than with malice, cooperates with God "the Lord of sciences,"

---

[97] Baillet, *Vie de Monsieur Descartes*, Book II.
[98] Baillet, *Vie de Monsieur Descartes*, Book II: "Il lui fit entendre qu'ayant reçu de
Dieu une force et une pénétration d'esprit avec des lumières sur cela qu'il n'avait pas
accordées à d'autres, il lui rendrait un compte exact de l'emploi de ses talents, et serait
responsable devant ce juge souverain des hommes du tort qu'il ferait au genre humain
en le privant du fruit de ses méditations."
[99] For a parallel case, see the "*Avertissement*" by Mother Angélique de Saint-Jean
Arnaud d'Andilly, as the forward to Mother Angélique Arnauld, *Relation*, published
in the series Chroniques de Port-Royal (Paris: Bibliothèque Mazarine, 1992), 10. When
the nuns failed to get Mother Angélique Arnauld to write down the story of the reform
of Port-Royal, they asked her spiritual director to command her to do it as a matter of
obedience.
[100] Bérulle, "Oeuvres de Piété" CLXXXI, in *Oeuvres Complètes*, II, 1078, col. 1245.

whether he appreciates the higher dimension of his deliberate *aksesis* or not. When Bérulle describes Copernicus as "an excellent mind," what else does he mean than a mind self-disciplined out of reverence for truth?

Bérulle's predilection for the heliocentric theory nicely illustrates the intellectual importance of "purity of heart." Typically, the soul is "pure in heart" when it suffers impulses (passions) without desire invading the will. Purity of heart can be taken at many levels. It requires simply that the soul remain focused on its own action in the face of either temptations or distractions, including divine consolations. Now, according to Bérulle, "an excellent mind of our century" has maintained that the sun illuminates the universe from its center, overriding immediate sensory impression. The heliocentric model, Bérulle points out, "satisfies all of the appearances that force our senses to believe that the sun revolves around the earth."[101] Copernican cosmology, in short, stems from the rational soul turning a deaf ear to sensory passions in order to focus on its own rational action. The mind's eye is unswayed by what the fleshly eye experiences. Reason acts with "purity of heart" since it ignores what sensations (passions) would dictate.

Far from rejecting new scientific initiatives, Bérulle was convinced that God had chosen the XVIIth century to "renew all sorts of sciences and dissipate the darkness of past centuries."[102] Like a number of leading figures of the Catholic Reform in Paris, Bérulle took active steps to stay abreast of new opinions—hence his presence at the papal nuncio's home to hear Chandoux. Francis of Sales, who visited Paris in 1618–1619,[103] defended a Barnabite friar who corresponded with Galileo, Dom Redente Baranzano, whose pro-Copernican *Uranoscopia seu de Coelo* was published in 1617 and again in Paris in 1618.[104] Given Bérulle's appropriation of the heliocentric model as a metaphor for Christocentrism and given Descartes's well-established mathematical proficiency, could Bérulle have failed to question him about the status of Copernican astronomy when they met privately in 1627?

Bérulle was convinced that the spectacular scientific renewal of his time signalled an imminent renewal of God's "own true science,"

---

[101] Bérulle, *De l'estat et des grandeurs de Jesus*, Discours II, in *Oeuvres Complètes*, I, 171.
[102] *La direction des supérieurs*, chap. 13, in *Oeuvres*, vol. I, 627.
[103] See Angélique Arnauld, *Relation*, 11, p. 41 and footnotes 103 and 104, p. 84.
[104] See A. Ravier's preface to Saint François de Sales, *Oeuvres* (Paris: Gallimard, 1969), Pléiade ed., xlix.

namely the science of how to direct the soul to spiritual perfection.[105]
Since the brunt of Descartes's intervention against Chandoux consisted
in contrasting his "beautiful natural method" with man-made dialectical arts capable of promiscuously defending every position,[106] Bérulle
may have recognized Descartes's desire to harmonize knowledge and
wisdom, science and virtue, by "combining the faculties of intellect and
will."[107] After meeting with Descartes, Bérulle apparently emphasized
the "purity" of Descartes's intentions and the likelihood that God Himself would bring them to fruition.[108]

By inviting us to regard the Cartesian *Regulae* as the most immediate result of Bérulle's encouragement, Marion invites us to see the
very idea of "clear and useful rules for directing the intelligence" in a
new light, namely as a promotion of orthopraxy. Appropriately limited to natural steps and to the acquisition of natural virtues, the
Regulae pioneers a new path in which scientific advance depends on
right practice and therefore involves a first level of spiritual reform.
Bérulle, Marion insists, simply helped Descartes "decide to become
himself, which meant, among other things, not to be Berullian."[109] This
is not only consistent with Bérullian direction, but corroborates Baillet's claim. The Berullian director is exquisitely careful never to impose
his own choices on the person whom he directs but helps him find
and follow his unique vocation.[110] Thus we start with a paradox: our
most important indication of Bérulle's influence on Descartes is that
he refrained from influencing him. Had Bérulle attempted to steer
Descartes towards apologetics, he would have disqualified himself as
a spiritual director and jeopardized his authority over Descartes's conscience. Instead, he turned Descartes's own chosen project into a sacred
duty and action of obedience.

---

[105] See *ibid.*: "Dieu qui a voulu perfectionner en ce siecle toute autre sorte de science,
dissipant les tenebres des siecles passez, veut aussi renouveller et perfectionner en nos
jours cette science vrayement sienne et propre à sa lumiere et à son esprit."

[106] See Baillet, *La vie de Monsieur Descartes*, Book II.

[107] See Baillet's account of Descartes's third dream on the night of November 11, 1619
(AT X, 184–185) and Baillet's description of *Studium Bonae mentis* (AT X, 190).

[108] As reported by Baillet, *La Vie de Monsieur Descartes*, Book II: "Il alla même jusquà
l'assurer qu'avec des intentions si pures … Dieu ne manquerait pas de bénir son travail,
et de le combler de tout le succès qu'il en pourrait attendre."

[109] Marion, *La théologie blanche*, 157.

[110] A nice synopsis of this aspect of Berullian guidance is found in the article "Direction Spirituelle en Occident," in *Dictionnaire de Spiritualité* (Paris: Beauchesne, 1957),
vol. III, cols. 1121–1123.

If Bérulle encouraged Descartes to publish his work, he must have felt confident that Descartes's "beautiful natural method" would guide others in the right path rather than lead them astray. Descartes's underlying theory of innate scientific "seeds" may have played a part in convincing Bérulle that Cartesian orthopraxy merited his support and would receive divine assistance. In *Regulae* Rule IV, Descartes speaks of innate rational notions as something mysteriously divine: *habet enim humana mens nescio quid divini.*[111] When, at the papal nuncio's home, Descartes made the audience "confess" that his principles were "more securely founded, more natural and more veridical" than others,[112] did he invoke his theory of innate rational seeds? Descartes's long-standing belief in "seeds of knowledge"[113] bears a significant affinity to Bérulle's emanationist theory of rational truths,[114] and to Augustine's theory of *rationes seminales*, according to which innate seeds of truth lie scattered in the recesses of spiritual memory and are "collected" through the process of rational cogitation.[115]

If Descartes invoked *semina scientiae* to justify the special infallibility of his method, this would explain Bérulle's desire for further clarification. Exactly how do Descartes's clear and distinct ideas relate to *rationes seminales*? What exactly is "divine" about *mens*? What, moreover, is Descartes's overall theory of human cognition?

---

[111] *Regulae*, Rule IV, AT X, 373: "Habet enim humana mens nescio quid divini, in quo prima cogitationum utilium semina ita jacta sunt."

[112] Letter to Villebrissieu, 1631, AT I, 213: "… combien mes principes sont mieux établis, plus véritables, et plus naturels, qu'aucun des autres qui sont déjà reçus parmi les gens d'étude."

[113] Going back at least to 1620. See *Cogitationes Privatae*, AT X, 217: "… sunt in nobis semina scientiae, ut in silice, quae per rationem a philosophis educuntur…"

[114] See Marion's detailed discussion of Bérulle's emanationist views in *La théologie blanche*, 143–149.

[115] See e.g. Augustine, *Confessions*, Bk. X, chap. XI.

CHAPTER TWO

PASSION AND ACTION IN RULE XII

Do the "divine" seeds buried in the *mens* give man unlimited access
to truth? Or does the Cartesian subordination of science to orthopraxy imply otherwise? After abandoning the *Regulae* in 1620, Descartes
returned to the project while living in Paris.[1] If we believe the explanation presented in the *Discours de la Méthode*, Descartes in 1620 believed
himself to be too immature, too rash, to use his method beyond algebra
for the renewal of natural philosophy.[2] He needed, first, to spend time
exercising himself in his prescribed method so as to have the firmest
possible grasp of it.[3] What new material emerges with the resumption of
the project? The last section of Rule VIII of the *Regulae*, which was written some time after 1626, sheds useful light.[4] Descartes ends Rule VIII
with two examples that illustrate the effectiveness of his method.[5] The
first example belongs to geometric optics (how to find the anaclastic
curve), but the second example is philosophical: how to determine the
class of truths that are attainable by natural reason.[6] Descartes describes
this second example as "the most noble of all": *omnium nobilissimum exemplum*. Anyone who seriously strives to have a good mind must ask himself this question at least once (*semel in vita*)—or so, at least, it seems to
him (*mihi videtur*).[7]

The last section of Rule VIII suggests that Descartes's period of
introspection and self-training provided him with a first philosophical

---

[1] See Gaukroger, *Descartes*, 111–112.

[2] AT VI, 21–22.

[3] *Ibid*.: "... Ie ne devois point entreprendre d'en venir à bout, que ie n'eusse attaint
(sic) un aage (sic) bien plus meur ...; et que je n'eusse, auparavent, employé beaucoup
de tems a m'y prepaper ... en m'exerçant touiours en la Methode que je m'estois
prescrite, affin de m'y affermir de plus en plus."

[4] See Jean-Paul Weber, *La Constitution du texte des Regulae* (Paris: PUF, 1964), 80ff; see
also Gaukroger, *Descartes: an Intellectual Biography*, 152–158.

[5] AT X, 393: "Haec omnia uno aut altero exemplo illustranda sunt."

[6] AT X, 395: "Si quis pro quaestione sibi proponat, examinare veritates omnes, ad
quarum cognitionem humana ratio sufficiat."

[7] *Ibid*.: "... quod mihi videtur semel in vita faciendum esse ab iis omnibus, qui serio
student ad bonam mentem pervenire."

area in which to apply his method beyond algebra, namely human cognition. Since Descartes could serve as his own experimental laboratory in this regard and since knowing how the knower knows logically precedes knowing anything else, Descartes must have felt confident that he was proceeding in the right order.[8] Did Descartes use his method to establish the limits of natural cognition before, or after, meeting privately with Bérulle? Nothing, Descartes proclaims in Rule VIII when he returns to the *Regulae*, "is more useful than inquiring how far human cognition extends."[9] Descartes's method promised both to vindicate natural reason as something "divine" but also limit its claim to encompass all of Truth. Precisely because of the Christian and mystical character of his own metaphysics, Bérulle had a clear stake in a rational investigation into the limits of human reason. How, then, does Descartes's method determine the scope of human cognition? How does Descartes both uphold the capacity of reason to secure true knowledge (against, say, skeptics and fideists) and limit its scope (against, say, free thinkers)? From Bérulle's point of view, a clarification of Descartes's general cognitive philosophy was in order.

Rule XII develops the material introduced in Rule VIII by providing a detailed theory of human cognition. As a result, the core axiom of Descartes's "beautiful and natural method," namely that scientific knowledge derives entirely from rational intuition and deduction, is consolidated. The format of Rule XII is expository, aimed at clarity: *dicimus primo… dicimus secundo…* Descartes addresses the reader directly, as an interlocutor. Thus after specifying that his cognitive model claims only to be a useful conceptualization, Descartes adds:

> "… and you do not have to believe it (*neque creditis*), unless you want to! But what prevents you from adopting the same hypotheses if they do not distort the truth and make everything much more clear? This is what you do when, in geometry, you make certain suppositions about a quantity. These hypotheses do not undermine the validity of the proof, even though you often have another idea of its nature in physics."[10]

---

[8] An interesting precedent is Kepler's elucidation of the lens-structure of the human eye—the astronomer's most basic tool—in *Paralipomena ad Vitellionem* (1604).

[9] AT X, 397: "At vero nihil utilius quaeri potest, quam quid sit humana cognitio et quousque extendatur."

[10] AT X, 412: "Neque creditis, nisi lubet, rem ita se habere; sed quid impediet quominus easdem suppositiones sequamini, si appareat nihil illas ex rerum veritate minuere, sed tantum reddere omnia loge clariora? Non secus quam in Geometria quaedam de quantitate supponitis, quibus nulla ratione demonstrationum vis infirmatur, quamvis saepe aliter in Physica de ejus natura sentiatis."

Strangely, Descartes then shifts from the plural *you* ("creditis, sequa-mini") to the singular *thou* ("supponas, negabis"), as though he were not sure whether to address his interlocutor with the French mark of formal respect ("vos") or, according to proper (Ciceronic) Latin form, as "tu".[11] To whom is Rule XII mentally addressed?

Unlike Rule VIII, Rule XII touches on theology twice: first to affirm that the natural light of reason is sufficient to establish God's existence by means of the entailment "*sum, ergo Deus est*"; and, second, to affirm the possibility of truths that exceed the reach of natural reason. In this last regard, Descartes says that propositions to which we "are impelled to assent by some higher force" (*per impulsum determinati a potentia aliqua superiora*) never deceive (*nunquam fallit*), but they surpass the competence of natural reason and therefore cannot be considered by Cartesian analysis.[12] The Cartesian method, in short, both claims the competence to provide theology with rational "preambles" and disqualifies itself from judging the veracity of truths that are known solely through Faith. What (or who) inspired Descartes to delineate so precisely the range of human reason with respect to theology?

Descartes's two positions with regard to theology conspicuously comply with Thomist doctrine. Descartes's first claim, that God's existence is known through a natural deduction, not only ratifies Thomas's endorsement of rational "preambles" to Faith, but satisfies Thomas's requirement that God's existence be proved by a demonstration *quia* (from effect to cause).[13] Descartes's second position, affirming the possibility of true knowledge received through a light superior to reason, is phrased in a sufficiently general way to accomodate, not only Scripture, but the continued activity of the Holy Spirit, as well as

---

[11] A few paragraphs later, AT X, 413: "colorem supponas esse quidquid vis, tamen extendum esse non negabis." Note that J.–L. Marion translates "vis" and "negabis," which are clearly singular, by the plural "vous," implying that the same singular person is addressed in both cases. See R. Descartes, *Règles utiles et claires pour la direction de l'esprit* (La Haye: Nijhoff, 1977), 41 and 42 ("encore que vous supposiez que la couleur soit tout ce que vous voudrez, voius ne nierez point, etc...") Marion does not mention the discrepancy in the Latin, or comment on it.

[12] *Regulae*, XII, AT X, 421 and 424, respectively.

[13] See Thomas Aquinas, *Summa Theologica*, Part I, Qu. 2, Art. 2, *Respondeo*; and *Summa Contra Gentiles*, Bk. I, chap. 3, section 2: "There are some truths which the natural reason is able to reach. Such are that God exists, that He is one, and the like. In fact, such truths about God have been proved demonstratively by the philosophers, guided by the light of natural reason." (Cited from Saint Thomas Aquinas, *Summa Contra Gentiles*, trans. Anto Pegis (Notre Dame: Notre Dame U. Press, 1975), vol. I, p. 63.)

Thomas Aquinas's doctrine of Angelic ministry, which Bérulle warmly endorsed.[14] Now, since Bérulle held the Angelic Doctor in special esteem and made it a habit to "follow St. Thomas as much as possible,"[15] and since Descartes showed special interest in establishing the cognitive scope of unaided human reason, we might be tempted to speculate that Bérulle took the opportunity of their meeting to remind Descartes of Thomas's doctrine. As Marion points out, spiritual directors did not, as such, discuss theology, but they gave advice, as we saw, *with regard to selecting useful authors.* Could Bérulle's authority be at the origin of the Thomist *Summa* that Descartes brought with him from France when he moved to Holland in 1629?[16]

Be this as it may, Rule XII proposes to explain, or at least to model, human cognition by following a broadly Scholastic/Thomistic agenda, namely by discussing (1) the nature of mind (*mens*), (2) the nature of body, (3) how the body is "informed" (*informetur*) by *mens*, and (4) "what faculties in the composite whole serve for the knowledge of things and how each of the faculties operates."[17] Quite apart from anticipating Descartes's mature discussion of metaphysical dualism and theory of man as a substantial composite,[18] Rule XII anticipates Descartes's later concern, equally rooted in scholastic philosophy, to divide mental events into *actions* and *passions.*[19] Wholly absent from the theory of cognition that is sketched in Rule VIII, the passion/action contrast that is invoked in Rule XII deserves careful scrutiny. As I will argue, Descartes's failure to solve a specific puzzle within this framework may have contributed to the final abandonment of the *Regulae.*

---

[14] See Thomas Aquinas, *Summa Theologica*, Part I, Qu. 111, Art. 1, *Respondeo*, and *Summa Contra Gentiles*, Bk. III, chap. 92, section 5: "Sometimes a man's understanding is enlightened by an angel." For Bérulle, see "Oeuvres de Piété," CXLVIII, in *Oeuvres* II, 1025–1026, cols. 1192–1193.

[15] See A. Molien, "Bérulle," in *Dictionnaire de la Spiritualité*, I, col. 1543; and J. Dagens, *Bérulle et les origines de la restauration*, 44.

[16] Letter to Mersenne, Dec. 25, 1639, AT II, 630. For Étienne Gilson's arguments that the *Summa* in question is the *Summa Contra Gentiles*, see *La liberté chez Descartes et la théologie*, 99–100.

[17] Descartes, *Regulae*, Rule XII, AT X, 411: "optarem exponere in hic loco, quid sit mens hominis, quid corpus, quo modo hoc ab illa informetur." For Thomas Aquinas, see *Summa Contra Gentiles*, Bk. 2, chap. 49: "That the intellectual substance is not a body" and chap. 68: "How an intellectual substance can be the form of the body." See also *Summa Theologica*, Part I, Ques. 75 and 76.

[18] See J.–L. Marion's discussion, in *Règles utiles et claires pour la direction de l'esprit*, 244.

[19] The first Part of Thomas's *Summa Theologica*, Part II, contains a Treatise on Human Acts followed by a Treatise on "The Passions, which are Acts Common to Man and Other Animals."

2.1. *Actions vs. Passions*

Descartes's interest in understanding how passions of the soul trigger behavior and how mental actions are connected (or not) to bodily movements dates back to 1619–1620. A few scattered statements in his private notebook testify to his curiosity regarding the mutability of passions (we go from sadness to anger, *a passione in passionem*) as well as regarding the deterministic character of animal actions (they are perfect and therefore, we suspect, not free).[20] Descartes in the same notebook also speculated enigmatically that "love, charity and harmony" are not three distinct principles but a "single active force" (*activa vis*).[21] These elements, transformed, resurface in Rule XII. Descartes in Rule XII no longer speaks of animal actions (*animalium actiones*) but of animal movements (*animalium motus*), suggesting that he now may wish to keep the term *actio* for a more restricted class. Rather than attribute the deterministic character of animal movements to a lack of freedom, Descartes in Rule XII argues that animal movements are performed without knowledge (*cognitio*). Animal movements, he argues, result from a purely corporeal imagination (*fantasia pure corporea*), as do the movements that humans perform without the "ministry of reason" (*ministerio rationis*).[22] In turn, the force (*vis*) that allows *cognitio* to take place, much like the *vis activa* of Descartes's early notebook, is indivisibly "one" (*unica*) despite its various manifestations.[23] In so far as Rule XII frames a general model in which *cognitio* plays the dividing role between humans and animals, what is Descartes's doctrine regarding the *actio/passio* contrast?

The first distinction drawn in Rule XII is the distinction between the action (*actio*) by means of which we apply our external bodily senses to some object and the passion (*passio*) through which we sense the object. *Actio* is identified here as "local movement" (*motus localis*).[24] Descartes's worry seems to be that the experience we have of displacing ourselves bodily in pursuit of sensory information masks the essential passivity of sensing. When we reach out to touch a surface, we act, but when a smooth or coarse texture affects our flesh, we do not act but

---

[20] AT X, 217 and 219 respectively.
[21] AT X, 218: "Une est in rebus activa vis, amor, charitas, harmonia."
[22] *Regulae*, XII, in AT X, 415.
[23] *Ibid.*
[24] AT X, 412: "Concipiendum est igitur, primo, sensus omnes externos, in quantum sunt partes corporis, etiamsi illos applicemus ad objecta per actionem, nempe per motum localem, proprie tamen sentire per passionem tantum."

passively suffer the action of the thing on us, we receive its mark, just as wax receives the shape of a seal. Descartes specifies that the sensory organ is "really modified" by what is sensed: diversely colored lights imprint various shapes on the eye, sound gives a new shape to the inner membrane of the ear, and so forth.

Descartes's next move radically transforms what is, so far, a standard Scholastic view. Substituting *figura* for the Aristotelian/Thomist *forma*, Descartes proposes to define all sensations generally as passions through which *shapes* are received: not a "nature," not a formal *quality*—color, temperature, sound or smell—but a purely semiotic *shape*. Red is a shape, yellow is another shape, F sharp is a shape, hot is a shape, salty is a shape. Since there are infinitely many possible shapes, Descartes argues, all sensible differences can be conceptualized solely as differences in shape. Apart from antecedents in Francis Bacon,[25] a possible source of Descartes's initiative is the late scholastic initiative to represent qualities geometrically, by means of graphs.[26] Descartes's argument implies that a small adjustment suffices to preserve the Aristotelian/Thomist framework by replacing the (rash, boastful) claim that essences (forms) are received with the more modest claim that *signs* only are received—signs that refer to things differentially without disclosing what these things are in an absolute sense. The move is radical. Sense perception apprehends only relevant differences among external objects, not their "quiddities."

Still in basic conformity with the Scholastic framework, Descartes next attributes the same passivity to perception by the common sense, imagination and memory, in so far as these faculties receive and store information. Depending on the "shapes" that are received by the common sense, which is to say depending on how nerves are stimulated, the "motor force" (*vix motrix*) is activated and the living organism (animal or human) reacts. Animal movements thus stem from the disposition of the animal's bodily parts and consist of bodily responses to sensory stimuli. Animals seek food and avoid predators and burrow in the ground without actual knowledge (*cognitio*) of anything. They live and move in perfect ignorance (innocence). Does this imply that animal movements are not, properly speaking, actions? If animal movements are passively triggered through a physiological chain-reaction, should they not be

---

[25] See Marion's commentary, in *Règles utiles et claires*, 229–230.

[26] See Edith Sylla, "Medieval Concepts of the Latitude of forms: the Oxford calculators," *Archives d'histoire doctrinale et littéraire du moyen-age* 40 (1973), 223–283.

counted as passions resulting from earlier passions? But then, *actio* and *motus localis* are not really synonymous, as first presumed. Descartes's analysis implies, moreover, that intentionality, or "goal-directedness," is insufficient, as such, to classify a local movement as a veritable action. If the perception, say, of a suitable prey triggers a predator's appetite and a series of movements aimed at capturing and eating the prey, there is a sense in which the predator has not "acted" but passively suffered bodily events, even though a goal is intended and even reached. Since Descartes specifies that the same analysis applies to human motions that are performed without the help of reason—*absque ullo ministerio rationis*—we must conclude that we humans, in turn, do not truly *act* but merely *suffer* the natural effect of thirst when we instinctively reach for water to quench a dry throat.

What new parameter, then, does knowledge, *cognitio*, introduce? Descartes argues that we know things, properly speaking, through a purely spiritual force (*vis pure spiritualis*), which is "no less distinct from the body than blood is from bone."[27] This cognitive force, moreover, is indivisibly one and the same force, whether (a) it *receives* shapes from the common sense, or (b) *applies itself* to shapes that are preserved by the memory, or (c) *forms* new shapes by "taking such complete possession of the imagination that often the imagination cannot, at the same time, receive the ideas that come to it from the common sense or transmit them to the motive force (*vis motrix*) according to purely bodily dispositions."[28] Case (a) depicts the cognitive force as receptive, implying that it is passively modified from the outside. Case (b), in its reflexivity, implies something like autonomy. Case (c) presumably describes someone who is so mentally focussed on a creative idea that he is temporarily oblivious to, and disconnected from, his physical surroundings. Descartes may have in mind a geometer imagining a triangle while proving a theorem, or an Ignatian exercitant focussed on practicing "guided imagination."[29]

---

[27] AT X, 415: "Concipiendum est, vim illam, per quam res proprie cognoscimus, esse pure spiritualem, atque a toto corpore non minus distinctam, quam sit sanguis ab osse."

[28] AT X, 415: "unicamque esse, quae vel accipit figuras a sensu communi simul cum phantasia, vel ad illas quae in memoria servantur se applicat, vel novas format, a quibus imaginatio ita occupatur, ut saepe simul non sufficiat ad ideas a sensu communi accipiendas, vel ad easdem ad vim motricem juxta puri corporis dispositionem transferendas."

[29] See e.g., *The Spiritual Exercises of Saint Ignatius*, The First Week, 54: "… the image will consist of seeing with the mind's eye the physical place where the object that we wish to contemplate is present. By physical place, I mean, for instance, a temple,

Case (c) thus captures the creative power of the cognitive force, which is capable of suspending outside sensation and/or sensory memory by taking over the imagination with its own deliberate thoughts. The implicit relevance of case (c) to physical movement (*motus localis*) must not be overlooked: Descartes's model implies that deliberate cognitive action can be used to inhibit instinctive responses. A person could, for example, form a mental picture powerful enough to override a flight response in the presence of danger. Similarly, a person could deliberately inhibit the *vix motrix* that pushes her to reach for a glass of water and instead give it to someone else. In short, by appropriating the imagination for itself and forming its own thoughts, the *vis pure spiritualis* through which we know things introduces a measure of independence with regard to instinctive and conditioned behaviors. Descartes's cognitive *vis* exempts us, for instance, from believing the sensory perceptions that "force" us to believe that the sun revolves around the earth.

The theory becomes more problematic when Descartes next specifies that, in all three cases,

> "The cognitive force (*vis cognoscens*) in turn suffers and acts (*interdum patitur, interdum agit*), sometimes imitating the wax, sometimes the seal."[30]

How are we to conceptualize a *passive* "force"?[31] The wax/seal comparison provides only an analogy, Descartes warns, since "absolutely nothing" among bodily things is like this force.[32] Still, a *vis activa* is easier to fathom than a *vis passiva*, since a *vis passiva*, by definition, passively undergoes the action of something acting on it. What exactly does Descartes have in mind? Rather than elaborate on this interesting passive/active duality of the cognitive force, Descartes instead seems to want to emphasize its autonomy. He goes on to use *applicare*—the same verb that defines case (b) and was used earlier for the action of applying a bodily sense to an object—to describe how the *vis cognoscens* applies itself (*applicet se*) to various entities with various functional results. Descartes draws a careful, hierarchical list. When the cog-

---

or mountain where Jesus or the Blessed Virgin is, depending on the subject of the contemplation."

[30] AT X, 415: "In quibus omnibus haec vis cognoscens interdum patitur, interdum agit, et modo sigillum, modo ceram imitatur."

[31] As Marion comments in *Règles utiles et claires*, 234, the source of Descartes's *vis cognoscens* is the Aristotelian *nous*, which is both *nous pathetikos* and *nous poietikos* (*De anima*, III, 5).

[32] AT X, 415: "neque enim in rebus corporeis aliquid omnino huic simile invenitur."

nitive force applies itself (1) to the common sense, it is said to see: *videre*, or to touch: *tangere* (and so on). When it applies itself (2) to the imagination as a reservoir of shapes, the cognitive force is said to remember: *reminisci*. When it applies itself (3) to the imagination as a blank slate for the purpose of inventing (*fingere*) new shapes, the cognitive force is said to imagine or conceive: *imaginari vel concipere*. Finally, when (4) it "acts alone," (*sola agat*), it is said to understand (*intelligere*). Although Descartes had initially stated that we have four faculties, he now clarifies that we have one indivisible "spiritual force" that manifests itself in four different ways. In these four functions, the cognitive force *applies itself*: in what sense does it "imitate sometimes the wax, sometimes the seal?" In what sense does it alternatively act and "suffer" (*patitur*)? In particular, when it acts alone, that is, when it understands, does it "suffer itself"?

2.2. *The Will in Action*

Descartes started by distinguishing between case (a), in which the knowing force *receives* shapes from the common sense, and case (b), in which the knowing force *applies itself* to shapes in the memory. Now he says that the "knowing force" applies itself in all of its functions. In particular, it sees or touches when it *applies itself* to the shapes in the common sense. Does this mean that we should dimiss case (a) altogether? Since animals do not have *cognitio*, they presumably merely perceive while we, humans, actually *see*. Does the autonomy, as such, of the cognitive force, explain the difference? Do we see because, unlike animals, we cannot see without knowing that we see? Perhaps Descartes means that the cognitive force intuits visible things precisely as external, temporal, intelligible, endowed with certain invariances, when it applies itself to shapes that have been optically received. While animals passively suffer visual stimuli, human beings, insofar as they apply themselves cognitively to stimuli, re-cognize patterns, order, abstract form, and therefore behold particulars as latent tokens of "universals." Over and beyond perception and empirical conditioning, human beings properly *see* nominal essences, which is to say, equivalently, that they "label" or "name" what they see. On this interpretation, the spiritual force through which we human beings properly know things—through which we see/remember/conceive/and understand things—is closely tied to linguistic ability. The question is, is the human capacity for language, as such, tied to a special capacity for action, distinct from the local movements that are triggered by bodily passions?

Descartes attributes a key importance to nomenclature. Properly labeling the different functions of the knowing force, Descartes insists, is what will allow the attentive reader accurately to estimate (a) what help to seek from each faculty and (b) how far human effort (*industria*) can be expected to overcome the defects of human intelligence (*ingenii defectus*).[33] Language as a classificatory tool and the ability deliberately to conduct mental activity according to the most effective order are thus intimately tied. Keeping a nominal record of how the knowing force divides into manifest faculties is a key step in making the intelligence (*ingenium*) more "apt." Rather than memorize blind syllogistic algorithms that weaken the intelligence,[34] the mind must methodically discover, describe and apply its cognitive force. Rule XII aims at putting the reader in touch with his own inner resources.

Descartes is eager to label each intellectual function as precisely as possible. When the knowing force acts alone (*sola agit*), it is said to understand (*intelligere*). Presumably, the intellect acts alone when it acts without having recourse to anything corporeal, including the imagination. Does this mean that the "pure intellect" is exempt from passivity? Or does it, instead, affect itself reflexively? In any event, the "pure intellect" is not the same, in Descartes's inventory, as the intelligence (*ingenium*). According to Descartes, the *ingenium* most properly describes the "knowing force" when it either (a) forms new ideas in the imagination or (b) considers those that have already been made.[35] The proper function of the intelligence (*ingenium*) is thus not to understand (*intelligere*), but to form new ideas in the imagination and to study them.

Descartes seems to draw a subtle distinction between "inventing" new forms (*novas formas fingere*), which describes the activity of the imaginative or conceiving faculty, and "forming new ideas" (*novas ideas formare*), which describes the activity of the *ingenium*. Is the latter a sort of specialized function of the former? Presumably, the key difference is that the *ingenium* does not produce just any "feigned" shape, such as a

---

[33] AT X, 416: "... horum nominum distinctio erit in sequentibus observanda. His autem omnibus ita conceptis, facile colliget attentus Lector, quaenam petenda sint ab unaquaque facultate auxilia, et quousque hominum industria ad supplendos ingenii defectus possit extendi."

[34] *Regulae*, Rule X, AT X, 406.

[35] AT X, 416: "proprie autem ingenium appellatur, cum modo ideas in phantasia novas format, modo jam factis incumbit."

chimera, but forms ideas possessed of a special logical consistency, such as triangles, circles and hexagons. Through the imaginative faculty, the mind is free to picture any concept at all, but through the *ingenium*, it pictures a subclass of logically constrained concepts for the "pure intellect" to understand.

Now, since the *ingenium* is precisely what the Cartesian method presumes to direct, exercise and improve, we should investigate in what sense the *ingenium* alternately "acts and suffers." The intellect (*intellectus*), Descartes explains, "can either be moved by the imagination or, on the contray, act on it."[36] In both cases, since the imagination has a sort of spatializing character, the intellect is related to extended things. It follows that when the intellect wants to act with regard to things in which nothing is corporeal, it cannot have recourse to the imagination, or to the memory or common sense.[37] It must neither move, nor be moved by, the imagination. In order to "act alone," the intellect must become "pure." Not only are the lower faculties of no help, Descartes says, they actually stand in the way. The intellect must therefore strive to detach itself from the senses and, as far as possible, from every distinct impression in the imagination.[38] Rather than let itself be moved by shapes invading the common sense, the intellect must *suspend* its receptivity to sensory input; rather than turn to shapes in the memory or form shapes in the imagination, it must *erase* all images. What role does the *ingenium* play in the process of purification? Since the "pure intellect" by definition acts alone, it cannot apply itself to anything but itself. The *ingenium*, presumably, must take charge of wiping the imagination clean. As we saw in Case (c), the *ingenium* has the power so forcefully to occupy the imagination with its own deliberate thoughts that sensory experience is suspended: does its power to override sensory images imply an equivalent power to suspend its own creations? While the intellect must act alone if it wants to contemplate immaterial things, it must, if it wants to examine something that is relevant to body, i.e., something characterized by extension, form an idea of it in the imagination.[39] This, as we know, is the proper function of the *ingenium*. Does the *ingenium* work best

---

[36] *Regulae*, Rule XII, 416.

[37] AT X, 416.

[38] *Ibid.*: "sed contra, ne ab iisdem impediatur, esse arcendos sensus, atque imaginationem, quantum fieri poterit, omni impressione distincta exuendam."

[39] AT X, 416–417: "Si vero intellectus examinandum aliquid sibi proponat, quod referri possit ad corpus, ejus idea, quam distinctissime poterit, in imaginatione est formanda."

if it first clears the imagination of sensory images? Is it more "apt" to form a *distinctissime* idea if the imagination is a *tabula rasa*? Independence from bodily sensation and from bodily memories benefits the special autonomy of the *ingenium* in a twofold way. First, whereas the faculty that invents chimeras draws on sensory memory, the *ingenium* draws its ideas strictly from itself. Independence from bodily memory allows the *ingenium* to supply itself with distinct concepts that transcend sensation (such as a mathematical point, "without length or breadth.") Secondly, the autonomy of the *ingenium* allows it to act beyond the sphere of private thought. The inner action of the *ingenium*, namely to form a distinct mental idea of something extended, is further aided, Descartes remarks, by our capacity physically to exhibit the extended thing to the external senses.[40] In other words, once the intellect has rid itself of sensory turmoil, it uses its intelligence to imagine geometric ideas, then physically to produce these ideas in symbolic form as an aid in furthering discovery. The *ingenium* thus acts inwardly and outwardly, mentally and physically, in a coherent performance. Through symbolic notation, the intelligence gives visible outward appearance to its inner industry. Not only does the intelligence act inwardly to "take hold" of the imagination as its own blank slate, it transforms external conditions as well. It takes hold of the bodily *vis motrix* for its own rational ends. It mobilizes gesture and sense to depict its own objects and present itself with visual stimuli of its own making.

When the geometer avails himself of a straight edge and compass to construct a geometric figure that no sense has previously perceived, an *actio*, a "local motion," is performed "with the ministry of reason." Just as imagining a geometric form is not a passion, but an action of the intelligence, the physical action of constructing geometric figures on paper is not triggered passively by sensory stimuli, but is initiated by the intelligence. Descartes goes on to distinguish between "proposing the things as such" to the external senses and proposing them in abbreviated form.[41] What he means is that symbolic notation lends itself to two basic forms, depending on the needs of the intelligence. A geometric symbol can be graphic, as when a pictogram is traced that exhibits

---

[40] AT X, 417: "ad quod commodius praestandum, res ipsa quam haec idea repraesentabit, sensibus externis est exhibenda."

[41] AT X, 417: "atque eodem modo, non tunc res ipsae sensibus externis erunt proponendae, sed potius compendiosae illarum quaedam figurae, quae, modo sufficiant ad cavendum memoriae lapsum, quo breviores, eo commodiores existent."

all of the relevant angles and proportions, or it can signify convention-
ally, as when a coherent set of properties is labeled/remembered "triangle A" or "triangle B." Intelligent actions originate as special sorts
of well-defined mental actions and culminate in physical actions that
revolutionize experience by bringing about new man-made sensibles,
designed to enhance rational ends. Descartes implies that the intelligence, both in acting mentally and physically, is characterized by a
very special autonomy that already announces the radical purity of the
understanding.

Rule XII comes as close as possible to implicating the free will in
human cognition, without taking the step of actually doing so. Mental
freedom is implied, in particular, as the key variable in distinguishing
mental activity from mental passivity, but is nowhere explicitly invoked
for this purpose. In earlier Rules I and III, where Descartes mentions
the will, freedom as such is not emphasized. Both of these earlier rules
draw a sharp distinction between the intellect and the will. Rule I
invokes the will to justify the whole project of the *Regulae*: increasing the
natural light is no vain project since it means that the intellect will be
able to show the will the best path in life to elect.[42] Rule III, conversely,
argues that what the intellect *cannot* show, the will may embrace on its
own. Thus we hold what is revealed to us by God to be unsurpassably
certain by means of an act of will (*actio voluntatis*) rather than through
our intelligence, precisely because faith concerns "obscure things."[43]
In both cases, the will is sharply contrasted to intellection rather than
implicated as an integral partner in the process of securing knowledge.

Rule XII reiterates the view adopted in Rule III, stating, this time,
that we are sometimes "carried" by our intelligence to believe certain things without being rationally persuaded, but instead determined
(*determinati*) either by some superior force or by "our own freedom" (*a
propria libertate*).[44] Presumably, Descartes means that we embrace certain
propositions, either because we are impelled by Grace (in which case
we never err) or because we freely choose to do so (in which case we
seldom err). An example of the first is embracing the "obscure things of

---

[42] AT X, 361: "... ut in singulis vitae casibus intellectus voluntati praemonstret quid
sit eligendum."

[43] AT X, 370: "... cum illorum fides, quaecumque est de obscuris, non ingenii actio
sit, sed voluntatis."

[44] AT X, 424: "Per impulsum sua de rebus judicia compunnt illi, qui ad aliquid
credendum suo ingenio feruntur, nulla ratione persuasi, sed tantum determinati vel a
potentia aliqua superiori, vel a propria libertate."

faith" based on supernatural help, an example of the second is embracing the same obscure things out of trust in one's teachers. Descartes new distinction in Rule XII clarifies that while Grace alone bestows unshakable certainty, the free will, as such, suffices for us to be able to overlook rational understanding and embrace Christian principles. Implied in Descartes's brief discussion is the idea that moral freedom, as such, prepares us for the supernatural light. By electing the best path in life according to the light of reason, and by therefore freely choosing to enhance the rational light, Descartes does not oppose the guidance of a higher light but instead exercises the inner resources that will allow him to cooperate with it.

The only explicit mention of volition in Rule XII occurs in the context of examining, not the knower, but the things "to be known": *res ipsae cognoscendae*. As far as the intellect is concerned, knowable things divide into simple things and composite things. Simple things, in turn, are either (a) purely intellectual, (b) purely material, or (c) common to both.[45] Volition is cited as an example of class (a). No corporeal idea, Descartes says, can represent to us what knowledge is, or doubt, or ignorance or the action of the will.[46] The action of the will, volition, is known through "a certain innate light."[47] Its relevance to cognition is simply to illustrate a type of known thing, not an activity of the knower. Volition in Rule XII plays no part in the cognitive activities that produce "all of human science" (*omnem humanam scientiam*). Neither the deliberate attentiveness required for the clear and distinct intuition of simple natures,[48] nor the fact that it is "in our power" (*in nostra potestate*) to refrain from a deductive step until we intuit its logical necessity,[49] leads Descartes to raise, as such, the question of freedom.

---

[45] AT X, 419: "Dicimus secundo, res illas, quae respectu nostri intellectus simplices dicuntur, esse vel pure intellectuales, vel pure materiales, vel communes."

[46] AT X, 419: "nec ulla fingi potest idea corporea quae nobis repraesentet, quid sit cognitio, quid dubium, quid ignorantia, item quid sit voluntatis actio, quam volitionem liceat appelare."

[47] *Ibid.*: "Pure intellectuales illae sunt, quae per lumen quoddam ingenitum, et absque ullius imaginis corporeae adjumento ab intellectu cognoscuntur."

[48] AT X, 425: "… et singulis seorsim defixa mentis acie intuendis."

[49] AT X, 424–425: "Sed hunc erorem vitare in nostra potestate fitum est, nempe, si nulla unquam inter se conjungamus, nisi unius cum altero conjunctionem omnino necessariam esse intuamur."

2.3. *Judging Simple Natures*

Descartes, at this stage in the development of his doctrine, considers the judgment to be a faculty of the intellect. To the division of the *vis cognoscens* into the four (or five) faculties described earlier, Descartes adds a new distinction, namely between the faculty through which the intellect, on the one hand, "intuits and knows," and the faculty through which, on the other hand, the intellect "judges, by affirming and denying."[50] The context in which the new distinction is introduced, is concerned, once again, with things *qua* known, rather than with the subject *qua* knower. Descartes invokes the distinction between the intellect's power of intuition and its power of judgment to prove the key axiom that "simple natures are all known *per se* and contain absolutely no falsity."[51] His argument is that we cannot form false ideas of simple natures since we cannot both cognitively apprehend a simple nature and judge it to be composed of what we know and of some unknown component. A simple nature is either known *per se* and with certainty or it is not known at all. The intellect, in one capacity, knows a simple nature and, in another capacity, judges that it knows of it everything that it can know. Thanks to its double function, the intellect not only knows simple natures but knows that it knows them as far as they are knowable, which is to say with the utmost certainty possible.

What is the source of Descartes's assumption that the judgment is a faculty of the intellect? His view is the standard scholastic doctrine, which divides the intellect into two distinct and successive operations, namely (1) apprehending the form of a thing, and then (2) judging the conformity of the mental form to the thing itself. Thomas Aquinas, for instance, appeals to these two distinct functions of the intellect when he discusses our knowledge of truth. He asks, specifically, which of the two functions of the intellect is responsible for our knowledge of truth—or, as he puts it, "whether truth resides only in the intellect composing and dividing."[52] Citing Aristotle,[53] he argues that the intellect first apprehends the form of a thing, but that this is insufficient by itself for its truth to be known. If the intellect then "judges that the apprehended

---

[50] AT X, 420: "... si distinguamus illam facultatem intellectus, per quam res intuetur et cognoscit, an ea qua judicat affirmando et negando."

[51] AT X, 420: "Dicimus tertio, naturas illas simplices esse omnes per se notas, et nunquam ulla falsitatem continere."

[52] *Summa Theologica*, Part I, Quest. 16, art. 2.

[53] *Metaphysics*, VI, 4 (1027b27).

form of the thing corresponds to the thing," it knows and affirms truth. Equating judgment with "composing and dividing," Thomas concludes that truth resides in the intellect judging, rather than in the intellect knowing "what a thing is." Judgment is thus a sort of meta-operation— the faculty of the intellect that ratifies or rejects what the intellect cognitively apprehends.

Descartes has a similar theory in mind when he appeals to the distinction between the faculty through which the intellect intuits a simple nature and the faculty through which it judges that what it knows is simple and, therefore, is known completely and securely. Since the judgment is a faculty of the intellect, its exercise is determined, Descartes implies, by the extent to which we pay careful attention to what we apprehend, which in turn is served by keeping track of mental operations and objects as presented by the Cartesian model. Thus in the case of composite things—things that are known as combinations of simple natures—Descartes argues that error arises specifically when we ourselves compose things, without the warrant of either logical necessity or experience. We avoid error, in turn, as long as we judge our compositions to be mere conjectures and refrain from affirming them as truths.[54] The key is to be able to recognize when we ourselves *propose* a connection among simple things rather than *intuit* a connection that ties simple things together independently of us. Exercising proper judgment and avoiding error thus depend on our willingness to let things impose their natures on us rather than imposing our distortions on them with our inventions. Once again, an antecendent is found in Francis Bacon, but also in Bérulle's stipulation that "submission of mind" to truth rather than "license and liberty" is a chief virtue of intellectuals.

At this stage of Descartes's thinking, avoiding error requires, not the exercise of human freedom, but practice in increasing the natural light—in cultivating the capacity to intuit simple natures by fixing the intelligence sequentially on each one. The intelligence becomes more "apt" to the extent that it trains itself to intuit, first simple natures, then the necessary connections that bind them into composite natures.

Judgment is not only a faculty of the intellect, without any involvement of the will, it is the faculty most aggressively transformed by Descartes's rules. By directing the intelligence first to analyse things

---

[54] AT X, 424: "non quidem nos fallit, si tantum probabile judicemus atque nunquam verum esse affirmemus."

into simple natures, then to intuit them as distinctly as the natural light allows, Descartes seeks to make the judgment at once more bold and more prudent. The result of following Descartes's rules is a new cognitive confidence. Fine-tuning his earlier statement that "all of human science derives from intuition and deduction," Descartes concludes that "all of human science consists in this alone, that we see (*videamus*) how these simple natures concur simultaneously in the composition of other things."[55] Science, in short, is identified to be a rigorous meta-sight, made up of coordinated insights. The things themselves—*res ipsae cognoscendae*—dictate to the sufficiently attentive and perspicacious intellect how judgment must be exercised. Analysis and synthesis mutually test veracity. This is why only deduction, which guarantees that we ourselves have not artificially joined simple natures together, allows us to synthesize simple things together in such as way as to be certain of their truth.[56] Deduction saves us from our own license. It prevents us from distorting what we see. It binds the judgment to what the intelligence intuits when it complies with the right rules—rules which the intelligence intuits, at least after Rule XII, as imposed by the natural operation of cognition and the order of mental faculties.

---

[55] AT X, 427: "Colligitur tertio, omnem humanam scientiam in hoc uno consistere, ut distincte videamus, quomodo naturae istae simplices ad compositionem aliarum rerum simul concurrant."

[56] AT X, 424: "superest igitur sola deductio, per quam res ita componere possimus, ut certi fimus de illarum veritate."

CHAPTER THREE

THE INSIGHTS OF ORTHOPRAXY

The cognitive theory outlined in Rule XII calls for further analysis in three basic areas: (1) metaphysics, so as to understand the nature of the *vis pure spiritualis* through which humans properly know things; (2) physics, so as to grasp the nature of body and the laws governing bodily change; and (3) human psychophysiology, so as to understand the human composite, its passions and actions. Most importantly, Descartes's cognitive theory implies that new knowledge is acquired by intentionally *conducting* the intelligence and conducting it *correctly*. Rule XII, which in itself proves that the Cartesian method achieves useful results, provides new means, in turn, of intellectual self-control, aimed at applying the mental faculties with the greatest possible efficiency. Understanding cognition is a first philosophical fruit of self-discipline that serves further to improve self-discipline.

Progress in science can no longer be divorced from the deliberate practice of spiritual virtues. The pursuit of truth implies inner vigilance and effort. The human desire to know,[1] it turns out, depends on a more fundamental human drive: the desire for moral perfection. Orthopraxy implies an inner rift, a mistrust of spontaneous behavior: the desire for moral perfection presupposes an awareness of imperfection, together with the will to act intentionally and vigilantly. The need for Method emerges from a raised consciousness about human failure and a determination to improve. The scientist must regard himself dynamically, as a *viator* striving to perform the correct steps. As Descartes himself had inscribed at the beginning of his private notebook: *Initium sapientiae timor domini.*[2]

The deep innovation of the *Regulae* consists in subordinating rational speculation (science) to orthopraxy (virtue).[3] Whether consciously

---

[1] Cf. Aristotle, Metaphysics, Bk. I (A), 980b23: "All men by nature desire to know."

[2] "Fear of God is the beginning of wisdom." See AT X, 8: "… et enfin quatre pages escrittes soubs ce titre: Praeambula. Initium Sapientiae timor domini."

[3] Cf. Baillet's account, cited earlier, of the *Studium Bonae mentis*, AT X, 191, in which Descartes wanted to harmonize "science and virtue."

or not, Descartes rejected the core premiss of Aristotelian naturalism, namely that truth is given to man "naturally." By harmonizing science and virtue, Descartes retrieved the Bonaventurian idea that the acquisition of knowledge cannot be divorced from a preliminary level of holiness and that "savoring" knowledge through intimate understanding results from orthopraxy. By emphasizing the primacy of method, Descartes transformed science from a worldly quest for expertise into a vocation for the inner life.

In the new Cartesian paradigm, the purpose of rational speculation is no longer to dazzle crowds, but to satisfy and enlighten the soul: first oneself, then others, viewed precisely as other selves, moral agents, *alter egos*. Reason, Descartes implies, will enlighten those who intentionally adhere to practical rules, by first restoring self-doubt (humility) and impartiality (justice). The urge to know *more* will be balanced by the hope of understanding *better*. The temptation to skip steps, to be rash, to circumvent effort, will be recognized and deliberately resisted. Presumption will recede. Vain curiosity (voyeurism) will be transformed into a legitimate quest for intellectual contemplation. Impatience will give way to reflection. Solving problems will nourish the soul with an enduring sense of inner joy rather than entertain it for a fleeting moment before returning it to its misery. Serenity, consequently, will replace ambition. Taking new delight in familiar and ordinary things, philosophers will no longer crave the exotic for its own sake or seek adulation. At its core, Descartes's predilection for mental orthopraxy shares the same basic principle as the devotionalist (Ignatian, Salesian, Berullian) theory of action: the slightest inner effort, exercised in the most ordinary setting, brings more contentment and "serves God" (reaches truth) better than dreams of martyrdom or exceptional mystical states.

During his most intensive period of discovery, roughly the ten years between the *Regulae* and the publication of the *Discourse on Method* in 1637, Descartes repeatedly wrote of the pleasure he found in "instructing himself."[4] The satisfaction of reaching new insights through his own inner pathways weaned him from what had perhaps been an inordinate desire for glory.[5] Orthopraxy transformed Descartes's inner-

---

[4] Cf. Descartes's letter to Mersenne of April 15, 1630, AT I, 137. Jean-Jacques Rousseau, an avid reader of the Cartesian Lamy, will elaborate on this pleasure in the *Rêveries d'un Promeneur Solitaire* (especially Walk VI).

[5] See, on this subject, G. Rodis-Lewis, *Descartes*, 65 and 328, ftn. 31. Rodis-Lewis's

most experience: "I now disdain most of the things that are ordinarily valued," he wrote to Balzac, "and value others that are usually disdained."[6] Descartes, it seems, had freed himself of the fear of anonymity. His greatest contentment, or so at least he claimed, lay in the special security of knowing that he conducted his intelligence as perfectly as possible.[7] In the "distant desert" where he had gone off to live, Descartes felt a new freedom.[8] Fidelity to his rules and furnishing his best inner effort on a daily basis, known only to himself, brought him unforseen satisfaction. Far from wishing for a keener intellect, Descartes embraced human limitations as an opportunity to practice patience. The experience of orthopraxy nurtured the special fortitude of the devout: Descartes became convinced that truth, even promulgated by an average person, would inexorably triumph over skillful lies.[9] He resurrected for philosophy the emblematic figure of the blind seer, who by advancing cautiously and alone comes to see beyond visible horizons.[10]

3.1. *The World Without Aristotle*

The purpose of this chapter is to unravel the connection between Descartes's commitment to inner orthopraxy and his controversial doctrine of the creation of mathematical truths. We will rely chiefly, although not exclusively, on Descartes's letters from July 1629 to the end of May 1630. The question to be answered is why Descartes adopted such an uncompromising position, even after being warned by Mersenne that

---

interpretation was independently corroborated for me by the Belgian psychoanalyst Henry Bauchau, who ventured that the etchings, in Descartes's third dream, represented, perhaps, a desire for worldly recognition and glory.

[6] Letter to Balzac, April 15, 1631, AT I, 198: "Ie suis devenu si philosophe, que ie méprise la plus-part des choses qui sont ordinairement estimées, et en estime quelques autres dont on n'a point accoustumé de faire cas."

[7] cf. *Discourse de la Méthode*, Part II, AT VI, 21: "Ce qui me contentoit le plus de cete Methode, estoit que, par elle, i'estois assuré d'user en tout ma raison, sinon parfaitement, au moins le mieux qui fust en mon pouvoir."

[8] cf. *Discours de la Méthode*, Part III, AT VI, 31, 12–13.

[9] cf. Descartes's letter to Mersenne, May 6, 1630, AT I, 149: "... la verité, expliquée par un esprit mediocre, devoit estre polus forte que le mensonge, fust-il maintenu par les plus habiles gens qui fussent au monde."

[10] Cf. *Discourse de la Méthode*, AT VI, 16–17; and *La Dioptrique*, AT VI, 83–84.

it compromised the theology of the Word. Since Descartes bases his position on natural reason, he implies that philosophy is competent to disqualify at least some attitudes elaborated in theology as *blasphemous*.

When he first moved to Holland, in late 1628 or early 1629, Descartes, as we know, was chiefly concerned with metaphysical issues.[11] Two ideas, in particular, sketched in Rule XII, namely the immateriality of *mens* and the proof of God's existence based on the subject's immediate intuition of self-existence (*sum, ergo Deus est*), begged to be more firmly substantiated. Did Bérulle or any other Oratorian, perhaps Gibieuf, press Descartes to focus on these two items? Descartes took care, as we saw, to arrange in Paris to have his metaphysical conclusions corrected by Gibieuf before publication. In July 1629, Descartes reminded Gibieuf of his promise and told him that he planned to send him a treatise in "two or three years."[12] The projected treatise, described later as a "beginning of metaphysics," turned out to provide a fairly detailed elaboration of the proof *sum, ergo deus est*, along with a proof of the immateriality of the human soul.[13] Looking back at this work in 1629, Descartes wrote to Mersenne that he "began his studies by trying to know God and to know himself," and that "he would not have known how to discover the foundations of physics if he had not sought them through this path."[14]

Three months after writing to Gibieuf, Descartes had shelved his plan to finish a treatise on metaphysics. By October 1629, excited by the prospect that his investigations into metaphysics had yielded new principles for philosophy, Descartes was at work on the colors of the rainbow. As he wrote to Mersenne, he now planned to compose a treatise explaining "sublunary phenomena" in order to offer a sample of his new principles to the public before venturing to publish a complete account of his philosophy.[15] The close interdependence of his rapidly accumulating conclusions soon argued against adopting a piecemeal

---

[11] For scholarly assessments of where Descartes spent the winter of 1628/9, see Gaukroger, *Descartes. An Intellectual Biography*, 187 and 443, footnote 1; and Rodis-Lewis, *Descartes*, 111–114.

[12] AT I, 17.

[13] See Descartes's letter to Mersenne, March, 1637, AT I, 350: "Il y a environ huit ans que i'ay écrit en latin un commencement de Metaphysique, où cela est deduit assez au long."

[14] Letter to Mersenne, April 15, 1630, AT I, 144.

[15] Letter to Mersenne, October 8, 1629. AT I, 23.

approach. By November, Descartes had once again revised his plan, deciding, this time, to go ahead and explain "all of Physics" in a treatise that would take him a year to write.[16] In the two years following Bérulle's encouragement to publish his method, Descartes had thus considered and abandoned three different formats before settling on the comprehensive project of *Le Monde ou Traité de la lumière*. Descartes was satisfied with his new plan: "my present plan gives me more contentment than any previous one, since I believe that I have found a way to present my thoughts so as to gratify some without giving others grounds for refutation."[17] Another reason, perhaps, for his satisfaction with the plan, was that he intended to give his new theory of light the central role in unifying cosmic phenomena.[18] The treatise proposed to explain, first, the sun and stars, which radiate light, then the transparent heavens, which transmit light, then the opaque mass of the earth, which scatters light—and finally man, who is light's spectator and the witness of the cosmic order.[19] A more Bérullian agenda is hard to imagine: Descartes's *World or Treatise on Light* would step beyond a baroque aesthetic to launch a new classical aesthetic by simultaneously placing the sun at the center of physical creation and God at the center of the spiritual realm. It was designed to evoke the six days of creation and remind the reader of what Adam saw when he first opened his eyes, radiant with innocence. Whatever its scientific merit, Descartes's final choice of format harmonized science and virtue into a contemplative *tour de force*.

The evolution of Descartes's plans testifies not only to his desire to reach a multi-faceted audience as persuasively as possible, but also to his increased confidence in the unified character of human science. Descartes's purely poetic hypothesis, proclaimed in Rule IV, that human wisdom is like sunlight illuminating various objects without loss of simplicity, seems to have been verified with every new discovery. The *vis pure spiritualis* through which we properly know things dispelled darkness

---

[16] Letter of November 13, AT I, 70.

[17] *Ibid.*: "Le dessein que i'ay me contente plus qu'aucun autre que i'aye iamais eû, car je pense avoir trouvé un moyen pour explorer toutes mes pensées en sorte qu'elles satisferont a quelques uns et que les autres n'auront pas occasion d'y contredire."

[18] Cf. Letter of November 25, 1630, AT I, 179, 5–10, where he says that he has been working on "the nature of colors and light" for six weeks. See also the letter of December 23, 1630, AT I, 194 13–21.

[19] See the summary given in *Discours de La Méthode*, Part V, in AT VI, 42.

everywhere it focused the same simple light, according to the proper rules. Orthopraxy made it more "apt" and more intense, but also tested its changeless coherence.

Shortly after announcing his new plan to write comprehensively on "all of physics," Descartes was queried by Mersenne about the theoretical possibility of inventing a universal language. Descartes answered that a universal language would require first discovering "the true philosophy," which alone analyzes all of human thoughts into distinct units and arranges them in the right order. If the true philosophy were to be discovered, the key to science would become universally available. Farmers would be able "to judge truth better than philosophers do now."[20] Provocatively, Descartes introduces a note of pessimism: "have no hope (*n'esperez pas*)," he tells Mersenne, "that you will ever see such a universal language come into use," since "the world would have first to become an earthly paradise, which is an idea fit only for novels."[21] *N'esperez pas*: Descartes knows full well that Hope is a theological virtue and that Mersenne, a Minim priest, professes to live by hope. The earth's redemption, to him, is no fiction. Does Descartes mean to imply that the new science must flourish hand-in-hand with moral reform— with the "science of the saints"?

In December 1629, Descartes warns Mersenne that his treatise on physics (*Le Monde*) will have to be reviewed by theologians before publication. The reason, he explains, is that theology has been so tightly welded to Aristotle that "it is almost impossible to describe a new philosophy without seeming at first to contradict the faith."[22] Descartes gives no indication that he himself wishes to engage in theological debate, quite the contrary. His worry, based on the success of anti-Aristotelian libertinism, is that some defendors of the faith might rashly confuse his rejection of Aristotelian principles with a rejection of Christian doctrine.[23] Descartes's solution is not to meddle in theology, but to ask professional theologians to ratify the idea that wrong Aristotelian premisses may be safely abandoned, provided they be replaced by true principles secured by theistic metaphysics. The agenda conforms

---

[20] Letter to Mersenne, November 20, 1629, AT I, 81–82.

[21] AT I, 82: "Il faudroit que tout le monde ne fust qu'un paradis terrestre, ce qui n'est bon à proposer que dans le pays des romans."

[22] Letter to Mersenne, December 18, 1629, AT I, 85–86.

[23] See, e.g., Tullio Gregory, *Genèse de la raison classique de Charron à Descartes* (Paris: PUF), Chap. I (Le libertinisme dans la moitié du XVIIe siècle), 13–61.

to the scholastic assumption that philosophy is the "servant" of theology: Descartes's plan is to disentangle Christian theology from the inadequate services it has received from Aristotle *faute de mieux* and give it a servant worthy of the name, namely *la vraye philosophie*. The subordination of philosophy to theology remains unquestioned. The duty of theologians to defend the non-irrationality of Christian truths is upheld. A month later, in January 1630, Descartes tells Mersenne that he plans to deny a standard scholastic/Aristotelian thesis regarding projectile motion and asks Mersenne to conduct independent experiments.[24] On February 25, again writing to Mersenne, he rejects the scholastic/Aristotelian claim that a ball bouncing back from a wall is kept in motion by the surrounding air and instead frames a formal rule for inertia.[25] Implicitly, Mersenne is given a chance, each time, to check for himself (a) that the Cartesian position fits nature better than the Aristotelian position, and (b) that it poses no threat to catholic faith. A letter of March 18 indicates that Descartes had resumed work on bodily passions and developed, against Aristotle's thesis that animals are "ensouled," an elegantly materialist model of animal motion and learning based on conditioned reflex.[26] By mid-April, Descartes was plunged in the study of "chemistry and anatomy combined," learning something "every day that he cannot find in books."[27] Aware that Mersenne opposed all forms of animism as idolatrous, Descartes gave birth to a new scientific paradigm that was not made up of arbitrary hypotheses but was rooted in principles obtained through inner orthopraxy—through the right use of spiritual faculties. Since every step and every link had to be established, progress turned out to be slower than anticipated. Every small problem that was raised by scholastic philosophy had to be explained according to new mechanistic principles: for example, by what mechanism does the mother's

---

[24] AT I, 113.

[25] Letter of February 25, 1630, AT I, 117: "ex hoc ipso quod una res coepit moveri, ideo pergit moveri, quamdiu potest; atque si non possit recta pergere, potius in contrarias partes reflectitur quam quiescat." ("From the very fact that a thing starts to be moved, it continues to be moved, as far as possible; and if it cannot pursue a straight course, it bounces back in other directions rather than come to a standstill.")

[26] AT I, 113–114. As we saw in an earlier footnote, a possible precursor is found, according to Maurice Nédoncelle, in John Barnes's *Dissertatio contra aequivocationes*. See Nédoncelle, *Trois Aspects du problème anglo-catholique au XVIIème siècle*, 19.

[27] AT I, 137.

imagination shape the foetus?[28] Descartes gave Mersenne the new completion date of 1633, adding that Mersenne could "reproach him" if he failed to meet it.[29]

3.2. *Mathematical Truths*

The letter in which this new deadline is set, written to Mersenne on April 15, 1630, occupies a special place in Descartes's correspondance because it contains Descartes's first statement on the creation of mathematical truths. As scholars from Gilson to Marion have consistently remarked, Descartes's doctrine flies in the face of cherished Scholastic notions.[30] Strikingly, Descartes not only announces that he plans to include the doctrine in his Physics,[31] he asks Mersenne to proclaim it publicly at every opportunity—without mentioning him (Descartes) by name.[32] What motivates this unexpected initiative? Descartes, who had deferred hitherto to theologians and given them the final word on metaphysical matters, suddenly seemed determined to assert a theological doctrine on his own, without consultation. He was clearly aware of its controversial character since he urged Mersenne to publicize it, in order that he, Descartes, could "learn what sort of objections could be made against it." A second reason to publicize the doctrine, even more surprising, was to "accustom the public to hear God mentioned with more dignity than He is mentioned by the majority of people, who

---

[28] At the end of May, 1630, Descartes told Mersenne that he was "no yet satisfied" that he understood this phenomenon. See AT I, 153, 27–30: "Pour le septiéme point, touchant les marques qui s'impriment aux enfants par l'imagination de la mère, j'avoue bien que c'est une chose digne d'estre examinée, mais ie ne m'y suis pas encore satisfait."

[29] *Ibid.*: "ie vous determine le tans pour m'y obliger davantage, et affin que vous m'en puissiés faire reproche si i'y manque."

[30] See e.g. F. Alquié, *La découverte métaphysique de l'homme chez Descartes* (Paris: PUF, 1960), 91: "Rien n'est plus opposé à la scolastique que la théorie de la création des vérités éternelles."

[31] AT I, 146; also, earlier, 145: "Mais ie ne laisseray pas de toucher en ma Physique plusieurs questions metaphysiques, et particulierement celle-ci: Que les verités mathematiques, lesquelles vous nommés eternelles, ont esté establies de Dieu et en dependent entieremant, aussi bien que tout le reste des creatures."

[32] AT I, 146: "l'espere escrire cecy, mesme avant qu'il soit 15 jours, dans ma physique; mais ie ne vous prie point pour cela de le tenir secret; au contraire ie vous convie de le dire aussy souvant que l'occasion s'en presentera, pourvu que ce soit sans me nommer."

almost always imagine Him as though He were something finite."[33] Why would Descartes venture to take on a mission of this kind, at the risk of alienating the theological establishment, starting with Mersenne himself?

The answer requires that we analyse Descartes's letter step by step. Mersenne had written to Descartes on March 14, and again on April 4, apparently troubled that he had not received an answer. The reproachful content of Mersenne's April 4 letter is readily gleaned from Descartes's answer: Why was it taking Descartes so long to write his treatise? Would he deliver it by November 1630, as pledged? Or was he going to abandon the project, like so many he had started and never finished? People were impatient to see his philosophy. Would it live up to their expectations? Meanwhile, while Descartes was procrastinating, a wicked book was circulating in manuscript form: atheists, apparently, had no problem finishing their projects and getting them to the public's attention!

Descartes's response is unusually long and personal. After reassuring Mersenne of his friendship and gratitude, Descartes shares his state of mind in considerable depth. First of all, he would prefer it if Mersenne lowered people's expectations—even removed expectations altogether. While he cares about his good reputation, he really wants, simply, to be forgotten. He fears fame more than he desires it. Fame robs a person of freedom and leisure, both of which he "possesses so perfectly and holds so dear" that there is "no monarch rich enough to buy them from him."[34] His anxiety in this regard will not prevent him from finishing "the little treatise I have started," but he wants to remain free, at all times, to "disown it."

Descartes, in short, seems to want to wrap himself in the *persona* of a Stoic sage to fend off Mersenne's pressure to publish. The presumed Stoic vestment, however, is contradicted by a crucial detail: Descartes explicitly says that if people have an opinion of him, he cares that it be a good one. He is not so uncivilized, uncouth, antisocial (*sauvage*) as to

---

[33] AT I, 146: "... et aussy que le monde s'accoustume a entendre parler de Dieu plus dignemant, ce me semble, que n'en parle le vulgaire, qui l'imagine presque touiours ainsy qu'une chose finie."

[34] AT I, 136: "Ie crains plus la reputation que ie ne la desire, estimant qu'elle diminue tousiours en quelque façon la liberté et le loysir de ceux qui l'acquerent, lesquelles deux choses ie possede si parfaitement, et les estime de telle sorte, qu'il n'y a point de monarque au monde qui fust assés riche pour les achepter de moy."

be without feelings in this regard.[35] He is not *impassible*, but a member of the human community, sensitive to his honor and to the duty of setting a good example. By showing his concern for *respectability*, Descartes distances himself from the elitist invulnerability of the Stoic and manifests instead his adherence to the norms of civility, or catholicity, of the *honnête homme*. What he rejects is not the favorable judgment of fellow human beings but the pursuit of fame. Descartes's *persona* is, in fact, the opposite of the Stoic sage: far from wishing to insulate himself against the judgment of others or the external whims of fortune, he wishes to rid himself of his own inner pride. What he specifically cherishes is *obscurity*, which reforms the soul, not the solitude of the Stoic, which nurtures an inhuman pride. Descartes's life of *otium*, in short, is really a clandestine *vie dévote*.

The cornerstone of Salesian, or Christian *honnêteté*, is the conviction that man's supreme dignity lies in living a perfectly average human life *well*. As Francis of Sales explains to *Philotée*, there is a duty to shun notoriety, be it in the form of praise or in the form of blame. Both undermine justice: to provoke the contempt of others is to tempt them, to provoke their adulation is to abuse them. The devout also must not seek to become emancipated from the legitimate demands of human opinion. Descartes thus assumes as his responsibility to prevent giving anyone cause to accuse him of presumption. On the other hand, to seek preferment, either in human eyes or in God's eyes, is to succumb to the root evil of pride. Francis of Sales, as we saw, warns Philothée against seeking to receive special marks of divine favor: better she focus on her actions, which are modest but in her power, than view herself as singled out, risking new levels of addiction and self-conceit. In the same way, Descartes recognizes fame as a threat to his inner agenda of orthopraxy because self-conceit sabotages orthopraxy at its core. His position does not reflect a Stoic *sauvagerie* but a distinctly Salesian and Berullian *honnêteté*. Other features corroborating this view surface in the account Descartes gives of his life. First, Descartes attributes the slow progress of his writing to the fact that he has discovered incomparable inner contentment: teaching himself, he learns every day what is not found in books, by which he means new philosophical results, but also the contentment itself that derives from obtaining the results methodically.

---

[35] AT I, 136: "Ie ne suis pas si sauvage que ie ne sois bien ayse, si on pense en moy, qu'on en ait bonne opinion."

Implied is a new intimacy with reason and with truth, penetrating the most ordinary facts. Orthopraxy reveals and confirms that the master of "those who know" is not Aristotle, but reason, the light within, the inner master. Examining plants, colors, snow, dreams and waking sensation with a purified intellect fills the heart with satisfaction. Time goes by effortlessly.[36] So rewarding is the inner agenda through which truth is discovered that other activities seem hardly worth the effort. Regulating the inner life is the chief vocation of human being and the chief way to use our faculties to find happiness.[37] What matters most, Descartes insists, what "occupies all of his care," is not to amuse himself with publications, but to "learn what is necessary for the conduct of my life:" *ce qui m'est nécessaire pour la conduite de ma vie.* Mersenne's reproach is turned back against him: what matters is to conduct oneself as perfectly as possible. Will Mersenne disagree?

Descartes explains that he has changed the format and scope of his project over the years simply because of the unexpected riches uncovered by the continuous application of his method. The final framework he has adopted, sufficiently wide to accomodate any new discovery and thus firmly rooted in the unity of science, is implicitly one of the method's most important fruits. Descartes implies to Mersenne that, far from being fickle, he has practiced *patience*. He has revised his expectations each time to suit new facts. He has attentively pursued new discoveries rather than focus on making a name for himself as quickly as possible. He has advanced cautiously rather than rashly, he has focused on truth rather than on himself. In the next paragraph, Descartes remarks that "there are people who think they know a subject perfectly as soon as they see a hint of light."[38] Descartes's pathway to the decision to write *Le Monde* and explain "all of Physics" was thus an exercise in subjection to truth. The cosmic spectator depicted in *Le Monde* emerged from a long practice in self-correction. By applying his method, Descartes used all of his faculties in the right order, as stipulated in Rule XII. He purified the imagination and practiced pure understanding. Orthopraxy, in short, led him to *le Monde* by restoring

---

[36] AT I, 137: "i'y travaille fort lentemant, pour ce que ie prens beaucoup plus de plaisir a m'instruire moy-mesme, que non pas a mettre par escrit le peuy que ie sçay…" And: "Au reste, je passe si doucement le tans en m'instruisant moy-mesme…"

[37] Cf. *Oeuvres de Piété*, 176, in Bérulle, *Oeuvres Complètes*, II, 1064.

[38] AT I, 138: "Il y a des gens qui pensent sçavoir parfaitement une chose, sitost qu'ils y voyent la moindre lumière."

some of the rectitude of the primitive state, in which "the lower powers
in man were subject to the higher, and were no impediment to their
action."[39]

The most notable testimony in Descartes's letter concerns his
changed experience of mathematics. To Mersenne's request for mathematical puzzles, Descartes answers that he will send him "a million,
for others, if you wish," but adds that he is so tired of mathematics and
holds them now in such little esteem that he will not go to the trouble of solving them himself.[40] What has distanced him from his own
mathematical virtuosity? Later in the letter, we learn that Descartes has
found a way to prove metaphysical truths "more evidently than the
proofs of geometry."[41] Is this why mathematics have lost their prestige
in his eyes? Are mathematical truths no longer the *nec plus ultra* standard
of certainty, as they appeared to Descartes in the *Regulae*? Or does he
mean to convey to Mersenne that he has moved beyond the need to
impress, to exhibit his superior skill, to be ranked among the gifted?

In the concluding section of the letter, Descartes proclaims that
mathematical truths, like all things, are made by God. Although Descartes explicitly anticipates objections and is aware, therefore, that the
doctrine will offend a number of people, he may have found support
in the Thomist *Summa* brought with him from France. Thomas indeed
affirms that "every being that is in any way is from God," including
mathematical beings, which "have an efficient cause," even though
their efficient cause (God) is not invoked in demonstration.[42] Be this as
it may, Descartes is uncharacteristically certain of a position that comes
as close as possible to theology. The context in which Descartes declares
the dependent status of mathematical truths provides a number of
possible clues. Mersenne's question prompting Descartes's declaration
is a theological question, reacting to the "wicked" book. We know
neither the content of the book, nor the nature of Mersenne's question.

---

[39] Cf. Thomas Aquinas, *Summa Theologica*, Part I, Q. 94, art. 4, *respondeo*.

[40] AT I, 139: "Ie suis si las des mathematiques, et en fais maintenant si peu d'estat,
que ie ne sçaurois plus prendre la peine de les soudre moi-mesme."

[41] AT I, 144: "au moins pense-ie avoir trouvé commant on peut demonstrer les
vérités metaphysiques, d'une façon qui est plus evidente que les demonstrations de
Geometrie."

[42] Thomas Aquinas, *Summa Theologica*, Treatise on Creation, Part I, Q. 44, art. 1:
"Whether It is necessary That Every Being Be Created by God?"; *respondeo* and Reply
to Obj. 3. One of Marion's chief claims in *La Théologie blanche* (pp. 58–59) is that
Descartes was cut off from Thomist theology and took Suarez and Vazquez as his point
of departure. This seems strange in light of the fact that he owns a Thomist Summa.

What can we surmise? Descartes shows great caution. Before answering Mersenne's question, he ascertains whether he should, in fact, answer it: although the question, he says, surpasses his intelligence, it does not exceed his professional competence as a philosopher, since it involves no truth that is based on Revelation. The question belongs therefore to metaphysics rather than theology, and must be examined by human reason.[43] Descartes then follows immediately with the statement: "Now, in my view, all those to whom God has given the usage of reason are under the obligation to use their reason chiefly to try to know Him and to know themselves."[44] Whatever the nature of Mersenne's question, Descartes in response invokes the *duty* of rational creatures to know the source (God) and nature of their rationality, and to know it prior to investigating other matters. Does he imply that duty in this regard belongs indivisibly to rationality? Does a rational being who fails in the obligation first to know God and himself fail to be perfectly rational?

Descartes goes on to give his own intellectual progress in example: (1) he started out his search for truth by addressing these two metaphysical questions; (2) he would not have discovered the foundations of physics otherwise; and (3) he devoted *most* of his effort to metaphysics, with satisfying results—in particular, he has discovered, he thinks, that he can prove metaphysical truths with even more evidence than geometric truths. The whole suggests that Mersenne asked Descartes something like the following: is it possible for the human intellect to pursue science as an independent body of internally demonstrable truths, in radical disjunction with higher questions regarding God and the spiritual realm? Descartes's response is to affirm that he, for one, did not proceed independently of higher questions and progressed successfully only because he first proved God's existence and the immateriality of the soul. Had he not *first* rationally determined the truth of God's existence and the immateriality of the soul, Descartes implies, he would never have figured out the true explanation of the colors of the rainbow.

---

[43] AT I, 143–144: "Pour vostre question de Theologie, encore qu'elle passe la capacité de mon esprit, elle ne me semble pas toutefois hors de ma possession, pource qu'elle ne touche point a ce qui depent de la revelation, ce que ie nomme proprement Theologie; mais elle est plustost metaphysique et se doit examiner par la raison humaine."

[44] AT I, 144: "Or i'estime que tous ceux a qui Dieu a donné l'usage de cete raison, sont obligés de l'employer principalement a le connoistre, et a se connoistre eus-mesmes."

Descartes next tells Mersenne that, although he had planned to publish his metaphysical results, he now judges that he should wait to see how his Physics are received. He adds:

> "If, however, the book that you mention were especially well-argued, I might feel obligated, were it to fall in my hands, to answer it on the spot; so false and, it seems to me, so dangerous are its contents, at least if the account you have heard of it is true."[45]

What is so dangerous and false? Does the book propose a plausible scientific project that does *not* require that God's existence first be rationally established? Does it claim, in particular, as Descartes did in the *Regulae*, that mathematical truths are *per se* certain and absolute? After volunteering to drop everything and refute the wicked book, Descartes adds that he plans to address the issue in his Physics:

> "But I will not fail to touch on a number of metaphysical questions in my Physics, most especially on the following: that mathematical truths, which you call eternal, have been established by God and depend on Him entirely, like all other creatures."[46]

Mathematical truths, which *you* call eternal: did Mersenne himself raise the theological problem of eternal truths, perhaps because the wicked book invokes the absolute necessity of mathematical truths, their logical independence, their self-subsistent validity, to defend a radically agnostic, or even atheistic, science? Descartes's chief argument against the absolute necessity of mathematical truths is that God is infinite and incomprehensible, while the human imagination is finite. Although we cannot conceive it, God has the power to *create* logical necessity. In close affinity to Oratorian sensibility, Descartes composes for Mersenne a sort of metaphysical *Magnificat*. We know that God is great, but we cannot comprehend His grandeur. The very incomprehensibility of God's grandeur benefits us since it inspires us to regard Him with awe. God's infinite elevation above creatures enhances His majesty and deepens our humility—provided, of course, that we securely know His existence and are preserved from ever thinking that we are without a king. Noth-

---

[45] AT I, 144–145: "Si toutefois le livre dont vous parlés estoit quelquechose de fort bien fait, et qu'il tombast entre mes mains, il traite des matières si dangereuses et que i'estime si fausses, si le rapport qu'on vous en a fait est veritable, que ie me sentirois peut-estre obligé d'y repondre sur le champ."

[46] AT I, 145: "Mais ie ne laisseray pas de toucher en ma Physique plusieurs questions metaphysiques, et particulièrement celle-cy: Que les verités mathematiques, que vous nommés eternelles, ont esté establies de Dieu et en dependent entiremant, aussy bien que tous le reste des creatures."

ing is prior to God. God has established his laws of nature the way a king decrees laws for his kingdom. God has inscribed mathematical truths on our souls the way a king would engrave his laws on subjects' hearts, if he could: as a consequence, there is no natural law that the human mind cannot discover if it applies itself to the task.

Descartes's reason for identifying rationality with a *duty* to know God and oneself—which is to say with the duty to prove God's existence and the immateriality of the human soul—is now clear: a chief example of human rational capacity is the knowledge of mathematical theorems, but we know mathematical theorems, as a matter of fact, only because God Himself has freely chosen to inscribe mathematical truths in the human soul. We should thus be content with the *relative* necessity of the quantitative truths that God has established in our minds to rule over us and lead us to knowledge, rather than arrogantly imagine that our theorems have absolute (infinite) necessity. To deny the dependence of mathematical truths on God's infinite power, Descartes implies, is to fall into disorder, ingratitude and presumption (*temerité*). If we forget the infinity of God's power, we underestimate divine incomprehensibility and commit a crime of *lèse-majesté*. We reduce divine logic to the measure of our own and wrongly think that what *we* cannot comprehend is impossible to God.[47] We forget that God is infinite. A chief reason to publicize the causal dependence of mathematical truths on God is to remind readers of God's infinity.[48] Descartes concludes with a question, put to him by Mersenne, about transfinite logic. Against Mersenne's rejection of an infinite line on the grounds that one infinity (the whole) would be larger than another infinity (the part), Descartes argues: what reason do we have to judge that this is impossible? The point is, the paradox exceeds our inductive ability, since the line would no longer be infinite if we could understand it.[49]

Descartes's next letter to Mersenne, written May 6, speaks again of the dangerous book. Descartes no longer requests a copy of it because it is too late to "execute his plan," which was to refute the book point by point and publish the refutations jointly with the book, so that readers would be "disabused" along with learning the false doctrine. Revealingly, Descartes worries that his counter-arguments might not be good

---

[47] AT I, 146.
[48] AT I, 146.
[49] AT I, 147: "Quelle raison avons-nous de iuger si un infini peut estre plus grand que l'autre, ou non? vû qu'il cesseroit d'estre infini, si nous le pouvions comprendre."

enough.[50] He clearly has the impression that the author is exceptionally skilled. All he can do is present the metaphysical proofs which have
persuaded him to hold the doctrine directly contrary to the one that is
taught in the dangerous book.[51] Since Descartes feels personally responsible for refuting the book point by point, should we venture that it was
written by a mathematician, in a Euclidean format? Since, moreover,
Descartes's doctrine is that God's existence and the immateriality of
the human soul are (1) rationally proved and (2) prerequisite for further
knowledge, should we venture to speculate that the dangerous doctrine
likely held the opposite, namely that nothing at all is known with certainty except mathematical truths, which have the singular advantage
that they are certain *per se* and do not require God, or imply God, or
depend on God in any way? If this interpretation is correct, the metaphysical status of mathematical truths play a decisive role. The point
is, Descartes is more likely, given the context, to be motivated to refute
atheist analysts than scolastic "univocity."

It seems that Mersenne sent Descartes a number of scholastic passages contradicting the Cartesian position about eternal truths, perhaps drawn from two of the eminent Jesuit philosophers, Suarez and
Vasquez.[52] Granted that Descartes thus was called to define his position
in precise scholastic terms, his emphasis remains focused on preventing mathematical idolatry. Descartes points out the absurdity of claiming that mathematical truths are so intrinsically true that they would
remain true *even if God did not exist*, since God's existence is the "first
and *most* eternal of all possible truths and the only source of all other
truths."[53] Logically speaking, Descartes is right: from a false premiss,
anything follows, which means that *si Deus non esset*, truth assignments
become entirely meaningless. Descartes does not formulate it in this
way, but he clearly means that the truth of God's existence is the first
truth and the most eternal because its contradictory makes logic itself
radically impossible. Moreover because God is infinite, knowing and
willing are a single indivisible and incomprehensible divine act. We
cannot comprehend the content of divine infinity, we can only love it

---

[50] Letter to Mersenne, May 6, 1630, AT I, 149: "Vous me direz, ie m'assure, que
c'est à sçavoir si i'eusse pû répondre aux raisons de cét Autheur."

[51] Letter to Mersenne, May 6, 1630, AT I, 149.

[52] See J.–L. Marion, *La Theologie blanche de Descartes*, 43–69, especially 59–60.

[53] AT I, 150: "Il ne faut donc pas dire que *si Deus non esset, nihilominus istae veritates essent
verae*; car l'existence de Dieu est la premiere et la plus eternelle de toutes les veritez qui
peuvent estre, et la seule d'où procedent toutes les autres."

and adhere to it through orthopraxy, which starts with the humility of recognizing God's incomprehensible infinity. Logic (rational orthodoxy), which is not God but depends causally on God, is comprehensible, and requires, in order to be understood, method and disciplined discourse, which is to say mental orthopraxy: the willingness to apply ourselves step by step to possess what is given to us to understand, namely the finite. Rather than fancy ourselves divine, we must cherish the necessity *quoad nos* of logic, the constructibility of geometric solutions and the inductive character of arithmetic.

The problem, Descartes repeats, is that most human beings fail to appreciate that God is infinite and incomprehensible. Those who do not "sufficiently know God" easily become atheists: it is no wonder that they fail to believe that mathematical truths depend on God, since they understand the truths of mathematics perfectly but not the truth of God's existence. Instead, they should consider the following argument: (1) God is a cause whose power exceeds human understanding; (2) the necessity of mathematical truths does not exceed our understanding; therefore (3) mathematical truths are something lesser than, and subject to, God's incomprehensible power. Is this one of the counter-arguments that Descartes had framed against the content of the wicked book?

Mersenne was clearly appalled by Descartes's answer and pressed him with new questions. What *sort* of causality does he think is involved? What necessitated God to create mathematical truths if they have no inherent necessity? What did God *do* to produce them? Do they emanate from God like rays from the sun? Once again, Descartes complies with Mersenne's requests, but his emphasis is elsewhere. His chief concern is to stress the difference between *savoir* and *comprendre*— between knowing and understanding. Insisting that God is the efficient and total cause of mathematical truths (*efficiens et totalis causa*), Descartes reasons as follows: I know that (a) God is the author of all things; (b) that eternal truths are something rather than nothing; and therefore (c) that God is their author.[54] Descartes then adds:

---

[54] Letter to Mersenne of May 27, 1630, AT I, 152: "Ie scay que Dieu est Autheur de toutes choses, et que ces veritez sont quelquechose, et par consequent qu'il en est Autheur." Cf. Thomas Aquinas, Treatise on Creation, *Summa Theologiae*, Part I, Q 44, *respondeo*; "I answer that, It must be said that every being that is in any way is from God. For whatever is found in anything by participation must be caused in it by that to which it belongs essentially, as iron becomes hot by fire ... Therefore all beings apart from God are not their own being, but are beings by participation. Therefore it must

> "I say that I know it, not that I conceive it or understand it; indeed
> we can know that God is infinite and almighty, even though our soul,
> being finite, cannot understand it or conceive it. Similarly, we can touch
> a mountain with our hands, but not embrace it as we would a tree, or
> anything that does not exceed the scope of our arms. To understand is to
> embrace a thing by means of thought; to know something requires only
> that thought touch it."[55]

The whole issue, in effect, is turned into a problem of right behavior—
of orthopraxy. To think is to act: to seek to *understand* God is to act with
presumption, since human thought is finite and God is infinite. Anyone who claims to *understand* God's infinite power (anyone who claims
that what *we* comprehend is *per se* absolute) has reduced God to finitude. The result of this disordered mental behavior is falsehood, and
more inner disorder: presumption, vanity, partiality, obstinacy, injustice.
The best the human mind can do by its natural effort is to *know* that
God is God—that God is infinite, incomprehensible, utterly beyond
human understanding. We are thus able to *touch* God sufficiently to
know that He exists, that He is the Author of all things, and that
he exceeds our *understanding*. This means that, from the very fact that
we *understand* mathematical truths, we also *know* that their necessity
is decreed, since we would not be able to understand them if they
belonged to God's essence and were God. If, however, we accept our
finitude and work with it rather than fight it, if we abstain from trying
to embrace God's infinity and instead rejoice that we *know* it, gratitude and duty will lead us to discover the created essences of creatures, which are nothing but these same eternal truths. Why, Descartes
implies, do we wish for what we cannot have, instead of cultivating
what is given to us? Once we accept the finitude of human science,
speculation conforms to orthopraxy: forsaking any claim to comprehend the infinite, we discover the laws (the limits) that are decreed
for us, incomprehensibly, providentially, by God's indivisible knowledge
and will, which is to say by God's love. We renounce the narcissistic
fantasy of rivalling God by claiming to understand absolute necessity
and instead are restored to justice by understanding what God wills:
namely the laws that govern our finitude and put in our hands the keys
of creation.

---

be that all things which are diversified by the diverse participation of being, so as to be
more or less perfect, are caused by one First Being, Who is most perfect."

[55] AT I, 152.

The last section of Descartes's letter, on a seemingly very different subject, confirms that the doctrine of the creation of eternal truths not only stems from orthopraxy (humility) but is designed to restore science from dogmatic and empty speculations to orthopraxy. Asked by Mersenne how to reconcile the fate of irrational beasts with Providence, Descartes says that God leads everything to perfection as a unified whole—*collective*.[56] The constant perishing and regeneration of individual animals is one of the universe's chief perfections.[57] Descartes says that he will explain all of this in his Physics and hopes that his account will be "so clear that no one will be able to raise doubts against it." Orthopraxy, which requires the demotion of speculative idols and the renunciation of appropriating God's infinity, gives back what it takes away a thousandfold.

---

[56] Letter to Mersenne, May 27, 1630, AT I, 154: "il n'est pas hors de mon sujet, et j'y répons que Dieu mene tout à sa perfection, c'est à dire: tout *collective*, non pas chaque chose en particulier." For a similar view, see François de Sales, *Traité de l'Amour de Dieu*, Livre II, chap. III, 415–420.

[57] AT I, 154: "car cela mesme, que les choses particulieres perissent, et que d'autres renaissent en leur place, c'est une des principales perfections de l'univers."

CHAPTER FOUR

A DISCOURSE ON RESOLVE

> "Il n'y a que l'acte où se
> trouve l'absolu."
>
> —Blondel

Descartes's theory of orthopraxy, as presented so far in the *Regulae*, is twofold. Descartes holds, first, that conducting the intelligence according to rules (cognitive orthopraxy) increases the intellect's ability to form good judgments. Secondly, he holds that when good judgments are presented to volition by the intellect, self-conduct improves in all of life's situations (general orthopraxy) since human beings, by definition, follow their better judgments. Thus in Rule I, as we saw, Descartes explains that the chief motivation for "increasing the natural light" is to insure that "in every circumstance of life, the understanding will show the will what course to adopt."[1] Two questions arise. First, what motivates the initial endorsement of cognitive orthopraxy before the intellect is sufficiently reformed to judge that cognitive orthopraxy ought to be endorsed? Secondly, is good judgment really all that is needed for orthopraxy? Recent debates over akrasia (weakness of the will; *lit.* "bad mixture") suggest that the connection between judgment and action is philosophically complex.[2] For example, if I know Descartes's rules for cognitive orthopraxy and fail to conduct my intelligence as directed, am I insufficiently convinced of their truth? Or am I weak-willed— insufficiently determined to seek truth and improve myself? Descartes's theory holds that failure of motivation in the will results from a failure of light in the intellect. Rational evaluation (by the intellect) and motivation (in the will) converge. Weak-willed action is not akratic so much as misguided or, rather, un-guided behavior. In the absence of convincing reasons to act, the will hesitates and remains undetermined—

---

[1] AT X, 361, lines 18–21.

[2] See, e.g., Arthur Walker's critical survey, "The Problem of Weakness of Will," *Noûs*, 23 (1989), 653–675; and Robert Audi, *Action, Intention, and Reason* (Ithaca and London: Cornell U. Press, 1993), 319–333.

abdicating agency in favor of appetites and conditioned desires. Conversely, the more rational and better informed the intellect is, the more firmly the will acts. The motivational force of a judgment lies precisely in the clarity and certainty of the truth it presents to the will.[3] As the *Regulae* attest, Descartes aimed, specifically, to increase the natural light *in each person*: only if individual judgment is reformed, sharpened, made firmer and more convincing, will each person embrace the better course of action "in every circumstance of life." What room does Descartes make for procrastination and the need for perseverence? Once a clear and distinct judgment has moved the will to action, does the motivation sustain itself? Or does motivation weaken over time? Descartes seems to deny the latter possibility.[4] In principle, once I judge that an action is desirable, I am moved to act accordingly, unless new reasons motivate me to stop and/or act differently.[5] Motivation cannot, as it were, slacken on its own. Something in the intellect must change, or weaken, for motivation to change or weaken. In the case of cognitive orthopraxy, Descartes was led to consider an analogous difficulty: why do conclusions reached through long chains of deduction fail to elicit the same intuitive certainty that is elicited by the self-evident premises from which they are derived? Descartes blamed memory and the inherently discursive character of human reasoning.[6] After the intellect forms a secure judgment, it may fail to remember the reasons for it, or turn to other matters and fail to keep the judgment in mind. Thus in the case of mathematical proofs, special mental effort is needed to remain focused on the logical necessity that connects the sequence of deductive steps leading to new axioms. If the mathematician forgets what prompted him to take any one of the steps in the chain of reasoning, he may doubt the evident nature of the con-

---

[3] A view that bears an affinity to Descartes's view is defended today by Frank Jackson, "Weakness of Will," *Mind* XCIII (1984), 13–14: "weak-willed action is action arising from wants and desires that have *not* evolved according to the dictates of the agent's reason."

[4] Cf. Arthur Walker, "Weakness of Will," 666: "There is a long tradition in philosophy, tracing back to Socrates, which denies the possibility of an imbalance between evaluation and motivation." For Descartes's explicit endorsement of the Socratic position, see his letter to Mesland, May 2, 1644 (?), AT IV, 117, line 20–21.

[5] See Descartes's letter to Mersenne, April 27 1637 (?), AT I, 367, lines 19–28, where Descartes argues that the resolution to act a certain way may be changed if conditions have changed, based on the axiom *sublata causa tollitur effectus*.

[6] Cf. Rule XVI, AT X, 454–459, which argues that symbolic notation will help to prevent memory failure.

clusion.[7] The inherent weakness of human memory and the need to proceed sequentially from one step to the next prevent us from grasping lengthy deductions as a single argument and, therefore, from transferring to the final outcome the immediate intuitive certainty of the premises.

Is there an analogous difficulty with the moral judgments that the intellect presents to the will? If the reasons supporting the truth of a moral directive are not immediately present, does the will lose its motivation? Or does the will contribute a weakness of its own? In the decade between the *Regulae* and the publication of the *Discours de la Méthode*, Descartes examined the problem of motivation as an intrinsic constituent of agent causation. Once again, we find a striking affinity between devotional theories of agency and the Cartesian theory. Descartes reached the conclusion that action depends for its strength and stability over time on the agent's underlying *resolve*. What is resolve and what motivates the will to impose an obligation on itself? An agent acts to bring about new conditions by willing to do so, but acts *resolutely* only if he perseveres in his plan in the face of obstacles and difficulty. Does this require a special initial act of self-determination, over and beyond the decision to act? The purpose of this chapter is to investigate the theory of agent causation that is elaborated by Descartes in the first three sections of the *Discourse on Method*. Why is resolve critical to the pursuit of truth and to Cartesian orthopraxy?

4.1. *Trying*

Let us first recall the special role of resolve in theories of the devout life. Francis of Sales, as we saw, argues that the devout soul is distinguished by its *prompt* execution of inner actions.[8] Not only does the devout soul examine itself, pray and fast according to the directives of inner orthopraxy, it does so diligently, attentively and joyfully. The devout soul seeks at all times, and in every way, to "do what it is desirable for

---

[7] Cf. Rule VII, AT X, 388: "Addimus autem, nullibi interruptum debere esse hunc motum; frequenter enim illi, qui nimis celeriter et ex remotis principiis aliquid deducere conantur, non omnem conclusionum intermediarum catenationem tam accurate percurrunt, quin multa inconsiderate transiliant. At certe, ubi vel minimum quid est paretermissum, statim catena rupta est, et tota conclusionis labitur certitudo."

[8] François de Sales, *Introduction à la vie dévote*, Part I, chap. I ("Description de la vraie dévotion") in *Oeuvres Complètes*, 31–33.

it to do," which is to please God. Invisible to the outside world, the devout soul is continuously active, continuously awake, continuously intent on perceiving and implementing God's will. Devotion is marked by a constant exercise of mindfulness, which is to say that every act expresses an intentional volition. Conditioned responses and impulsive behaviors are intentionally replaced by *intentionally* intentional actions.

The interpretation offered by devotionalists is that the devout soul, strengthened and illuminated by grace, is sufficiently free from the effect of original sin to know and love its spiritual faculties, which is also to love the divine will above all things and strive to implement all of the divine counsels, starting with the reform of inner actions.[9] What must a person do to embark on the path of spiritual liberation? According to Francis of Sales, the novice, after reflecting on the brevity of human life, the desirability of heaven and the abyss of hell, must resolve to "elect" the devout life. Although the will naturally seeks what the intellect presents to it as good (eternal happiness) and shuns what the intellect presents to it as harmful (hell), a special act must be performed that transforms the will's natural motivation into a permanent resolve. The novice must sign a formal contract pledging to serve God, putting an individual first person behind the pledge by declaring it to be "*my* will, intention and irrevocable decision."[10] Strikingly, the autonomy and power of the individual soul is *constituted and established* by the voluntary assumption of contractual obligation, raised above temporal vicissitudes to an absolute level: *I, the undersigned, constituted and established in the presence of eternal God and the whole celestial court...*[11]

The Salesian contract "dedicates the soul and all of its faculties" to God's service and includes the pledge not to be deterred by setbacks.[12]

---

[9] See François de Sales, *Traité de l'Amour de Dieu*, Livre I, chap. XVII, in *Oeuvres*, 400–403.

[10] See François de Sales, *Introduction à la vie dévote*, Part I, chap. XX, in *Oeuvres*, Part I, chap. XXI, 70.

[11] *Ibid.*: "Je, soussignée, constituée et établie en la présence de Dieu éternel et de toute la cour céleste." For the historic importance of contracts and the philosophical underpinnings, see Charles Fried, *Contract as Promise* (Cambridge, Ma.: Harvard U. Press, 1981), especially 1–27. See also 126: "The restitutionary principle is more primitive, closer to what justice in general requires in dealing between unconnected strangers. By making promises, strangers may supplant that primitive regime with a voluntary regime of their own making."

[12] *Ibid.*: "Mais hélas, si par suggestion de l'ennemi ou par quelqu'infirnité humaine, il m'arrivait de contrevenir en quelquechose à cette mienne résolution et consécration, je proteste dès maintenant, et me propose, moyennant la grâce du Saint-Esprit, de m'en relever aussitôt."

Since, moreover, the contract serves in effect to replace a regime based on restitution (the sinner deserves to be condemned) with a voluntary regime initiated by God's love (the "New Dispensation"), the core resolution is to reform the self by striving to accomplish God's will, which is to say to embrace orthopraxy. By a special inner act, the will determines itself not only to follow what the intellect presents as the better path, but to identify itself with the better path so thoroughly that alternative paths are henceforth preemptively denied. Rather than suffer the eternal oblivion (separation, damnation) that it deserves under a restitutionary regime, the soul commits itself to act mindfully in cooperation with good judgments and renounce akrasia.[13]

The Salesian contract defines, in effect, a promise of perpetual cooperation with moral directives. Since the experience of falling short only helps to uproot pride and therefore foster new gratitude and resolve, discouragement, under the promissory regime, is impossible.[14] The contract insures that the first fruit of devotion is humility, which corrects human narcissism by emphasizing the value of effort over the self-flattering motivation of success. The human will finds its dignity and contentment in *trying* to please God. Devotion explicitly cherishes the "small virtues" that God proposes to our "care and labor."[15] Content to strive to accomplish what lies in its power, the will endorses orthopraxy as its own distinctly human region of trial, perpetual effort and agency.

Francis of Sales warns against *ersatz* zeal that mimics devotion but is fueled by human vanity. In such cases, action is aimed at self-glorification rather than God's will.[16] Restlessly eager to impose its way on the world, the will relies on itself and, once the goal is reached, loses its motivation. In contrast, the devout soul acts limitlessly, on the strength of grace. Its motivation is inexhaustible. And while inner reform is carried out in the privacy of the individual heart, a beneficial influence radiates outward to others and sustains them in their capacity for resolve and autonomy. Thus the ideal spiritual director (Bérulle) is prompt to assist anyone who seeks truth (Descartes) but also serenely

---

[13] Charles Fried, in *Contract as Promise*, 1, argues that "the promise principle … is that principle by which persons may impose on themselves obligations where none existed before."

[14] See François de Sales, *Introduction à la vie dévote*, Part III, chap. VI, in *Oeuvres*, 145–147.

[15] François de Sales, *Introduction à la vie dévote*, Part III, chap. II, 132.

[16] Cf. François de Sales, *Introduction à la vie dévote*, Part IV, chap. IX, in *Oeuvres*, 272.

detached.[17] He intervenes only to bear witness to the intrinsic dignity of
trying, to convey to his directee the beneficial force of duty. Bérulle,
as we saw, attempted to motivate Descartes to publish his work by
invoking his debt to God for the intellectual gifts he had received.[18]
How far did he succeed?

4.2. *Promise and Akrasia*

A letter to Mersenne in July 1633 reveals the extent to which Descartes
struggled with procrastination when he was called upon to finish a
manuscript for publication. Once the discovery phase was over and
the thrill of new insight was gone, Descartes experienced "great difficulty" in applying himself to writing. In contrast to the zeal he felt for
"instructing himself," the tedium of redaction weighed on him heavily.
Mersenne had long suspected the problem and had pressed him peri-
odically to complete his projects. In April 1630, as we saw, Descartes
promised to send Mersenne a finished manuscript "at the beginning of
1633," adding that the promise was designed specifically to put pressure on himself.[19] In November 1630, new discoveries on the nature of
light gave Descartes an opportunity to try to renegotiate his promise,[20]
but Mersenne, it seems, held him to his commitment. In July 1633,
Descartes was at work finishing his treatise, but confessed that, had he
not promised to finish it, he "might not get to the end of it."[21]

Short as the letter is, it vividly conveys Descartes's lowered energy. To
sit down at his desk to write required an almost insurmountable effort:
i'ay tant de peine a y travailler.... What obstacle did he face? Nothing
prevented him physically from accomplishing a task to which he had

---

[17] See François de Sales, *Introduction à la vie dévote*, Part III, chap X, 159–160.

[18] See Baillet's account, in *Vie de Monsieur Descartes*; for the importance of meditating
on the gratitude owed to God for gifts received, see Francis of Sales, *Introduction à la vie
dévote*, Part I, Chapter XI (Meditation III), in *Oeuvres*, 50–52.

[19] AT I, 137, lines 12–17.

[20] Letter to Mersenne, November 25, 1630, AT I, 179, lines 11–13: "... en sorte que je
pretens qu'elle me servira pour me dégager de la promesse que ie vous ay faite, d'avoir
achevé mon Monde dans trois ans."

[21] Letter of July 22, 1633, AT I, 268, lines 13–14: "Mon Traitté est presque achevé,
mais il me reste encore à le corriger et à le décrire; et pource qu'il ne m'y faut plus rien
chercher de nouveau, i'ay tant de peine a y travailler, que si ie ne vous avois promis, il y
a plus de trois ans, de vous l'envoyer dans la fin de cette année, ie ne croy pas que i'en
pusse de longtemps venir à bout; mais je veux tascher de tenir ma promesse."

freely appointed himself. Presumably, when he made the promise, he had good reasons to judge that this was the proper course of action to adopt. What changed? Did his judgment change? Or had he underestimated the tedium of writing? Did a rift, in short, declare itself between judgment and motivation when *sustained* motivation became required? Two years later, having cancelled the plan to publish *le Monde* and decided instead on the new format of the *Discourse on Method*, Descartes once again complained, this time to Huygens, of the "impossibility" of applying himself to writing.[22]

Descartes in his youth experienced mildly morbid episodes of both lowered vitality and bursts of "enthusiasm." In a private notebook, he recorded that sadness and anxiety (depression) caused him to eat and sleep excessively, while good spirits induced anorexia and wakefulness.[23] He speculated that moral failures (vices) were forms of mental illness, analogous to physical illness but less easily diagnosed.[24] In July 1633, when he struggled to apply himself to finish writing *Le Monde*, how did Descartes interpret his condition and what remedy did he adopt?

While he may have suspected a physiologic factor,[25] Descartes construed his inaction as a moral failure. Availing himself of his promise to Mersenne, he formulated a directive for himself: *je veux tascher de tenir ma promesse*—"I want to try (labor) to keep (hold on to) my promise." By promising to send Mersenne a finished manuscript by a definite date, Descartes had imposed an obligation on himself, and by now resolving to *try* to keep his promise, he translated the obligation into a moral directive calling for immediate daily compliance. He forced himself to regard his inaction as akratic: unlike the failure to *keep* his promise, which could conceivably stem from any number of obstacles, the failure to *try* to keep it could only derive from his own weakness of will. Indeed if procrastination is akratic and culpable, this implies, by defi-

---

[22] Letter to Huygens of November 1, 1635, AT I, 330: "Il faut que je vous fasse des plaintes de mon humeur; sistost que je n'ai plus esperé d'y rien apprendre, ne restant plus qu'a les mettre au net, il m'a esté impossible d'en prendre la peine, non plus que de faire une préface que j'y veux joindre."

[23] AT X, 215, lines 14–17: "Adverto me, si tristis sim, aut in periculo verser, et tristia occupent negotia, altum dormire et comedere avidissime; si vero laetitia distendar, nec edo nec dormio."

[24] See AT X, 215, lines 11–13: "Vitia appello morbos animi, qui non tam facile dignoscuntur ut morbi corporis, quod saepius rectam corporis valetudinem experti sumus, mentis nunquam."

[25] See what he writes to Huygens about blaming his *humeur* or temperament, AT I, 330, cited above.

nition, that nothing prevents the exercise of proper agency. The agent
is assumed to be capable of making the required effort—in short, of
trying.

Philosophically, Descartes's self-remedy raises a host of important
questions about akrasia. If he fails to make the necessary effort, in what
sense was it ever in his power to make it? Is it an axiom that *trying*
is inherently in our power? Two immediate consequences regarding
the definition of akratic action follow from Descartes's directive, which
interprets a promise as a moral injunction to *try* to keep it. First,
Descartes's implicit definition of akrasia is philosophically broad. If he
goes for a walk instead of working on his treatise, the action is akratic.
If he sits at his desk and stares into space, his *in*action is akratic. If he
stares into space because he fails to form the intention of writing, his
mental inaction is akratic. Descartes's "promissory paradigm" implicitly
defines akrasia broadly enough to include acts of omission as well as
acts of commission, mental acts as well as physical acts. Descartes
defines akrasia, in short, as a root failure of agent causation—a failure
to initiate the volition to act in the right way.[26]

A second consequence of Descartes's promissory paradigm is that
self-control, more than logicality of content, is the central issue. Failure
to try to keep a promise offends reason only because a rational agent is
assumed to be able to exercise control over what he tries to do or not
do. At stake is not the rationality of the agent but the underlying causal
agency without which rational action is impossible.[27] What motivates
the will to try to keep a promise is the dignity of intentional agency, not
the content of the promise.[28] This is why reasons that are invoked to
break a promise usually appear suspect. Suppose someone promises to
visit a hospitalized friend and then finds a reason to go to the movies
instead. The failure to visit the hospitalized friend is not a failure to

---

[26] Cf. Robert Audi's definition of akrasia as "volitional failure to direct myself in the
right path." In *Action, Intention and Reason* (Ithaca and London: Cornell U. Press, 1993),
322.

[27] For a discussion and brief bibliography, see C. Fried, *Contract as Promise*, 137, ftn.
9. As Fried summarizes, other explanations for promissory obligation appeal to the
principle of reliance (F.S. McNeilly, "Promises Demoralized," 81 *Philosophical Review*
63 [1972]); the value of veracity (G.J. Warnock, *The Object of Morality* [London: 1971]);
and the (interpersonal) value of trust (Don Locke, "The Object of Morality and the
Obligation to Keep a Promise," 2 *Canadian Journal of Philosophy* 135 [1972]).

[28] The self-imposed nature of the obligation is emphasized by Joseph Raz, "Voluntary Obligations and Normative Powers," *Proceedings of the Aristotelian Society*, supp. vol. 46
(1972), 79–102.

think rationally but a failure to live up to a self-imposed obligation, which is to say a failure to dignify one's power of self-determination.[29] Note that if the person *tries* to go to the hospital, but gets into a traffic jam and is prevented, he is not culpable in the same way as if he fails to *try*. The inner action, the volition itself, the "active directing of myself in the right path," is the crucial Cartesian standard of akrasia. As long as Descartes *tries* to keep his promise to Mersenne, he avoids blame.

By the middle of November 1633, Descartes intended to keep his promise only *partially*, by sending Mersenne a portion of his manuscript at year's end, while begging for a little more time to deliver the remainder, "like creditors when their payments are due."[30] How much of a promise must be kept for it to count as a *bona fide* attempt? Half? More than half?[31] Did Descartes not *try* hard enough to try—raising the possibility that trying, as a model of action, leads to infinite regress?

The news of Galileo's condemnation disrupted Descartes's plans and prompted the decision, first to postpone, then to cancel sending a finished manuscript to Mersenne. Descartes's three letters on the subject are revealing. In November 1633, after explaining his decision not to publish *le Monde*, Descartes insisted that he still intended to send Mersenne his manuscript, but needed *one more year delay, please, in order to revise it and polish it*.[32] In February 1634, having received no response, Descartes assumed that Mersenne's "good will" towards him had cooled because of his failure to keep his promise.[33] The point is, Descartes himself was unsure whether he was to blame or not. By April, however, he argued that Mersenne (being a priest) should be "the first" to applaud his "resolve" not to show his work to anyone or seek to publish it.[34] Descartes not only considered himself to have

---

[29] I thus suggest that Descartes would disagree with Don Locke that responsibility to others is more fundamental than responsibility to one's self. See Don Locke, "The Object of Morality, and the Obligation to Keep a promise," 142: "The stronger and more specific requirement to do as I promised arises only because by promising I did explicitly undertake to act in that way. So I incur the obligation by taking responsibility for the doing of something, and thus laying my reliability and trustworthiness on the line." Locke concludes that we must concentrate on "the essentially social and interpersonal aspect" of morality. But why must trustworthiness be essentially interpersonal? Why is self-trust not more fundamental?

[30] Letter to Mersenne of November 1633, AT I, 270, lines 1–10.

[31] For a discusion of "substantial performance," see C. Fried, *Contract as Promise*, 120–122.

[32] Letter to Mersenne of November 1633, AT I, 271–272.

[33] Letter to Mersenne of February, 1643, AT I, 281, lines 1–12.

[34] Letter to Mersenne of April, 1634, AT I, 285, lines 5–11.

been exonerated of his promise, but to have imposed a new and higher obligation on himself. He was not prevented from keeping his promise by circumstances beyond his control (the traffic jam model,) but by a higher duty of obedience to the Church. His resolution to publish *Le Monde* was annuled and superseded by the resolution to comply with "persons whose authority over my actions weighs no less than the authority of my own reason over my thoughts."[35] As Descartes saw it, self-control now required that he *refrain* from publishing *Le Monde*, in spite of his rational convictions regarding Copernican astronomy.

A year and a half later, in November 1635, Descartes had decided to salvage parts of his writing and prepare the collection of treatises that we know as the *Discourse on Method*.[36] Once again, he bound himself by promises (this time to Huygens) in order to force himself to meet a deadline,[37] and once again complained of the "impossibility" of finishing and asked for extensions. Finally, in March 1636, Descartes wrote to Mersenne that he was ready to publish. The book, he explained, consisted of four treatises, all in French. The title would be: "Project of a universal science capable of raising our nature to its highest degree of perfection."[38] When Mersenne ventured to suggest a change in format, Descartes protested, with obvious good humor: "You must consider me to lack firmness and resolve in my actions…"[39] These very words, firmness and resolve, appear prominently in the *Discourse on Method*—prompting us to ask the following question: what role does acting resolutely play, if any, in "raising our nature to its highest degree of perfection"?[40]

---

[35] As Descartes will explain in *Discours de La Méthode*, Part VI, AT VI, 60, lines 7–10: "… des personnes, a qui ie defere, et dont l'authorité ne peut gueres moins sur mes actions, que ma propre raison sur mes pensées."

[36] Letter to Huygens of November 1, 1635, AT I, 330.

[37] See Huygens's letter to Descartes, December 5, 1635, AT I, 333, lines 18–20: "Souvenez-vous de la solemnité des promesses, s'il vous plaist, et hastez-vous au miracle de rendre la vue aux aveugles."

[38] Letter to Mersenne, March 1636, AT I, 339, lines 16–25.

[39] Letter to Mersenne of March, 1637, AT I, 348, lines 1–3: "Ie trouve que vous avez bien mauvaise opinion de moi, et que vous me iugez bien peu ferme et peu resolu en mes actions…"

[40] The full title of the first edition, published by Ian Maire in Leyden in 1637, is: "Discours de la methode pour bien conduire sa raison, et chercher la verité dans les sciences. Plus La Dioptrique. Les Meteores. Et La Geometrie. Qui sont des essais de cete Methode." The frontispiece shows a bearded man at work tilling the soil, illuminated and assisted by the sun casting its rays from heaven.

4.3. *Resolve and Self-Reform*

Consisting "more in Practice than in Theory,"[41] the *Discours de la Méth-ode* opens with the famous declaration that all men are equally endowed with reason. Since reason, however, is defined as the "power to judge well and to distinguish what is true from what is false,"[42] the mere possession of reason is not enough for the pursuit of knowledge. Reason must be exercised correctly, which means that reasoning is an action and requires that rules be followed: *"Ce n'est pas assez d'avoir l'esprit bon, mais le principal est de l'appliquer bien."*[43] The need for cognitive orthopraxy stems not only from the distinction between potency and act (between having the capacity to reason and reasoning) but from the added feature that passing from potency to act depends critically on a first-person agent. The rational capacity that is in me cannot give rise to actual reasoning unless *I* reason. Reasoning is not caused in me by some prior chain of events, or by some faculty operating deterministically, but is an action that *I* undertake and which *I* alone cause to take place.

Reasoning requires not only that *I* undertake to apply my reason but that I take responsibility to apply it *well*. Descartes captures the project of cognitive orthopraxy with a metaphor: "those who walk slowly, but who keep to the right/straight path (*le droit chemin*) without wavering, are able to advance much further than those who run and go astray."[44] As the metaphor implies, reasoning presupposes a causal agent who reasons by exercising rational self-control and taking responsibility for every step. The *I* who reasons must first cause its actions to fall under its own intentional jurisdiction. I reason by acting intentionally, which is to say, by causing myself to intend each rational step. In contrast, those who fail to constitute themselves as first-person agents by first exercising self-control are carried away by rash impulses and go astray. Cognitive orthopraxy, Descartes implies, requires that the first-person agent be the *sole* source of action. When action is caused exclusively

---

[41] Letter to Mersenne of March 1637, AT I, 349, line 21.

[42] *Discours*, Part I, AT VI, 5–7.

[43] "It is not enough to have a good mind, what matters chiefly is to apply it well." *Discours de la Méthode*, Part I, AT VI, 2, lines 11–12.

[44] *Discours de la Méthode*, Part I, AT VI, 2, lines 15–18: "ceux qui ne marchent que fort lentement, peuvent avancer beaucoup davantage, s'ils suivent toujours le droit chemin, que ne font ceux qui courent, et qui s'en esloignent."

by the first-person agent, it becomes responsible ("slower") and goal-directed ("straighter").

Descartes's metaphor raises an immediate question with regard to the theory that motivation in the will results from light in the intellect: what judgment motivates the resolve to suspend impulsive behavior and initiate self-control?[45] The question harkens back to Plato's cave and the initial conversion (*tropein*) of the Socratic hero away from shadows towards truth. How does Descartes propose to solve the "paradox of uphill self-control"?[46]

Although the first-person narrative of the *Discours* stems from an earlier project to produce a *History Of My Mind*,[47] its chief purpose is philosophical. The hero of the *Discours* is not Descartes but the first person as such, the agent *I*, embarked on a quest of self-discovery. The story of this agent *I* unfolds through trials and adventures in which causal agency is discovered and tested, culminating in the project of cognitive orthopraxy. Descartes's theory of action is, first and foremost, a theory of autonomy. Rational autonomy develops out of personal autonomy, which emerges from a first, purely existential resolve to come-of-age. As soon as the hero is old enough to break away from his tutors and act on his own behalf, he severs himself from the body of collective learning through a dramatic first decision:

> "I turned away entirely from the study of books and resolved to seek no other knowledge than what I could find in myself or in the great book of the world."[48]

The hero's first action does not respond to knowledge presented to the will by the intellect, but rather to an intimate subjective stirring in which rational autonomy is valued as a pure possibility. Is the hero's first action irrational? The action abruptly terminates an age of passivity and ushers in a deliberate quest. The will is motivated to shun one

---

[45] cf. Arthur Walker, who, in "Weakness of Will," 671, remarks that the akrates fails "to endorse, or endorse strongly enough, the directive premiss 'I am to do what is desirable for me to do'." He adds: "It may be difficult to explain, in a non-question-begging way, why a failure to endorse this directive is irrational, but there is little doubt that it is."

[46] To use Alfred Mele's expression in *Irrationality: An Essay On Akrasia, Self-Deception, and Self-Control* (New York: Oxford U. Press, 1987), 32.

[47] Letter of Balzac to Descartes, March 30, 1628, AT I, 570, lines 22–25: "Souvenez-vous, s'il vous plaist, *De l'hystoire de vostre esprit*. Elle est attendue de tous nos amis, et vous me l'avez promise en presence du Pere Clitophon."

[48] *Discours*, Part I, AT VI, 9, lines 17–23.

state ("turn away") and embrace a new one ("and seek") through the
hope of acquiring autonomy. The hero's resolve splits his life in two,
past and future, which is to say into a realm of determined fact on the
one hand and a realm of open possibility on the other. Action thus creates, by seizing it, a unique "now" of time in which the agent *I* emerges,
interferes, and alters the course of events. Rejecting all that is scripted
(books), the hero embraces the unknown (the future, myself, the world)
as the region that uniquely befits agent causation. What motivates the
hero's resolve to come of age is the conviction that to live is to act,
starting with the resolve to act.

The *I* cannot constitute itself, Descartes implies, without first *risking*
itself. By definition, action that risks itself disobeys all familiar guidelines
and responds to an unknown judgment, which it sets above existing
knowledge as a vanishing point. In a private separation rite, the hero
destitutes himself of horizons *that no longer suit him* in order to prepare
himself to take on a new identity. Should we say that the hero's resolve
to come of age expresses an active mastery of the inevitable passage
of time? Since hesitation is fatal, the resolve must be unconditional.
The *I* cannot appropriate the fleeting "now" of agency except boldly
(from the point of view of the will) and recklessly (from the point of
view of the intellect). The hero's first action is precisely a gamble. The
outcome, by definition, is unpredictable.

The hero of the *Discours* resolves very specifically to apply "the rest
of his youth" to travel the world, mingle with armies, explore the
diversity of human cultures and *test himself*. By resolving to test himself
in the world, the hero has tested himself already. The resolve to act—
as opposed to the *intention* to act or the mere *wish*—constitutes the
first trial of autonomous agency. Interrupting the whole momentum of
passive behaviors, the hero affirms his autonomy by refusing to comply
with directives (tutors, books) that provide him with infantile safety and
abrogate his autonomy. The act of resolve, as such, both produces and
endorses the basic axiom of moral autonomy, namely: "I am to do
what it is desirable for me to do." Just as a promise brings about an
obligation where none existed before, a resolution brings about the
intentional self-control through which *I* intend myself (know myself)
and value myself (love myself) as a matter of practice. The directive
to come of age—to "do what it is desirable for *me* to do"—implies
the intentional emergence of a first-person agent and can only be *my*
directive by trumping all earlier directives and associated frameworks.
Only by acting against the sway of the ordinary motives do *I* give

myself the moral autonomy to value the *I* who will cause itself "to do what it is desirable for me to do."

Does causal agency first declare itself in a resolve that opposes the agent *I* to all other causes? Does Descartes mean to imply that the moral axiom is either endorsed directly through action, specifically through *agere contra*, or never endorsed at all?

The hero's rejection of intellectual subjection (tutors, books) in favor of the unknown (living world) ushers in a transitional phase in which *I* exist "betwixt and between," dangerously bereft of identity.[49] The implied vulnerability to mistakes, shame, wounds, defeat, prompts an incubation period of deliberate anonymity. Stepping up on the stage of the world destitute of identity, *I* constitute myself, first, as spectator.[50] Descartes, in his youth, invoked wearing a mask: *ne in fronte appareat pudor ... larvatus prodeo*.[51] Self-masking serves a double function, allowing the novice a period of apprenticeship and confering protection (disguise) against regressive urges. Birthing myself through my own resolve and without warrant, *I* intentionally conceal myself from the telluric forces that compete with my causal agency and would cause my autonomy to abort.

Severed from books and plunged into the world, the hero-spectator observes the actions of living agents as they go about their life's business. He forms the opinion that worldly truth is pragmatic: judgments that are tested through action and corrected on the basis of adverse consequences likely contain more truth than speculations divorced from practice.[52] By the same token, the many effective ways in which living agents transform the world mean that he, too, must decide on a course

---

[49] I am drawing on the ideas pioneered by Arnold Van Gennep, *The Rites of Passage*, translated from the German by Monika Vizedom and Gabrielle Calle (Chicago: The University of Chicago Press, 1960) and elaborated by Victor Turner, *The Forest of Symbols* (Ithaca and London: Cornell U. Press, 1967).

[50] *Discours*, Part III, AT VI, 28, lines 25–27: "... ie ne fi autre chose que rouler cà et là dans le monde, tashant d'y estre spectateur plutost qu'acteur en toutes les Comedies qui s'y jouent."

[51] *Cogitationes Privatae*, AT X, 213, lines 4–7. Dated January 1, 1619.

[52] *Discours*, Part I, AT VI, 9–10: "Il me sembloit que je pourrois rencontrer beaucoup plus de verité, dans les raisonnemens que chascun fait touchant les affaires qui luy importent, et dont l'evenement le doit punir bientost après, s'il a mal jugé, que dans ceux que fait un homme de lettres dans son cabinet, touchant des speculations qui ne produisent aucun effect et qui ne luy sont d'autre consequence, sinon que peutestre il en tirera d'autant plus de vanité qu'elles seront plus esloignées du sens commun."

of action—*his* course, marked by his own irreducibly individual agency. Autonomy thus implies responsibility.

The judgment that worldly truth is pragmatic, and therefore that autonomy calls for acting responsibly, motivates the hero to a second resolve, namely to turn away from visible actions to inner actions. If visible actions test the inner intentions of the agents who perform them, all the more will inner actions serve to test the very source of intentionality, the agent *I* who forms the intentions behind visible actions. The hero's second resolve severs his ties to the "great book of the world" and plunges him into a new unknown realm:

> "After spending a few years studying in the book of the world and working on acquiring experience, I resolved one day to study inside of myself and to employ all of the forces of my mind to choose the paths that I ought to follow."[53]

Descartes's narrative is very specific regarding the physical detachment that is called for by the second resolve. Famously, the hero is "locked up all day in a small heated room (*poêle*)," severed from the world and distraction. The setting bears an obvious affinity to an Ignatian retreat.[54] Like the Ignatian retreatant, the hero of the *Discours* focuses on the inner power of self-determination: how is this power exercised and what responsibility does it entail? The aim, in both cases, is to purge the retreatant/hero of worldly attachments in the hope of motivating a "firm resolve" to embrace self-reform through orthopraxy. Through a series of mental acts, the *I* intends itself in new ways, clarifies its values, and originates a new breakthrough in autonomy.[55]

Serving as his own retreat-director, the Cartesian hero does not passively respond to random thoughts[56] but intentionally considers ideas

---

[53] *Discours*, I, AT VI, lines 26–31: "Mais aprés que i'eu employé quelques années a estudier ainsi dans le livre du monde, et a tascher d'acquerir quelque experience, ie pris un jour (la) resolution d'estudier aussy en moymesme, et d'employer toutes les forces de mon esprit a choysir les chemins que ie devois suivre."

[54] See *The Spiritual Exercises of Saint Ignatius*, Annotation XX, 43: "… He will profit all the more if he is separated from all of his friends and from all worldly cares; for example, if he moves from the house where he lives and chooses another home or room where he may dwell as privately as possible." On Descartes's annual retreats at La Flèche, see Rodis-Lewis, *Descartes*, 36.

[55] Both Robert Persons's *First Booke of the Christian Exercise, Appertayning to Resolution*, known by his contemporaries simply as *The Resolution*, and Francis of Sales's *Introduction à la vie dévote*, Part I, aim at popularizing the content of the First Week of the Ignatian Exercices. For more context, see Victor Houlistan's Introduction to *The Christian Directorie*, xxii.

[56] In sharp contrast to Montaigne.

that lead to inner transformation.[57] In particular, he considers the distinctive features that mark agent causation and present it to the will as valuable.[58] Reflecting that artifacts are shaped either by agents, or chance, or both,[59] the hero remarks that whatever is conceived and executed by a single agent manifests a distinct coherence. This is true of a building raised from scratch by a single architect, of the true religion instaured by God, of legislative codes and scientific disciplines. Monstrosity, in contrast, results from a plurality of causes operating at cross purpose. Strange and crooked shapes arise over time through accidents, through *ad hoc* additions made by various hands and piecemeal amendments produced at different periods, without regard for overall consistency. The hero reasons further that unplanned growth of this type is inevitable and even adaptive in the case of large systems comprising intractably numerous individuals. Whole cities, states and societies have stabilized through compensatory accretions over time and are not good candidates for rational reconstruction from the ground up. The best candidate for rational reform, he concludes, is "myself."

What action does the new insight motivate? The hero reasons that he must act as his own metaphorical architect and undertake, first, to purge himself of all the beliefs he has accumulated from various sources since childhood.[60] Although the judgment is rational, it is, however, insufficient, by itself, to motivate the will to comply. Why? A reasonable fear of failure inserts itself between what reason dictates and the will. The hero acknowledges that *the resolve to discard all of the opinions that one has previously received into one's belief is not an example that everyone should*

---

[57] Cf. the choice of words, AT VI, 11, lines 13–14: "Je m'avisai de considérer"—I advisedly chose to consider. The method of "consideration" is vividly illustrated by the Meditations proposed by Francis of Sales in *Introduction à la vie dévote*, Part I (*Oeuvres Complètes*, 47, 49, 51, 53, 55, 57, 60, 61, 63, 65). For a discussion of the transformative power of the Ignatian Exercises, from which the method of consideration is drawn, see W.W. Meissner, "Spiritual Exercises," in *Psyche and Spirit*, eds. W.W. Meissner and C.R. Schlauch, 119–152.

[58] Cf. Richard Taylor, who appeals to "agent causation" to describe "causation of events by beings or substances that are not events" in *Metaphysics* (Englewood Cliffs, NJ: Prentice Hall, 1963), 52; and Roderick Chisholm, who claims that we have agent causation when "there is some event, or set of events, that is caused, *not* by other events or states of affairs, but by the man himself, the agent." "Freedom and Action," in *Freedom and Determinism* ed. K. Lehrer (New York: Random House, 1966), 17. See also R. Clarke, "Towards a Credible Agent-Causal Account of Free Will," *Noûs* 27 (1993), 191–203.

[59] AT VI, 11, lines 13–22.

[60] AT VI, 13, line 26.

follow.[61] It now seems that not everyone *ought* to comply with what reason dictates, even though everyone possesses the power of reason. The problem is that reason implies a paradox: the foolhardy will rush into action blindly and fail, while the appropriately modest will prudently abstain, preferring to stick with existing authority.[62] Thus a person will resolve to act rationally if and only if he is unreasonable. A rational directive does not, as such, lead to the formation of a rational intention to act if the act does not lie within the agent's *reasonable* competence.

How, then, does the hero transcend prudence without embracing folly? On what rational grounds does he risk himself and commit himself to a dangerous course? He judges, not that he has a better chance than others of pulling through, but that he has no choice: too much exposure to too many contradictory guides has left him no alternative but to undertake to guide himself.[63] The resolve to act is reached by blocking the option of inaction. The directive of rational self-reform now motivates the will by presenting itself as the *only* rational course, despite its drawbacks. Strictly speaking, rational self-reform is thus endorsed by default—because the opposite course of action cannot be rationally intended.

Far from being a fully warranted *best* course of action, rational self-reform is thus only the *better* course of action, and this is sufficient for the hero rationally to intend to carry it out. Since, moreover, the hero is forced to undertake to guide himself precisely because he hitherto lacked a single master (*un seul maître*), the resolve to proceed by default coincides precisely with coming under the guidance of a single master, namely reason, for the very first time. As soon as the hero resolves to risk himself, prudence appears to be mere hesitation, a worldly attachment to safety, the product of having been guided so far by convention and appetites. Had the hero indeed been guided by reason alone from birth, *as he is now for the first time*, his judgments would be "solid and pure," there would be no need for rational self-reform and no need, for that matter, to justify rationalism.[64] By resolving to proceed

---

[61] AT VI, 15, lines 13–15.

[62] AT VI, 15, lines 15–31.

[63] AT VI, 16, lines 1–29.

[64] *Discours*, Part II, AT VI, 13, lines 4–12. Cf. Pierre de Bérulle, *De la vie de Jesus*, Chap. IV, in *Oeuvres*, II, 453, who asserts that the Virgin Mary was "gifted with the use of reason" from birth: "Elle est conceue sans peché. Elle est sanctifiée dés le premier moment de son estre. Elle est douée deslors de l'usage de raison et de grace."

with rational self-reform as his best bet, it may turn out that the hero gives himself more than he intended or could have intended.

The directive to discard all existing judgments providentially brings the hero face to face with human weakness. Precisely because it is taken by default, the resolve to carry out cognitive purgation leads to the key resolve behind cognitive orthopraxy, namely the resolve to exercise continuous self-control:

> "I resolved to advance so slowly and to exercise such care in all things that, slow as my progress may be, I would at least keep myself from falling."[65]

The (worldly) imprudence of acting autonomously, "guided only by reason," puts the *I* at perpetual risk. The agent discovers his insufficiency—his tendency to presumption, rashness, error. Recognizing his weakness, he resolves to act against his own nature. The first step of self-control is thus motivated by rational self-doubt, which springs in turn from the perceived hiatus between what the Sole Master (Reason) commands and what *I* have in my power to accomplish. Inner reflection has yielded the judgment that the *best* I can do that lies in my power as a causal agent is avoid falling. The axiom that was initially endorsed as a bold gamble of self-constitution—"*I* must do what it is desirable for me to do"—now implies that *I* must rigorously submit myself to myself in order to submit myself to reason and reform myself. *I* must exercise continuous self-control if *I* am to act at all. The directive to avoid falling is absolute: dread is transported to the sphere of mental agency, where it constitutes the directive to *act responsibly*. Since reasoning, as such, is the intentional action that underlies all further intentional acting, rules of cognitive orthopraxy (patience, circumspection, order, thoroughness) immediately follow, including the "firm and constant resolve" to follow the rules of cognitive orthopraxy at all times.[66]

---

[65] AT VI, 16, line 30 – 17, line 3: "Mais, comme un homme qui marche seul et dans les tenebres, ie me resolu d'aller si lentement, et d'user de tant de circonspection en toutes choses, que, si ie n'avançois que fort peu, ie me gardeois bien, au moins de tomber."

[66] AT VI, 18, lines 13–15: "… pourvu que je prisse une ferme et constante resolution de ne manquer pas une seule fois a les observer."

4.4. *Betting on Agent Causation*

A series of resolutions thus culminates in the resolution to exercise self-control "in all things" and embrace cognitive orthopraxy. Over and beyond solving new problems, the hero feels a special contentment in the certainty of "using my reason in all things, if not perfectly, at least as best as lies in my power."[67] He experiences, moreover, that cognitive orthopraxy "progressively accustoms the mind to conceive its objects more clearly and more distinctly."[68] The hero's pragmatic theory of truth is transferred to the realm of mental actions: the judgment that reasoning requires a causal agent who first exercises self-control is validated in practice. Confident now that he has discovered a viable way to achieve rational self-reform, the hero sets out to uproot false beliefs by deliberately suspending all of the judgments that he has upheld so far. This means a new turning point, since volition, for a period of time, will be unguided. Stranded in a sort of rational no man's land, the hero builds himself a "temporary shelter" of moral maxims designed to prevent his actions from becoming "irresolute."[69]

The question confronting the hero is basically the following: if I judge that I cannot formulate a *best* judgment, which is to say a rationally unimpeachable directive, does reason require that I refrain from acting? The hero's answer is that we have, on the contrary, a "very certain" rational duty to "act according to probable opinions when it eludes our power to have truer ones." Reason mandates that *I* act *reasonably* when I am not in a position to act *rationally*.

Why does this judgment escape purgation and present itself as a "very certain truth"—*une vérité tres certaine*?[70] Is it self-evident? Is it a law of nature, somehow inscribed on our hearts? Or is it the first fruit of practical self-control, which reveals to a sharper discernment that self-control, *unnatural as it is*, is inherently more desirable for a causal agent than license?

---

[67] AT VI, 21, lines 18–21.

[68] AT VI, 21, lines 22–24: "... ie sentois, en la pratiquant, que mon esprit s'accoustumoit peu a peu a concevoir plus netement et plus distinctement ses obiets."

[69] *Discours*, Part III, AT VI, 22, lines 16–29.

[70] AT VI, 25, lines 4–6: "C'est une vérité tres certaine que, lorsqu'il n'est pas en nostre pouvoir de discerner les plus vrayes opinions, nous devons suivre les plus probables."

In the absence of certifiably true judgments, *I* must obey reasonable judgments with firm resolve.[71] The Cartesian criteria for reasonable action reflect the special dignity of agent causation and aim at
protecting it. The hero's provisional maxims prevent him from engaging in wanton behaviors that lure him away from seeking his perfection
in the self-conduct that underlies the inner life. Exotic mores must not
be adopted, excess must be avoided, fickleness must not be indulged.
Worst of all is presuming to change the world rather than adjusting
one's expectations. Since "nothing is entirely in our power but our
thoughts," we must consider that whatever we fail to achieve in the
external world, once we have tried our best to achieve it, is absolutely
impossible in our regard.[72] The hero's provisional maxims, in short, aim
at *dis*–motivating wishful behaviors that undermine self-control. Irrational desires lead to vanity, frustration and regret, while reasonable
maxims lead to serenity and self-empowerment. Since "thoughts alone
lie in our power," we are responsible for *trying* rather than for succeed-
ing. Whatever lies beyond our best effort is not meant for us, nor does it
diminish our dignity to renounce it, on the contrary. Volition, which is
more intimately ours than anything external or dependent on external
things, is the mark and seat of human dignity. In so far as effort presupposes self-control and stems from reasonable intentions, *trying* forges
a (cautious and deliberate) path of causal agency between determinism and randomness. Responding to stimuli without being determined
by them, intentional action exhibits creativity, by which we specifically
mean action that is marked simultaneously by new initiative and coherence. Two more "provisional" maxims enhance the self-control that is
required for creativity. The first protects the agent from the entanglement of promises and the second calls for the agent to conceive a stable long-term plan. Unlike contracts, which legitimately "remedy the
inconstancy of the weak-willed (*esprits faibles*)," promises interfere with
the freedom to evolve new judgments and must therefore be avoided.[73]
Yet there is a reasonable duty for an agent not to squander agency in

---

[71] Cf. Robert Audi, *Action, Intention and Reason*, 320–321: "Our better judgment need
not be our *best*, in either of the senses of 'best judgment' most relevant to incontinence
… A judgment can play the crucial *directive* role whether warranted or not."

[72] AT VI, 25, lines 22–28: "… et generalement, de m'accoustumer a croire qu'il n'y
a rien qui soit entierement en notre pouvoir, que nos pensées, en sorte qu'aprés que
nous avons fait nostre mieux, touchant les choses qui nous sont exterieures, tout ce qui
nous manque de nous reussir est, au regard de nous, absolument impossible."

[73] AT VI, 23–24.

incoherent initiatives. The hero must review his options and "try to elect" the best long-term occupation: *tâcher à faire choix de la meilleure occupation.*[74] To the extent that the hero's volition is now neutral—unmoved by irrational wishes and false motives—he is in a special position to elect "cultivating his reason" as his life's project.

The hero's endorsement of cognitive orthopraxy thus harmonizes with the *reasonable* maxim that his life's agenda ought to be *rational,* which is to say both intentional and coherent, possessed of the special unity that marks the project of a single creative agent. The choice of science—"to advance in the knowledge of truth"—is rationally justified on three grounds: (1) it provides immediate contentment that is "sweet and innocent"; (2) it honors the "light given to each of us by God to discern truth from falsehood"; and (3) it promises to put "all true goods" and virtues within reach since "the will embraces what the intellect represents to it as good."[75] By offering these three reasons, the intellect, in effect, presents the pursuit of truth to the will as a good, motivating it to act. But note that the pursuit of truth is a rational good precisely because it reforms the will. The hero's chosen agenda outlines an "uphill battle of self-control" through which the will accedes to virtue.

Descartes's provisional maxims ask us, in effect, to bet on the dignity of human volition, which is to say, to bet that exercising self-control is the first step toward rational self-reform. With every new resolve, the hero brings about an inner transformation that enhances his self-control and his power to apply reason well. When the hero resolves to "study within himself" and reflect over the special value of causal agency, he tests the value of causal agency in practice, since the beauty and coherence of his reflection are the same as emanate from rational artifacts. The further resolve to purge himself of opinions that he himself has not rationally caused himself to hold, and which therefore motivate his will incoherently, without his sanction, marks the beginning of a radical exercise of autonomy, fueled by the very resolve that initiates it. The "bet" is that rational self-conduct (cognitive orthopraxy) will bring about true judgments, which in turn will retroactively justify the initial resolve and raise volition "to the highest degree of natural perfection."

---

[74] AT VI, 27, lines 3–6.
[75] AT VI, 28, lines 1–14.

4.5. *Basic Action*

The hero's four successive resolutions share a number of common features. In each case, the action is purely mental and brings about a purely internal transformation. In each case, the resolve is made by an agent who conceives and executes it, standing as its sole cause. In each case, the agent causes the will to respond in a radically new way to habitual directives—namely by ignoring them. The will is mobilized to interrupt the determining force of previous beliefs and create a hiatus in which the agent determines that he will initiate a new course. Resolve is thus defined as an internal action through which the agent causes himself to be the exclusive determinant of his will and actions.

With each Cartesian resolve, the degree of intentional reflexivity increases. In the first resolve, namely the resolve to "come of age," the hero constitutes himself as a physically autonomous agent by rejecting the authority of other human beings over his actions and determining himself to seek the knowledge that he needs in order to act under his own authority. Although the resolve, as such, already illustrates in practice the radical inner autonomy to which he aspires, its internal structure remains intentionally opaque. Not until the second resolve, which is the resolve to study within himself and mobilize inner powers for the sake of choosing his life's agenda, does the hero begin to constitute himself intentionally as the sole cause of his actions.

Causal agency is now studied at its source. The privileged status of volitions as "lying entirely within my power" and the special coherence that marks the result of intentional action caused by a single rational agent converge to mobilize the agent's innermost creativity. Autonomy is now identified as a practical inner agenda of self-reform, leading to the third resolve, which is to purge the mind of unfounded opinions. The "rebellion" against subjugation that was initiated by the first resolve is transported to the realm of mental action and radicalized. Once again, the hero faces risk, but of a mental rather than physical nature. He risks losing his way *morally* rather than *existentially*.

The new level of risk coincides with a new level of intentional reflexivity in which the agent beholds his weaknesses and limitations in the face of the task that he intends to accomplish. The resolve through which the hero overcomes inaction (worldly prudence) marks an internal point of no return, analogous to the first emancipation from tutors and safeguards. This time, however, the agent's innermost causal power is intentionally and consciously at stake. It follows that a fourth resolve must be made, through which the agent assumes the burden of self-responsibility without which creativity is impossible. As soon as he resolves to "advance alone and in darkness," the hero resolves to re-place spontaneity with self-control. Born of self-doubt, the resolve cul-minates in cognitive orthopraxy, which completes the search for auton-omy by making it consist in permanently intentional action. Intentional self-control and causal power are fused into a continuous (open-ended) project of creative agency.

The question that naturally poses itself is whether Descartes means to assign a special place to resolve in his overall theory of action. Within the narrative of the *Discours*, does resolve play the part, in some sense, of basic action, defined as action that is not carried out by means of some other action?[76] A recent theory has argued that volitions are *causally* basic actions, since volitions, unlike physical actions, bring about intrinsic changes rather than extrinsic results.[77] Thus whereas I move my hand *by raising* it, and raise it *by willing* to raise it, my volition as such is not the result of a prior action.[78] In so far as Cartesian resolve is a volition, an inner mobilizing of agency, it qualifies as a causally basic action. The question is whether resolve should count as a basic action in yet another sense.

In an exchange of letters with Mesland, Descartes concedes that "there is in the will a real and positive power of self-determination."[79] Presumably resolve is the reflexive exercise of just such a power: what-ever its content, each act of resolve on the hero's part seeks to block causal factors other than agency so as to better isolate and implement self-determination. How does resolve differ in this regard from ordinary volitions? Whereas a volition may or may not succeed in overcoming the interference of other factors, such as appetites, habits and fatigue, a

---

[76] Voting, for example, is *not* a basic action, since it requires that I pull a lever, make a mark, etc. See A. Danto, "Basic actions," in *The Philosophy of Action*, ed. A.R. White (Oxford: Oxford U. Press, 1968), 43–58; John Searle, in *Intentionality* (Cambridge, UK: Cambridge U. Press, 1983), 100, offers the following definition: "*A* is a basic action type for an agent *S* iff *S* is able to perform acts of type *A* and *S* can intend to do an act of type *A* without intending to do any other action by means of which he intends to do *A*."

[77] See Hugh McCann, "Volition and Basic Action," *Philosophical Review* 83 (1974), 451–473.

[78] See H. McCann, "Volition and Basic Action," 465–466: "Whether an act is causally basic is a matter not of whether it itself is caused, but of whether it involves a causal sequence wherein its result is caused by a more fundamental action."

[79] Letter of May 2 1644, AT IV, 116, lines 15–19.

resolve is precisely the act that both acknowledges and combats whatever tries to move the will outside of the agent whose will it is. Resolve
puts the power of self-determination in the hands of the determining *I*,
who alone makes *self*–determination an act of genuine autonomy.

The effect of resolve is thus to secure agency as such against the
contrary pull of determinisms that escape the agent's control. Descartes
stigmatizes "irresolute" actions precisely because a lack of firmness implies a divided will and diminished agency. The resolve to exercise
cautious self-control is thus the very opposite of the tendency to hesitate: responsible caution is the essence of causal agency since the agent
employs self-determination intentionally to suspend action before a sufficiently rational judgment is available to guide it. Irresolute actions, on
the contrary, manifest a deficiency of self-control. While the irresolute
agent gives way to spontaneity in the absence of a clear directive, the
resolute agent deliberately *refrains* from acting.

Ordinary language describes agents as acting more or less firmly,
with more or less resolve. By definition, "degrees" of resolve apply to
volitions, not to resolve. A marginally firm volition is one that applies
little effort to a plan and gives up at the first obstacle, while a supremely
resolute volition is one that perseveres in carrying out its objective in
spite of all adversity. An equivalent description is to say that volitions
are more or less strengthened by the agent's intrinsic power of self-
determination: a supremely resolute volition is determined to determine its own course of action, while a less firm volition hesitates and
changes course in the presence of alternative motives. Still a third
equivalent description is to say that a supremely resolute will is one
which is determined to carry out the agent's plan (self-determination),
while an irresolute will remains indeterminate at its core.

It follows that volitions are more effective *qua* volitions if they are
based on a prior resolve, and less effective *qua* volitions if they are initiated by an agent who has not first determined himself to determine
his volition. This means, in turn, that the very causal power of volitions presupposes a prior act, namely an act of resolve. If volitions are
causally basic, they are more or less causally *successful* depending on
how firmly the agent wills himself to will in the first place. Resolve, the
act through which the agent determines himself to ignore motives that
are not self-determined, underlies all subsequent volitions as their wellspring. Resolve is thus not more basic than volition, but a more basic
volition and the root volition that institutes volitions as causally basic
actions.

As we know from Descartes's correspondence, the *Discours* gives only a very abbreviated version of the method of systematic doubt. To critics who objected that the method had not been elaborated in sufficient detail, Descartes answered that too much risk was involved in a vernacular text offered to a broad public. Not until the publication of the Latin *Meditationes* does Descartes's full theory of resolve come to light.

CHAPTER FIVE

TEMPUS AD AGENDUM: THE TIME TO ACT

Although scholars and philosophers agree that Descartes's 1641 masterpiece, the *Metaphysical Meditations*, marks a critical turn in the history of philosophy, controversy continues to rage with regard to the character, meaning and philosophical merit of its content.[1] Heralded since Hegel as marking the birth of modern philosophy, the *Meditations* has been subjected to radical deconstruction, notably by Michel Foucault and Jacques Derrida,[2] as well as charged by Feminist critics with enshrining masculinist ways of knowing.[3] The most enduring questions fall broadly into three categories. First, from a strict internalist perspective, are Descartes's arguments valid? Is the *cogito* self-evident? Is God's existence really "proved"? Is Descartes's "foundationalist" agenda for science not in fact wrong-headed?[4] Moreover is Descartes to blame for a nefarious mind/body split that has plagued Western thinking for centuries?[5]

---

[1] A useful sample of perspectives on the *Medidations* is found in Amélie Oksenberg Rorty, ed., *Essays on Descartes's Meditations*; Roger Ariew and Marjorie Grene, eds., *Descartes and His Contemporaries: Meditations, Objections, and Replies* (Chicago: U. of Chicago Press, 1995); Olivier Depré and Danielle Lories, eds., *Lire Descartes Aujourd'hui* (Louvain/Paris: Institut Supérieur de Philosophie, 1997); and Delphine Kolesnik-Antoine, ed., *Union et Distinction de l'Âme et du Corps: Lectures de la VIe Méditation* (Paris, Kimé, 1998).

[2] See Michel Foucault, "Mon corps, ce papier, ce feu," appendix to *Histoire de la folie à l'âge classique* (Paris: Gallimard, 1972), pp. 583–603; and Jacques Derrida, "Cogito et histoire de la folie," in *L'écriture et la différence* (Paris: Seuil, 1967), pp. 51–67. See also the useful review article and discussion by James A. Winders, "Writing Like a Man (?): Descartes, Science, and Madness" in *Feminist Interpretations of Descartes*, ed. Susan Borno (University Park, PA: The Penn. State U. Press, 1999), pp. 114–140.

[3] See e.g. Luce Irigaray, *Speculum de l'autre femme* (Paris: Minuit, 1974), Evelyn Fox Keller and Christine Grontkowski, "The Mind's Eye," in Sandra Harding and Merill Hintikka eds., *Metaphysics, Methodology, and Philosophy of Science* (Dordrecht: D. Reidel, 1983); and Susan Borno, *The Flight to Objectivity: Essays on Cartesianism and Culture* (Albany: State U. of New York Press, 1986).

[4] For a recent example of this view, see e.g. Stephen Toulmin, *Cosmopolis: The Hidden Agenda of Modernity* (Chicago: U. of Chicago Press, 1990).

[5] See e.g. G. Ryle's famous attack on "the Ghost in the Machine" in *The Concept of Mind* (London: Hutchinson, 1949); and Antonio Damasio, *Descartes's Error: Emotion, Reason, and the Human Brain* (New York: Putnam, 1994).

Closely related to philosophical assessment is the problem of Descartes's purpose. Perhaps Descartes does not mean to demonstrate God's existence in a rigorous analytic sense, but to show that his new mechanistic ontology is *compatible* with Christian theology? Or perhaps the *Meditations* should be seen as a case of radical dissimulation, serving to mask the atheistic character of Descartes's mechanistic framework?[6] Perhaps Descartes's chief purpose is epistemological, namely to "recount a journey from pre-philosophical common sense to metaphysical enlightenment"?[7] Perhaps he means to provide "cognitive exercises" that will help wean the reader from naive Aristotelian empiricism?[8] Perhaps he means to enlist St. Augustine's authority against the iron grip of Peripatetic physics?[9] Or perhaps the real aim is to lay the foundation of scientific medicine?[10] Perhaps Descartes proposes a new theodicy to vindicate God's Goodness—to show that God is no more responsible for human error than he is for human evil?[11]

Finally, there is the problem of Descartes's choice of format. A source of derision already to his early opponents,[12] and a recurrent stumbling-block to analytic philosophers, Descartes's meditational format has provoked a lively debate among scholars, opposing those who consider it centrally to shape Descartes's project[13] to those who view it instead as a relatively superficial allusion to a traditional genre, leaving the content unaffected.[14] Since arguments on both sides are persuasive

---

[6] See e.g. Louis Loeb, "Is there Radical Dissimulation in Descartes's *Meditations?*" In *Essays on Descartes's Meditations*, ed. Amélie O. Rorty, pp. 243–270.

[7] See Michael Williams, "Descartes and the Metaphysics of Doubt" in *Essays on Descartes's Meditations*, ed. Amélie O. Rorty, p. 117. Cf. also Ferdinand Alquié, *La découverte métaphysique de l'homme* (Paris: Vrin, 1950).

[8] See Gary Hatfield, "The Senses and the Fleshless Eye: The Meditations as Cognitive Exercises," in *Essays on Descartes's Meditations*, ed. A. Rorty, pp. 45–79.

[9] See Stephen Menn, *Descartes and Augustine* (Cambridge: Cambridge U. Press, 1998).

[10] See Annie Bitbol-Hespériès's, "La médecine et l'union dans la *méditation* sixième," in *Union et distinction de l'âme et du corps: lectures de la VIe Méditation* (Paris: Kimé, 1998), pp. 18–36.

[11] See Etienne Gilson, *La Doctrine Cartésienne de la liberté* (Paris: Alcan, 1913) and, recently, Zbigniew Janowski, *Cartesian Theodicy* (Dordrecht, Boston and London: Kluwer Academic Publishers, 2000).

[12] See *Voiage du monde de Descartes* (Paris, 1690); cited by Bradley Rubidge in "Descartes's *Meditations* and Devotional Meditations," *Journal of the History of Ideas* 51 (1990), p. 27.

[13] See Amélie O. Rorty, "The Structure of Descartes's *Meditations*" and Gary Hatfield "The Senses and the Fleshless Eye: The Meditations as Cognitive Exercises," both in *Essays on Descartes's Meditations*. ed. A.O. Rorty, pp. 1–20 and 45–79, respectively.

[14] This is the view put forth by Bradley Rubige's in "Descartes's *meditations* and Devo-

without being compelling—clearly key features of the *Meditations* are absent from devotional literature, but clearly the mystic's "triple way" shapes the overall design—is there some fruitful third way to look at Descartes's meditational format?

Spread like creation over a period of six days, the *Meditations* appropriates the traditional meditational form for a new purpose.[15] Descartes's meditational regimen claims explicitly to embody a "once in a lifetime" event—an ordeal to be conducted *semel in vita*.[16] The Cartesian journey of self—discovery proposes to transform the meditator in a way that is both unique and irreversible. The journey intended by Descartes's *Meditations* is far more than a "journey from common-sense to metaphysical enlightenment" (Michael Williams) and it offers far more than "cognitive exercises" (Gary Hatfield): fraught with danger and haunted by specters, Descartes's journey initiates the meditator into a new realm of spiritual action, in which the wound of biological mortality is healed by a new perspective of trust and gratitude. Descartes's theory of action stands at the core of the transformation since the immaterial soul knows itself and loves itself through acting spiritually. The outcome of the meditational journey is to relinquish the self-centered narcissism of biological consciousness and adopt a position of mature engagement by freely adhering to the cosmos "as a small part."

Let us first review indications of Descartes's preoccupation with the brevity of human life. During the famous night of November 11, 1619, when he was twenty-three years old, Descartes dreamt of a book in which was inscribed a single verse of poetry, inviting him to choose a path in life: *Quod vitae sectabor iter?* In the dream, Descartes was eager

---

tional Meditations," cited in ft. 11. Stephen Gaukroger endorses Rubige's conclusion in *Descartes: an Intellectual Biography* (Oxford: Oxford U. Press, 1995), p. 336, and p. 459, ftn. 149.

[15] On Descartes's formal ties to the tradition of Christian meditation, see Amélie Rorty, "The Structure of Descartes's Meditations," in *Essays on Descartes's Meditations*, 1–20. A useful study of Renaissance meditational form, with ties both to John Cassian and to the *devotio moderna*, is given by Kent Emery Jr. in "Denys the Carthusian and Traditions of Meditations," reprinted in *Monastic, Scholastic and Mystical Theologies from the later Middle Ages* (Aldershot, G.B.: Variorum, 1996) IV, 2–26.

[16] This aspect of Descartes's *Méditations Métaphysiques* is nicely emphasized by Daniel Garber in "*Semel in vita*: The Scientific Background to Descartes's *Meditations*"; published in *Essays on Descartes's Meditations*, pp. 81–116. For the view that the Ignatian exercises were originally meant, also, to occur "semel in vita", see Dom John Chapman, *Downside Review* XLVIII (1930), pp. 4–18.

to tell some unknown man that he recognized the verse as belonging to Ausonius's *Idylls*.[17] The Idyll in question, Idyll XV, depicts human existence in stark, despairing terms. Human life stretches from the infirmity of infancy to the infirmity of old age: every stage of life has its burden, no age brings contentment.[18] The last line of the poem declares that "for man it is good not to be born, or to die right away."[19] In short, the difficulty of making a life-choice lies in the fact that *no* choice frees us from suffering and death.

Now, in Descartes's dream, Idyll XV is explicitly recommended as "excellent," along with a further Ausonian Idyll, *Est et Non*, which also depicts human life as arbitrary and futile.[20] In the *Regulae*, two images from pagan antiquity surface somewhat uncongruously, both intimately connected with mortality, namely the image of Theseus in Minotaur's labyrinth, and the image of the Sphinx. Descartes depicts his method as the thread that will save us from Minotaur,[21] and applies his method to solve the Sphinx's riddle.[22] Descartes in Rule XIII also invokes Socrates, himself an image of the new Theseus (in Plato's *Phaedo*,) charged with confronting and vanquishing death.

Descartes's acute sense of the brevity of life resurfaces again in October 1637, when he writes to Huygens that his hair is rapidly turning grey.[23] In January 1638, he wrote again to Huygens, that he was more focused than ever on self-conservation, expressing the hope that through diet and healthy habits we might "reach a much longer

---

[17] See Baillet's account, AT X, p. 183: "à l'ouverture du livre, il tomba sur le vers *Quod vitae sectabor iter?* etc. Au même moment il apperçût un homme qu'il ne connoissoit pas, mais qui lui présenta une pièce de vers, commançant par *Est et Non*, et qui la lui vantoit comme une pièce excellente. M. Descartes lui dit qu'il sçavoit ce que c'étoit, et que cette pièce étoit parmi les Idylles d'Ausone…"

[18] Idyll XV, cited here from Ausone, *Oeuvres*, ed. Max Jasinski (Paris: Garnier), I, p. 166, lines 10–17: "Omne aevum curae, cunctis sua displicet aetas." See also: "Sensus abest parvis lactantibus et puerorum … Ipsa senectus/ Exspectaba diu votisque optata malignis/ Objicit innumeris corpus lacerabile morbis." For speculation about the edition known to Descartes, see AT X, pp. 182–183, footnote (a).

[19] "Non nasci esse bonum aut natum cito morte potiri." Cited from ed. Max Jasinski, p. 168, line 59.

[20] Cf. the last line: "Qualis vita hominum, duo quam monosyllaba versant!" Ed. cit., p. 173.

[21] Rule V.

[22] Rule XIII.

[23] See Descartes's letter to Huygens dated October 5, 1637, AT I, p. 434: "Les poils blancs qui se hastent de me venir m'avertissent que je ne dois plus estudier a autre chose qu'aux moyens de les retarder…"

and happier old age than we do now."[24] We learn from this last letter that he was working on an epitome of medicine and needed "a lot of time and experiments" to find ways to slow down the effects of aging.

When, a year later, Descartes isolated himself in order to produce the final version of his metaphysics in the form of the *Meditations*, he told Mersenne that his motto was "to love life without fearing death,"[25] an attitude which he would later explicitly view as one of the chief fruits of his Meditations.[26]

There is a special urgency about the *Meditations* that is absent from the *Discourse on Method*. Having waited to be "of such a mature age that no better age would follow,"[27] Descartes felt that he was under obligation to act and could no longer procrastinate: Meditation I declares that *I would henceforth be at fault if I continued to consume in deliberation the time left for me to act.*[28] Time has turned into a precious resource, a finite quantity that calls for the responsibility to act—before time runs out to come to terms with time and transcend it.

What special opportunity presents itself at the "right" age and must resolutely be seized? Descartes's six-day meditational regimen proposes to lead the meditator through a "once in a lifetime" passage from a naive addiction to having and owning to the liberation of autonomy and the desire to act. Like the coming-of-age rites studied by anthropologists,[29] and like the Ignatian Exercises and the Salesian Meditations,[30] Cartesian meditation enlists the asymmetry of human time to highlight human mortality and the need for deliberate self-engagement. The theme of successive ages and of seizing the appropriate age for radical action is raised in the *Discours*, but emphasized more explicitly in the *Meditations*. While the *Discours* says that the hero at the age

---

[24] Letter to Huygens dated January 1638, AT I, p. 507.

[25] Letter to Mersenne, January 9, 1939, AT II, p. 492. For evidence that this coincides with the period during which the *Meditations* are composed, see Geneviève Rodis-Lewis, *Descartes*, pp. 183–184.

[26] See Descartes's letter to Huygens of October 13, 1642, AT III, pp. 579–580.

[27] Meditation I, AT VII, p. 17: "aetatem expectabam, quae foret tam matura, ut capessendis disciplinis aptior nulla sequeretur."

[28] Meditation I, AT VII, p. 17: "si quod temporis superest ad agendum, deliberando consumerem."

[29] The classic introduction is Arnold Van Gennep's *Les rites de passage* (1908), available in English translation by Monika Vizedom and Gabrielle Caffee as *The Rites of Passage* (Chicago: U. of Chicago Press, 1960).

[30] See *The Spiritual Exercises of Saint Ignatius*, Week I, Exercise 5, 59; and François de Sales, *Introduction à la vie dévote*, Part I, chap. XIII, Meditation V, in *Oeuvres*, 55–57.

of twenty-three was too "precipitous" or rash to embark on the quest
for new philosophical principles,[31] Meditation I specifies that the best
age to undertake the task is an age "so mature" (*tam matura*) that no
age more "apt" (*aptior*) for his "once in a lifetime" decision will follow.[32]

Beyond Descartes's initial wish to ward off those readers who might
be led astray by the novelty of his method,[33] the explicit injunction to
wait for the right age before "seriously meditating" appears increasingly
to be imbued with psychophysical elements. Descartes's evolution in
this regard starts with a letter written in March 1637, possibly to his
friend Jean de Silhon.[34] Descartes explains that, while he refrained from
presenting his metaphysical doctrine in greater detail in the *Discourse on
Method* out of caution for "weak minds," he had hoped that "you, sir,
and those like you, who are among the most intelligent, would draw
the same conclusions as I did if you made the effort not only to read
but also to meditate on these things, dwelling for a long time on each
point…"[35] While the *Discourse* specifies that the author waited to be
cured of youthful "rashness" to undertake serious meditational work,
it presents, not the author's method of meditation, but a summary of
the results.[36] Descartes hoped to occult the meditational structure of his
project from "weak minds," while hinting to "the most intelligent" that
he had proceeded by means of meditation.

In the *Discours*, the concern for chronological maturity is overshad-
owed by a more immediate concern to distinguish between those who
are not sufficiently *educated* to be safely initiated into Cartesian meditations and those whose training should allow them spontaneously to
turn the brief metaphysical exposition in Part IV of the *Discours* into

---

[31] *Discourse on Method*, II, AT VI, p.

[32] Meditation I, AT VII, p. 17: "aetatem expectabam, quae foret tam matura, ut
capessendis disciplinis aptior nulla sequeretur." In French translation, AT IX, p. 13:
"j'ai attendu un âge qui fût si mûr, que je n'en pusse espérer d'autre après lui, auquel je
fusse plus propre à l'exécuter."

[33] See Letter CIX, AT I, p. 560.

[34] Secretary of Mazarin and author of *Les deux vérités, l'une de Dieu et de sa providence,
l'autre de l'immortalité de l'âme* (1626) and of *L'Immortalité de l'Ame* (1634). See Letter LXXI,
AT I, pp. 352–354.

[35] AT I, p. 354: "Et pour vous, Monsieur, et vos semblables, qui sont des plus
intelligents, j'ay esperé que s'ils prennent la peine, non seulement de lire, mais aussi
de méditer par ordre les mesmes choses que j'ay dit avoir méditées, en s'arrestant assez
lon-temps sur chaque point, pour voir si i'ay falli ou non, ils en tireront les mesmes
conclusions que i'ay fait."

[36] See *Discourse on Method*, last paragraph of III and first paragraph of IV.

meditational exercises. The new specification in Meditation I that the meditator be of "an age so mature that no better age will present itself," testifies to a fine-tuning of Descartes's reflection. Indeed since the *Meditations*, written in Latin, are safely out of the reach of the vernacular "weak-minded" who might abuse the Cartesian method, why maintain and even strengthen the criterion of maturity?

Descartes may have wished to present the author of the *Meditations* as appreciably older and more seasoned than the thirty-one year-old meditator presented in the *Discourse*, but also to address the *Meditations* not only to theologians, but to those on the Paris faculty who had reached a special seniority and authority, such as the Oratorian Gibieuf, in whom Descartes placed special hope for obtaining official approval. Gibieuf had been a member of the Sorbonne since 1609 and was forty-nine in 1640, when the *Meditations* appeared, just five years Descartes's senior.[37] Arnauld on the other hand, who did not join the Sorbonne Faculty of Theology until December 19, 1641, at the age of thirty-eight,[38] will be explicitly praised by Descartes for his good judgment *in spite of* his lack of seniority.[39] Moreover, Descartes implies that the right age to meditate must be reached *and not exceeded*. What does Descartes have in mind, exactly, by an "age so mature" (*aetas tam matura*) that no age "more apt" for self-discovery will ever "follow" (*sequetur*)?

Descartes elsewhere speaks of the optimal age for metaphysical discovery as a certain "limit" (*terme*) that marks the advent of a new "age of knowledge" (*l'âge de la connaissance*) and must be seized "as soon as" (*sitôt*) it is reached.[40] Since the limit in question marks not only the starting-point but also the end-point of maturity (*"tam matura ... ut aptior nulla sequetur"*), it seems that Descartes has in mind a fairly well-circumscribed age, similar to a "now" of time, to be seized or

---

[37] See Letter CCXV, to Gibieuf, November 11, 1640, AT III, pp. 237–238; and Letter CCXLIV, to Mersenne, 23 June 1641, AT III, p. 388: "Ie suis grandement ayse de ce que le pere Gibieuf entreprend mon parti et tasche de me faire avoir approbation des Docteurs."

[38] See AT III, p. 473, footnote (b).

[39] See Letter CCLXII, to Gibieuf, of January 19, 1642, AT III, p. 473.

[40] See *Recherche de la Vérité*, AT X, p. 508: "Il faudrait que chaque homme, sitôt qu'il a atteint un certain terme qu'on appelle l'âge de la connaissance, se résolût une bonne fois d'ôter de sa fantaisie toutes les idées imparfaites qui y ont été tracées jusques alors, et qu'il commençât tout de bon d'en former de nouvelles." The date of this work is unknown, but the majority of scholars agree that it was probably composed after the *Meditations* (Adam: 1641; Gaukroger: 1642; Gouhier: 1647; Cassirer and Rodis-Lewis: 1649–1650).

forever lost, like a philosophical *carpe diem*. By specifying that any age of *lesser* maturity would be premature but that no age of *greater* maturity will ever be available, Descartes implies that human beings attain a sort of natural *apex aetatis* that must be consciously embraced. Writing to Huygens in 1637 at the age of forty-one, Descartes, as we saw, not only remarked on the "haste" with which his hair was turning grey but also that the whitening of his hair constituted a "warning" (*avertissement*) to devote himself more exclusively to philosophy.[41] Just as he experienced himself at twenty-three to be too young and "rash" to embark on methodical doubt, he interpreted visible signs of bodily decay after forty as a reminder that he would one day be too old and feeble. In January 1639, as we know, he resolutely set everything aside to complete the *Meditations*.[42] In a letter reassuring Mersenne that his sudden silence was not due to bad health, Descartes observes that he has been free from illness for thirty years (which implies that he viewed his state in 1619 to have been morbid)[43] and that he finds himself "as it were, further removed from death now than in my youth" since age had "taken away that heat in the liver which used to make me like the profession of arms…"[44] He then expresses the hope that he would live long enough either "to avoid the nuisances of old age through science or suffer them patiently."[45]

Two features of the letter stand out: first, Descartes implicitly regarded himself in the winter of 1639, at forty-three, to be quasi "equidistant" from the precarious health he suffered in his youth and the inevitable infirmity of old age. Secondly, in a more universal sense, he regarded himself as having reached a special age of physiological equilibrium, in which his body is relieved of the impetuous "fire" of youth while not yet troubled by the "nuisances" of old age. At forty-three, Descartes felt he had reached a brief and precious safe-harbour. Far from regretting the "ardor" of his youth, he welcomed being cured of it and the folly of dreams of glory. Without regretting having been attracted once to the "profession of arms," he now joked to

---

[41] AT I, p. 434, vide supra footnote 6.

[42] See G. Rodis-Lewis, *Descartes*, pp. 183–184.

[43] This self-assessment would tend to confirm Stephen Gaukroger's assessment, in *Descartes: An Intellectual Biography*, pp. 109–110.

[44] Letter to Mersenne, 9 January 1639, AT II, p. 480: "l'aage (sic) m'a osté cete chaleur de foye qui me faisait autrefois aymer les armes."

[45] AT II, p. 480.

Mersenne that "today, I profess only cowardice,"[46]—knowing that the saintly Minim would hear him to profess the opposite: *today I wage battle for truth and life*. The letter indeed finished on a singularly affirmative declaration that offers us the best clue to what Descartes has in mind by the *nec plus ultra* of human maturity: *I live, I am healthy, I philosophise*.[47]

The optimal age for self-discovery would thus be the point of equilibrium at which human beings are briefly poised between growth and decay, with perspective on both. In Aristotelian terms, such an *apex aetatis* corresponds to the natural resting point of the perfectly developed human form, the prime of life where intact physical vigor combines with a mature awareness of the passage of time and therefore a new kind of boldness and responsibility. The adult who is neither pre-mature nor post-mature, is, in a sense, most paradigmatically and "actually" human, exemplifying the perennial form through which the human species through eternity imitates the deathless revolutions of the stars.[48] In Virgil's Arcadia, a special place is given to the shepherds who discover a tomb in the foliage "mid-way" on their journey,[49] and in XVIIth century depictions of the scene, such as Guercino's painting (1618) or Nicolas Poussin's famous masterpiece (1639), the shepherd who acts to touch the tomb and decipher its riddle is typically the distinctly mature, bearded shepherd, rather than the youths who surround him.[50] Descartes, we think, wrote a *Pastorale* for Queen Cristina's birth-

---

[46] Letter to Mersenne of January 9 1639, AT II, p. 480: "ie ne fais plus profession que de poltronnerie."

[47] AT II, p. 492: "vous croyerez toujours, s'il vous plait, que ie vy, que ie suis sain, que ie philosophe."

[48] See e.g. Aristotle, *Parva Naturalia* 479a28–31; trans. G.R.T. Ross, in *The Complete Works of Aristotle*, ed. Jonathan Barnes (Princeton: Princeton U. Press, 1984), I, p. 761: "Youth is the period of growth of the primary organ of refrigeration, old age of its decay, while the intervening time is the prime of life."

[49] Virgil, *Eclogues*, ed. Robert Coleman (Cambridge: Cambridge U. Press, 1977), Ecloga IX, 59–60: "hinc adeo media est nobis via; namque sepulcrum/ incipit apparere Bianoris." Cf. Theocritus, *Idyll* VII, 10–11: "We had not yet reached half way and the tomb of Brasilas was not visible to us."

[50] Guercino's painting is in Rome, at the Galleria Nationale. Poussin's first painting of the *Shepherds of Arcadia*, dated c. 1627, is at Chatsworth, England, in the collection of the Duke of Devonshire and the Chatsworth Settlement Trustees. Like his second, more famous version of the theme, which is in the Paris Louvre, it shows the bearded, mature shepherd closest to the tomb. For reproduction, (tentative) dates and commentary, see *Nicolas Poussin, 1594–1665*, eds. Pierre Rosenberg et Louis-Antoine Prat (Paris: Réunion des Musées Nationaux, 1994), pp. 142–143 and pp. 283–285. Insofar as Poussin had close interactions with Paris Jesuits, for whom he painted six works in July 1622 to celebrate the canonization of Ignatius and Francis Xavier, Descartes may have been

day in 1649, featuring young soldiers who come to recognize that the love of military glory must give way to a supremely more mature love of "eternal wisdom, justice and peace."[51]

Did Descartes have a precise chronological age in mind to define the human *apex aetatis*? His earliest assessment of maturity contrasts school boys (*pueri*) to those who are of a "sufficiently mature age" to conduct themselves rationally without external guidance, i.e. who are old enough to "withdraw their hand from under the schoolmaster's rod."[52] In the *Discourse on Method*, however, as we saw, Descartes declares the age of twenty-three to be too young for genuine intellectual undertaking and places intellectual maturity at over thirty.[53] He knew that the age of thirty traditionally marked a new age of maturity for the ancients, as indicated by "Tiberius, or maybe Cato," whom he will one day cite to Berman: "a man of thirty no longer needs a doctor since he has enough experience by then to be his own."[54] Descartes removed to the Netherlands near or when he turned thirty-three, "traditionally considered to be the age reached by Christ," as Geneviève Rodis-Lewis remarks, mindful of the importance of *Imitatio Christi* in Jesuit religious culture.[55] Familiar to Descartes as well, perhaps, was Psalm XC, which places mid-life at thirty-five,[56] the age picked by Dante *nel mezzo del cammin di nostra vita* for spiritual reform and self-discovery.[57]

---

aware of him. Descartes's pupil Queen Cristina, after abdicating the throne of Sweden, founded the *Accademia del Arcadia* in Naples. On the importance of the Arcadian theme in XVIIth century French literature, see *Et in Arcadia Ego*, ed. Antoine Soare (Paris, Seattle and Tubingen: papers on Seventeenth Century Literature, 1996). In particular, the opening paper by Jean-François de Raymond, *Ego cogito: Le mémorial de Descartes*, pp. 19–24.

[51] This is pointed out by Geneviève Rodis-Lewis in *Descartes*, p. 275, who gives good arguments in defense of Baillet's report in *La vie de Monsieur Descartes*, II, p. 395. For the opposing view, endorsed by Gaukroger, that Descartes did not compose this work, see Richard A. Watson, "René Descartes n'est pas l'auteur de *La Naissance de la Paix*," in *Archives de philosophie* 53 (1990), pp. 389–401.

[52] Regula II, AT X, p. 364: "aetate satis matura manum ferulae subduximus."

[53] *Discourse*, II, AT VI, p. 22.

[54] Interview with Berman, 16 April 1648, AT V, p. 179: "Nemo trigenarius medico opus habere debeat, quia ea aetate satis per experientiam, quid sibi prosit, quid obstet, scire potest, et ita sibi medicus esse."

[55] See *Descartes*, pp. 333–334, footnote 5.

[56] "The days of our years are three score years and ten." Descartes brought a Bible with him to the Netherlands, "from France" (i.e. Catholic) as he testifies to Mersenne, AT II, p. 630.

[57] "Midway upon the journey of our life I found myself in a dark wood, where

While puberty rites are designed to initiate youths into new identities dominated by sexual polarities, Descartes's "age-of-knowledge"
rites aim at a sort of reverse initiation: *meditatio* will disengage the self
from biological imperatives and gendered identity.[58] Descartes's own
sexual liaison with Hijlena Ians in October 1634, resulting in the birth
of a daughter in July 1635, may have inspired new insights with regard
to sexual consciousness and new philosophical resolve.[59] In particular, Descartes's insight that sexual hormones affect the brain, distorting self-perception and presenting sexual union as the "highest good
imaginable," may date from this period and bolster the observation in
Meditation III that natural impulses are "blind".[60] Significantly, in 1631,
at thirty-five, Descartes described himself to Balzac as detached from
"most" worldly goods,[61] but not from sensual gratification, at least as
far as "a philosopher can allow himself without offending his moral
conscience."[62] Descartes at the time indulged in a rich fantasy life, pursuing imaginary pleasures in daydreams.[63] When Voetius denounced
him for fathering illegitimate children, Descartes answered (1643): "Not
long ago (*nuper*) I was indeed young (*juvenis fui*), and was then a man as
I am now, nor have I ever taken a vow of chastity or presumed to be
more saintly than others."[64]

---

the right way was lost." *Divina Commedia*, Inferno, Canto I, lines 1–3: "Nel mezzo del
cammin di nostra vita / mi ritrovai per una selva oscura / che la diritta via era ta."

[58] See in this regard Stanley Clarke's article "Descartes's 'Gender'" in *Feminist Interpretations of René Descartes*, ed. Susan Bordo, pp. 82–102.

[59] See the account of what is known about Descartes's liaison given by G. Rodis-
Lewis in *Descartes*, pp. 194–200.

[60] See AT VII, p. 40: "ex caeco aliquo impulsu." For Descartes's theory of sexual
psychophysiology, see *Les Passions de l'âme*, AT XI, p. 395: "En un certain âge et en un
certain temps on se considere comme defectueux et comme si on n'estoit que la moitié
d'un tout, dont une personne de l'autre sexe doit estre l'autre moitié: en sorte que
l'acquisition de cete moitié est confusement representée par la Nature, comme le plus
grand de tous les biens imaginables."

[61] See Descartes's letter to Balzac of April 15, 1631, just two weeks after his thirty-
fifth birthday, AT I, p. 198: "ie suis devenu si philosophe, que ie méprise la plus-part
des choses qui sont ordinairement estimées."

[62] *Ibid.*: "ie ne suis pas si severe, que de leur (i.e. mes sens) refuser aucune chose
qu'un philosophe leur puisse permettre, sans offenser sa conscience."

[63] See in the same letter, AT I, p. 199: "apres que le sommeil a longtemps promené
mon esprit dans des buys, des iardins, des palais enchantez, où i'éprouve tous les plaisirs
qui sont imaginez dans les Fables, ie mesle insensiblement mes réveries du jour avec
celles de la nuit."

[64] AT VIII–2, p. 22: "nuper enim juvenis fui, et nunc adhuc homo sum, nec unquam
castitatis votum feci, nec sanctus prae caeteris volui videri."

The youthful fire that impelled him to military glory at twenty seems to have been succeeded by a preoccupation with sexual pleasure in his mid-thirties. The maturity that Descartes experienced in January 1639 coincides above all with self-possession, relative to both aggressive and libidinal impulses. Descartes is reported to have viewed his liaison with Hijlena as a "dangerous entanglement" and apparently resolved to remain celibate while choosing to live in close quarters with her between October 1637 and 1640.[65] We recall that October 1637 also marks the time when Descartes took his rapidly greying hair as a "sign" that he should devote *all* of his time to philosophy. By the winter of 1639, when he sat down to compose the *Meditations*, he had concrete reason to feel that he had reached a new level of self-mastery and had matured not only beyond the youthful "heat" that once pushed him to war, but also beyond the propensity to imaginative *rêverie* that had marked his thirties with *otium* and procrastination. His appetite for the "charms of solitude," which he diagnosed in himself in 1619,[66] had sought satisfaction later in dreams of "bushes, gardens and enchanted palaces" in which, as he told Balzac, he experienced "all of the plea-sures that are imagined in Fables".[67] Maturity meant overcoming both impetuosity and the seduction of imaginary gratification. Descartes's conspicuous concern to wean the mind from rashness and from the lures of imagination, while present in the *Regulae* and the *Discourse on Method*, reaches a new level of articulation in the *Meditations* and forms the basis of a new theoretical step.

Descartes's claim in Meditation I that he waited to reach the limit of maturity before inviting others to "seriously meditate" with him is thus far less rhetorical than first appears and constitutes the culmination of a life-long quest for philosophical maturity.[68] Three months before his forty-third birthday, in the winter of 1639, Descartes had reached

---

[65] Baillet bases his account on a written report by Clerselier that Descartes told Chanut in 1644 that "God had rescued him ten years earlier of this dangerous entan-glement and preserved him so far from slipping again." See Baillet, *La vie de Monsieur Descartes*, II, p. 90. See also Letter LXXXIII, dated August 30, 1637, AT I, pp. 393–394, in which Descartes says he wants "Hélène to come here as soon as possible, hopefully before *la Sainte Victor* (October 10)."

[66] See Baillet's account of Descartes's analysis of his first dream, AT X, p. 185; and Sigmund Freud's speculation that he was preoccupied by sexual fantasy, reported by Maxime Leroy, *Descartes, le philosophe au masque*, (Paris, 1929, I, p. 90).

[67] *"où j'éprouve tous les plaisirs qui sont imaginez dans les Fables"*, AT I, p. 199, cited above in footnote 34.

[68] Cf. *Discourse*, I, AT VI, p. 5.

a new state of psychophysiological equilibrium, of autonomy and self-possession. He was sane of mind and vigorous of body, free of immature ardor and of the tendency to "mix daydreams with night dreams," capable of sexual continence—ready, in short, not only to put his metaphysical ideas into final meditational form but to take responsibility for initiating others into the "age of knowledge."

Rites of passage are designed safely to guide the initiand through the trials and perils that are the necessary conditions for self-transformation. Symbolic rebirth requires some sort of symbolic death. The Cartesian transition from dependent, bodily awareness to spiritual action involves, similarly, symbolic death and rebirth, requiring structured initiation and expert guidance. Descartes's six-day journey of ordered meditation leads the initiand through steps that the author himself took and survived. The reader is invited to repeat Descartes's own path to self-initiation by "seriously meditating with him."[69] Descartes's innovative format, so distinct from the narrative synopsis of the *Discourse*, does not so much clarify *Discourse* Part IV as recast it into a special initiatory rite. Rather than provide new arguments, the *Meditations* provide a new series of actions through which the initiand advances along an "unbeaten and remote path" that cannot be safely divulged to "everyone."[70] Actions require time, and time, as such, becomes an integral factor in helping the meditator gradually assimilate inner change. Only those who devote sufficient time to "seriously meditate" and practice new action step by step will experience first-hand the inner transformation through which they become authors of their own *meditationes*. Personal agency and increased concentration on the meditator's part, rather than more abundant explanations, are the critical new features that will deliver Cartesian results. Initiatory motifs abound in Descartes, starting as early as the *Regulae*, where, as we saw, he evokes Theseus's descent into the Labyrinth of the Minotaur.[71] Risk is an inherent feature of initiatory rites, trial a defining means to confer legitimacy. The element of danger and the risk of failure are precisely what allow the same initiatory rite to be effective for each new initiand. When he promised

---

[69] *Praefatio ad Lectorem*, AT VII, p. 9: "serio mecum meditari."

[70] *Praefatio ad lectorem*, AT VII, p. 7: "viamque sequor ad eas explicandas tam parum tritam atque ab usu communi tam remotam, ut non utile putarim ipsam in gallico et passim ab omnibus legendo scripto fusius docere, ne debiliora etiam ingenia credere possent eam sibi esse ingrediendam."

[71] Respectively, Regula II, AT X, p. 366: "rectum veritatis iter"; and Regula V, AT X, p. 380.

Balzac to write a "history of my mind" in 1628, Descartes presented it
as an adventure yarn, complete with battling Giants.[72] In the *Discourse
on Method*, Descartes warns that systematic doubt is not for the faint-
hearted.[73] To join him in the quest for autonomy requires abandoning
familiar paths and scaling steep cliffs and deep precipices.[74] Whoever
clings to received opinions will soon abandon the quest, judging it "too
perilous to wade into water so deep that no foothold is possible."[75] As
Descartes seems to have recognized all along, but never fully conveyed
until the *Meditations*, his method of universal doubt has the initiatory
force of an ordeal. Descartes, however, promises safe-passage because
he is the guide who has been there and back: "You must not be afraid
to cross after me."[76]

---

[72] See Balzac's letter to Descartes's of March 30, 1628, AT I, pp. 570–571: "Souvenez-vous, s'il vous plaist, DE L'HISTOIRE DE VOSTRE ESPRIT. Elle est attendue
de tous nos amis, et vous me l'avez promise en presence du Pere Clitophon... Il y aura
plaisir à lire vos diverses avantures dans la moyenne et dans la plus haute region de
l'air; à considerer vos proüesses contre les Geans de l'Escole, le chemin que vous avez
tenu, les progrez que vous avez fait dans la verité des choses, etc."

[73] See e.g. *Discourse on Method*, Part II, AT VI, p. 15: "Je crains que [mon dessein]
ne soit déjà trop hardi pour plusieurs. La seule résolution de se défaire de toutes les
opinions qu'on a reçus auparavant en sa créance n'est pas un exemple que chacum
doive suivre." See also *Praefatio*, AT VII, p. 7.

[74] Preface to the Meditations, AT VII, p. 7, and the *Discours on Method*, II, p. 15.

[75] *Recherche de la Vérité*, AT X, p. 512: "J'avoue qu'il y auroit du danger, pour ceux
qui ne connoissent pas le gué, de s'y hasarder sans conduite, et que plusieurs s'y sont
perdus."

[76] *Recherche de la Vérité*: "J'avoue qu'il y aurait du danger, pour ceux qui ne connais-
sent pas le gué, de s'y hasarder sans conduite, et que plusieurs se sont perdus; mais vous
ne devez pas craindre d'y passer après moi."

CHAPTER SIX

BASIC ACTION REVISITED

Descartes compares the method of universal doubt to being plunged into deep water where firm ground vanishes and trusted footholds disappear.[1] Heir to the revival of Pyrrhonism in the second-half of the sixteenth-century,[2] familiar with fideistic uses of Montaigne's *Que sçay-je?*,[3] Descartes was quick to distance himself from sceptics who "doubt for the sake of doubting and affect to remain forever irresolute."[4] His goal, he emphasizes, is the opposite, namely to discover solid "rock under shifting earth and sand."[5] Descartes, as we saw, devised maxims to insure that a firm volition be maintained during the time that judgment is suspended. In Meditation I, central features of Sextus Empiricus's "zetetic, ephectic and aporetic" discipline[6] are appropriated and transformed into a distinctive *via purgativa* that cleanses the meditator of cognitive attachments until a *tabula rasa* is reached.

Descartes's appropriation of the Pyrrhonic project of "doubting all things"[7] is, however, re-directed from the aim of achieving *ataraxia* to an entirely new Cartesian aim: restoring the primacy of action. The key,

---

[1] See e.g. Meditation II, AT VI, p. 24 and in *Recherche de la Vérité*, AT X, p. 512.

[2] See Richard Popkin, *The History of Scepticism from Erasmus to Descartes* (Assen: Van Gorcum, 1960) and *The History of Scepticism from Erasmus to Spinoza* (Berkeley and Los Angeles: U. of California Press, 1979).

[3] See Popkin, *The History of Scepticism*, and Harry Bracken's summary in "Bayle's Attack on Natural Theology: the Case of Christian Pyrrhonism" in Richard Popkin and Arjo Vanderjagt, eds., *Scepticism and Irreligion in the Seventeenth and Eighteenth Centuries* (Leiden: Brill, 1993), p. 255: "Thus in Montaigne and Huet, sceptical arguments are employed to destroy intellectual pride and rational pretense, so that one finally becomes totally humble. Once one's mind is a blank tablet, God may choose to write His revealed truths upon it." Descartes's familiarity with Montaigne's follower, Pierre Charron, is attested by Frédéric de Buzon's documentation (Bulletin Cartesien, 1991, *Archives de philosophie*) that a copy of *La Sagesse* was given to Descartes in 1619 by a Jesuit father of Neuburg. See also Geneviève Rodis-Lewis, Bulletin cartésien 21, *Archives de philosophie*, 1993.

[4] *Discours de la Méthode*, Part III, AT VI, 29.

[5] *Ibid.*: "car au contraire mon dessein ne tendoit qu'a m'assurer, et a rejetter la terre mouvante et le sable, pour trouver le roc ou l'argile."

[6] See *Outlines of Pyrrhonism*, Bk. I, chapter III.

[7] See Sextus Empiricus, *Outlines of Pyrrhonism*, Bk. I, c. XVI.

as we shall see, is a new evaluation of the sceptic *epoche* or suspension of judgment. Granted that *epoche* invites man to renounce cognitive certainty, what does the initiative to suspend judgment imply about the autonomy of human action?

Drawing on lines of inquiry suggested by Jean-Luc Marion,[8] but insufficiently explored with regard to the initial phase of the Cartesian journey, this chapter will argue that Meditation I seeks to reveal, through direct experience, that mental action (volition) is more fundamental than perception (cognition). Meditation I uproots cognition in order to isolate causal agency at its source. Pushing scepticism to a critical new extreme, hyperbolic doubt forces the meditator to confront his own unintelligibility and dissolves the last foothold of cognitive pretense. Is anything left in the meditator's power, after he surrenders himself to hegemonic uncertainty—symbolically, to a depth without lower or upper limit?[9]

Meditation I is structured to serve as a separation rite. The mind is gradually divested of the totality of its perceptual contents. The plan is to collapse the "theater of the world" and rip away the meditator's masks, in the hope of retrieving and transforming the spiritual *pudor* of primordial agency into an affirming flame.[10] The first day of meditation is designed to break down denial and dis-cover the agent *I* prior to perceptual self-constitution. As the meditation progresses, the meditator will be shorn of his adopted selves (*personae*) and suffer the anguish of disintegration. Cartesian desconstruction, however, does not culminate in despair, but in vigils—*laboriosa vigila*. Why? Does the day's agenda of "overturning everything" (*omnia esse evertanda*) overturn the primacy of cognition and provoke an unanticipated discovery? An affirmative answer will force us, in the next chapter, to revise standard interpretations of Cartesian foundationalism.

Our first step is to examine the final and definitive parameters of Cartesian seclusion. Consistent with the aim of appropriating the method of sceptic doubt for a new end, Meditation I modifies Montaigne's legacy by bringing a personal experience of Ignatian retreats

---

[8] In *Sur le prisme métaphysique de Descartes* (Paris: PUF, 1987), Chapter V.

[9] See Meditation II, AT VII, pp. 23–24: "tanquam in profundum gurgitem ex improviso delapsus, ita turbatus sum, ut nec possim in imo pedem figere, nec anatare ad summum."

[10] Cf. Descartes's private self-perception of 1619, AT X, p. 213: "Ut comoedi, moniti ne in fronte appareat pudor, personam induunt: sic ego, hoc mundi theatrum conscensurus, in quo hactenus spectator existi, larvatus prodeo."

to bear on it. Descartes transforms the Pyrrhonist's permanent retreat from the world[11] into an acute, but temporary crisis. Structurally, the Ignatian retreat reproduces for others the two crises that marked Ignatius's own journey "from spiritual childhood to spiritual adulthood".[12] Descartes absorbed the Ignatian model to bring about a break, not only with worldly conventions, but with permanent inner indecision, epitomized by Montaigne's ethos of interminable debate.[13] Descartes indirectly rebukes Montaigne by specifying that a limit must be put on *deliberatio*. The resolve to meditate is a resolve to act, lest one's whole life be wasted ("consumed") in weighing the pros and cons of acting. Both the sceptic's "double-life" and the *otium* advocated by Montaigne as an age-appropriate retirement from worldly responsibilities[14] are subsumed by Descartes under the Ignatian model of a vocational crisis, requiring a bold, but entirely temporary, break with conventional life. The innovation of Meditation I is to reduce scepticism to a transitional stage, beneficial to the epistemologic subject precisely because it contains, when made sufficiently virulent, the seed of its own demise. Meditation I treats scepticism as a spiritual *crisis of motivation*, requiring a re-configuration of spiritual identity.

Initiation rites over a wide range of cultures typically begin with some form or other of retreat as a rite of separation. The novice is isolated from his village, parents and relatives, secluded in forest or bush, made to wear special clothes and follow special dietary restric-

---

[11] In the form, namely, of a "double-life" of inner freedom and outward conformity. See e.g. Pierre de Charron, *La sagesse*, I.14 and II.2; and François La Mothe Le Vayer, *Dialogues faits à l'imitation des anciens*, ed. A. Pessel (Paris: Fayard, 1988), pp. 242 and 273.

[12] Citing Robert Gleason, S.J., introduction to *The Spiritual Exercises of St. Ignatius* (New York: Doubleday, 1964), p. 11. Ignatius's first confinement was at his family home in Loyola in 1521, following a leg wound; the second was at Manresa from March 1522 to February 1523. For the importance of seclusion, see Direction 20: "In these Exercises, as a general rule, he will profit all the more if he is separated from all of his friends and from all worldly cares; for example, if he moves from the house where he lives and chooses another home or room where he may dwell as privately as possible..." Trans. Anthony Mottola, op. cit., p. 43.

[13] See Montaigne, "L'art de conférer", *Essais* II, viii. Charles Larmore suggests that this sceptical ethic was Montaigne's second important contribution to scepticism. It replaced, in effect, the ancient sceptical goal of *ataraxia* with the more vigorous ideal of feeling at home in interminable controversy. See "Scepticism," *The Cambridge History of XVIIth Century Philosophy*, p. 1150. Cf. as well Rorty's recent ethos of open-ended "conversation".

[14] See e.g. *Essais*, Bk. I, c. 8 and c. 39; in Oeuvres Complètes, ed. Pléiade, 33-34 and 232–242.

tions. He is torn from the habitual matrix of familiar surroundings and stripped of his ordinary social identity.[15] Separation may also, as in reported cases of spontaneous shamanic vocations, take the form of mental symptoms, physical ailments, dreams, fever, depression or social withdrawal.[16] Whether physical or emotional or both, separation enacts a period of symbolic death before rebirth.[17] Meditation I explicitly depicts the meditator as removed from the world through a first voluntary act: *solus secedo*.[18] Descartes specifies that he is installed by a fire, dressed in a housecoat—*hyemali toga indutum*.[19] The resolve to "meditate seriously" requires that the meditator first divest himself of social status, of worldly roles and of the garments that signify these roles and allow social interaction. The Cartesian meditator must confine himself indoors, in a cocoon-like setting, like someone afflicted with illness. All ties with country, family, friends, occupation and rank, must be temporarily broken off. Schedules and clocks vanish, reference points recede, day and night imperceptibly merge into an ambiguous twilight. Meditation I distills and crystallises Descartes's earlier separation initiatives, from the famous *poêle* where he stayed "locked up all

---

[15] See Arnold van Gennep, *The Rites of Passage*, 74: "The first act is a separation from the previous environment, the world of women and children. The novice is secluded in the bush, in a special place, in a special hut, etc…" Victor Turner, in "Betwixt and Between: The Liminal Period in *Rites de Passage*," reprinted in *The Forest of Symbols*, 93–111, gives the following nice summary on p. 94: "Van Gennep has shown that all rites of transition are marked by three phases: separation, margin (or *limen*), and aggregation. The first phase of separation comprises symbolic behavior signifying the detachment of the individual or group either from an earlier fixed point in the social structure or a set of cultural conditions (a "state"); during the intervening liminal period, the state of the ritual subject (the "passenger") is ambiguous; he passes through a realm that has few or none of the attributes of the past or coming state; in the third phase the passage is consummated."

[16] In connection with the night of November 10, 1619, Gaukroger suggests that Descartes may have been suffering from melancholia, or "nervous exhaustion, perhaps breakdown." In *Descartes: an Intellectual Biography*, p. 110.

[17] See Arnold van Gennep, *The Rites of Passage*, p. 75: "In some tribes, the novice is considered dead, and he remains dead for the duration of his novitiate. It lasts for a fairly long time and consists of a physical and mental weakening which is undoubtedly intended to make him lose all recollection of his childhood experience." Also, p. 81: "The novice is separated from the previous environment, in relation to which he is dead, in order to be incorporated into his new one. He is taken into the forest, where he is subjected to seclusion, lustration, flagellation, and intoxication with palm wine, resulting in anesthesia."

[18] Meditation I, AT VII, 18: "Opportune igitur hodie mentem curis omnibus exsolvi, securum mihi otium procuravi, solus secedo…"

[19] Meditation I, AT VII, p. 18.

day alone with his thoughts" in 1619[20] to the "remote desert" where he removed in 1629,[21] and finally, in January 1639, to the severing of all communication in order to "philosophize."[22]

The Cartesian meditator is now cast in stone for posterity: dressed in a housecoat, removed from the stage of the world and re-located to a private stage indoors, "next to a fire" as its symbolic center. He has cast away external cares and secured for himself a "safe repose:" *securum mihi otium procuravi*.[23] The *hiemali toga* that exempts him from social inter-action also protects him symbolically against all that is wintry (*hiemalis*): not unlike the Socratic sage cherished by humanists and by Montaigne, the Cartesian meditator appears to have found shelter from the fray.[24] In his *robe de chambre*, he is at once self-sufficient and regressed, "free and serious" (*serio et libere*).[25] Not only does the Cartesian meditator emerge in Meditation I with a new defining visibility, the precise elements that mark his seclusion are integrated into the meditational work. Each new meditator is invited to assume the same *persona* through a clever optical illusion. The new meditator will indeed be asked, each time, to consider for himself whether he is *really* "sitting in his housecoat by the fire": Is he sure? Is he not dreaming?[26]

The point is, the initial *persona* is soon revealed to be yet another posturing of the human self, another mask of disguise assumed on the stage of life. The "safe" *otium* soon turns dangerous. The real Cartesian rites of separation are psychological and metaphysical, shattering the sceptic's earnest pseudo-separation. Confinement indoors and loss of contact with the outside world provide an illusory safeheaven only the

---

[20] *Discours*, II, AT VI, p. 11.

[21] *Discours*, III, AT VI, p. 31: "aussi solitaire et retiré que dans les desers les plus escartez."

[22] Letter of January 9, 1639, AT III, p. 523. For arguments that this marks the decisive redaction of the *Meditations*, see Geneviève Rodis-Lewis, *Descartes*, 183–184.

[23] Meditation I, p. 18: "mentem curis omnibus exsolvi, securum mihi otium procu-ravi". Descartes's translator, de Lyunes, writes (AT IX, p. 13): "*un repos assuré dans une paisible solitude*". The effect, whether intended or not, is to affiliate the Cartesian medi-tator with Montaigne.

[24] *Republic*, VI, 496D-E. Note that Thomas More, in *Utopia*, I, lines 9–14, recalls the image of the Platonic sage who "stays indoors and is content to keep himself dry". See *Utopia*, p. 100.

[25] The sculptor Auguste Rodin resurrected the Cartesian meditator, quite uncon-sciously, in his famous statues of Balzac.

[26] See AT VII, p. 18: "alia sunt de quibus dubitari plane non potest: ut jam me hic esse, foco assidere, hyemali toga esse inditum." And p. 19: "quam frequenter vero usitata ista, me hic esse, toga vestiri, foco assidere…"

better to despoil the meditator of his "quiet repose" and subject him to
increasingly stressful forms of identity loss.[27] From the self-confident figure who initially sits by the warmth of a fire to the dismembered victim
of demonic rage at the end of the ordeal, an immense trajectory is tra-
versed. The key insight—namely, the primacy of action—emerges only
after the perceptual world has been engulfed in a distinctly Cartesian
apocalypse.[28] Meditation I is a classic descent into the underworld. The
meditator who resolves to "overturn everything" will have to traverse a
symbolic death.

Before examining how this progressive descent into the abyss is
orchestrated, we must briefly point out the new role played by the
moral *conscience* in motivating the decision to embark on self-reform.
Why *not* consume the whole of life in debate? In the *Discours*, as we saw,
the decision to proceed with self-purgation, despite the danger involved,
is taken by default as the only rational course open to a hero who finds
himself crippled by confusion. He decides to *risk* acting, as his best bet.
In Meditation I, a new motivation is given: the mature subject *would be
at fault* if he failed to take action.

The notion of *culpa* is invoked to construe inaction as akratic. The
mature person has a moral duty to break with indecision (indolence)
and act before time runs out. Implied is the axiom that prudence
decays into procrastination when prolonged without limit (Montaigne)
and that procrastination, in turn, is unworthy of mature human being
"when the time to act" is running out. Does Descartes's appeal to duty
in the face of human finitude echo the encouragement he heard long
ago from Bérulle? This time around, accountability to some higher
human dignity inspires the two related decisions, first, to "overturn
everything" (*omnia esse evertenda*) and second to undertake the task by
means of a formal meditational retreat (*solus secedo*). Both are decisions to act and make action an implicit imperative of conscience: the
meditator would be culpable if he *continued to postpone* the "formidable
entreprise" (*ingens opus*) of overthrowing "everything" while there still is
"time to act." What has changed? The meditator's moral conscience,

---

[27] In "Betwixt and Between" (96) Victor Turner points out that in the liminal phase,
the novice is "at once no longer classified and not yet classified." Separation rites,
therefore, aim at achieving de-classification.

[28] For the argument that extending sceptic doubt to the external world is Descartes's
chief methodological innovation, see Myles Burnyeat, "Idealism and Greek Philosophy: What Descartes Saw and Berkeley Missed," *Philosophical Review* 91, 1982, pp. 3–
40.

in effect, has caught up with him. Although he has indeed "long been aware" (*anidmaverti*) of "admitting" (*admiserim*) falsehoods into his belief as though they were truths (*falsa pro veris*), he was not mature enough to redress the situation, nor, implicitly, to recognize the *moral* dimension of endorsing error. Now that he is old enough, he has the capacity to redress the situation and would therefore be at fault if he shied away from the task. Meditation I starts with an imperative issued by the moral conscience, addressed to the moral subject and forcing him to accountability for his actions.

Meditation I draws a subtle contrast between moral conscience and reason. While conscience regally summons the meditator to act "while there is time," reason speaks softly, in the voice of counsel. No sooner has the meditator decided to embrace systematic doubt, than "reason persuades" (*persuadet*) him to adopt a first rule, namely the uncompromising "rule of indubitability." The rule requires the meditator to reject what is the least bit dubitable as though it were manifestly false. How does reason succeed in introducing this rule? As Charles Larmore has pointed out, the pure pursuit of knowledge, as such, does not require that this rule be adopted.[29] If, however, as Larmore argues, the rule shows that the goal of avoiding falsehoods simply counts more, for Descartes, than the goal of acquiring truths,[30] we must ask: why? The answer is that the Cartesian meditator, since he has made the decision to meditate, is already convinced that unlimited debate (indecision) is unworthy once the capacity is there. Like the initial decision to meditate, the rule of indubitability is itself a *resolve* to banish indecision rather than wallow in inaction. The rule of indubitability empowers the meditator to extricate himself from the interminable sway of indecision by giving him the rational prerogative to assign a definite truth-value, namely the value "false," to any opinion that fuels debate by presenting itself as debatable. While the moral conscience inspires the determination to act decisively, reason provides the first tool, namely a decision procedure that divides the set of all opinions into two non-overlapping

---

[29] See Charles Larmore, "Scepticism," *The Cambridge History of XVIIth Century Philosophy*, I, p. 1165, and Bernard Williams, *Descartes: the Project of Pure Enquiry* (Hassock, Sussex: Harvester, 1978).

[30] See "Scepticism", in *ibid.*: "The idea of pure enquiry involves the pursuit of (at least) two distinct cognitive goals—the acquisition of truths and the avoidance of falsehoods. But in itself it leaves open how these two goals are to be ranked or balanced against one another. Descartes's unwillingness to run any risk of error shows that for him the second goal always counts more than the first."

sets, namely the set of truths (which might be empty) and the set of falsehoods. The rule, in effect, disallows the "probable" set of the sceptics.

Would a sceptic protest that the Cartesian meditator is too easily persuaded by Reason? By providing a decision procedure, the rule of indubitability puts an end to the passive suffering of *involuntary* doubt. The meditator has been dissatisfied with his knowledge "for several years already." The question is not to doubt or not to doubt: *the fact that you are afraid of doubting your knowledge,* Descartes says elsewhere to someone who shies away from meditation, *tells me that you already doubt it.*[31] The rule of indubitability is a form of active-mastery: a passive, chronic vulnerability to doubt, like a low-grade fever, is suddenly reversed by a decision procedure that banishes the doubtful together with the false. Inaction is replaced by action. Reason gives the meditator a way to "make up his mind" rather than vacillate forever.

At a first level, Meditation I is designed to rule out sensory experience as a basis for science.[32] Descartes believes that toppling first-order empiricism, i.e. the premiss of Aristotelian physics, requires that the mind be weaned of sensibles and regards methodical doubt as one of the means to achieve this—*abducere mentem a sensibus.*[33] At a deeper level, Descartes retrieves the Augustinian idea that the mind's attachment to sensibles is as much an affective disorder as an intellectual one. The problem is not so much that we naively trust our perceptions of color, flavor and sound, but that we cherish what we perceive and develop an addiction to the bodily self-identity that we form through the flesh. The force of Aristotle's axiom, *nothing in the intellect that was not first in the*

---

[31] See *Recherche de la Vérité*, AT X, 513: "C'est un indice, que votre science n'est point si infallible, que vous n'ayez peur qu'elles (i.e. les raisons que j'ai dites) en puissent saper les fondements, en vous faisant douter de toutes choses; et par conséquent que vous en doutez déjà…"

[32] Descartes's anti-Aristotle agenda is explicitly revealed in his letter to Mersenne of January 28, 1641, AT III, p. 298: "Ces six meditations contiennent tous les fondemens de ma Physique. […] J'espere que ceux qui les liront, s'accoutumeront insensiblement a mes principes, et en reconnoistront la verite avant que de s'appercevoir qu'ils detruisent ceux d'Aristote." On Aristotelian first-order empiricism as Descartes's target in Meditation I, see Charles Larmore, "Scepticism," *The Cambridge History of Seventeenth-Century Philosophy* (Cambridge, UK: Cambridge U. Press, 1998), I, pp. 1165–1173; also Gary Hatfield in "Reason, Nature, and God in Descartes," in *Essays on the Philosophy and Science of René Descartes*, ed. Stephen Voss (New York and Oxford: Oxford U. Press, 1993), pp. 259–287.

[33] See Descartes's letter to Vatier, 22 February, 1638, AT I, 560, lines 13–25.

senses,[34] stems, not from any logical dictate, but from our attachment to the flesh and material things.

Sensibles must be, not simply critiqued but actually *decathected* before progress can me made.[35] Meditation I guides the meditator through progressive decathexis. At first, Descartes invokes well-established cases in which our senses fail us, such as the sight of a stick in water which appears broken due to refraction—examples that force us to reflect on sensory evidence but leave our attachment intact. What if we have to take the next logical step, and generalize, and reject *all* sensory evidence? The meditator's resistance stiffens dramatically when he is asked to doubt his own body:

> "These very hands and this whole body—what reason could I have to deny that they are mine?"[36]

The question is a recurrent motif of the meditational journey and will receive many successive levels of answer before a final response is framed in Meditation VI. In Meditation I, the question functions to break the bond that ties the meditator to his perceptible *persona*, to "these hands" and "this whole body," as though estranging him from himself, nullifying his very claim to have anything at all that is *his own*. Self-identity and bodily perception are so intimately fused that to negate *my* hands and *my* body would indeed amount to becoming

> "Like the insane, whose brains are so ruined by the stubborn vapors of bile, that they claim to be kings when they are paupers; to be clothed in royal purple when they are quite naked…"[37]

Maybe the entire meditational venture is pathological, triggered by neurological imbalance? Reason, having persuaded the meditator against compromise, now seems to guide the meditator to insanity. Although Descartes's allusion to morbid states may bear a trace of

---

[34] Cited explicitly by Descartes in Meditation VI, AT VII, p. 75.

[35] I am appealing to Sigmund Freud's term *Besetzung* in its standard English translation. Cf. Freud's 1914 essay "On Narcissism: an Introduction," in Peter Gay, ed., *The Freud Reader* (New York and London: W.W. Norton, 1995), 547. Cathexis, derived from the Greek verb "to occupy" describes the ego's capacity to invest itself emotionally in objects or ideas. A cathexis may also be withdrawn and directed to new objects and ideas. The work of withdrawal is what I call "decathexis."

[36] Meditation I, AT VII, p. 18: "Manus vero has ipsas, totumque hoc corpus meum esse, qua ratione posset negari?"

[37] *Ibid*.: "nisi me forte comparem nescio quibus insanis, quorum cerebella tam contumax vapor ex atra bile labefactat, ut constanter asseverent vel esse reges, cum sunt pauperrimi, vel purpura indutos, cum sunt nudi."

the symptoms he experienced in 1619,[38] what matters is that Descartes picks a very specific illustration of insanity. The meditator must compare himself to someone who insanely believes that he is *a king, dressed in purple when he is poor and destitute.*

Reason and irrationality seem dangerously to merge, leaving the meditator completely disoriented. Descartes implicitly suggests that he, too, confidently believing that "this whole body" is and is *his*, may be little more than a demented *roi imaginaire*, lulled by a lifetime of self-delusion and comforted by false riches. The meditator is forced to question the false security—*these hands, this whole body*—with which he has clothed himself and disguised his wretchedness to give himself stature and weight.

The meditator protests, resists—as would his demented counterpart: *But what? These men are mad—I would be no less demented if I copied their example.* Resistance takes the form of denying that there could be any similarity between myself and that demented other, while moving ahead requires that the similarity be recognized and overcome. Faced with a demented *alter ego*, the meditator must ask himself whether he has not always been insane to believe himself secure and possessed of royal attributes (knowledge, evidence) when in reality he was defenseless and naked. The metaphor of royal purple hiding desolation recalls Descartes's early indictment of the world as mere theater where roles (*persona*) are assumed in order to cover shame[39] as well as a long tradition of humanist reflection on the same topic.[40]

As a rite of separation, the choice between remaining demented by refusing to doubt sensory information or becoming demented by giving it up serves to establish a point of no return that tests the meditator's resolve. The meditator, in order to advance, must acknowledge his dementia. Symbolically, he must renounce "the imaginary kingship of

---

[38] See in this regard Gaukroger, basing himself on Baillet, *Descartes: An Intellectual Biography*, pp. 109–110.

[39] AT X, p. 213: "Ut comoedi, moniti ne in fronte appareat pudor, personam induunt: sic ego, hoc mundi theatrum conscensurus, in quo hactenus spectator existi, larvatus prodeo."

[40] Cf. Thomas More, *Utopia*, II, 27–30: "At illi tamen, tamquam natura non errore praecellerent, attollunt cristas et sibimet quoque pretii credunt inde non nihil accedere." ("Yet they strut about and think their clothes make them more substantial, as if they were exalted by nature herself, rather than their own fantasies.") Ed. and trans. by George M. Logan, Robert M. Adams and Clarence H. Miller (Cambridge, UK: Cambridge U. Press,1995); also Montaigne, *Essays*, Bk. III, c. 6 and c. 7, in Oeuvres, 876–898.

the world," and face his destitution with sober eyes.[41] Not only must he face his nakedness, he must prefer destitution to illusion. He must *deny* (*negari*) that "this body, these very hands" are his. The Cartesian rite of separation dissolves the narcissistic bond that ties the meditator to his sensory body by casting it as the product of excited bile. The task of *abducere mentem a sensibus* succeeds by penetrating psychic defenses organized to protect narcissism and resist change.

The Cartesian *via purgativa* uses analytical strategies to transform the meditator's intimate affective core. In order to be successfully weaned of sensory self-attachment, the meditator must choose to comply with what reason persuades. The meditator's fidelity to reason guides him beyond common sense into new darkness. Tempted to cling to sensory perception when distress is acute, the meditator is reminded that ordinary dream-life involves the same sort of delusions that morbidly afflict the insane.[42] Descartes cleverly plunges the meditator into a new labyrinth of role-confusion by exclaiming: *how often have I dreamed that I was sitting by the fire in my housecoat when I was really naked in bed!* Illusionism and suggestibility reach their peak. The meditator who tries to keep track of images and self-images, of self and other, of dream and reality, loses his footing and is engulfed in a theater of the absurd. Since he cannot prove that he is awake, (or that he is not Descartes) he is forced to regard all sensory information as so much dream-appearance. The implication is that his life, up to now, has been little better than a prolonged slumber.[43]

Assaulting the citadel of the meditator's resistance, Descartes once again cunningly pretends to forestall further descent into nihilism. Granted that we must renounce the certainty of being awake, can we not claim that, independently of wakefulness or sleep, *two added to three make five* with indubitable certainty? This is a pivotal moment in Descartes's analysis, since it seems that the desired foothold of certainty has been reached:

---

[41] I'm using here Simone Weil's phrase: "Se dépouiller de la royauté imaginaire du monde." In *La pesanteur et la Grâce* (Paris: Plon, 1988), p. 20.

[42] See, also, what Descartes says about dream-images in *Les Passions de l'âme*, art. 26, in ed. Pléiade, p. 708.

[43] In connection with this idea, see *Entretien avec Burman*, ed. Pléiade, p. 1360: "L'esprit dans l'enfance est tellement enseveli dans le corps qu'il n'a de pensées que celles qu'il tire de l'affection du corps." And: "L'esprit, dans l'enfance, est enseveli dans le corps au point de ne penser rien que de corporel; le corps qui *trouble toujours l'esprit* (my italics) dans ses pensées, le trouble surtout pendant l'enfance."

"For whether I am awake or asleep, two and three together make five, and a square has no more than four sides; and it seems impossible that such evident truths be suspected of any falsity or uncertainty."[44]

Are mathematical truths indubitable? In the earlier, unpublished *Regulae* Descartes seemed to affirm that they are.[45] In the *Discours*, he rejected the indubitability of "even the most simple" mathematical theorems on the ground that "some human beings commit paralogisms."[46] What is new in Meditation I is the move to generalize by invoking against mathematical truths the idea of a creator-god *qui potest omnia.*[47] This is equivalent to arguing that *all* human beings may be engaged in commiting paralogisms without knowing it. Over and above the desire to outdo Sceptic doubt,[48] hyperbolic doubt traces the epistemological problem of mathematical certainty back to the more fundamental question of human origin: where do we come from, what makes us rational and why should we trust reason? The meditator indeed must concede that his nature is such that he is *sometimes* deceived: so what assures him that he is not *always* deceived? Moreover if human nature is not the work of an omnipotent God, but instead the work of a lesser deity, or the product of chance, or the result of blind material processes, then he has even *less* reason to trust in human reason and in the absolute validity of mathematical deductions. The chief innovation of the *Meditations* rel-

---

[44] Meditation I, ed. cit., p. 62: "Nam sive vigilem, sive dormiam, duo et tria simul juncta sunt quinque, quadratumque non plura habet latera quam quatuor; nec fieri posse videtur ut tam perspicuae veritates in suspicionem falsitatis incurrant."

[45] See *Règles pour la direction de l'esprit*, Rule II, in ed. cit., p. 41: "Parmi les sciences déjà connues seules l'arithmétique et la géométrie sont exemptes de fausseté et d'incertitude." Notice, however, that in a later paragraph, Descartes's statement is less absolute, since he says only that "l'arithmétique et la géométrie sont beaucoup plus certaines que les autres sciences"—implying that they are *relatively* more certain than other sciences, not that they are certain *simpliciter.*

[46] *Discours*, IV, AT VI, p. 32: "Et pourcequ'il y a des hommes qui se méprennent en raisonnant, mesme touchant les plus simples matieres de Geometrie, et y font des paralogismes … ie reiettay comme fausses toutes les raisons que i'avois prises auparavant pour Demonstrations."

[47] Some scholars argue that Descartes's further deconstruction is added *ex post facto* purely for the purpose of religious apologetics. See e.g. Louis Loeb, "Is There Radical Dissimilation in Descartes's *Méditations?*" in *Essays on Descartes's Meditations*, op. cit., pp. 243–270.

[48] See e.g. *Interview with Burman*, AT V, p. 147: "Reddit hic auctor hominem tam dubium, et in tantas dubitationes conjicit ac potest; ideoque non solum objicit illa quae objici solent a Scepticis, sed etiam omnia illa quae objici possunt, ut ita plane omnes dubitationes tollat; et in eum finem genium hic introducit, quem sursum dari aliquis objicere potest."

ative to the *Regulae* and the *Discours* is to bring the question of human
origin from the periphery to the center. Hyperbolic doubt brings the
meditator face to face with ontological doubt. The purpose, as revealed
by the end of the Meditation, is to purge the meditator of cognitive
hope in order to elicit a pure moral act.

Characteristic of a descent into hell is that man is cut off from any
intelligible evidence of divine goodness. Estranged from divine love,
convinced only of the possibility of divine omnipotence, the meditator,
walking "alone and in darkness," is confronted by a new dilemma:
should he deny the existence of an almighty Creator in order to rescue
the certainty of mathematics, or should he affirm an almighty Creator
and give up all hope of human science? As in most separation rites,
the choice is really an ordeal, designed to test the initiand's fibre as he
ventures into unfamiliar territory.

Critics who dismiss Descartes's hyperbolic doubt as either philosophically unsound or as a gimmick to court Church approval miss the true
liaison of Descartes's analysis and consequently gain "little benefit" from
it. The sufficiently attentive meditator should, at this junction, experience the anguish of a double temptation to nihilism. The apparently
"hopeful" side of the dilemma is a snare since both paths lead equally
to defeat. The choice is either to affirm divine omnipotence and give
up human science, or deny divine omnipotence and give up human
science. Faced with what seems to be a negative *consequentia mirabilis*,[49]
what course will the meditator follow—*quod vitae sectabor iter?*[50]

The Augustinian theologians on the Paris theology faculty, notably
the Oratorian Gibieuf and Arnauld, would be able to recognize the
affective scheme underlying the dilemma. In Augustinian terms, the
meditator must choose between "love of self," which culminates in
contempt of God (denial of divine omnipotence), or "love of God,"
which culminates in contempt of self (renunciation of human science).
From this point of view, the dilemma is a test of the intentional aim
of the meditator's desire rather than a test of logic. Yet Descartes's
rational framework reveals that "love of self" is futile, since it leads
to contempt of God and therefore the loss of any hope of providing

---

[49] A implies B and not-A implies B; therefore B. Descartes's *cogito* also follows this
structure. Either I know that I am, or I doubt it. If I know it, then I am. If I doubt it,
then I am. Therefore I am. On the *Consequentia Mirabilis* and its vogue among Jesuits,
see William and Martha Kneale, *A History of Logic* (Oxford: Clarendon Press, 1962),
pp. 172–174 and 346–348.

[50] From Ausonius, as discussed earlier, and Descartes's dream, AT X, 216.

the self with the certainty that it desires. The "abysmal" temptation to deny an almighty Creator is rationally unmasked as a false solution. The certainty of arithmetic is no more absolute if we deny, than if we posit, an omnipotent Creator.

At this critical point, the meditator makes the right choice. He decides to affirm the existence of an omnipotent Creator and accept the consequence that science may be beyond human reach: *Quid igitur erit verum? Fortassis hoc unum, nihil esse certi.*[51] What motivates the meditator's decision? What light in the intellect moves the will to take the right path? The alternatives lead to the same negative outcome but are asymmetric from a rational point of view. There is indeed no rational basis to *deny* the (purely rational) possibility of an omnipotent evil creator. While the existence of an omnipotent evil creator is entirely doubtful, the *possibility* of such an existence has not been disproved and must, therefore, be admitted. By trusting reason "blindly" (i.e. without regard for consequence), the meditator has been saved from a fatal abyss. Had he opted to deny the logical possibility of divine omnipotence, he would now face a dead end. Instead, he faces a new predicament.

The meditator now concedes the hypothesis that an omnipotent Creator exists, but has no reason to believe that this Creator is *good*, since the phrase "omnipotent creator" does not analytically imply benevolence. The meditator must therefore concede that this Creator, who has absolute power, has the power systematically to deceive him. What action will he take in the face of this hegemonic power of deception? Faithful to his initial resolve to remain free of error, the meditator decides to renounce all knowledge. In order to thwart the demon's assault, he actively prevents familiar opinions from "occupying his mind against his will."[52] Rather than collude with the demon, rather than submit to deception, the meditator gives up his body and surrenders everything that can be used by the demonic force to plunge him into error.

The first day of *meditatio* thus ends with a dark night and savage dismemberment. The initiand gives everything up: sky, earth, colors, figures and sounds, his hands, eyes, flesh and blood.[53] Abandoned to

---

[51] "What, then, will be true? Perhaps this alone—that nothing is certain." Second Meditation, (AT VII, p. 24; IX, p. 19).

[52] AT VII, 22: "assidue enim recurrunt consuetate opiniones, occupantque credulitatem meam tanquam longo usu, fere etiam me invito."

[53] Meditation I, AT VII, 22–23: "Putabo caelum, aerem, terram, colores, figuras, sonos, cunctaque externa nihil aliud esse quam ludificationes somniorum, quibus insi-

the demon's fury, he clings to Truth apophatically, as an inaccessible and utterly unknown ideal.

It is useful at this point to remember that Descartes inherited stark symbols and self-techniques from his schooldays at La Flèche, starting with the Ignatian prayer:

> "Suffer me not to be separated from Thee; From the malignant enemy defend me; In the hour of my death call me."[54]

Againt overwhelming peril (temptation, death), the soul appeals *de profundis* for supernatural help—and the prayer, as such, *is* the help needed and the source of spiritual strength. The Ignatian Exercises, as we saw, also taught Descartes the method of *agere contra*—of deliberately opposing the evil spirit and/or disordered attachments by "contrary action."[55] In Meditation I, the meditator adopts the same strategy. Since doubtful opinions have sway over his mind because of habit and because they present indeed more reasons to be believed than to be denied,[56] he will never overcome his spontaneous tendency to believe them until he adopts the contrary view and preemptively regards them all as false.[57]

Hyberbolic doubt is thus part of a general determination to *agere contra*.[58] Precisely because the proposition "$2+3 = 5$" imposes itself on the mind with such force, the meditator must prevent himself from believing it by raising an almost imperceptible (*valde tenuis*) metaphysical objection. The meditator's strategy also closely resembles Ignatian *agere contra* in its aim, namely to achieve "indifference." Like the Ignatian exercitant, the meditator seeks deliberately to neutralize his biases by adopting counter-biases.[59] The hypothesis of the evil demon (*genium malignum*), like the practice of guided imagination in the Ignatian exercises, provides instrumental help in defining the target and the condi-

---

dias credulitati meae tetendit: considerabo meipsum tanquam manus non habentem, non oculos, non carnem, non sanguinem, non aliquem sensum…"

[54] "Anima Christi," in *The Spiritual Exercises of St. Ignatius*, 36.

[55] Ignatian Direction 16, in *The Spiritual Exercises of St. Ignatius*, 41.

[56] AT VII, 22: "… quas multo magis rationi consentaneum sit credere quam negare."

[57] Meditation I, AT VII, 22: "non male agam, si, voluntate plane in contrarium versa, me ipsum fallam."

[58] Note that Myles Burnyeat overlooks obvious Jesuit sources in his discussion of Descartes's innovation.

[59] AT VII, 22: "… donec tandem, velut aequatis utriumque parejudiciorum ponderibus, nulla amplius prava consuetudo judicium meum a recta rerum peceptione detorqueat."

tions for *agere contra*. In the violent scenario of the demonic assault, the rule of indubitability takes on a new, personal force. The meditator's most intimate causal agency is vividly brought to the fore. The meditator reasons that, since he cannot help himself from believing what he perceives, he will deceive himself instead: *me ipsum fallam*. Contrary to what his perceptions dictate, namely that they are veridical, he will suppose that they result from a deliberate agenda of systematic deception. This requires that he intentionally depart from truth and suppose, not that there is God, divine fountain of Truth, but the counter-hypothesis of a Creator who is both almighty and evil (*malignum*), namely intent on deceiving rather than enlightening his creature.[60]

Descartes also learned from Ignatian retreats the "rules for the discernment of spirits" and the purgative effect of "contrition of the heart."[61] The Cartesian meditator, like the Ignatian exercitant, actively cooperates with reason to "awaken the conscience to remorse." Spontaneous biases, such as the belief that "these hands, this body, are mine" or that "2 + 3 = 5," must be acknowledged, lamented and purged, the same as disordered attachments or any bad habit (*prava consuetido*) that pushes us away from the right path. If we briefly return to Baillet's report that Descartes himself experienced an episode of acute contrition in 1619, the contritional design of Meditation I becomes clear. On the night of November 11, following the famous nightmare in which he was pushed into a church against his will by an evil spirit (*a malo spiritu*), Descartes reflected on the goods and evils of this life for a few hours, prayed for protection from punishment for his sins, then drifted into sleep only to wake up again terror-stricken.[62] This experience of terror, Descartes believed, "marked his *synderesis*, by which he meant remorse over his past sins".[63] Significantly, Descartes's contrition was triggered by the fear that "some bad spirit was attempting to seduce him" while

---

[60] AT VII, 22: "Supponam igitur non optimum Deum, fontem veritatis, sed genium aliquem malignum, eundemque summe potentem et callidum, omnem suam industriam in eo posuisse, ut me falleret."

[61] See *The Spiritual Exercises of St. Ignatius*, Rules for the Discernment of Spirits, Week I, Rule 1: "The good spirit acts in these persons (i.e. who go from mortal sin to mortal sin) in a contrary way, awakening the conscience to a sense of remorse through the good judgment of reason."

[62] AT X, p. 182.

[63] See Baillet's account, in AT X, p. 186: "L'épouvante dont il fut frappé dans le second songe, marquoit, à son sens, sa syndérèse, c'est–à–dire, les remords de sa conscience touchant les péchez qu'il pouvait avoir commis pendant le cours de sa vie jusqu'alors."

the terror he experienced due to his "remorse of conscience" was followed by a roll of thunderous lightning signifying that "the Spirit of Truth had descended to take possession of him."[64] We recognize in the account not only Descartes's assimilation of Ignatian "discernment of spirits" but also his conviction that remorse, if sufficiently radical, (1) effectively cleanses the soul of past sins (biases, *prava consuetudino*); (2) protects the soul from "evil seduction," and (3) makes possible a new communion with Truth.[65]

By sacrificing his flesh, eyes and limbs rather than surrender to demonic deception, the meditator is cleansed of his susceptibility to be swayed by perceptions and makes a radical discovery. Besieged on all sides by what he firmly regards to be sensory delusions, ravaged by a demon "as malevolent as he is powerful," the meditator discovers that, while he is cut off from knowledge, he is not cut off from Truth. On the contrary, voluntary renunciation of knowledge and of the power to know anything at all reveals that he possesses a power that the demon cannot bend: *in me est, ne falsis assentiar.*[66] As long as the meditator remains resolute and gives up all knowledge rather than cling to his "body of death," the demon is powerless to force him into error. The meditator is admonished to stay "obstinately fixed" on his resolve: however powerful (*quantumvis potens*), however cunning (*quantumvis callidus*), the demon cannot compel him.[67]

The radical *kenosis* through which the meditator escapes the demon's deception reveals that causal agency, as such, is radically independent of perception and, therefore, escapes the very possibility of perceptual deception. Bereft of hands, eyes, flesh, the meditator is emptied of all cognitive hope but not of the hope of adhering to Truth since he has—and exercises—the power to abstain from succumbing to error. The meditator's power to suspend judgment (*epoche*) defies the demon's power absolutely and shows that the demon's power is narrowly con-

---

[64] *Ibid.*: "La foudre dont il entendit l'éclat, étoit le signal de l'esprit de vérité qui descendoit sur luy pour le posséder."

[65] See in this regard the First Week of the Ignatian Exercises, especially the First Exercise ("I shall ask for pain, tears, … shame and confusion … how often I have deserved to be damned eternally for the many sins I have committed.") Also the Second Exercise; "Let me see myself as a sore and an abscess whence have come forth so many sins, so many evils, and the most vile poison." An additional directive specifies: "When I wake up … I shall be filled with confusion for my many sins."

[66] AT VII, 23.

[67] AT VII, 23.

fined to the perceptual/cognitive realm. The demon has power over the soul's passions, but has no power over the soul's *will to act*. It follows that the very hypothesis of an omnipotent malicious deity falls apart. When put to the test, the premiss proves to be incoherent. The meditator's power to suspend judgment indeed disproves the possibility of a creator who is *both* almighty and a deceiver. This means, in turn, that the power of *epoche* and the non-impossibility of truth are logically indivisible.

Let us review what has transpired. The meditator supposes that there is a creator who is omnipotent, based on the impossibility of denying that such a creator is possible. He then supposes that this omnipotent creator is an evil deceiver, based on the impossibility of deriving benevolence from "omnipotence." The result is the hypothesis that there is an omnipotent and evil creator. Since "from a false premiss, anything at all follows," hyperbolic doubt holds: the premiss that there is an omnipotent evil demon implies that $2+3 = 6$, that $2+3 = 1425$, that green is red, and so forth. The falsity of the supposition, however, is not ascertained *until the meditator disproves the omnipotence of the evil demon by exercising his power to suspend judgment.*

In other words, the meditator's action proves that the premiss "there is an omnipotent and evil demon" is false, and by the same token, disproves the impossibility of truth. By remaining "obstinately resolved" to thwart the demon's power, the meditator indeed succeeds in thwarting it where he least expected it. No truth becomes known or affirmed, but the coherence of Truth is upheld, since the proposition from which the incoherence of Truth derived is certifiably false (as opposed to merely doubtful and *regarded* as false). The meditator's set of truths is still empty—but his set of falsehoods now contains at least one *provably* false element, namely the proposition "there exists a creator who is both omnipotent and evil." The (indubitable) falsity of the demonic hypothesis rules out the necessity that "my nature might be such that I am *always* deceived"—as indeed the exercise of *epoche* attests, since the demon, try as he may, cannot compel me to be deceived as long as I remain determined to suspend judgment. Sceptical *epoche*, the act of suspending judgment, is thus the most basic of all rational actions: it proves, as such, that the belief that Truth is possible cannot be proved to be false. The project of assigning truth-values is, therefore, inherently coherent.

Is it any surprise that Descartes hesitated to introduce casual vernacular readers to this analysis, worrying that they might lose their

way and drown?[68] The Cartesian meditator who survives the ordeal
and triumphs over the nocturnal "river demon," like Jacob Israel, is
permanently wounded in his bodily flesh (he can no longer trust sensation naively) but gains a radically new "celestial" perspective. He possesses the power to "resolutely keep himself" (*obfirmata mente cavebo*) from
endorsing error.[69] This means that he possesses the power to resist and
defeat the evil deceiver he has conjured, which in turn means that the
evil deceiver cannot be the author of his origin. By discovering *in me est,
ne falsis assentiar*, the meditator awakens from a deep slumber, a state of
receptive passivity—painfully, and plagued with a regressive tendency
to revert to somnolence.

Like a slave who enjoys in his sleep an imaginary freedom and
conspires with his dreams to resist waking up, the meditator "spontaneously reverts to his old opinions" (*sponte relabor in veteres opiniones*).[70] A
tension arises between the resolve to act—to keep guard against error—
and the passive habit of a lifetime to believe spontaneously whatever
perceptions are received. Like a monk in the Egyptian desert, the meditator is summoned to undertake "arduous vigils" (*laboriosa vigila*) without any guarantee that his efforts will accede to new knowledge or be
sufficient to dispel the present darkness. The meditator, in short, faces
a last test of his resolve: he is called to watch over his mind and keep
error away for the sake of Truth, without any known truth in sight. He
must exercise his inalienable power to *love* Truth without any reason to
believe that he will ever *know* Truth. Descartes's *laboriosa vigila* involve
a willingess to endorse orthopraxy for the inherent dignity of it, prior
to the hope of reward, even if the hope of reward, which is the hope
of acquiring authentic knowledge, emerges irrepressibly from exercising
rightful vigilance.

---

[68] Cf. Descartes's letter to Mersenne, March 1637, AT I, 350: "Ce que j'ai obmis
tout à dessein, et par consideration, et principalement à cause que i'ay écrit en langue
vulgaire, de peur que les esprits foibles venant à embrasser d'abord avidement les
doutes et scrupules qu'il m'eust fallu proposer, ne pussent apres comprendre en mesme
façon les raisons par lesquelles i'eusse tasché de les oster, et ainsi que ie les eusse
engagez dans un mauvais pas sans peut-estre les en tirer."

[69] AT VII, 23.

[70] AT VII, 23.

CHAPTER SEVEN

I REFRAIN, THEREFORE I AM

Meditation II famously presents the Cartesian *cogito* as an Archimedean leverage point, sufficiently firm to allow "the earth's orb to be moved from its place to a new one."[1] Implicitly, the new Cartesian fulcrum will help to wean the meditator from geocentrism and make it possible for him epistemologically to inhabit a Copernican cosmos. The human *ego*, by discovering itself as the inititator of its own rational activity, is delivered from its terrestrial dependence on place.[2] How does this Cartesian revolution proceed? The key to Meditation II is that the certainty of the *cogito* and the immateriality of the *ego* are inseparable. The *ego* recognizes and adopts itself as a new epistemologic center precisely because its presence to itself is given through its own immaterial intervention. When Descartes was asked to clarify the difference between the Cartesian *cogito* and the Augustinian *cogito*, he explained that the goal of the Cartesian *cogito* is not, like Augustine's, to argue that the soul is an image of the Trinity, but to establish that the *ego* is an immaterial substance.[3]

The purpose of Meditation II is to reverse the scholastic/Aristotelian axiom that "nothing is in the intellect that was not first in the senses" by bringing the meditator to recognize that mind is better and more immediately known (*notior*) than body.[4] Descartes hoped that the meditator would devote "months or at least weeks" to Meditation II, not because of the difficulty of its subject matter, but because of its therapeutic power in correcting the habit of confusing intellectual and mate-

---

[1] Meditation II, AT VII, 24: "Nihil nisi punctum petebat Archimedes, quod esset firmum et immobile, ut integram terram loco dimoveret; magna quoque speranda sunt, si vel minimum quid invenero quod certum sit et inconcussum."

[2] Cf. Meditation II, AT VII, 24: "corpus ... locusque sunt chimera."

[3] Letter of November, 1640, AT III, 247: "... au lieu que je m'en sers pour faire connoistre que ce *moy*, qui pense, est *une substance immaterielle*, et qui n'a rien de corporel." Augustine's *cogito* is in *De Civitate Dei*, Book XI, chap. 26.

[4] As the subtitle of Meditation II indicates: *De natura mentis humanae: quod ipsa sit notior quam corpus*. The same threefold plan is outlined in *La Recherche de la Vérité*, AT X, 505, lines 11–14 and 510, lines 4–11.

rial things.[5] Meditation II, Descartes insists, offers a "unique" means of detaching the mind from the senses.[6]

What role, if any, does the *cogito* play in the process of therapy? If we recall that the distinction between mind (*mens*) and body was derived in the *Regulae* from *intelligo*,[7] and that *intelligere* was taken to denote the mind's activity when acting alone,[8] we have a precise starting point from which to examine how the Cartesian *cogito*, in the forms in which Meditation II presents it, lays the ground for the *ego*'s self-discovery. Scholars have typically argued against Descartes that the claim *I think, therefore I am* fails because Descartes lacks an adequate concept of himself.[9] Since the verb *cogitare* covers a variety of Intentional states, from volitions (doubting, supposing) to perceptions (sensing light or heat),[10] we must try to specify what type of thinking initiates self-discovery and, therefore, the Cartesian revolution.

7.1. *Ego and Agency*

Meditation II does not present the formulation *cogito, ergo sum*, but offers instead four carefully-worded variations, as though Descartes meant for the meditator to test its certainty by examining it from four different angles. At the start of the second day, the meditator finds himself at a point of no return. He is "so full of doubts" that he can neither turn back nor make progress.[11] As though suddenly fallen (*delapsus*) into deep

---

[5] Second Answers, AT IX, 103.

[6] Second Answers, AT IX, 104: "Le vrai, et, à mon jugement, l'unique moyen pour cela [sc. éloigner l'esprit des sens] est contenu dans ma seconde Meditation."

[7] AT X, 421–422: "Intelligo, ergo mentem habeo a corpore distinctam."

[8] AT X, 416, 4: "si denique sola agat [sc. vis illa per quam res proprie cognoscimus], dicitur intelligere."

[9] See Peter Mackie, "The Cogito and its importance," in *The Cambridge Companion to Descartes*, 164–165: "In all, then, Descartes leaves us wondering how he thinks of himself when he forms his certain beliefs about his thought and existence. He seems committed to the view that he thinks of himself by conceiving some concept of himself. Yet, no adequate concept of him seems to be available."

[10] Descartes offers a number of lists, but one is especially useful, found in his letter to Mersenne of April 27, 1637, AT I, 366, lines 1–6: "Pour ce que vous inferez que, si sa nature de l'homme n'est que de penser, il n'a donc point de volonté, ie n'en voy pas la conseqence; car vouloir, entendre, imaginer, sentir, etc., ne sont que diverses façons de penser, qui apartiennent toutes à l'âme."

[11] AT VII, 23: "... ut nequeam amplius earum oblivisci, nec videam tamen qua ratione solvendae sint."

water, he is so disoriented (*turbatus*) that he can neither find a footing nor swim to the surface.[12] What does he decide to do? He remains firm in his resolve to act rationally and to doubt whatever presents itself "until something certain is discovered," even if the only certainty that he succeeds in reaching turns out to be that "nothing is certain."[13] The rule of indubitability, reason's gift (*ratio persuadet*), guides the meditator through treacherous depths by requiring that he act deliberately, vigilantly, and with constant steadfastness. Rational orthopraxy, aimed at rejecting error, is preferred over the possession of faulty knowledge. Watching his every step, refraining from a myriad tempting but forbidden fruits (reasonable beliefs), the meditator conscientiously strives (*enitar*) to doubt all things for the sake of Truth. The method of systematic doubt means that the meditator deliberately *tests* whatever presents itself as a candidate for veracity and rejects it (*removendo*) if the slightest ground of uncertainty is dicovered. The emphasis is on the rational effort conducted by the meditator to block his ordinary beliefs, most especially those that result spontaneously from sensory perception. When we say that the meditator systematically doubts (*dubito*) whatever impinges on his consciousness, we mean that he tirelessly rejects as false whatever he can rationally challenge. He thus deliberately prevents himself from believing what his senses dictate. He prevents himself as well from believing what his "mendacious memory" (*mendax memoria*) represents to him as having once existed. Reason, in the form of the rule of indubitability, turns out to be a call to action—a summons deliberately to subvert, by means of thought-experiment, the spontaneous process through which sensory ideas are received by the mind as veridical. In a determined effort of *agere contra*, the meditator relentlessly interferes to stop perception from resulting in the belief that what is perceived is real.

As Descartes stressed in the *Discours*, the meditator does not just happen to think that whatever enters his mind is false, he *decides* to think thus, *wills* himself, against the spontaneity of ordinary perception, to think thus: "je *voulais* ainsi penser que tout était faux."[14] In the systematic sense in which Descartes uses the term, *dubito* means a

---

[12] AT VII, 23–24: "Tanquam in profundum gurgitem ex improviso delapsus, ita turbatus sum, ut nec possim in imo pedem figere, nec enatare ad summum." Cf. Montaigne, *Essais*, Bk. II, c. 1, in Oeuvres, 315–321.

[13] AT VII, 24: "pergamque porro donec aliquid certi, vel, si nihil aliud, saltem hoc ipsum pro certo, nihil esse certi, cognoscam."

[14] This is the first formulation of the *cogito* in the *Discours*, AT VI, 32: "Je pris garde

deliberate mental action, carried out knowingly and intentionally by
the meditator against the habit in him of receiving ideas passively and
indiscriminately.

Because the Cartesian *epoche* makes special use of thought-experiment (the demonic hypothesis) rational thought is substituted for perception with regard to the causal genesis of beliefs. Rather than allow
beliefs to be caused in him as a result of sensory perception, the meditator supposes that perception is deceptive: "I suppose therefore that
all that I see is false"—*suppono igitur omnia quae video falsa esse*. By deliberately supposing that what he sees is false, the meditator thwarts the
ordinary causal impact of extramental things on the mind and takes
rational control of what he believes. To suppose deliberately that visible things are false is to override rationally the passive process of perception. When we say that we see a table, what we mean is that we
have a certain mental experience that includes the experience that the
experience is caused by the real table that we see.[15] Conversely, to
suppose that the perception is false is to make oneself believe, on a
provisional basis and knowingly, that the experience is *not* caused by
anything real. Descartes correctly extends the same analysis to sensory
memory. Rather than regard his memories as veridical, the meditator
believes (*credo*) that nothing represented to him by memory ever existed.

He denies his senses, meaning that he supposes them not to function
as senses: *nullos plane habeo sensus*. Consequently, he regards body, figure,
extension and place to be mere illusions (*chimera*). The meaning of
abducere mentem a sensibus comes to light. The mind's rational capacity
to disbelieve sensory input is isolated from the mind's passive tendency
to believe sensory perception. The mind's "abduction" from sense is an
auto-abduction, an inner struggle between what reason conjectures and
what sense spontaneously dictates. The rule of indubitability provides a
"unique" means to detach the mind from sense because it requires the
mind to rebel against its own perceptual passivity by mobilizing and
exercising its rational agency.

Descartes, in 1638, remarked that advancing from the *cogito* to the
proof of God's existence required that the reader be proficient in think-

---

que, pendant que je voulais ainsi penser que tout était faux, il fallait nécessairement
que moi, qui le pensais, fusse quelque chose."

[15] Paraphrasing John Searle, *Intentionality*, 123; "When I see a flower, part of the
content of the experience is that this experience is caused by the fact that there is a
flower there."

ing independently of sense.[16] To what extent does Meditation II seek to develop rational proficiency to facilitate the *cogito*? Meditation II draws a subtle new connection between *abducere mentem a sensibus* and *credere*.

Descartes, as we know, initially distinguished between, on the one hand, rational truths, which we know by an act of intellect (*ingenii actio*), and, on the other hand, revealed truths, which we believe (*credamus*) by an act of will (*voluntatis actio*).[17] In Meditation II, the verb *credo* is given a new rational meaning. When the meditator, in the name of the rule of indubitability, intends to deny that sensory memories imply that any real extramental things ever existed, he carries out his intention by believing the opposite, namely that they imply nothing. *Credo* denotes an act of will, authorized by reason for the purpose of rational conjecture. The meditator is free rationally to *suppose* or *believe* that his sensory memories imply nothing more than illusions precisely because he does not yet have rational grounds to *know* or *understand* them to be veridical (caused by real extramental things). Rational belief ("my memories are illusions") weans the meditator from irrational prejudice ("my memories imply the real things that they represent").

In general terms, the meditator's rational thought-experiment of "supposing that what I see is false" serves as a blueprint for overriding immediate sense impressions (*ideae adventitiae*) with rational hypotheses (*ideae factae vel factitiae*)—such as when I deny that the sun's visible motion implies its revolution around the earth, or, for that matter, deny that the sight and taste of bread in the transubstantiated host imply the presence of bread.[18] In both cases, a deliberately endorsed *belief* supersedes immediate sense *data*, displaying the mind's ability to

---

[16] See e.g. Descartes's letter to Father Vatier, February 22, 1638, AT I, 560: "La principale cause de son obscurité [sc. de ce que j'ay écrit de l'existence de Dieu] vient de ce que je n'ai pas osé m'étendre sur les raisons des sceptiques, ny dire toutes les choses necessaires *ad abducendam mentem a sensibus*."

[17] See *Regulae*, Rule III, AT X, 370: "Quod tamen non impedit quominus illa, quae divinitus revelata sunt, omni cognitione certiora credamus, cum illorum fides, quaecumque est de obscuris, non ingenii actio sit, sed voluntatis."

[18] For Descartes's description of the Copernican hypothesis as an *idea facta vel factitia*, as opposed to "adventitious" sensory impressions, see his letter to Mersenne, June 16, 1641, AT III, 383: "Par le mot *Idea*, i'entends tout ce qui peut estre en nostre pensée, et que i'en ay distingué de trois sortes: à savoir, *quaedam sunt adventitiae*, comme l'idée qu'on se fait vulgairement du Soleil; *aliae factae vel factitiae*, au rang desquelles on peut mettre celle que les astronomes font du Soleil par leur raisonnement." For Descartes's interest in transubstantiation and his commitment to the Catholic doctrine, see his letter to Mersenne of January 28, 1641, AT III, 295–296.

act independently of sense perception. Bérulle, as we saw, praised the Copernican theory on precisely this ground. The rule of indubitability, in short, trains the meditator *ad abducendam mentem a sensibus* by requiring that he rationally *form* beliefs ("what I perceive is an illusion") rather than passively *receive* beliefs from sense ("what I perceive is a real body causing me to perceive it."). Let us further scrutinize the contrast between *supposing* and *perceiving*—between intentionally *forming* beliefs and *receiving* them from sense.

The contrast is similar to the contrast between deliberately forming a mental image of a table and perceiving a table. In the first case, a mental action is required and the person performing the action—forming the image—knows himself to be the author or source of the image, while in the second case, the image impinges on the mind from elsewhere.[19] When the meditator blocks perceptual beliefs by supposing the opposite, he replaces ideas that are received from elsewhere (*ideae adventitiae*) with ideas of his own making (*ideae factae vel factitiae*). He prevents himself from "suffering" the effects of what stimulates his senses by believing what he himself wills himself rationally to believe. In Meditation II, the reversal is operated by the decision to act reflexively: *me ipsum fallam*. By definition, my belief that things are real result from my perceiving them ("what I see is a table causing me to see it"). If I believe, instead, that they are illusions, I remove myself from being cognitively affected by perception and constitute myself rationally as both the source and recipient of my ideas. By deceiving myself, I bring about ideas of which I am knowingly the sole author. Elsewhere, Descartes explicitly distinguishes between perceptions that are *caused* by body and perceptions that are deliberately caused by the mind.[20]

Does the distinction imply, in turn, that my deliberate action of self-deception is immune to deception and uncertainty? Our analysis conforms to Descartes's view that the contrast between acting and perceiving is a contrast between *actio* and *passio*. Descartes holds that there are two basic types of Intentional events or *cogitationes*: perceptions and volitions. Appealing to the "wax and seal" metaphor, he insists that perceptions are *passions*, whereas volitions, and volitions alone, are

---

[19] See Searle, *Intentionality*, 124, ftn. 9: "Imagine the difference between forming an image of the front of one's house as a voluntary action, and actually seeing the front of the house ... The voluntarily formed images we would experience as caused by us, the visual experience of the house we would experience as caused by something independent of us."

[20] *Des Passions de l'âme*, I, Art. XIX, AT XI, 343.

actions.[21] Even more significantly, Descartes also holds that deliberate action implies, indivisibly, the knowledge that one is acting.[22] To act deliberately, according to Descartes, is precisely to act "knowingly." Descartes sometimes speaks of having the "idea" of acting while one is deliberately acting (*le savoir par une idée*), sometimes of "perceiving our volitions" (*perceptions de nos volontez*).[23] In any event, his view is that any action on a person's part that involves a volition implies the person's knowledge/perception of acting. From the soul's point of view, a volition is an *actio*, but it is also a *passio* for the soul to perceive its volition.[24] Descartes concludes that a volition is *both* an action and a perception indivisibly, but is called *action* because a thing is always to be denoted by its nobler aspect.[25]

Does the meditator, by acting deliberately to deny perceptual beliefs, necessary know, perceive, intuit his action? Is *this* perception open to doubt? Can the meditator doubt that he acts while he deliberately acts?

We are now sufficiently practiced in *abducere mentem a sensibus* to approach the *cogito*. The meditator, struggling in deep water, searches for something indubitable. He wonders if his thoughts do not logically imply God, or some agent like God, as their cause: *qui mihi ipsas cogitationes immittit*. The implication is rejected on the grounds that he, the meditator, could himself be the "author of his thoughts."[26] Let us pause to note that, without the thought-experiment of *supposing* that what he sees is false, without the experience of constituting himself as the deliberate author of his thoughts, the thought that he *could* be their

---

[21] Letter to Mesland, May 2, 1644, AT IV, 113: "Et comme ce n'est pas proprement une action, mais une passion en la cire, de recevoir diverses figures, il me semble que c'est aussi une passion en l'ame de recevoir telle ou telle idée, et qu'il *n'y a que ses volontés qui soient des actions*." (Emphasis added).

[22] See Descartes's letter to Mersenne, January 28, 1641, AT III, 295: "Nous ne sçaurions rien vouloir, sans sçavoir que nous le voulons, ny le savoir par une idée; mais ie ne mets point que cette idée soit differente de l'action mesme."

[23] The first is cited from the previous footnote, AT III, 295; the second is in *Des Passions de l'âme*, I, Art. XIX, AT XI, 343: "Nos perceptions sont aussi de deux sortes, et les unes ont l'âme pour cause, les autres le corps. Celles qui ont l'âme pour cause, sont les perceptions de nos volontez… Car il est certain que nous ne sçaurions vouloir aucune chose, que nous n'apercevions par mesme moyen que nous la voulons."

[24] *Ibid.*: "Et bien qu'au regard de nostre ame, ce soit une action de vouloir quelque chose, on peut dire que c'est aussi en elle une passion d'apercevoir qu'elle veut."

[25] *Ibid.*: "Toutefois, à cause que cette perception et cette volonté ne sont en effect qu'une mesme chose, la denomination se fait tousjours par ce qui est le plus noble; et ainsi on n'a point coustume de la nommer une passion, mais seulement une action."

[26] AT VII, 24: "Quare vero hoc putem, cum forsan ipsemet illarum author esse possim?"

author might not have suggested itself. Until he acted deliberately to
oppose perceptual beliefs by replacing them with rational conjectures,
the very issue of the source of beliefs remained entirely opaque. The
training in detaching the mind from sense revolved, in effect, around
the causal question: "who, or what, sends these thoughts into me?"—
qui mihi ipsas cogitationes immittitne?

The meditator considers, next, whether the possibility that he himself is the author of his thoughts implies, in turn, anything certain. Does
it imply that *he*, at least, must be something instead of nothing?[27] At
first, the meditator objects that he, too, must fall under the general
decision to invalidate all perceptions. Since indeed he has persuaded
himself (*mihi persuasi*) that all of his perceptions are false—that there
are no bodies and no minds—it seems that he, too, must be nothing.[28]
The question of whether possible authorship implies an actual author
reduces to the question of whether the author of the thought "all that
I perceive is nothing" is able to persuade himself that he, the author of
the thought, is also nothing while persuading himself thus. The meditator can deny that "these hands, this body, are mine," but can he deny
that the denying implies a rational agent, himself, to perform it?

The first formulation of the *cogito* is presented as a conditional. It
is formulated in the past tense, presumably to emphasize that the
inference is valid independently of memory and time:

> "Imo certe ego eram, si quid mihi persuasi"—I most certainly was, if I
> persuaded myself thus.[29]

Two features of this first formulation warrant the meditator's special
attention. First, the conditional form brings to light a pure, rational
necessity. No claim is made that my memory is accurate and that I
actually deceived myself. The claim is conjectural: *if* I deceived myself,
then I who performed the mental act of deceiving myself must have
existed. The second important feature is that the *ego* as such is disclosed
by the inference. Since the Latin *eram* means "I was," adding *ego* before
eram emphasizes the first-person implied by the inference, as though
the discovery that *I* existed took precedence over the conclusion that
I *existed*. The *ego* grasps itself precisely as the agent implied by rational
action.

---

[27] AT VII, 24: "Nunquid ergo saltem ego aliquid sum?"
[28] AT VII, 25: "nonne igitur etiam me non esse?"
[29] AT VII, 25.

Descartes's inference depends on the assumption that a rational action cannot occur without a rational agent/*ego* to perform it. It claims, moreover, that this assumption is rational. Part of what it means to be a first-person rational agent (*ego*), Descartes implies, is that the logical connection between acting deliberately and the existence of a deliberate agent is rationally known. Does Descartes elaborate this assumption further and shed additional light on the concept of *ego* that emerges with the *cogito*?

The second formulation of the *cogito* is also presented as a conditional. In contrast to the first formulation, the second formulation invokes the alien action of the hypothetical evil demon on the *ego*, not the *ego*'s action on itself. The argument, framed in the present tense, starts with the premiss that "there is an evil deceiver who strives to deceive me always (*me semper fallit*)." Based on this premiss, the meditator concludes:

"Without doubt, therefore, I myself am, if he deceives me."[30]

How is the existence of my *ego* implied by the fact that an evil demon deceives me always? Only the most patient meditator will unravel Descartes's argument. Once again, since the argument is conditional, no claim is made about whether or not a specific event, namely the demon's action of deceiving me, is actually taking place. The claim is simply that *if* the demon deceives me, *then* I exist. Two new features of the rational *ego* are brought to light. First, the conditional clause (*si me fallit*) has a more hypothetical character than the conditional clause of the first formulation (*si mihi persuasi*). While the first inference extracted logical necessity from a materially possible fact, the second formulation extracts logical necessity from a pure thought-experiment. The first inference involves an *abstract* condition, the second inference involves an *ideal* condition. The second formulation, in effect, is a counterfactual.

We know from Meditation I that the hypothesis of the omnipotent deceptor is inconsistent. Strictly speaking, the second formulation should read as follows: "If it *were* possible for an evil demon to deceive me always, then if he *were* deceiving me, I *would* have to exist." The second formulation, if the inference is valid, underscores, therefore, that rational thought-experiments are appropriate means of isolating and disclosing rational connections. The rational *ego* reasoning in abstraction of what can be realized materially, discovers valid truths. The question is: is the inference valid?

---

[30] AT VII, 25: "Haud dubie igitur ego etiam sum, si me fallit."

What, exactly, is Descartes's argument? How is the *ego*'s existence conditionally proved? Since the demon, by hypothesis, deceives me always (*me semper fallit*), his victim, namely myself, cannot obtain the concept "Truth" from experience. Yet the concept "Truth" is required by the clause *if he deceives me* since the idea of deception is formed privatively from the prior idea of Truth.[31] The hypothesis *si me fallit* requires, therefore, that the demon's victim know and value Truth intrinsically. But only a rational and existing *ego* knows and values truth intrinsically.[32] Only a rational *ego* intrinsically possessed of the idea of Truth is capable of conducting a thought-experiment in which it supposes itself to be *deceived*. The hypothesis of hegemonic deception thus implies the existence of a rational *ego*, disclosed in its inalienable power to conceive of Truth.

So far, Descartes has proceeded analytically by asking what is implied by (a) the supposition that I acted rationally on myself and (b) the second-order hypothesis that I supposed myself to be the victim of hegemonic deception. A third formulation now establishes the *ego*'s actual existence and living presence to itself as rational agent and rational intellect:

> "Try as he might, the deceiver will never bring it about that I am nothing as long as I think that I am something."[33]

Instead of being joined by a condition (*si*), the two clauses are joined by simultaneity in the present tense (*quamdiu*). We note that "thinking myself to be something" is, as it were, a single thought with two aspects, comprising both *actio* and *passio*: the *ego* both acts mentally (forms an idea) and grasps the result of acting (knows an idea). Since the thought is self-referential, we must presumably assume that it presents the *ego* to itself as the agent of the idea that is formed. The action through which the *ego* forms a positive concept of itself, and the intellection through which the *ego* grasps itself in the positive concept that it has deliberately ("knowingly") formed, jointly imply the *ego*'s existence. Formulations (1) and (3) combined constitute, in effect, the infer-

---

[31] Cf. Descartes's remark, AT X, 218 in his private notes, that the statement in Genesis that God separated light from darkness cannot be taken litterally, since a "privation cannot be separated from a habit" (*non potest separari privatio ab habitu*).

[32] Cf. the definition given by Descartes of reason as "the power to distinguish the true from the false," (*la puissance de distinguer le vraye d'avec le faux*), in *Discours de la Méthode*, Part I, AT VI, 2.

[33] AT VII, 25: "Fallat quantum potest, nunquam tamen efficiet, ut nihil sim quamdiu me aliquid esse cogitabo."

ence: *if the first, then the second; but the first, therefore the second.*[34] Formulation 1 established the conditional "if the first (if I acted on myself), then the second (I existed)." Formulation 3 now adds: "but I am acting on myself, therefore I exist." Formulation 3 establishes that a first-person rational action is actually occuring ("I think of myself as something") and, therefore, that a first-person rational agent exists ("I am not nothing"). The meditator's immediate intuition of acting deliberately explains the logical impossibility that he recognizes—namely the logical impossibility that he himself who is solely responsible for the action is "nothing" as long as he intuits himself to be performing the action.

Much confusion over whether *ego sum* is meant to be an immediate intuition or a deduction,[35] is dispelled once we consider that, to Descartes, acting deliberately means acting "knowingly." The *ego* that knowingly thinks of itself as something intuits its action precisely as a first-person volition that logically requires a first-person agent, namely itself. Similarly, the *ego* that knows itself in a concept that it forms grasps logically that it is what forms the idea (thinks) and grasps it (thinks).

The "thinking" invoked in Formulation 3, at once *actio* and *passio*, comes as close as possible to fusing together the two Intentional states of acting and knowing. The demon cannot "make me" (*efficiet*) into nothing as long as I deliberately act to disclose myself to myself as rational agent and intellect. Rational action that originates with the *ego* and terminates in the *ego*'s positive self-ideation as a rational agent that acts and knows itself by acting lies beyond the demon's scope. I can doubt the veracity of my perceptions since I am not their "author," just as I can doubt that $2 + 3 = 5$, since I am not the author, either, of mathematical axioms. What I cannot doubt is that I myself am the author of my mental actions while I am knowingly and willingly conducting them. The *ego* intuits itself indirectly as the necessary cause of its own volitions and, reflexively, as the witness of its agency. The *ego* discovers its existence indivisibly as agent and knower.

The *ego*'s initiative to "think myself something" is imbued with an almost redemptory flavor: *I* rescue myself from inexistence and self-doubt only as long (*quamdiu*) as I act deliberately to know myself as the agent of my actions and the knower of my agency. The *ego* by

---

[34] For the Stoic origin of this schema and its availability to Descartes through both Sextus Empiricus and Cicero, see Kneale and Kneale, *The Developement of Logic*, 163.

[35] See Peter Markie's discussion in "The Cogito and its importance," 143–152.

deliberately conceptualizing itself independently of sense triumphs over the nothingness to which the demon would confine it.

The fourth and final formulation completes the exercise of existential self-discovery by opening a bridge between the *ego* and the external world. Framed in the present tense, the final formulation argues that the conclusion—*I am, I exist*—is implied by the first-person speech act that declares it (*profertur*), or, equivalently, by the mental act that conceives it (*mente concipitur*):

> "Therefore, all things having been carefully and sufficiently examined, it must be established that the proposition: *I am, I exist* is necessarily true everytime I pronounce it or conceive it mentally."[36]

Is the argument valid? In contrast to the Liar's paradox, in which the self-referential proposition "I am a liar" remains undecidable because it is true if and only if it is false,[37] the self-referential proposition "I exist" is, as it were, hyper-decidable or *self*-evident. The first-person speech act through which the *ego* declares itsef to exist, or, equivalently, the "inner" speech act or *verbum mentis* through which the *ego* conceptualizes the proposition "I exist," presents itself as self-validating because its contradictory appears to be self-refuting.[38] Each time I tacitly conceptualize that "I exist" and/or declare *viva voce* that "I exist," I seem to bear witness to the truth of my claim. Unlike Formulation 3, which is wholly private and based on private intuition, the final *cogito* implies the possibility of public validation. Why?

Descartes's argument depends on the assumption that human speech acts imply agent causation.[39] The self-referential speech act "I exist" strikes us as irrefutable only because the first-person who is represented

---

[36] AT VII, 25: "Adeo ut, omnibus satis superque pensitatis, denique statuendum sit hoc pronuntiatum, Ego sum, ego existo, quoties a me profertur, vel mente concipitur, necessario esse verum."

[37] Descartes may have been familiar with Cicero's formulation of The Liar, *De Divinatione*, ii. II: "A man says that he is lying. is what he says true or false?" Cited by Kneale and Kneale, *The Development of Logic*, 114.

[38] See Kneale and Kneale, *The Development of Logic*, 599: "Whereas 'You do not exist' and 'This does not exist' are merely self-stultifying remarks, 'I do not exist' is self-refuting. For here the denial of existence is incompatible not only with the existential proposition implied by the use of the subject term, but also with the fact that the remark has been made."

[39] Cf. the definition proposed by R. Chisholm, 'Freedom and Action,' in K. Lehrer, ed., *Freedom and Determinism* (New York: Random House, 1966), 17: we have agent causation when "there is some event, or some set of events, that is caused, not by other events or states of affairs, but by the man himself, the agent."

in the speech-act is assumed to be the causal agent without whom the speech-act would not be performed. We assume, in short, that it is authentically *self*-referential. Only if the *ego* causally brings about the speech-act "I exist" does the speech-act in question testify to the *ego's* existence. The person who points to himself and says "I exist" is the very agent without whom the speech-act would not occur.[40] Were we, instead, to suppose a machine that could be made mechanically to emit the sequence of sounds "I exist," the existential import would hardly be comparable. We would object that the machine is programmed—that the sound "I" fails to denote a causal agent producing the sound in order to refer to itself. Descartes's argument requires that the first-person concept/proposition "I exist" be not only self-referential but self-*caused*. If the concept "I exist" is caused by a random brain muta-tion or if the sound-sequence "I exist" is caused by impersonal events that do not originate in the *ego's* volition, the conclusion that "I exist" cannot be drawn. Only if *I* actually exist *and cause myself to declare it* does the declaration "I exist" prove that *I* exist each time that I declare it.

In the final formulation, the verb *cogitare* does not appear as such. Instead, a deliberate declaration (*pronuntiatum*), whether made tacitly to myself (*mente concipitur*) or proferred publicly (*a me profertur*) is what implies the *ego's* existence. The shift from *cogito* to *concipio sive profero pronunciatum* sheds light on a puzzle raised by Peter Markie: "What is it about Descartes's self-awareness when he clearly and distinctly perceives that he thinks that makes his awareness an awareness of *him*?"[41] The meditator's self-referential speech-act "I exist" discloses the *ego's* rational agency with special force. Far from having "no adequate concept of himself," as Markie claims, the meditator discovers himself as the causal agent of his own speech-acts and, more generally, of his deliberate thoughts. As Markie correctly argues, he neither thinks of himself through a concept that identifies him by physical traits nor by one that identifies him relative to mental traits. Instead, he thinks of himself through the concept of causal agent—a concept that he forms *by acting* and exercising his causal agency.[42]

---

[40] Cf. Chisholm, "Human Freedom and the Self," in Watson, ed., *Free Will*, 32: "Each of us, when we act, is a prime mover unmoved. In doing what we do, we cause certain events to happen, and nothing—and no one—causes us to cause those events to happen."

[41] Peter Markie, "The Cogito and its importance," in John Cottingham, ed., *The Cambridge Companion to Descartes*, 162.

[42] Peter Markie, in "The Cogito and its importance," 164–165, writes: "In all, then,

In *Discours* Part V, Descartes had already appealed to language as evidence that human beings are causal agents rather than very complex automata.[43] Unlike animals, human beings use signs deliberately and appropriately to declare their thoughts to others. Human beings do not merely emit noise out of instinct, they deliberately form thoughts and compose semiotic strings at will to convey them. Writing to Newcastle in 1646, Descartes will reiterate that human speech-acts attest to the fact that human beings possess a rational soul and are causal agents in their own right.[44] While physical systems *react* involuntarily to changes in conditions that affect their material components, human beings *respond* to new conditions both creatively and appropriately—or at least have the innate capacity to do so.[45]

Does Descartes imply that human beings are causal agents precisely because human beings are rational? On this view, the *ego* that is revealed to itself existentially by declaring "I exist" or tacitly conceiving the thought "I exist," is strictly the *ego* that conducts itself rationally and detaches itself from the senses in order to discover a leverage point of truth. The intrinsic rationality of the Cartesian *ego* removes one of the main objections that has been raised against agent causation, namely that the radical indeterminism claimed at the source jeopardizes the possibility of explaining the constraints that mark the result.[46] On Descartes's account, automatic or conditioned behaviors

---

Descartes leaves us wondering how he thinks of himself when he forms his certain beliefs about his thought and existence. He seems committed to the view that he thinks of himself by conceiving some concept of himself. Yet, no adequate concept of him seems to be available. He does not think of himself through a concept that identifies him by his physical traits. He does not think of himself by one that identifies him relative to his mental traits. What is left?"

[43] *Discours de la méthode*, Part V, AT VI, 56–58.

[44] See the Letter to Newscastle, November 23, 1646, AT IV, 574: "Il n'y a aucune de nos actions exterieures, qui puisse assurer ceux qui les examinent, que nostre cors n'est pas seulement une machine qui se remue de soy-mesme, mais qu'il y a aussi en luy une ame qui a des pensées, excepté les paroles, ou autres signes faits a propos des suiets qui se presentent, sans se raporter à aucune passion."

[45] AT VI, 56, line 24 to 57, line 3. Cf. Noam Chomsky, *Language and Mind*, 36: "Descartes noticed that certain phenomena do not appear to fall within the mechanical philosophy. Specifically, he argued, no artifact could exhibit the normal properties of language use; the fact that it is unbounded in scope, not determined by external stimuli or internal state, not random but coherent and appropriate to situations though not caused by them—a collection of properties that we may call 'the creative aspect of language use.'"

[46] See Robert Kane, "Two Kinds of Incompatibilism," *Philosophy and Phenomenological Research*, Vol. I, No. 2, December 1989, 225: "The basic problem is this: given the

do not imply causal agency and do not, as such, imply the presence of a rational *ego* (even though the perception that one is acting involuntary requires a rational *ego*.)[47] Causal agents, by definition, interrupt the momentum of event causation by interfering to act rationally, initiating a new set of events that are neither deterministic nor random—which is to say that these agent-caused events are "appropriate to situations though not caused by them."

Descartes's theory of agent causation implies that the *ego* discloses its agency and therefore its existence by acting deliberately. It implies, moreover, that deliberate action is rational action to the extent that the *ego* initiates action independently of event-causation. The *ego*, in short, acts most conspicuously and understands itself best when it "acts alone." When the meditator declares "I exist" or mentally conceives it, nothing but the *ego* acts or is known or exists. Descartes concluded in the *Discours* that the rational soul is immaterial and, therefore, is not produced biologically as the result of material events: "the rational soul cannot be drawn from the potency of matter … but must be specially created."[48] Descartes returns to the question of the nature and origin of the rational soul in the first three Meditations. Meditation I invokes the problem of human origin to cast doubt on the certainty of arithmetic, precipitating the demonic hypothesis; Meditation II establishes the immateriality of *mens*, while Meditation III, in turn, will derive the doctrine of special creation. Earlier, in the *Regulae*, Descartes, as we know, asked the question *quid sit mens hominis* and spoke of *mens* as the "purely spiritual force" through which we know things, "no less distinct from body than blood from bone or hand from eye."[49] He insisted, moreover, on the essential unity of this force (*una et eadem est vis*) through

---

requirement that free choices or actions be undetermined, it becomes difficult to satisfy … the Explanation Condition": and 227: "Agent Cause theorists like Taylor disallow any explanations of agent causation in terms of reasons or causes. But, this leaves them without any answer to the critical question: 'Why did the agent do A rather than B or B rather than A?'".

[47] See the letter to Newscastle, cited earlier, AT IV, 573: "C'est tellement sans user de notre raison que nous repoussons les choses qui nous nuisent, et parons les coups que l'on nous porte, qu'encore que nous voulussions expressement ne point mettre les mains devant nostre teste, lors qu'il arrive que nous tombons, nous ne pourrions nous en empescher."

[48] AT VI, 59: "J'avois descrit, après cela, l'ame raisonnable, et fait voir qu'elle ne peut aucunement estre tirée de la puissance de la matiere, ainsi que les autres choses dont j'avois parlé, mais qu'elle doit expressement estre creée."

[49] *Regulae*, XII, in AT X, 415.

various types of mental activities, comparable in some incomparable way to both the seal and the wax depending on whether the mental activity under consideration is forming thoughts or perceiving thoughts, imagining new shapes or understanding purely intelligible ideas.

Presumably, the logical necessity that I, the *ego*, exist each time I declare "I exist" or form the proposition mentally, is grasped by a pure act of *intelligere*. The *ego* does not "feel" its existence but understands its existence as rationally implied by the deliberate speech-act that it initiates (causes) and perceives. The self-referential character of the declaration "I exist" serves to convey publicly the agent's immediate and private intuition of acting deliberately. The *ego* and the idea of the *ego* and the *ego*'s manifest agency, first to itself and, through speech-acts, to others, form a single discovery. I could not initiate new events from scratch and know myself to be their deliberate cause if I did not carry the idea of myself in myself and deploy it in my agency. To what extent does the indivisible *vis pure spiritualis* of the *Regulae* re-emerge in Meditation II precisely as the *ego*—the causal "force" or agent without whom rational inquiry and rational understanding could not occur—and which cannot, therefore, itself be an event, a material thing among others, deterministically moved by events, if it is to have the characteristic agency that the *ego* knows itself to have?

7.2. *Ego and Immateriality*

The four different formulations of the *cogito* at the start of Meditation II constitute a critical preamble to investigating the *ego*'s nature by providing the *ego* with a privileged opportunity to "act alone." The *ego* bracketing perception cannot bracket its perception of bracketing perception and discovers itself as the cause of its own mental activity. Once the *ego* grasps itself as the agent implied by actions of which it is the sole cause (*mihi persuasi*), its *passiones* also verify that *ego sum, ego existo*. The *ego* that deliberately opposes the effects of sensation recognizes itself to be the epistemologic subject that suffers the effects of sensation: *Idem ego sum qui sentio*—"I am the same *ego* who senses."[50] Whether *cogito* signifies a volition (*actio*) or a perception (*passio*),[51] *I* grasp myself as equally implied

---

[50] AT VII, 29: "Idem denique ego sum qui sentio, sive qui res corporeas tanquam per sensus animadverto: videlicet jam luce video, strepitum audio, calorem sentio."

[51] Cf. Descartes's clarification to Elizabeth, October 6, 1645, AT IV, 310: "On peut

by all of my thoughts since *I* grasp my thoughts precisely as *mine* to the extent that I grasp myself as capable of causing them and of rationally reflecting on them, whatever their origin.[52]

The *cogito* implies that the *ego*'s presence to itself as source of rational action and intellectual light distinguishes human beings from animals. While animals coordinate sensation through natural impulse, through reflex response and conditioning, the human *ego* suffers sensation precisely as the same *ego* that is capable rationally of questioning its veracity and blocking its impact.[53] Because human beings are rational agents and are gifted with rational intuition (*intuitus mentis*) over and beyond natural instinct, they inherently personalize experience in a way that animals cannot.[54]

Once the *ego* discovers its existence, it wants to know more about itself, as though irresistibly driven to further self-knowledge by its own light. The rational soul, jealous of its dignity, does not want to mistake itself for what it is not. Inspired by a secret new hope, the *ego* enquires: *sed quid sum?* Even before establishing the *cogito*, the *ego* showed a sort of natural distaste for conceiving of itself as dependent on body: *Am I really so bound to body and sense that I cannot be without them?*[55]

The second half of Meditation II is the classic adventure of the *ego*'s self-recognition through meditating on a skull and the brevity of fleshly life. The Cartesian meditator, speaking in the first-person, speaking as *I who exist and know myself to exist and embrace the certainty of my*

---

generalement nommer passions toutes les pensées qui sont ainsy excitées en l'ame sans le concours de sa volonté, et par consequent, sans aucune action qui viene d'elle."

[52] See Descartes's letter to Mersenne, October 16, 1639, AT II, 598: "L'ame acquert toutes ses connoissances par la reflexion qu'elle fait, ou sur soy mesme pour les choses intellectuelles, ou sur les diverses dispositions du cerveau auquel elle est jointe pour les corporelles, soit que ces dispositions dependent des sens ou d'autres causes."

[53] Without raising the concept of causal agent, Husserl speaks of *ego cogito* as a "living presence of the *ego* to itself." See his *Meditations Cartésiennes* (Paris: Vrin, 1996), 49: "dans cette expérience, l'*ego* s'atteint lui-même de façon originelle… Ce noyau, c'est la présence vivante du moi à lui-même, telle que l'exprime le sens grammatical de la proposition: *Ego cogito*."

[54] See Descartes's letter to Mersenne, October 16, 1639, AT II, 599: "Pour moi, ie distingue deux sortes d'instincts; l'un est en nous en tant qu'hommes et est purement intellectuel; c'est la lumiere naturelle ou *intuitus mentis*, auquel seul ie tiens qu'on se doit fier; l'autre est en nous en tant qu'animaux, et est une certaine impulsion de la nature a la conservation de notre corps, a la jouissance des voluptez corporelles etc., lequel ne doit pas tousiours estre suivi."

[55] AT VII, 24: "Sumne ita corpori sensibusque alligatus, ut sine illis esse non possim?"

existence, reviews his previous attempts at self-identity. He reflects that he took himself up to this point to be "a man," possessed of a face, hands, arms—possessed in short, of "the whole machine of limbs that we call body, the same *as appears in a corpse*."[56] Repulsed by the alien image of *my death*, the meditator urges the *ego* to self-elucidation: Am *I* really so thoroughly bound (*alligatus*) to the body and the senses that *I* cannot be without them?[57] Is it rationally possible that *I*, who grasp the intelligibility of my existence as a rational force and a rational light, be *mortal*?

The hypothesis of the evil demon, initially framed to purge the *ego* of its naive *hubris*, is now invoked to secure the *ego* against despair. Supposing once again that a powerful demon is bent on deceiving him, the meditator searches for evidence that anything belonging to the nature of body belongs to the *I* who searches to define its own nature. Three mental actions—*attendo, cogito, revolvo*—fail to uncover any bodily feature in the first-person agent conducting the search: *nihil occurit*. No trace of anything that is subject to mortality is found in the *ego* that mobilizes itself apprehensively to scrutinize itself—no extension terminated by a shape, nothing that is circumscribed in a place, nothing that is sensible to taste or smell, or touch or eyesight.[58]

When the meditator turns next to "those things that he has until now attributed to the soul (*anima*),"[59] he denies that any capacity that depends on corporeal or extended entities belongs to the essential nature of his *ego*. Neither physical autonomy (eating and walking) nor sensory perception belong by nature to the *ego* that grasps itself reflexively in the *cogito*. The meditator next considers thinking as such—*cogitare*:

> "How about thinking? That's it. Thinking is it! Thinking alone cannot be separated from me (*a me divelli*). I am, I exist; this is certain. But how long? As long as I think; for it might well be the case that, if I were to stop thinking, I would wholly and immediately cease from being."[60]

---

[56] AT VII, 26: "Nempe occurrebat primo, me habere vultum, manus, brachia, totamque hanc membrorum machinam, qualis etiam in cadavere cernitur, et quam corporis nomine designabam."

[57] AT VII, 24–25: "Sumne ita corpori sensibusque alligatus, ut sine illis esse non possim?"

[58] AT VII, 27: "per corpus intelligo illud omne quod aptum est figura aliqua terminari, loco circumscibi, spatium sic replere, ut ex eo aliud omne corpus excludat; tactu, visu, auditu, gustu, vel odoratu percipi."

[59] AT VII, 27: "Quid vero ex iis quae animae tribuebam?"

[60] AT VII, 27: "Cogitare? Hic invenio: cogitatio est; haec sola a me divelli nequit.

The *cogito* that reflexively established the *ego*'s existence is turned into a conditional that establishes the *ego*'s essential connection with thinking. The discovery of the *ego* is perfected by the new insight: *Sum autem res vera, et vere existens; sed qualis res? Dixi, cogitans.*[61] The *ego*'s challenge is now to defend its essential identity against added attributes, especially against any *picturable* attributes. The *ego* deliberately mobilizes its imagination, only to exclude from its essence whatever lends itself to being imagined. Not without a certain exultation does the *ego* profess:

> "*I* am not that assemblage of limbs that we call the human body, *I* am not some ethereal substance diffused throughout those same limbs, *I* am not a breath, not a vapor, not a flame, nor anything at all that is imaginable to myself (*quidquid mihi fingo*), since indeed *I* have supposed that whatever is imaginable is nothing and yet the fact remains that *I* am something."[62]

The *ego* cannot think of itself as nothing, but neither can it picture itself, *feign* itself—produce an idol of itself, equivalent to a visual, extended self-impression. Whereas the *ego* successfully conceives the thought "I exist," the same *ego* fails in the attempt to imagine itself.[63] Meditation II, in effect, supplements the *ego sum, ego existo* of the *cogito* with the corollary that *non me effingere possum*.

The analysis through which imagining is excluded from the essence of the *res cogitans* implies that the *cogitare* through which the *ego* identifies itself as a *res cogitans* is a very pure type of thinking. Writing to Gibieuf in 1642, Descartes will concede that imagining and sensing belong to the soul since both are types of thought (*des espèces de pensées*), but will insist that they belong to the soul only *qua* joined to the body and that the "pure" soul can be conceived, without these faculties.[64] Must we

---

Ego sum, ego existo; certum est. Quandiu autem? nempe quandiu cogito; nam forte etiam fieri posset, si cessarem ab omni cogitatione, ut illico totus esse desinerem."

[61] AT VII, 27.

[62] AT VII, 27: "Imaginabor: non sum compages illa membrorum, quae corpus humanum appellatur; non sum etiam tenuis aliquis aer istis mebris infusus, non ventus, non ignus, non vapor, non halitus, non quidquid mihi fingo; supposui enim ista nihil esse. Manet positio: nihilominus tamen ego aliquid sum."

[63] Descartes explains that the very meaning of *effingo* should have admonished him, since "to imagine means to contemplate the figure, or image, of a corporeal thing." AT VII, 28: "Atque hoc verbum, *effingo*, admonet me erroris mei: nam fingerem revera, si quid me esse imaginarer, quia nihil aliud est imaginari quam rei corporeae figuram, seu imaginem, contemplari."

[64] Letter to Gibieuf, January 19, 1642, in AT III, 479: "... sans lesquelles on peut concevoir l'ame toute pure."

understand the *cogitare* that belongs to the *ego* inseparably to be the *intel-ligere* defined in the *Regulae* as the mind's activity when it "acts alone"? Moreover, is the understanding that I think, the deliberate I-thought that is invoked in the premiss "I think," of the same order as the understanding of the truth *I think, therefore I am?* Writing to Newcas-tle in 1648, Descartes will argue that the truth of the *cogito* is known by a rational intuition so immediate and pure that it prefigures the intuitive knowledge of God in the beatific vision.[65] This suggests that the *ego* does not discover itself through some sort of "self-feeling," but knows itself by rational intuition as posed in "unimaginable" existence by its very act of self-understanding. The *ego*, it seems, succeeds in identifying itself as a pure *res cogitans* precisely because it "acts alone" when it grasps itself rationally as what can neither be sensed nor imag-ined.

While the *ego* discovers its existence and nature by rational insight, Descartes repeatedly maintains that the human soul (*anima*) thinks at all times, even in the womb, since the very essence of *res cogitans* is to think.[66] Descartes speculates that the soul in the womb is entirely "occupied" by sensations of pain and pleasure, hot and cold, but insists that the idea of self is possessed latently, along with all other *per se nota* truths. Presumably, this means that the *ego* ignores itself as such until reason, strengthened with age (*crescente aetate*), persuades *me*, at the apex of maturity, to detach *myself* deliberately from the senses and seriously meditate. The inalienable power that belongs to the *ego* to act rationally, which is brought to light by direct exercise in connection with the demonic thought experiment, culminates in the *ego*'s rational self-discovery as a purely rational entity or *res cogitans* in Meditation II. By resolutely implementing the rule of indubitability, which is to say by conducting "arduous vigils" without promise of return, the *ego* has awakened from its slumber to "enjoy (*fruatur*) the freedom to think" about immaterial things, starting with itself.[67] The pure *intelligere* that is the *ego*'s essence is at once a rational self-volition and self-insight. Existing latently in the depths of the body, the *ego* spawns a series of

---

[65] Letter to Newcastle, March or April 1648, AT V, 138.
[66] Letter to Hyperaspistes, August 1641, AT III, 423: "Nec etiam sine ratione affir-mavi, animam humanam, ubicumque sit, etiam in matris utero, semper cogitare: nam quae certior aut evidentior ratio ad hoc posset optari, quam quod probarim eius natu-ram sive essentiam in eo consistere, quod cogitet?"
[67] See Letter to Hyperaspistes, AT III, 424: "vigens animus fruatur libertate cogi-tandi de aliis, quam quae ipsi a sensibus offeruntur."

preliminary first-person identities until deliberate meditational exercises succeed in isolating it from sense and imagination and bring it to light as the radical fulcrum needed to "move the earth's orb from its place."

7.3. *Light (Reason) and Fire (Death)*

Granted that the *ego* has emerged from latency and knows itself to exist immaterially, does the *ego* know itself *better*, more distinctly and immediately, than it knows corporeal things (*res corporeas*)? Aware that this new claim contradicts the scholastic-Aristotelian axiom that the "quiddity" of material things is what is most immediately known to human being, Descartes designs the final exercise of Meditation II as a veritable conversion of the *ego* to its own rational light.

The exercise begins with a confession: The meditator concedes that *he-I* cannot abstain from believing that corporeal things, which are concretely sensed and mentally pictured, are better known to *him-me* than the elusive "I know not what of me" (*istud nescio quid mei*) that cannot be imagined. *Nec possum abstinere*: at the start of the exercise, the *ego*'s power is in bondage, a pure intelligence unable to *abstain* from the empirical assumption that it must reason from the sensible to the intelligible, rather than the other way around.

Descartes starts with a diagnosis. The problem, he says, is that the human mind delights (*gaudet*) in straying from the right path: *gaudet aberrare mens mea*. The postlapsarian flavor of *gaudet* suggests that the mind—*my* mind—is in some sense depraved, denatured, finding pleasure in transgression, rebelling against the necessity to stay within the limits of truth.[68] The *ego*'s powerlessness to resist the priority claim of sensory experience is really a failure since childhood to take responsibility for its actions—but how could the *ego* love itself sufficiently to take responsibility for its action so as long as it lay riveted to bodily sense and was ignorant of itself?

The cure is to place the *ego* above its cognitive activity, so that the *I* can lucidly behold the mind's propensity for dereliction of duty and redeem it by claiming it as *my* mind. Like a skilfull rider who learns to guide and control his horse, the *ego* will devise ways to make its cog-

---

[68] AT VII, 29: "Sed video quid sit: gaudet aberrare mens mea, necdum se patitur intra veritatis limites cohiberi."

nitive faculties more amenable to reason and more easily governed.[69]
The metaphor of horse-and-rider and, specifically, of *relaxing* the reins
in order for the *ego* to gain better control over its faculties by understanding them, implies that the the *ego*'s rational agency is at the root of
knowledge.

The chief exercise framed by Descartes to cure the *ego* of its weakness
for what is given in sense is the famous thought experiment of the
piece of wax. The aim of the experiment is to transform the *ego*'s
self-understanding into self-cathexis. Two lights are juxtaposed in close
proximity on the same stage: the immaterial light of reason and the
material light of fire, the *ego* that knows and the flame that burns and
destroys. While the experiment is designed at one level to teach the
meditator that even the knowledge of bodily things does not depend on
sense impression, at a deeper and higher level it seeks to put the *ego* face
to face with the private apocalypse of bodily death. The *ego* cures itself
of its dependence on sense by surviving the trauma of sacrifice.

"Let us consider an ordinary body, one that we touch and see, for
example *this* piece of wax."[70] The Ignatian technique of guided imagination is used philosophically to emphasize the real (Aristotelian) particular that is given in perception, but also to highlight the aesthetic
qualities that keep the *ego* under their spell. This concrete and particular piece of wax, recently taken from the beehive, has "not yet lost the
taste of honey."[71] It retains (*retinet*) the scent of the flowers from which
it was gathered.[72] Its color and shape are visible to the eye. Its surface
is hard and cool to the touch. When struck, it emits an audible ring
(faint echo of distant church bells in the countryside). All five senses are
rapturously stirred, converging to seduce the *ego* into believing that the
piece of wax is known to it empirically, (syn)aesthetically.

The guided imagination exercise now takes a new turn, at once
visible and fatal: *Sed ecce, dum loquor, igni admovetur*. Here is the wax and
here it is, moved, as I speak, to the fire. The vivid qualities with which it
enchanted the mind begin to mutate and disappear. The scent expires
(*expiret*), the taste evaporates, the color changes, the shape vanishes, the

---

[69] AT VII, 29–30: "Adhuc semel laxissimas habenas ei permittamus, ut, illis paulo
post opportune reductis, facile se regi patiatur."

[70] AT VII, 30: "Consideremus res illas quae vulgo putantur omnium distinctissime
comprehendi: coprora scilicet, quae tangimus, quae videmus… Sumamus, exempli
causa, hanc ceram."

[71] AT VII, 30: "nondum amisit omnem saporem sui mellis."

[72] AT VII, 30: "nonnihil retinet odoris florum ex quibus collecta est."

hardness liquifies and no sound will ever be drawn from it again.[73] As though anticipating Husserl's thought-experiment of the destruction of the world,[74] patterns dissolve and vanish into opposites. Is the fate of body implicitly tied to the directionality of time, to the imperceptible rush that destroys, already, always too soon, the flowers and scents of summer? More than the insufficiency of sensory qualities to yield the *ego*'s knowledge of the metamorphosed wax, itself a symbol *par excellence* of *res extensa*, the goal of the exercise is to force the *ego* to recognize the knot that binds sensory life to the passage of time (*tempus fugit*)—the very predicament invoked at the beginning of Meditation I to trigger a sense of urgency.

Remanet cera: nothing that is sensed remains that is not thoroughly transformed, yet the wax remains. The *ego*'s rational perception that the same piece of wax survives (*supersit*) liquification and that the wax, strictly speaking, is not a bundle of fleeting qualities, but an extended thing capable of undergoing "innumerable mutations," is an insight that sense cannot supply. Nor could the imagination have supplied it, since "innumerable" mutations are not, as such, imaginable.[75] The *ego* knows the piece of wax through rational inspection alone: *solius mentis inspectio*.[76] Descartes stresses that the concrete particular, the same piece of wax that I see and touch and imagine, not the abstract concept "wax," is what is "perceived only by the mind."[77] The rational *ego* frames its own rational understanding of even the most ordinary and concrete material thing by turning, not to sense or the imagination, but to itself.

Exactly what mental faculty is exercised by the *ego* when it conceives of the piece of wax over and beyond what is sensed or imagined? For the first time in the Meditations, the verb *judicare* appears. At the heart of the *ego*'s confusion, Descartes argues, is a confusion of terms. We typically say that we *see* a piece of wax when one is before us, not, as we should, that we *judge* that a piece of wax is before us, based on the

---

[73] AT VII, 30: "saporis reliquiae purgantur, odor expirat, color mutatur, figura tollitur ... nec jam, si pulses, emittet sonum."

[74] Husserl, *Ideas* I, section 49; see also Herman Philipse, "Transcendental Idealism," in Barry Smith and David Woodruff Smith, eds., *The Cambridge Companion to Husserl* (Cambridge, UK: Cambridge U. Press, 1995), 256–259.

[75] AT VII, 31: "Nam innumerabilium ejusmodi mutationum capacem eam esse comprehendo, nec possum tamen innumerabiles imaginando percurrere."

[76] AT VII, 31: "Ejus perceptio non visio, non tactio, non imaginatio est ... sed solius mentis inspectio."

[77] AT VII, 31: "Quaenam vero est haec cera, quae non nisi mente percipitur?"

color and shape it presents.[78] The distinction between *videre* and *judicare* is brought to light by the "happenstance" that, looking out the window, I see a procession of passers-by in coats and hats: I cannot say that I *see* men since all I see are hats and coats moving, but I judge that they are men. Descartes concludes: "Only by the faculty of judging (*sola judicandi facultate*) that is in my mind (*in mente mea*) do I know (*comprehendo*) what I thought I saw with my eyes."[79] Is *judicare* an *actio mentis* rather than a *passio mentis*? Does the *ego* "act alone" when it judges and knows by judging? How does *judicare* differ from *intelligere*?

The Meditation ends with a lyrical self-address by the *ego* to itself, a series of questions that foster its conversion to itself as first knower and first thing known. Even when an error of judgment is still possible (even when *judicare* has not been yet defined), the human intellect, *mens humana*, not sense, is the light that brings knowledge. While appearances are sensed by even the least among animals, the human mind strips an ordinary piece of wax of its "outer garments" and considers it naked.[80] What, then, can the *ego* say of "this mind itself, which is myself?"[81] What will I say of myself, of the *ego* that is seen to conceive so distinctly of this wax? Do I not know myself better—more truly, more certainly, more distinctly? If I judge that a piece of wax is before me, does it not follow far more evidently that I myself exist? Every sensation, every act of imagination, now converge to point to the *ego*'s rational capacity to know things by "acting alone," *a solo intellectu*. It follows, *a fortiori*, that I, the *ego*, perceive myself, *my mind*, more easily and evidently than anything else. To seal the conversion, to imprint the *nova cognitio* deeply in the memory, the meditator pauses to meditate at greater length before moving on.

---

[78] AT VII, 32: "Dicimus enim nos videre ceram ipsammet, si adsit, non ex colore vel ex figura eam adesse judicare."

[79] AT VII, 32.

[80] AT VII, 32.

[81] AT VII, 33: "Quid autem dicam de hac ipsa mente, sive de me ipso?"

CHAPTER EIGHT

INDUCTION AND INFINITY

Claudam nunc oculos: the *ego*'s resolve to turn away from all "vain and false" images marks a decisive step, on the third day, in the project of self-inquiry. Will the *ego*, severed from sensory stimuli and from the power of imagination, wander off into illusion? Or will it discover and exercise its most basic and innate rational abilities? In a soliloquy worthy of Augustine,[1] the *ego* seeks to become familiar with itself by "conversing with myself alone," only to discover the rational necessity of logical necessity and the existence of God—*existentiae meae author*.

There is an important sense in which Meditation III appropriates for philosophy the Augustinian formula *Noverim me, noverim te*.[2] Seeking to know myself, I discover the paradox that reasoning about myself implies "that I am not alone in the world"—*non me solum esse in mundo*. What distinctive features mark the *ego*'s journey to the true infinite—*Itinerarium mentis in Deum*?[3] While embracing the spirit of Augustinian interiority, Meditation III rejects the solipsistic subjectivism of introspection and firmly pursues the Thomist agenda of proving God's existence *a posteriori* by the natural light.[4] Like Thomas, Descartes in Meditation III reasons from an immediately known effect to a necessary first cause.[5] As though determined to harmonize Augustine and Thomas, the *ego*, which is to say *mens*, chooses a distinctly Augustinian starting point for a distinctly Thomist proof: God's mark of Infinity on the rational soul, "more intimate than my most intimate self."[6] Rather than start with the sensory evidence of extramental motion and discover a cosmic prime mover, the *ego* starts with the idea of the actual infinite and discovers a logical prime mover, source of all rational thought. Exhilerated and

---

[1] Compare Descartes, *"meque solum alloquendo"* (AT VII, 34) with Augustine, *"cum solis nobis loquimur"* (Soliloquies, II, 7, 14).

[2] St. Augustine, *Soliloquies*, I, 1, 1. See also *Confessions*, X, 1, 1.

[3] Citing Bonaventure's title *Itinerarium mentis in deum*.

[4] See, e.g., Descartes's letter of dedication, AT VII, 2.

[5] Cf. "First Answers," AT IX, 90.

[6] Citing St. Augustine, *Confessions*, III, 6: "tu autem eras interior intimo meo et superior summo meo."

astonished, the *ego* conducts the same proof twice, as though testing (tasting) the absolute.[7]

Meditation III is a meditation on the rational operations that spring from the *ego*'s undeserved possession of an axiom of infinity. Judging (*judico*) that "God is infinite in act, such that nothing can be added to his perfection,"[8] the *ego* marvels at an axiom that befalls it as a pure gift. How is the judgment that there is a true infinite possible? What does the idea signify? Is it coherent? How does the *ego* discern it and distinguish it from figments? By addressing and answering these questions, the *ego* will transform the Augustinian belief, based on Revelation, that the soul is restless because it is "born to know an infinite Good"[9] into the theory that the soul is rational and capable of mathematical induction because "the perception of the infinite is somehow (*quodammodo*) in me prior to the perception of the finite."[10]

Rather than dismiss Descartes's *via analytica* on the grounds that his proof makes use of scholastic principles, rather than assume a fallacy, we will focus on the rational operations by means of which the *ego* succeeds in judging that "there is an infinite totality" and the radical change in perspective that the judgment implies: how do *I* come to grasp myself as *finite*? How is it possible that *I*, a finite rational agent or force, succeed in framing ideal elements at infinity? The Cartesian *ego* pulls itself out of solipsism not by reasoning inductively about sense experience but by reasoning about induction itself and asking: how is induction possible?

8.1. *The power to reason unrestrictedly*

The *ego* in Meditation III strives (*conabor*) to make itself gradually (*paulatim*) better known to itself through "deeper" introspection (*penitius inspiciendo*). The verb *conabor* and the many comparatives (*penitius, magis*

---

[7] First Answers, AT IX, 84: "C'est pourquoi, outre cela, j'ai demandé, savoir si je pourrais être, en cas que Dieu ne fût point, non tant pour apporter une raison différente de la précédente, que pour expliquer la même plus exactement (*absolutius*)."

[8] AT VII, 47: "Deum autem ita judico esse actu infinitum, ut nihil ejus perfectioni addi possit."

[9] See, e.g., Bonaventure, I, Sentences, 3, 2, conclusion; in *Doctoris Seraphici S. Bonaventurae Opera Omnia* (Quaracchi, 1882–1902), I, 40: "Nata est anima ad percipiendum bonum infinitum, quod Deus est, ideo in eo solo debet quiescere et eo frui."

[10] AT VII, 45: "... ac proinde priorem quodammodo in me esse perceptionem infiniti quam finiti, hoc est Dei quam mei ipsius."

notum) imply a project that is at once deliberate and open-ended. The *ego*'s first step in making itself more familiar to itself (*mihi magis familiarem redere*) is to posit a general hypothesis about itself—to exercise the power it finds within itself to frame universal laws.

Reflecting that the indubitability of the *cogito* rests on the "clear and distinct perception of what I affirm," the *ego* reasons that such indubitability would not be possible if what the *ego* perceives clearly and distinctly could be false.[11] Implicitly, the *ego*, which is to say *mens sive ratio*, divides all possible propositions into two distinct and complementary sets, namely the set of whatever is clear and distinct to reason and the set of everything else. The *ego* concludes that it is reasonable to establish (*statuere*) a general rule: "whatever I perceive very clearly and distinctly is true."[12] *Pro regula generali*: the seemingly self-enclosed *cogito* gives rise to a universal axiom. The *ego* seeks to frame laws that admit of no exception—laws that claim to hold over an unlimited range, covering, in advance, every case (*illud omne*).

No sooner does the *ego* affirm its existence as an extramental fact implied by its mental agency than it claims the right to reason unrestrictedly, perceiving in itself a clear and distinct propensity to frame general laws. The *ego*, in short, recognizes itself as *ratio*—a universal instrument.[13] The set of clear and distinct propositions now possesses two members, namely the *cogito* and the "truth rule," which combine to affirm that a rational agent implies that what is known rationally is true.

The *ego* must now test the unrestrictedness of its rule, which means that the *ego* must turn its attention once again to arithmetic truths. The proposition "$2 + 3 = 5$," unlike the nebulous content of sensations, seems, like the *cogito*, to be "sufficiently clearly intuited" (*satis perspicue intuebar*) to fall within the scope of the truth rule.[14] Why does the *ego* stop short of declaring the arithmetic proposition to be unconditionally true, like the *cogito*? Once again, the *ego* finds itself blocked by the rational

---

[11] AT VII, 35: "... si posset unquam contingere, ut aliquid, quod ita clare et distincte perciperem, falsum esset."

[12] AT VII, 35: "jam videor pro regula generali posse statuere, illud omne esse verum, quod valde clare et distincte percipio."

[13] Cf. *Discours de la Méthode*, Part V, AT VI, 57: "Car, au lieu que la raison est un instrument universel, qui peut servir en toutes sortes de rencontres, ces organes ont besoin de quelque particuliere disposition pour chaque action particuliere."

[14] AT VII, 36. See also, a few lines further: "in iis quae me puto mentis oculis quam evidentissime intueri."

possibility of an omnipotent Creator. Unlike the *cogito*, which is self-evident in the precise sense that the *ego* cannot simultaneously think it and deny it, the proposition "$2 + 3 = 5$," the *ego* insists, is vulnerable to deception. Why?

The only perception that escapes the Deceiver's power, as Meditation I revealed, is the *ego*'s perception that it acts when it suspends judgment, since acting deliberately and perceiving the action is indivisibly the same thing. But how about the logical necessity that binds the *ego*'s self-perceived causal agency to its existence—the *ergo* of the *cogito*? How is it known undubitably? And how does it differ from the logical necessity that connects "$2 + 3$" to "5"? Part of the *ego*'s experience of acting deliberately—of suspending judgment—is the rational (i.e. clear and distinct) intuition that the newly produced effect, namely the suspended judgment, requires a cause. Since the effect of the *ego*'s acting is given as actual in immediate self-perception, the causal agent, the *ego* itself, must exist. The *ego* perceives (subjectively) that it causes a certain effect in itself by acting and knows (objectively) that it therefore exists. In the special case of the *cogito*, the *ego* is thus able to pass from subjective experience to rational necessity and from acting mentally (*cogito*) to extramental fact (*ergo sum*).[15] In contrast, the logical necessity that "$2 + 3 = 5$" stands outside of the *ego*'s causality and cannot be secured in the same self-referential way.

The truth rule thus remains hostage to further inquiry into reason and its source because the *ego* cannot by itself validate rational intuition unrestrictedly, much as the *ego* feels entitled to do so, based on the logical necessity that it grasps in the *cogito*. Before the *ego* can embrace the truth rule unconditionally and declare that *everything* that reason intuits clearly and distinctly is true, the *ego* must prove that rational intuition as such is free of restrictions. Why does the *ego* rationally intuit that the validity of rational intuition depends on ruling out the possibility of an omnipotent Deceiver? Does an omnipotent Creator exist? Does *anything* exist other than myself?

Before the idea of a true infinite can be fruitfully considered, the *ego* must conduct three preliminary investigations into the nature and properties of its ideas. The *ego* must establish (1) that ideas, unlike judgments, are not *per se* deceptive; (2) that some ideas are not artifacts

---

[15] This explains the apparent confusion in Descartes's various accounts of the *cogito* as both noninferential and inferential. See Peter Markie's discussion in "The Cogito and its Importance," *The Cambridge Companion to Descartes*, 141–148.

invented by the *ego* and that the *ego* is able to distinguish between the two; and (3) that sensory ideas are insufficiently clear and distinct to serve as the starting point of a rational argument.[16]

Looking deeper into its own rational nature, the *ego* starts by dividing its thoughts into two classes, namely: (1) ideas, which are "like images of things," and (2) "thoughts that include additional features," such as when "I will, reject, fear, affirm, deny."[17] Class-1 thoughts (ideas) simply present a content for the *ego* to consider, while Class-2 thoughts relate (*complector*) the *ego* to one or several Class-1 thoughts (ideas.)[18] Is the *ego*'s mental act of dividing thoughts into two classes itself a Class-2 thought? Since dividing thoughts into classes relates the *ego* to at least three new Class-1 thoughts, namely (a) the idea of ideas, (b) the idea of thoughts-that are more than ideas and (c) the idea of classes of ideas in general, it seems that the *ego*, when "conversing with itself alone," discovers itself to be innately generative. To become familiar with itself as *mens sive ratio* is, first and foremost, to exercise a native immaterial power to divide and combine. Far from passively contemplating itself, the *ego* conducts operations and "converses" with itself by collecting its thoughts into sets and including certain sets into others.

The *ego* reasons as though reason supplied it natively with axioms of extension and specification.[19] Thus among Class-2 thoughts, some, the *ego* pursues, are called volitions (*voluntates appellantur*) or affections (*affectus*), but others are called judgments (*judicia*).[20] By emphasizing that these are labels, the *ego* presumably means to remind itself that the classification is preliminary and that a more precise meaning of "volitions," "affections" and "judgments" remains possible at some

---

[16] Descartes explains his threefold preliminary agenda to Clerselier in a letter of April 23, 1649, AT V, 354–355: "J'ay crû estre obligé de distinguer, premierement, toutes nos pensées en certains genres ... pour remarquer lesquelles ce sont qui peuvent tromper...; J'ay du aussi distinguer entre les idées qui sont nées avec nous, et celles qui viennent d'ailleurs, ou sont faites par nous...; De plus, j'ay insisté sur le peu de certitude que nous avons de ce que nous persuadent toutes les idées que nous pensons venir d'ailleurs..."

[17] AT VII, 37: "ut, cum volo, cum timeo, cum affirmo, cum nego."

[18] *Ibid.*: "semper quidem aliquam rem ut subjectum meae cognitionis apprehendo, sed aliquid etiam amplius quam istius rei similitudinem cogitatione complector." The distinction thus distantly recalls the distinction between "defective" and "complete" *lekta* in Stoic logic. See Kneale and Kneale, *The Development of Logic*, 144–145.

[19] For an especially clear and sensitive discussion of these axioms, see Paul Halmos, *Naive Set Theory* (Princeton, London and new York: D. Van Nostrand Company, Inc., 1960), 1–7.

[20] *Ibid.*: "et ex his aliae voluntates, sive affectus, aliae autem judicia appellantur."

later time. For now, the *ego* reasons, since neither ideas nor volitions, when taken strictly as such, make any extramental claim,[21] falsehood "is to be feared" only in the case of judgments.

What is special about judgments? When passing judgment, the *ego* does not simply perceive, or react to, an idea. Rather, the *ego* deliberately relates itself to a mind-independent relation that brings two or more ideas together in a distinctive configuration.[22] In the case of the *cogito*, for example, the *ego* relates itself to the necessity that relates the *ego*'s causal agency to the *ego*'s actual existence. The mind-independent necessity (relation of necessity, implication) to which the *ego* relates itself is thus self-evident and is exhibited in the act of judgment itself. If, however, the mental proposition under consideration is not manifest to reason, if the relation binding the terms lacks evidence, the *ego* must refrain from joining itself to it. Moreover, as long as a metaphysical "cloud" hangs over the universality of reason, the *ego* can never be assured, except in the case of the *cogito*, that relating itself to a mind-independent relation is justified. The general rule that "all judgments warrant caution" thus clarifies that the truth rule is a judgment and a mind-independent claim about rational intuition and truth.

Having established that ideas, taken as such, without extramental reference, are not susceptible of error, the *ego* focuses, next, on ideas. What is known about their origin? The *ego* proposes at this point simply to examine the Intentional experience through which ideas become present to it. Bracketing rational intuition in the hope of spying on its emergence, the *ego* proceeds introspectively, only to stumble, as we shall see, against the rational limit of introspection.

Some ideas, the *ego* reports, seem (*videntur*) to be innate because "*I* understand (*intelligam*) what a thing is (*res*), or what truth is (*veritas*), or what thought is (*cogitatio*) from no other source than from my own nature."[23] Part of the *ego*'s experience of understanding itself rationally as a *res cogitans* is the experience that the very concepts through which it understands itself belong to it as a *res cogitans*. The *ego* does not have to learn what truth is empirically, or look to convention to know what

---

[21] AT VII, 37: "... si solae in se spectentur, nec ad aliud quid illas referam."

[22] The merit of Descartes's classification of judgments in Class-2 is easily recognized in light of Bertrand Russell's discussion in *The Problems of Philosophy* (London: Oxford U. Press, 1977), 125: "The relation involved in *judging* or *believing* must, if falsehood is to be duly allowed for, be taken to be a relation between several terms, not between two."

[23] AT VII, 38: "nam quod intelligam quid sit res, quid sit veritas, quid sit cogitatio, haec non aliunde habere videor quam ab ipsamet mea natura."

thought is. Such concepts emerge from the understanding fully-formed, like Athena from the forehead of Zeus. They seem to be categorical in the precise sense that the *ego* would not be a *mens sive ratio* without them.

A second class of ideas is specified introspectively by the experience of deliberate effort. In sharp contrast to innate ideas, which emerge through reasoning, some ideas are laboriously and deliberately "made by me" (*a me ipso factae*), such as the idea of the Syren or the Hippogriff. Part of the *ego*'s experience of a fabricated ("made up") idea is the experience that the *ego* itself must author it, determine its features and properties. Whereas reason knows innately what counts as "truth" or "thought," presumably human convention alone decides what counts as a "Syren" or a "Hippogriff." Introspection thus leads from the private experience of origin to the rational notion of cause. If the idea of a Syren differs from the idea of truth because the *ego* knowingly *invents* the idea of siren but does not invent the idea of truth, should we conclude that innate ideas, as far as introspection can tell, are *uncaused*?

The introspective experience of origin raises the question of causality all the more sharply in yet a third class of ideas, namely "adventitious ideas," which seem to impinge on the *ego* from outside. The *ego* experiences (*experior*) that sensory ideas "do not depend on my volition and therefore do not depend on me:" *non a mea voluntate nec proinde a me ipso pendere.*[24] Part of the *ego*'s experience of sensory ideas is the experience that they are received involuntarily (*sive velim, sive nolim*). Sensory ideas thus seem to be generated in the mind without the *ego*'s agency, which suggests that the *ego* is not their cause. The *ego*, as a result, is prompted to believe that sensations are caused by extramental things that imprint images of themselves on the mind.[25] But what *rational* ground supports the belief? What clear and distinct connection is perceived between sensations and extramental things?

---

[24] AT VII, 38. Compare to Kant, *Groundwork of the Metaphysics of Morals*, ed. Mary Gregor, English trans. Christine Korsgaard (Cambridge, UK: Cambridge U Press, 1999), Section III, 4:451, p. 56: "... the difference noticed between representations given us from somewhere else and in which we are passive, and those that we produce simply from ourselves and in which we show our activity." Cf., further, John Searle's argument in *Intentionality*, 124, ft.9: "Suppose we had the capacity to form visual images as vivid as our present visual experiences ... The voluntarily formed images we would experience as caused by us, the visual experience of the house we would experience as caused by something independent of us."

[25] AT VII, 38: "Experior illas non a mea voluntate nec proinde a me ipso pendere ... ut jam, sive velim, sive nolim, sentio calorem, et ideo puto sensum illum, sive ideam caloris, a re a me diversa, nempe ab ignis cui assideo calore, mihi advenire..."

Introspection by itself yields no self-evident or logically necessary connection. The *ego* discovers that nothing *clear* is established by this method about the origin of ideas. All ideas, the *ego* concedes, may well turn out to be innate, or invented, or adventitious.[26] Introspection thus reveals, as it were, its own limits. Epistemologically, introspection, as such, does not lead very far. Its chief importance is to alert me to the radical difference between blind inclinations that commit me to beliefs and the natural light, which shows me that something is actually true.[27] The *ego*'s belief, based on inner experience, that sensations imply an extramental universe of hot, cold and colored things in motion stems from a "blind impulse," not a "sound judgment."[28] The involuntary character of sensations is insufficient for *mens sive ratio* to conclude that sensory ideas imply real extramental things resembling them. Implicitly, the Thomist proof of God's existence based on the sensory evidence of extramental motion is made hostage, not only to the problem of sensory veracity, but to the radical impossibility of extracting anything like causal necessity from phenomenal inspection.[29]

8.2. *Magnitude and Order*

Having discarded introspection and "natural inclinations," the *ego* forges a new path (*via*) by framing a second, purely rational classification. The *ego* argues that, while ideas are all equally mental modes from a formal point of view, they nonetheless vary conspicuously with regard to what they represent.[30] Since some ideas represent dependent things while other ideas represent more elaborate, self-sustaining entities, the *ego* proposes to compare and rank its ideas according to the

---

[26] AT VII, 38: "Vel forte etiam omnes esse adventitias possum putare, vel omnes innatas, vel omnes factas: nondum enim veram illarum originem clare perspexi."

[27] AT VII, 38: "Cum hic dico me ita doctum esse a natura, intelligo tantum spontaneo quodam impetu me ferri ad hoc credendum, non lumine aliquo naturali mihi ostendi esse verum."

[28] AT VII, 39–40: "non hactenus ex certo judicio, sed tantum ex caeco aliquo impulsu."

[29] Cf. First Answers, AT IX, 84–85, where Descartes explains that two reasons led him "not to follow Thomas in all things," the first being that "j'ai pensé que l'existence de Dieu était beaucoup plus évidente que celle d'aucune chose sensible."

[30] AT VII, 40: "Quatenus una unam rem, alia aliam repraesentat, patet easdem esse invicem valde diversas."

varying "quantity of objective reality" that they exhibit.[31] For example, ideas that represent substances, the *ego* reasons, exhibit "more objective reality" than ideas that represent accidents,[32] while the idea that represents an infinite substance contains, in turn, "more objective reality" than the idea that represents a finite substance.[33]

The *ego* is thus able to rank concepts based on a notion of magnitude. About each concept, reason asks: how much do I (*mens sive ratio*) perceive in the content that is clear and distinct, which is to say, that is recognizably and *per se* rational? In the idea of wax, for example, over and beyond many ill-defined and nebulous features drawn from sense experience, the separate or purely rational *ego* distinctly perceives extension and shape: these rational properties mark the idea of wax as representing a positive or real entity in its own right. In contrast, when examining the (materially false) idea of heat, the *ego* perceives nothing clear and distinct and therefore has no reason to count "heat" as more than "nothing."[34]

A concept that exhibits clear and distinct rational features represents a possible, if not an actual, entity.[35] Regardless of whether any actual piece of wax exists or ever will exist, the *ego* regards wax as rationally possible, while "heat" is viewed as no more than a subjective illusion.[36] By the same token, the idea of wax represents something that is rationally "more possible" than what is represented by the idea of "shape,"

---

[31] As Descartes clarifies in the First Answers, a thing has "objective being" when it exists as an object of thought, in contrast to actual, extramental being (AT VII, 102–103). On Descartes's notion of "objective being," see Calvin Normore, "Meaning and Objective Being: Descartes and His sources," in A. Rorty, ed., *Essays on Descartes's Meditations*, 223–241.

[32] AT VII, 40: "Nam proculdubio illae quae substantias mihi exhibent, majus aliquid sunt, atque, ut ita loquar, plus realitatis objectivae in se continent, quam illae quae tantum modos, sive accidentia, repraesentant." Descartes defines "substance" in the Fourth Series of Answers, AT VII, 222, as follows: "haec ipsa est notio substantiae, quod per se, hoc est absque ope illius alterius substantiae possit existere." Again, in Principles of Philosophy, I, 51 (AT VIII-1, 24): "Per substantiam, nihil aliud intelligere possumus quam rem quae ita existit, ut nulla re indigeat ad existendum."

[33] AT VII, 40: "rursus illa per quam … infinitum … intelligo, plus profecto realitatis objectivae in se habet, quam illae per quas finitae substantiae exhibentur."

[34] AT VII, 43, and AT VII, 44, respectively.

[35] Cf. Calvin Normore's conclusion in "Meaning and Objective Being: Descartes and His sources," 238: "The objective reality of an idea of something is then just the possible existence of that thing."

[36] Cf. Fourth Answers, AT VII, 234: "Propter hoc tantum illam materialiter falsam appello, quod, cum sit obscura et confusa, non possim dijudicare an mihi quid exhibeat quod extra sensum meum sit positivum, necne."

since the idea of wax represents something that is "apt to exist *per se*,"[37] while the idea of shape represents something that depends on something else for its existence, namely on a prior substance. A new landmark in rational self-familiarity has been reached. Rational knowledge of the logically possible, and of the logical *order* of the logically possible, is even more fundamental to the *ego*, more intimate to reason, than introspective knowledge of the existing self.

As de Luynes's French translation suggests[38] and as Arnauld's explicit citation of Augustine's *De quantitate animae* confirms,[39] the abstract quantity conceived by the *ego* to compare and rank concepts is, in effect, the *quantitas perfectionis* invoked by scholastic theory to rank entities in a vast *scala entis* according to the intrinsic degree of metaphysical perfection possessed by each entity.[40] What is new is the implicit claim that the notion of quantity is innate to human reason, inspiring and shaping the *ego*'s rational activity before the *ego* is explicitly aware of it.[41] For the *ego* to become "more familiar with itself" is, first and foremost, for it to discover and deploy its rational predilection for quantitative order, indistinguishable, Descartes implies, from reason itself.

How far does the *ego*, "conversing with itself alone," become conscious of the rational principles of order that constitute its power of logic and access to truth? Does the notion of order logically precede the notion of quantity, or is quantity what inspires ordering? Is it possible for the *ego* to conceive of "variable" magnitude without conceiving of "absolute" magnitude, or to conceive of the latter without the notion of ordinality? These are the questions that confront the *ego* as soon as it turns away from introspection and focuses on the pure structure of what is logically possible as opposed to what is empirically given. As we shall see, the discovery of the actual infinite and its logical priority over the *ego*'s power of induction will transform the *ego*'s self-understanding.

---

[37] AT VII, 44: "nam cogito lapidem esse substantiam, sive esse rem quae per se apta est existere."

[38] AT IX, 32: "... c'est-à-dire participent par représentation à plus de degrés d'être ou de perfection, que celles qui me représentent seulement des modes ou des accidents."

[39] Fourth Objections, AT VII, 205.

[40] See Edith Sylla, "Medieval Concepts of the Latitude of Forms: The Oxford Calculators," *Archives d'histoire doctrinale et littéraire du moyen-âge* 40 (1973), 223–283; and my own *Measure of a Different Greatness: the Intensive Infinite, 1250–1650* (Leyden: Brill, 1999).

[41] Descartes will stress this implicit priority to Berman, AT VI, 153: "Quamvis hoc non fecerit explicite, fecit tamen implicite."

Basic to the *ego*'s reasoning about order is the notion of *containment*. As we saw, the *ego* spontaneously divided its thoughts into classes, implicitly collecting ideas into one class and judgments into another, which implies in turn that one class contains ideas as its elements while the other contains judgments. The *ego*, in effect, now starts with the collection of its ideas and considers three distinct members that conveniently illustrate the notion of *quantitas realitatis*, namely the amount a exhibited by the concept of accident, the amount s exhibited by the concept of finite substance, and the amount *s-infinite* exhibited by the concept of infinite substance. How can these three distinct elements be put in order of increased perfection, namely in the order a, s, *s-infinite*?

One solution is to regard the more perfect item as containing in itself the perfection of less perfect items, culminating with infinite perfection, which "contains (*continetur*) wholly in itself every perfection whatever."[42] The notion of containment stems indivisibly from what reason *perceives* and what reason *supplies*: because the *ego* is rational and unmarred, at this point, by sensory confusion, the *ego* perceives a rational possibility in its objects and cooperates with reason to construct new objects that actualise the possibility. The *ego* forms the notion of degree by conceiving of each spot in the ordering as the collection of the amounts that occur at or before that spot.[43]

In the two finite cases cited by the *ego*, degree a and degree s, degree s is higher/greater/later than degree a because degree s contains in itself the perfection of degree a while degree a does not contain the perfection of degree s. By conceiving of "less and more" through containment, the *ego* frames, out of its initial collection, a new collection whose elements are sets—*degrees*, collections of amounts rather than amounts. A special feature of the new collection is that its elements are not only sets but "nested" sets, namely the sets $[a]$, $[a, s]$ and $[a, s, s\text{-}infinite]$. The smallest or first element, namely the singleton $[a]$, is included in the two others; the next smallest or second element, namely $[a, s]$ is included in the third, and the third or greatest element includes in itself all of the preceding sets. Without invoking number, the *ego* has the means to order three distinct concepts as first, middle and last by iterated containment.

---

[42] AT VII, 46: "quidquid clare et distincte percipio, quod est reale et verum, et quod perfectionem aliquam importat, totum in ea (sc. idea entis summe perfecti et infiniti) continetur."

[43] Cf. Paul Halmos, *Naive Set Theory*, 22.

Since the degrees in question mark successive values taken by one and the same abstract quantity (*quantitas realitatis*), does order not depend logically on the notion of quantity? Do rational "amounts" present a rational possibility of being ordered in ways that arbitrary items do not? The *ego*, after all, first converted its concepts into "amounts" before ordering them by magnitude. But would the *ego* have done so—have conceived of its concepts quantitatively—if the idea of substance were not rationally perceived already as "higher in rank" than the idea of accident? The notion of containment as deployed by the *ego* to frame a quantitative scale culminating in an infinite term seems to weld together indivisibly the asymmetric notion of rank and the notion of quantity, as though ordinality and cardinality were rationally fused. The result of the *ego*'s operation is that the Real, taken in the broadest sense of the logically coherent, presents itself as a special sort of mathematical structure, namely as the domain of the reflexive, antisymmetric and transitive relation "less than or equal to."[44]

We must note that the elements of the domain are not metaphysical things such as accidents and substances, but degrees—sets of amounts that characterize metaphysical things *logically and to the mind's eye*. The finite/infinite contrast invoked to characterize "substance" logically implies an open-ended range of finite degrees predecing the infinite term. This means that the collection "containing in itself the totality of every perfection" has infinitely many finite elements. The collection must be written, not as [*a, s, s-infinite*] but, more precisely, as [*a, s, ..., s-infinite*]. The *ego* thus conceives of the Real as an infinite structure with properties reminiscent of a "chain" (*catena*)—similar to the "series of numbers" invoked by Descartes in his youth to speculate that the soul remembers best what has the structure of a progression.[45] The *ego*'s chief focus is not establishing the individual "measure" of this or that substance or accident, nor even the "measure" of any individual concept, but the relation under which the rational truth exhibited by concepts forms a unified rational structure.[46]

---

[44] See Paul Halmos, *Naive Set Theory*, 54–55.

[45] See *Cogitationes privatae*, AT X, 215: "Catenam scientiarum pervidenti, non difficilius videbitur, eas animo retinere, quam seriem numerorum."

[46] Cf. Paul Benacerraf, "What numbers could not be," in *Philosophy of Mathematics*, ed. Paul Benacerraf and Hilary Putnam, 2nd ed. (Cambridge: Cambridge U. Press, 1983), 290: "'Objects' do not do the job of numbers singly; the whole system performs the job or nothing does."

Some features of the *ego*'s *scala realitatis*, or, perhaps more clearly and more originally, "scale of positivity,"[47] are especially noteworthy. First, the collection of degrees possesses a least element since the concept of "nothing" (*nihil*) exhibits precisely "zero" amount of perfection and therefore defines a degree that is not itself preceded by any degree. Second, for all degrees (o, a, s, ..., s-*infinite*) if a degree belongs to the domain, then the degree that immediately supersedes it also belongs to the domain. Third, no successor degree is equal to zero. Fourth, if two degrees immediately surpersede the same degree, then they are one and the same degree. Except for the transfinite degree s-*infinite*, which is problematic since it succeeds *all* finite degrees as a whole, the *ego*'s quantitative ordering of the Real possesses some of the properties of the progression or "chain" of natural numbers.[48]

8.3. *Causation*

Things existing as ideas in the mind have only representational being, not actual being. The diminished status of representational being inspires the *ego* to regard the logical content of its ideas precisely as *effects*. Why? On the one hand, minimal as representational being is, something with rational features existing as an object of thought is not "nothing."[49] Whatever is possessed of rational features has a measure of positivity in the logical order. This means that it requires an explanation: why is this rational feature conceived, rather than some other?[50] On the other hand, representational being, like an image reflected in a pool, is so vastly inferior to actual being, that ideas as such cannot account for the rationality of their own content. For example, the idea of a "very artful machine" cannot form itself of its own accord from scratch but must result from elsewhere, receiving its rational fea-

---

[47] Descartes in his answer to Arnauld will speak of God as "positive" rather than as "real" to emphasize the purely logical character of his argument. See Fourth Answers, AT VII, 236–237.

[48] Compare to Halmos's discussion of the Peano axioms in *Naive Set Theory*, 46–49.

[49] AT VII, 41: "quantumvis imperfectus sit iste essendi modus, quo res est objective intellectu per ideam, non tamen profecto plane nihil est." Cf. First Answers, AT IX, 82: "laquelle façon d'être est de vrai bien plus imparfaite que celle par laquelle les choses existent hors de l'entendement; mais pourtant ce n'est pas un pur rien, comme j'ai déjà dit ci-devant."

[50] See First Answers, AT VII, 103: "... sane indiget causa ut concipiatur, et de hac sola quaestio est."

tures either from the thinker's inventive genius, or from his knowledge of mechanics, or from his having seen a similar machine in existence.[51]

Since rational things existing as objects in thought are sufficiently
real to warrant explanation but insufficiently real to be self-explanatory,
the *ego* concludes that the content of ideas results from a cause. How
does the *ego* innately conceive of cause? As the *cogito* indicates, the *ego*
knows itself as the causal agent implied by such deliberate acts as suspending belief and judgment.[52] A rational act (*dubito*) implies a rational
agent to bring it about by causing it to occur (*ergo sum*). In this paradigmatic case, the *ego* knows itself, moreover, specifically as the "total and
efficient" cause of its own suspended judgment, meaning that nothing
less, but also nothing more, than a first-person agent (the *ego*) existing actually is needed for a first-person mental act to be performed.
A "total and efficient" cause is defined indeed in Meditation III as
"containing enough perfection to produce every aspect of its effect"
by "communicating to the effect whatever amount of reality the effect
possesses."[53]

Since the *ego* explicitly says that it knows what a substance is *ex hoc
quod sim substantia*,[54] we must presume that the *ego* implicitly knows what
a "total and efficient" cause is *ex hoc quod sim causa*. Part of the argument
of the *cogito* is that a cause is as efficacious as it is *real*, which means
that a thing's degree of perfection is, equivalently, its degree of "causal
efficacy."[55] Since my judgment is suspended, a free rational effect is
brought about, implying logically a sufficiently real/efficacious cause,
which implies a free rational agent existing extramentally: *ergo sum*.

Just as the *ego* framed a general truth rule based on the clarity of
the *cogito*, the *ego* now frames a general function relating effect to cause.
No claim is made about the philosophical meaning of causation, or
its empirical conditions, or temporal parameters. The *a priori* axiom of
causality, "manifest to the natural light," simply claims, as a matter of

---

[51] Cf. First Answers, AT VII, 103–104.

[52] Descartes will defend his position to Arnauld that "there is nothing in our mind
of which we do not have knowledge" by clarifying that he means "operations," not
powers. See AT VII, 232: "Tertim denique est, *quod nihil in mente nostra esse possit cujus non
scimus conscii*; quod de operationibus intellexi, et ille de potentiis negat."

[53] the best example is given at AT VII, 41: "making a stone now begin to be (*nunc
incipere esse*) where none existed before."

[54] AT VII, 45.

[55] AT VII, 40: "Nam, quaeso, unde nam posset assumere realitatem suam effectus,
nisi a causa? Et quomodo illam ei causa dare posset, nisi etiam habere?"

pure logical necessity, that a "total and efficient" cause must have "at least as much (reality) as its effect."[56] *Jam vero lumine naturali manifestum*: given an effect of a certain magnitude, a cause of at least equal magnitude is implied. The function relates, not metaphysical terms, but quantities. The only claim made is that a quantity a implies a quantity b that contains it (i.e. that is equal to a or greater than a). Must a cause precede its effect? Reason does not dictate that causation must be restricted to cases in which temporal precedence characterizes the cause.[57] Must the terms related be distinct? Arnauld will try to argue that a relation generally implies two distinct related terms.[58] Descartes will answer that such a requirement, again, is equivalent to restricting causality arbitrarily to the finite case. Reason balks at arbitrary restrictions: *dictat lumen naturae nullam rem existere, de qua non liceat petere cur existat.*[59] As we will see, just as *mens sive ratio* must discard the empirically-inspired part-whole axiom that restricts magnitude and number to finitude, the *ego*, conversing with pure reason, must discard empirically-based restrictions on causation in order to frame a universal, "infinitist" theory. For the pure *ego* "conversing with itself," causation picks out, for every degree on its scale, the degree of its maximum possible effect. A first consequence, as the *ego* points out, is that "nothing is produced by nothing." If there is no efficacy in a cause, no effect is possible. The special case in which the cause has *no* power and therefore can only produce *nothing*, corresponding to the scholastic/Aristotelian axiom that *nihil posse ex nihilo fieri*, does not stand out as an exception but is included in the function as a limiting case.[60] The range of possible effects commanded by degree 0 (zero) of perfection (*nihil*) is the null set, with no elements. A second consequence, prohibiting circularity, is that "whatever has more perfection cannot be brought about by what has less."[61] Since representational being, as we saw, is too minimal or "unreal" to cause itself, every idea implies a cause that contains in actuality (*formally*) at least the same

---

[56] AT VII, 40: "Jam vero lumine naturali manifestum est tantumdem ad minimum esse debere in causa efficiente et totali, quantum in ejusdem causae effectu." De Luynes adds: "pour le moins autant de réalité."

[57] First Answers, AT VII, 108: "non videtur ita esse restringenda."

[58] Fourth Objections, AT VII, 210: "Causa omnis est effectus causa, et effectus causae effectus, et proinde mutua est inter causam et effectum habitudo; at habitudo nonnisi duorum est."

[59] First Answers, AT VII, 108.

[60] AT VII, 40: "Hinc autem sequitur, nec posse aliquid a nihilo fieri."

[61] AT VII, 40–41: "... nec etiam id quod magis perfectum est, hoc est quod plus realitatis in se contineant, ab eo quod minus."

magnitude as is contained in the idea representationally.[62] This means that every object of thought whose content "is not nothing" implies a cause existing extramentally.

A cause must possess at least as much perfection as its effect, if not formally, then *eminently*.[63] The idea of eminence enshrines the doctrine that a given degree of causal efficacy contains the entire range of degrees below it. Eminence means, in particular, that the philosophical (Aristotelian) notion of "form" is superseded by the purely logical notion of degree. Whereas a formal cause brings about an effect with properties similar to its own, an eminent cause brings about an effect that shares in its "quantity of reality" without participating in its "form." Just as the number 8 may be viewed as including in itself the number 5 eminently but not formally, since 8 possesses properties that 5 does not, a cause eminently contains all of the causes below it without formally possessing their properties. Causes are thus stripped of irrelevant metaphysical connotations and recast strictly as "spots" in a universal ordering. Eminence, in short, underscores that each new degree of causal efficacy must be regarded as the set of all of its predecessors.[64]

A case in point is the *ego* and its ideas. The *ego* asks whether any of its concepts exhibits such a high degree of representative reality that it implies a cause of greater efficacy than the *ego* itself. If such an idea is found, implying a "spot" in the chain of causes that supersedes the *ego*, then, the *ego* argues, "I am not alone in the world"—*non me solum esse in mundo*.[65] As a free causal agent and existing *res cogitans*, the *ego* acts deliberately, reasons unrestrictedly, establishes universal laws, perceives and classifies its thoughts. Unaware of depending on anything but itself for these operations and finding nothing in itself that is extended or divisible, the *ego* grasps itself as an immaterial substance. Although the *ego* does not possess either extension or figure, the *ego* recognizes in itself more reality, more perfection, than the "very little" (*perpauca tantum*) amount that it perceives clearly and distinctly to belong to extended substance. The *ego* concludes, therefore, that it possesses

---

[62] AT VII, 41: "Quod autem haec idea realitatem objectivam hanc vel illam contineat potius quam illam, hoc profecto habere debet ab aliqua causa in qua tantumdem sit ad minimum realitatis formalis quantum ipsa continet objectivae."

[63] See Second Answers, Axiom IV, AT VII, 165: "Quidquid est realitatis sive perfectionis in aliquâ re, est formaliter vel eminenter in primâ et adaequatâ ejus causa."

[64] See Paul Halmos, *Naive Set Theory*, 56.

[65] AT VII, 42: "... sed aliquam aliam rem, quae isitus ideae est causa, etiam existere."

enough "eminent" perfection to produce in itself the idea of a material substance and its accidents. In the scale that measures causal efficacy with regard to ideas—with regard, that is, to producing things that have representative being only—the *ego* holds a rank of considerable eminence: the most complex machines, cities, worlds, stars, angels, beasts, all lie within the *ego*'s constructive mental power, as the *ego*'s "eminent" domain of mental effects. Nothing in these ideas exceeds the *ego*'s causal efficacy. The *ego* possesses enough eminent perfection to produce, of itself, the content of all of its ideas—except one, the idea of God.

8.4. *Infinity*

By the name "God," the *ego* understands "a certain infinite substance" —*substantiam quandam infinitam*.[66] The more diligently the *ego* examines the magnitude of perfection exhibited by the idea of an infinite substance, the more the *ego* reflects that, although "the idea of substance is in me from the very fact that I am a substance," the idea of an infinite substance "would, nonetheless, not be in me, who am finite, if it did not proceed from some actually infinite substance."[67] Is the conclusion valid? Does the idea really exceed the *ego*'s causal efficacy? If so, does it imply that "the *ego* is not alone in the world"?

The *ego* must carefully inspect the content of the idea in order to rule out any possible error. First, is the infinite a mere figure of speech? Do I "perceive the infinite" by means of a "true idea," or does it merely represent privation?[68] By conceiving of reality logically as a quantitative progression, the *ego* "manifestly knows" that there is "more reality in an infinite substance than in a finite substance."[69] *Manifeste intelligo*: the positivity of the infinite signified by the name of God is evident to the *ego* because the *ego* has framed for itself an infinite structure in which one and the same abstract quantity progresses from zero, through an

---

[66] AT VII, 46.

[67] AT VII, 45: "Nam quamvis substantiae quidem idea in me sit ex hoc ipso quod sim substantia, non tamen idcirco esset idea substantiae infinitae, cum sim finitus, nisi ab aliquâ substantiâ, quae revera esset infinita."

[68] AT VII, 45: "Nec putare debeo me non percipere infinitum per veram ideam, sed tantum per negationem finiti, ut percipio quietem et tenebras per negationem motus et lucis."

[69] *Ibid.*: "manifeste intelligo plus realitatis esse in substantia infinita quam in finita."

open-ended series of finite degrees, to infinity. The first fruit of the *ego*'s
shift away from metaphysical musings to an abstract science of relations
is thus the ability to conceive of the infinite positively, as what exceeds
every finite measure.[70]

As soon as the *ego* comes face to face with the infinite positivity
implied by the idea of God, the *ego* identifies itself precisely by its *lack*.
The self-conferred notion of "substance" gives way to a more precise
formulation. Unlike *quantitas realitatis*, which is sufficiently abstract to
take on the value "finite" or "infinite," the term "substance" cannot
apply "univocally" to both finite substance and God. Finite *perseity*,
starting with the *ego*'s own self-subsistence, now appears to be limited,
relative, imperfect—*analogous* to God's absolute *perseity*, but in such an
infinitely lower order as to lose its essential meaning.[71] By recognizing
the positivity of the infinite perfection exhibited by the idea of God, the
ego grasps its essential finitude and understands that

> "the perception of the infinite is somehow in me prior to the perception
> of the finite, which is to say that the perception of God is prior to my
> own self-perception."[72]

Just how radically is the *ego*'s self-understanding revised? The *ego*'s initial, even provisional, idea of substance (*substantiae quidem idea*) stemmed
from self-perception (*ex hoc ipso quod sim substantia*) and therefore occulted
its essential incomprehensibility. The *ego* knows, now, that the idea of
infinite substance is valid and knows that its content is incomprehensible.[73] Substance is defined, not by the *ego*'s case, but by the infinite case:
"By infinite substance, I understand ... the very essence of substance
taken absolutely."[74] As soon as the *ego* recognizes the logical priority of

---

[70] In 1649, Descartes will clarify his doctrine of the positive infinite to Clerselier:
"Il faut remarquer que ie ne me sers iamais du mot d'*infini* pour signifier seulement
n'avoir pas de fin, ce qui est négatif ... mais pour signifier une chose réelle, qui est
incomparablement plus grande que toutes celles qui ont une fin."

[71] Cf. Principles of Philosophy, I, art. 51: "Per *substantiam* nihil aliud intelligere
possumus, quam rem quae ita existit, ut nulla alia re indigeat ad existendum. Et quidem
substantia quae nulla plane re indigeat, unica tantum potest intelligi, nempe Deus.
Alias vero omnes, non nisi ope concursus Dei existere posse percipimus. Atque ideo
nomen substantiae non convenit Deo et illis *univoce*, ut dici solet in Scholis." (AT VIII–
1, 24).

[72] AT VII, 45: "ac proinde priorem quodammodo in me esse perceptionem infinit
quam finiti, hoc est Deus quam mei ipsius."

[73] AT VII, 46: "est enim de ratione infiniti, ut a me, qui sum finitus, non comprehen-
datur."

[74] Letter to Clerselier of April 23, 1649, AT V, 355–356: "Per infinitam substantiam,

infinite substance over finite substance, *perseity* ("*per se*–ness") itself takes on an essentially quantitative meaning, limited and therefore logically contingent in finitely possible entities, infinite and therefore logically necessary in the infinitely possible or *per se* case, God.[75] Far from clinging to a residual scholastic prejudice,[76] the *ego* renders the scholastic term "substance" *unusable*.[77]

Since the paradigmatic case of *perseity* ("per se-ness") is, as such, incomprehensible to the finite *ego*, only the logical (or mathematical) term at infinity remains clear and distinct, grasped in the rule, now explicit, that knowledge of what is limited and imperfect presupposes knowledge of what is absolute: *omnis autem defectus et negatio praesupponit eam rem a qua deficit, et quam negat.*[78] We will see that the finite case, particularly of magnitude and of causation, will also be logically revised in light of the transfinite case. But could the idea of infinity be materially false, like the idea of heat, representing nothing as though it were something—derived, therefore, from the *ego*'s admixture of *nihilitas*? The turn to logic—the shift from thinking metaphysically about "substance" to reasoning logically about unrestricted order—allows the *ego* to grasp that the case at infinity, representing what is infinitely real because infinitely rational, constitutes the standard of veracity without which reason itself loses meaning. The limited rational features found by reason in the idea of wax imply and presuppose the infinite rationality of the absolute case. In sharp contrast to materially false ideas,

---

intelligo substantiam perfectiones veras et reales actu infinitas et immensas habentem. Quod non est accidens notioni substantiae superadditum, sed ipsa essentia substantiae absolute sumptam, nullisque defectibus terminateae; qui defectus, ratione substantiae, accidenta sunt; non autem infinitas et infinitudo." Cf. Jean-Luc Marion, "The Essential Incoherence of Descartes's Definition of Divinity," in *Essays on Descartes's Meditations*, 307: "The definition of substance is therefore articulated; the infinite."

[75] Cf. Fourth Answers, AT VII, 222, where Descartes points out that the notion "substance" loses its power to signify if stripped of the attributes based on which substance is known: "si vero postea eandem illam substantiam spoliare vellemus iis attributis ex quibus illam cognoscimus, omnem nostram de ipsa notitiam destrueremus; atque ita verba quidem aliqua de ipsa possemus proferre, sed non quorum significationem clare et distincte perciperemus."

[76] As Husserl accuses Descartes in *Méditations Catésiennes* (Paris: Vrin, 1996), Section 10 ("Comment Descartes a manqué l'orientation transcendentale,") 50–52.

[77] As Jean-Luc Marion remarks in "The Essential Incoherence of Descartes's Definition of Divinity," 306, Descartes "never succeeds in conceptualizing two different meanings of this unique term. He upholds the same concept, while juxtaposing two contradictory usages."

[78] Conversation with Berman, AT V, 153.

which present a content so confused that reason recognizes nothing in it that is rational, the idea of an infinity of rational perfection is "supremely clear and distinct." The idea contains "more objective reality" than any other idea and is therefore "truer" than any other idea.[79] The idea of the infinite, in short, exhibits, not what is confused to reason's scrutiny, but what is distinctly *incomprehensible*—what is so positively rational (real) as to exceed the conceptual power of finite reason. Far from failing to represent something rational, the idea contains in itself indivisibly the full totality of every possible rational possibility— of everything that the *ego* distinctly perceives to be real and true.[80] This means that the range of what is logically possible, which is to say what is finitely "real" because possessed of more or less rational coherence, is bounded at either end by what has no rational possibility of being and is therefore *per se* impossible and what has infinite rational possibility of being and is therefore *per se* necessary. The *ego*, beholding logical necessity as such, cannot comprehend the excess of truth exhibited by the idea, but needs only to know and judge (*intelligere ac judicare*) that everything (*illa omnia*) that is rationally clear and distinct, along with innumerable other unknown perfections, belongs to God "either formally or eminently," in order for the idea of God to be the most distinct, the clearest and truest "of all ideas that are in me."[81]

The idea of God thus represents an infinite totality of degrees of being supremely rational and logically self-evident. This means that the idea of God is equivalent to an innate axiom of infinity: reason claims that there is a collection, given to reason alone, that contains o and contains the successor of each of its elements.[82]

But is such an axiom of infinity really above the *ego*'s efficient reach? Does the *ego* not simply extrapolate from its own open-ended power of increase to the infinite case? The *ego* experiences that it has the power to augment its knowledge gradually and sees (*video*) no obstacle to augmenting it to infinity: *magis et magis augeatur in infinitum*.[83] Is the

---

[79] AT VII, 46: "cum maxime clara et distincta sit, et plus realitatis objectivae quam ulla alia contineat, nulla est per se magis vera."

[80] AT VII, 46: "quidquid clare et distincte percipio, quod est reale et verum, et quod perfectionem aliquam importat, totum in ea continetur."

[81] AT VII, 46: "... ut idea quam de illo habeo sit omnium quae in me sunt maxime vera, maxime clara et distincta."

[82] Cf. Halmos, *Naive Set Theory*, 44.

[83] AT VII, 47.

potential infinity that the *ego* finds itself capable of bringing about not enough for it to frame the idea of an actual infinite?

Three (equivalent) arguments refute the possibility of deriving the axiom of infinity by adding finite increments. First, granted that the *ego*'s potential for perfection is limitless, such a potential infinite is irrelevant to the idea of divine infinity, in which "nothing at all is potential." Indeed the very fact that the *ego* actualises its potential only gradually, step by finite step, implies imperfection.[84] This means that a successor function, by itself, is powerless to collect *all* successors into a totality. Secondly, the finite *ego*, for all its eminence, cannot complete an infinite process. The *ego*'s self-acquired perfection never actually reaches infinity since it never increases to the extent that it cannot be further increased, whereas "I judge God to be infinite in act, in such a way that nothing can be added to his perfection."[85] The best the *ego* can do is increase its perfection *forever*, it cannot increase it *unsurpassably*. The *ego* thus brings to light a key property of an actually infinite magnitude, which is that it cannot be increased by finite addition (reflexivity). Since this property is equivalent to suspending the part-whole axiom, whoever admits the idea of an infinite magnitude implicitly concedes that the part-whole axiom does not hold universally.[86]

Finally, the potential infinite that lies within the *ego*'s power is not anything that actually exists and therefore does not contain in itself the actual efficacy required to cause the idea of the actual infinite.[87] The infinite totality of perfection that is exhibited in the idea of God cannot be reached by counting and is therefore inaccessible to the *ego*'s constructive operations. It must be given as a totality—embraced as a gift that the *ego* cannot give itself. By the axiom of causation, it implies a cause that possesses actually the same absolute infinity that is represented in the idea. Incomprehensibly, in the limit when logical possibility is infinite, necessary Truth necessarily exists. The *ego*, imperfect

---

[84] AT VII, 47: "… nihil tamen horum ad ideam Dei pertinet, in qua nempe nihil omnino est potentiale; namque hoc ipsum, gradatim augeri certissimum est imperfectionis argumentum."

[85] AT VII, 47: "Etiamsi cognitio mea semper magis et magis augeatur, nihilominus intelligo nunquam illam idcirco fore actu infinitam, quia nunquam eo devenietur, ut majoris adhuc incrementi non sit capax; Deum autem ita judico esse actu infinitum, ut nihil ejus perfectioni addi possit."

[86] As Descartes explains to Mersenne as early as 15 April 1630, AT I, 146–147.

[87] AT VII, 47: "Ac denique percipio esse objectivum ideae non a solo esse potentiali, quod proprie loquendo nihil est, sed tantummodo ab actuali sive formali posse produci."

and finite, no only strains to behold a conclusion that it cannot actually fathom but easily forgets the logical necessity that derives it.[88]

Just how radically is the notion of *cause* revised once the *ego*'s innate axiom of infinity is made explicit? As though seeking to implant the knowledge of God's existence as firmly as possible in its innermost consciousness, the *ego* repeats the proof by asking whether "I myself who have the idea of God could exist if such a God did not exist."[89] Three arguments establish the *ego*'s dependence on God, giving a final and full expression to the implication sketched so many years earlier in the discarded *Regulae*, Rule XII: *sum, ergo Deus est.*[90] All three arguments center on agency—on the *ego*'s experience of its agency and on God's infinite, *a se*, agency. The first argument establishes that the *ego* did not bring itself into existence. If the *ego* had produced itself (i.e. produced an immaterial substance possessed of an axiom of infinity) from nothing, it would have a high enough degree of efficacity to give itself a multitude of perfections (i.e. accidents) that it lacks.[91] Better, the *ego* would have no difficulty in giving itself the infinite perfections that it perceives to be contained in the idea of God,[92] since indeed, if a difficulty were encountered in this regard, the *ego* would experience (*experirer*) an upper limit to its efficacy.[93] Implicitly, if the *ego* had created itself from nothing, it would have also created the idea of an actual infinite in itself, and would thus implicitly have infinite efficacy, since nothing finite, as we saw, is capable of producing the idea of an actual infinite. Therefore the *ego* is insufficiently efficacious to give itself infinite perfection. Therefore the *ego* did not bring itself into existence *ex nihilo*. Part of what it means for the *ego* to be rational is that it recognizes its imperfection, recognizes that it recognizes its imperfetcion *because* of an innate absolute standard, and recognizes, in conclusion, that "I myself am not God."[94] Since I

---

[88] AT VII, 47–48: "cum minus attendo, et rerum sensibilium imagines mentis aciem excaecant, non ita facile recordor."

[89] AT VII, 47–48: "ulterius quaerer libet an ego ipse habens illam ideam esse possem, si tale ens nullum existeret."

[90] AT X, 421.

[91] AT VII, 48: "manifestum est longe difficilius fuisse me, hoc est rem sive substantiam cogitantem, ex nihilo emergere, quam multarum rerum quas ignoro cognitiones, quae tantum istius substantiae accidentia sunt, acquirere."

[92] *Ibid.*: "nulla difficiliora factu mihi videntur."

[93] *Ibid.*: "siquidem reliqua quae habeo, a me haberem, quoniam in illis potentiam meam terminari experirer."

[94] AT VII, 48: "Si a me essem, omnes enim perfectiones quarum idea aliqua in me est, mihi dedissem, atque ita ipsemet Deus essem."

"doubt and desire," I experience that I cannot give myself the infinite perfection that I see in God, which is to say that I experience that my agency reaches only higher and higher finite terms, not the actual infinite to which I aspire. Reason illuminates the *ego* by teaching it, in short, that finitude is a wellspring of wisdom: *Thy perfection in my weakness.*

The second argument confirms the same illuminating rational humility by establishing that the *ego* is not the *current* cause of its own existence. Since the *ego*'s existence at time *t* does not necessitate its existence at a later time *t'*, the *ego*'s continued existence requires a cause to sustain it and produce it *de novo* at every instant in time.[95] Does the *ego* sustain itself? The *ego*, by definition, is always conscious of acting when it acts.[96] Yet the *ego* experiences (*experior*) no force or operation on its part that causes it to endure from one moment to the next.[97] Therefore the *ego* knows "most evidently" that it depends on some being other than itself.[98] Only because the *ego* is a causal agent in its own right who cannot exert a force or conduct an operation without knowing itself to be the causal agent exerting the force or conducting the operation in question, does it recognize that some force or agency is bearing it continuously through an infinity of temporal "nows" since it persists in time through no action of its own.[99] The *ego* recognizes that it is born into existence again and again at every instant, carried through time effortlessly, in what feels to it like an inertial motion but is really the effect of an (inexhaustible) agency from elsewhere.

The third argument rules out the possibility that the cause of the *ego*'s current existence is finite and establishes that the *ego* is created and sustained at every instant by an infinitely perfect being—God. Unlike the well-known arguments that wrongly deny infinite series of prior causes,[100] the argument proceeds by "eminence" to claim that increase in perfection cannot proceed "without limit" but implies an actually

---

[95] AT VII, 49: "adeo ut conservationem sola ratione a creatione differre, sit etiam unum ex iis quae lumine naturali manifesta sunt."

[96] *Ibid.*: "si quae talis vis in me esset, ejus proculdubio conscius essem." Cf. Descartes's clarification to Arnauld that the *ego* is always conscious of its operations, not of its latent powers. Fourth Answers, AT VII, 232.

[97] *Ibid.*: "Sed et nullam esse experior."

[98] *Ibid.*: "Ex hoc ipso evidentissime cognosco me ab aliquo ente a me diverso pendere."

[99] For Descartes's embrace of the infinite divisiblity of magnitudes, see e.g. Conversation with Berman, AT V, 155.

[100] See First Answers, AT VII, 106, for Descartes rejection.

infinite term at infinity. *Nullum hic dari potest progressum in infinitum*:[101]
increase in perfection is necessarily linear and therefore progresses until
it becomes infinite, marking a saturation point that cannot be exceeded.
The *ego* treats cardinality and ordinality as inseparable: since the actual
infinite cannot be increased in *size* by a new increment, it cannot be
superseded in *rank*. How does this infinite progression that stops at
infinity and defines an intelligible but incomprehensible supreme term
illuminate causality?

The *ego* reasons that no finite cause is absolute—"uncaused"—since
every finite cause is surpassable and implies therefore something with
greater causal efficacy (more reality) than itself. Once the *ego* has determined that the infinite is logically prior to the finite, lower degrees that
are contained in higher degrees are regarded as logically *posterior* to the
higher degrees that contain them. But what is logically *posterior* to something is logically *dependent* on what is prior to it. This means that lower
degrees depend logically on higher degrees. As though moving down
the scale it had previously climbed by constructing nested sets, the mind
now regards each whole as logically prior to the parts that it contains,
rather than regarding the parts as logically prior to the whole. On this
view, the paradigmatically absolute whole, the only complete totality,
which is to say the only independent term, is the term at infinity—
the term that contains in itself the perfection of infinitely many terms
and is contained in turn by no higher term. Once the perspective is
inverted, the *ego* ascends the scale once again by asking of each candidate cause whether it implies a higher cause on which it depends (a
greater whole which contains it) or not. Since the effect to be explained,
namely the *ego*, possesses the notion of unsurpassable perfection, no
cause that depends on a higher cause is adequate to create and sustain the *ego* from instant to instant, since no imperfect cause is able to
cause the idea of absolute perfection. The *ego* is thus able to leap over
the whole class of imperfect, finite, dependent causes (existing *ab alio*) to
find a logical "resting place" at infinity: a cause that is inaugmentably
perfect—that depends logically on no other cause and therefore exists
a se.

Is the term at infinity *un*–caused or *self*–caused? Faced with a battery
of criticisms over implying that God is his own efficient cause, Descartes
will insist that the *ego* is rationally entitled to ask about everything unre-

---

[101] AT VII, 50.

strictedly whether it exists *a se* or *ab alio*. The *ego* is able to conclude by this procedure that God exists, without further specifying how "existing *a se*" is to be understood.[102] The key is to calculate a result, not hold onto to what is comprehensible. What seems called for is a new concept, intermediary between *efficient cause* strictly speaking and *no cause at all*, namely the concept of

> "*a thing's positive essence*, to which the concept of efficient cause may be extended, in the way that in geometry we extend the concept of the greatest imaginable curve to the concept of a straight line, or the concept of a rectilinear polygon with indefinitely many sides to the concept of a circle."[103]

The concept of a thing's positive essence, unlike the notion of efficient cause, is purely quantitative and can take the value finite or infinite unproblematically. This allows the notion of efficacy to be extended beyond finite parameters. Finite causes, by definition, imply a higher cause on which they depend. This means that every finite cause receives whatever finite degree of positivity/efficacy it possesses from above, which means that it exists *ab alio*. No finite cause possesses therefore sufficient efficacy to cause *itself* since its being, its positive essence, depends on a greater efficacy. A finite efficient cause is limited to causing effects that are distinct from it, even if the effect is equal to it in perfection. By the same token, a finite efficient cause is logically prior to its effect.

If, however, we extend the concept of efficacy to the infinite case, the features of priority and distinctness that characterize the finite case disappear. Infinite efficacy is so inexhaustible and unsurpassable and radically independent that cause and effect merge "incomprehensibly" in an indivisible excess of self-affirming positivity.[104] God is "without cause" because he causes himself, as it were, infinitely. By appealing to

---

[102] Fourth Answers, AT VII, 238: "Quaerendum igitur est de unaquaque re, an sit *a se*, vel *ab alio*; et quidem per hoc medium existentia Dei concludi potest, etsi non expresse explicetur quo modo intelligendum sit aliquid esse *a se*."

[103] Fourth Answers, AT VII, 239: "Existimo necesse ostendere inter *causam efficientem* (sic) proprie dictam et *nullam causam* esse quid intermedium, nempe *positivam rei essentiam* (sic), ad quam causae efficientis conceptus eodem modo potest extendi, quo solemus in geometricis conceptum lineae rectae, vel conceptum polygoni rectilinei, cujus indefinitus sit numerus laterum, ad conceptum circuli extendere."

[104] See First Answers, AT VII, 109: "Plane admitto aliquid esse posse, in quo sit tanta et tam inexhausta potentia, ut nullius unquam ope eguerit ut existeret, neque etiam nunc egeat ut conservatur, atque adeo sit quodammodo sui causa" and further clarification in answer to Arnauld, Fourth Answers, AT VII, 330: "Cumque illa inexhausta

the positivity in a thing's essence and increasing it mentally beyond all finite measure, the *ego* is thus free to extend the notion of "efficacy" to the seemingly paradoxical case at infinity, just as geometers are free to extend the notion of curve to include a straight line as the case of infinite curvature, or extend the notion of polygon to include the circle as an infinitely-many sided polygon. Elsewhere, in the same vein, Descartes will say that our idea of the divine intellect differs from our idea of the human intellect only "as the idea of infinite number differs from the idea of binary or quadruple number," implicitly abstracting the notion of "number" from the experience of counting in order to "extend" the notion of number to the infinite case.[105]

The innate axiom of infinity that marks the *ego* as God's handiwork and image[106] retroactively explains why the *ego* reasons inductively. The *ego* now recognizes, first, that the paradigmatic idea of unity, of a complete totality, is the idea of the infinite totality of perfections that belong to God.[107] Without the innate idea of God, the *ego* would not have the rational notion of whole and part, or know its finitude, or aspire to indefinite increase and conceive of the natural numbers as an open-ended progression. The *ego* perceives that it can count forever without reaching a last number, which means that something regarding number eludes its power. Once God's existence is known explicitly, the *ego* concludes that the power to conceive that *a number greater than any thinkable number is thinkable* cannot be given to the *ego* by the *ego* itself but must be received from a more perfect being.[108]

---

potentia, sive essentiae immensitas sit quammaxime *positiva* (sic), idcirco dixi rationem sive causam ob quam Deus non indiget causa, esse *positivam* (sic)."

[105] See Second Answers, AT VII, 137: "nisi tantum ut idea numeri infiniti differt ab idea quaternarii aut binarii." See also Conversation with Berman, AT V, 155: (O) "Sed sic daretur numerus infinitus?" (R) "Quid absurdi?"

[106] AT VII, 51. See also Annette Baier's essay, "The Idea of the True God in Descartes," in A. Rorty, ed., *Essays on Descartes's Meditations*, 359–387, especially 368.

[107] Second Answers, AT VII, 137: "In Deo intelligimus absolutam immensitatem, simplicitatem, unitatem omnia alia attributa complectentem, quae nullum plane exemplum habet, sed est, ut ante dixi, *tanquam nota artificis operi suo impressa* (sic)." See also 140.

[108] Second Answers, AT VII, 139: "necessario concludi, non quidem numerum infinitum existere, ut neque etiam *illum implicare*, ut dicitis, sed me istam vim concipiendi majorem numerum esse cogitabilem quam a me unquam possit cogitari, non a meipso, sed ab aliquo alio ente me perfectiore accepisse." See also Conversation with Berman, AT V, 157: "inter numerandum me non posse pervenire ad numerum maximum, sed semper esse cogitabilem majorem numerum quam a me cogitari possit."

The power to reason inductively—to think the unthinkable without reducing it to what is thinkable—stems from the axiom of infinity that stems from God and is known to the *ego* "by the same faculty with which I know myself." Before reaping further fruits, the *ego* deliberately pauses—suspends its conversation with itself—in order to dwell (*immorari*) for a moment in contemplation of God. Contemplation consists in weighing (*expendere*) God's attributes and "intuiting, admiring and adoring" (*intueri, admirari, adorare*) the beauty of God's immense light.[109] With the first action, *immorari*, the *ego* suspends discursive reasoning and puts itself deliberately in God's presence.[110] With the second action, *expendere*, the *ego* does not so much enumerate God's numberless perfections as internalize their unfathomable density.[111] Finally, with the triad "intuit, admire and adore," the *ego* focuses attention on God's unity until contemplation becomes at once uninterrupted and effortless. Taken together, the *ego*'s five contemplative actions "magnify God" and further detach the *ego* from inferior pleasures.[112] The *ego* indeed testifies, by way of conclusion, that contemplation of this kind affords "the greatest rapture (*voluptas*) of which we are capable in this lifetime."[113]

---

[109] AT VII, 52: "Placet hic aliquandiu in ipsius Dei contemplatione immorari, ejus attributa apud me expendere, et immensi hujus luminis pulchritudinem intueri, admirari, adorare."

[110] Cf. the devotional technique recommended by Francis of Sales as a preparation for meditation in *Introduction à la vie dévote*, chaps. IX-XVIII, in *Oeuvres*, I, 46–67.

[111] Cf. the contrast, in Cicero, between "weighing" (*expendere*) arguments and merely "counting" (*enumerare*): *de Oratore* 2, 309 ("cum colligo arumenta causarum, non tamen ea numerare soleo quam expendere"). See also what Jean-Marie Beyssade argues about Cartesian "induction" in "The idea of God and proofs of his existence," in *The Cambridge Companion to Descartes*, 188–190.

[112] Cf. Francis of Sales, *Traité de l'Amour de Dieu*, Chap. VII, in *Ouvres*, I, 585–587, especially 585: "avec une attention toujours plus soigneuse et ardente, elle (sc. l'âme) va remarquant toutes les beautés et perfections qui sont en lui (sc. Dieu)."

[113] AT VII, 59: "maximam, cujus in hac vita capaces sumus, voluptatem percipi posse experimur."

CHAPTER NINE

ACTION AND INDIVIDUATION

By the start of the fourth day, the *ego* is so used to withdrawing from the senses[1] that focusing on purely intelligible things no longer presents any difficulty.[2] This means, among other things, that the *ego* is in a new position to investigate volition, which "cannot be represented by anything physical."[3] What sort of power is the will and what is known by the *ego* about its own agency?

Since the *ego*'s idea of the human mind (*mens humana*) is now incomparably clearer than the idea of any bodily thing,[4] the question *sed quid sum?*[5] has been answered to the extent that an answer is naturally possible. The *ego* is an incorruptible spiritual substance, wholly independent of matter, but also a contingent and finite spiritual substance, a *mens humana*, wholly dependent on God. The *ego* has discovered both its dignity and its finitude—its emancipation from matter and its bond to God. The special combination of perfection and imperfection that marks *mens humana* as "a sort of mean between God and nothingness"[6] calls for a new investigation into the *ego*'s powers. While the *ego*'s anxiety over its origin has been laid to rest (the *ego* results neither from blind material forces nor from an imperfect demiurge), God's very perfection raises new questions. If God is "the author of my origin"—*meae authorem*

---

[1] Meditation IV, AT VII, 52–53: "Ita me his diebus assuefeci in mente a sensibus abducenda."

[2] *Ibid.*: "ut jam absque ulla difficultate cogitationem a rebus imaginabilibus ad intelligibiles tantum, atque ab omni materia secretas, convertam."

[3] See *Regulae* Rule XII, AT X, 419, where volition is cited as a prime example of something that is purely intelligible and cannot be represented by the idea of anything physical: "Pure intellectuales illae sunt, quae per lumen quoddam ingenitum, et absque ullius imaginis corporeae adjumento ab intellectu cognoscuntur: tales enim nonnullas esse certum est, nec ulla fingi potest idea corporea quae nobis repraesentet, quid sit cognitio, quid dubium, quid ignorentia, item quid sit voluntatis actio, quam volitionem liceat appellare."

[4] AT VII, 53: "Sane multo magis distinctam habeo ideam mentis humanae quam ideam ullius rei corporae."

[5] Meditation II, AT VII, 26 ("Quid autem nunc?") and 27 ("Sum autem vera res et vere existens, sed qualis res?").

[6] Meditation IV, AT VII, 54: "Me tanquam medium quid inter deum et nihil."

originis[7]—does anything in me, over and above my metaphysical status *per se*, attest to my origin? Following the contemplative pause that concludes Meditation III and reveals an unforseen capacity for contentment (*voluptas*), the *ego* must harvest (*colligi*) the implications of bearing God's "image and resemblance,"—*ad ejus imaginem et similitudinem.*[8] Is the *ego*, innately driven to seek greater perfection, in some sense personally destined, or reserved, or called, to find contentment by (re)uniting with God, "on whom my whole existence depends every single moment"?[9] Ascending from the universal idea of *res cogitans* to the idea of the personal *ego ipse* that "I myself" am, Meditation IV starts a new inquiry into spiritual selfhood.

How does the *ego*, with its many thoughts and ideas, grasp itself reflexively as indivisible? Presumably, the *ego* knows itself to be numerically the same *ego* whether "doubting, affirming, imagining or sensing"[10] because the innate idea of God supplies the underlying notion of unity. Since indeed God is paradigmatically one,[11] and since the idea of God logically precedes the *ego*'s idea of itself,[12] the *ego* grasps its essential unity in light of God's own supreme simplicity. God, in whom a chief perfection is that all perfections are one, creates and sustains the *ego* in the image of his own divine indivisibility. The idea of self and the idea of God are tied at the root: I could not have the idea of myself without the idea of God, since I would not *be* myself without it.[13]

The newly personal sense in which the *ego* investigates itself coincides with a shattering of solitude. Not only is the *ego* "not alone in the

---

[7] Meditation VI, AT VII, 77.

[8] Meditation III, AT VII, 51.

[9] AT VII, 53: "ab illo singulis momentis totam existentiam meam dependere." Cf. Francis of Sales, *Traité de L'Amour de Dieu*, I, chap. XVIII, in *Oeuvres*, I, 404–405. Speaking of the soul's innate inclination to love God as a "memorial of our first principle and Creator," Francis elaborates the following allegory: "Tout de même que les cerfs auxquels les grands princes font quelquefois mettre des colliers avec leurs armoiries, bien que par après ils les font lâcher et mettre en liberté dans les forêts, ne laissent pas d'être reconnus par quiconque les rencontre."

[10] Meditation III, AT VII, 34: "Ego sum res cogitans, id est dubitans, affirmans, imaginans etiam et sentiens."

[11] Meditation III, AT VII, 50: "unitas, simplicitas, sive inseparabilitas eorum omnium quae in Deo sunt, una est ex praecipuis perfectionibus quas in eo esse intelligo."

[12] AT VII, 45: "manifeste intelligo [...] priorem quodammodo in me esse perceptionem infiniti quam finiti, hoc est Dei quam mei ipsius." For the idea in which the *ego* grasps itself, see 42: "illa [idea] quae me ipsum mihi exhibet."

[13] Meditation III, AT VII, 51: "nec etiam opus est ut nota illa (sc. artificis) sit aliqua res ab opere sua diversa" and "illamque similitudinem, in qua Dei idea continetur."

world"[14] since God necessarily exists, but God's infinite creative power implies that innumerable souls besides the *ego* are possible.[15] An open-ended plurality of finite *mentes*, like the *ego* in nature but numerically distinct from it, must be admitted, at least conceptually. In sharp contrast to God, who is single absolutely,[16] finite *mentes* are single multiply, capable of co-existing under the same generic name.

How then are immaterial individuals distinguished from one another? What principle determines, so to speak, "where one *mens sive ratio* leaves off and another *mens sive ratio* begins?"[17] What criteria of identity establish that a particular *mens* remains numerically the same *mens* as thoughts change and knowledge increases? A further question concerns the discernibility of immaterial individuals: is the distinctness of *mens X* and *mens Y* discernable to a third *mens Z*?[18] Is *mens X* ever manifest, as such, to other *mentes*? Descartes, who studied Law in Poitiers between 1615 and 1616,[19] was no doubt familiar with the assumption made by legal theory that contractual promises could be regarded as manifest volitions—as evidence of the existence of a promisor endowed with a stable individual identity and, therefore, liable for future damages in case of breach.[20] Later in this chapter we will show that the problem of the individuation of *mentes humanas* merges with the problem of moral and legal identity—with defining and validating the self who is able to declare "I, the undersigned."

In Descartes's doctrine, the soul is at once indivisible, substantial and incorruptible.[21] Unlike the bodily things of sensory experience, which are clusters of accidents that form and dissolve according to

---

[14] AT VII, 42: "necessario sequi non me solum esse in mundo."

[15] AT VII, 56: "Non possum tamen, ex quo immensam Dei potentiam animadverti, negare quin multa alia ab illo facta sint, vel saltem fieri possint."

[16] In Second Answers, AT VII, 140, Descartes emphasizes that the divine unity is not the same as generic unity: God's unity is a real and positive perfection in God, while generic unity adds nothing real to the singular individuals that come under the same generic name.

[17] Praphrasing W.V.O. Quine, *Ontological Relativity and Other Essays* (New York, NY: Columbia U. Press, 1969), 10.

[18] The point of departure for a fresh scrutiny of these questions remains Geneviève Lewis's doctoral work, published as *L'individualité selon Descartes* (Paris: Vrin, 1950).

[19] See G. Rodis-Lewis, *Descartes*, 41, and AT XII, 40.

[20] On the emergence of the "will theory of promises" in the late XVIth and XVIIth centuries, especially the innovative view of promises put forth by Hugo Grotius (1583–1645) against François de Connan (1508–1551), see P.S. Atiyah, *The Rise and Fall of Freedom of Contract* (Oxford: Clarendon Press, 1979), 138–165.

[21] Synopsis, AT VII, 14: "Omnes omnino substantias, sive res quae a Deo creari

mechanical laws, each human soul (*mens humana*) is "a pure substance" (*pura substantia*), created and sustained immediately by God.[22] Because of its special status as pure substance, each human soul is by its very nature numerically one and remains numerically the same soul despite changes in volitions and perceptions.[23] A fortiori, the soul's numerical identity is not affected by changes in the body that the soul informs. Rather, a human being of flesh and blood remains numerically the same human being only because *mens* remains numerically the same *mens* even though the flesh grows, changes its material constituents and decays.[24]

Each and every finite *res cogitans* is thus immediately created by God as the individual substance that it is, distinct from every other substance and incorruptible by nature. The critical Cartesian distinction is the distinction between "pure" substances and things "that consist of accidents."[25] Stones, plants and animals are examples of the latter, emerging as provisional aggregates determined by the various motions that agitate matter. While *res extensa*, taken as a seamless spatio-material manifold, depends immediately on God and is, therefore, *per se* one and incorruptible, extended things taken apart from the whole (stones, plants, animals) have no essential individuality. They arise and disappear, generated and destroyed according to invariant laws. From an Aristotelian-scholastic point of view, Descartes's main problem is with the individuation of material things rather than with the individuation of spiritual things (*mentes*).[26]

---

debent ut existant, ex natura sua esse incorruptibiles, nec posse unquam desinere esse, nisi, ab eodem Deo concursum suum iis denegante ad nihilum reducantur."

[22] AT VII, 13–14: "mentem vero humanam non ita ex ullis accidentibus constare, sed puram esse substantiam."

[23] *Ibid.*: "etsi enim omnia ejus accidentia mutentur, ut quod alias res intelligat, alias velit, alias sentiat, non idcirco ipsa mens alia evadit."

[24] See Descartes's Letter to Mesland, 9 February 1645, AT IV, 166–167. John Locke's objection to this Cartesian doctrine is in *Essay on the Human Understanding*, II, c. XXVII, 6, "The identity of man;" "For if the identity of soul alone makes the same man; and there be nothing in the nature of matter why the same individual spirit may not be united to different bodies, it will be possible that those men, living in distant ages, and of different tempers, may have been the same man."

[25] Descartes emphasizes that both the soul's immortality and "all of physics" depend on this distinction. See AT VII, 13: "quia praemissae, ex quibus ipsa mentis immortalitas concludi potest, ex totius Physicae explicatione dependent."

[26] See G. Rodis, *Individualité selon Descartes*, 39 and her citation of Hamelin, *Le système de Descartes*, 305: "La matière ne comporte donc pas d'*individua* au sens etymologique du terme." On the special problem of how finite bodies are individuated, see Emily

What argument does Descartes offer to justify the claim that human *mentes*, unlike bodies, are pure substances? In the *Discours de la Méthode*, as we know, Descartes cites the evidence of human language to argue that the human soul cannot be "elicited from the potentiality of matter."[27] The power to originate speech acts, which is to say, to bring about effects that are neither deterministic nor random, testifies to something in human being that is uniquely creative and cannot be reduced to mechanistic principles.[28] While material things generate effects deterministically and are themselves material effects, rational beings produce deliberate effects and must, therefore, be "expressly created" rather than generated materially—or so at least Descartes argues.[29] Human language, according to Descartes, implies the soul's free agency, which in turn implies the soul's immateriality and special status as a pure substance immediately created and conserved by God.

The argument that is sketched in the *Discours*—aimed, in particular, at refuting any trace of reason/free will in brutes[30]—is developed in great detail in Meditation III. Inquiring after its origin, the *ego* discovers that no fleshly parents could have produced it or could now sustain it, since nothing finite has the power to produce an immaterial substance endowed with the idea of an actual infinite (or, equivalently, "made in God's image.")[31] If the *ego*'s existence proves that God exists (*sum, ergo Deus est*),[32] the impossibility that the *ego* be caused by anything *but* an infinitely perfect agent (God) implies, conversely, that the *ego* is a "pure substance."

Grosholz, "Descartes and the Individuation of Physical Objects," in Kenneth Barber and Jorge Gracia, eds., *Individuation and Identity in Early Modern Philosophy* (Albany, NY: State U. of New York Press, 1994), 41–58.

[27] AT VI, 59.

[28] For a modern version of the same argument, see Noam Chomsky, *Language and Thought*.

[29] AT VI, 59: "l'ame raisonnable ne peut aucunement estre tirée de la puissance de la matiere, mais doit expressement estre creée."

[30] Could Descartes mean to correct Grotius? Compare Descartes, AT VI, 58–59 ("ce qu'ils [sc. les animaux] font mieux que nous ne prouve pas qu'ils ont de l'esprit mais plutot qu'ils n'en ont point, et que c'est la nature qui agit en eux") to Hugo Grotius, *De jure Belli ac Pacis* (Paris, 1625), Bk. I, chap. 1, XI: "If ever justice is attributed to brutes, it is done improperly, from *some shadow and trace of reason they may possess*."

[31] AT VII, 50: "Quantum denique ad parentes attinet, ut omnia vera sint quae de illis unquam putavi, non tamen profecto illi me conservant, nec etiam ullo modo me, quatenus sum res cogitans, effecerunt."

[32] See *Regulae*, XII, AT X, 421.

How innovative is Descartes's doctrine that pure substances are individuated as such—requiring no further "principle" of individuation beyond God's immediate creative act? Descartes's key distinction between "pure substances" and "things consisting of accidents" (*ex accidentibus constare*) recalls Aristotle's distinction between *entia per se* and *entia per accidens*.[33] For Descartes, accidental things have no *per se* unity, while pure substances, such as immaterial *mentes*, are indivisibly what they are in virtue of their essence. Jarring as Descartes's mechanistic doctrine of plants and animals may be for Aristotelians, his claim regarding the *per se* individuality of *mentes* amounts to regarding *mentes* as *entia per se* and thus fits with scholastic theory, most notably with the cautious and conciliatory doctrine elaborated by Suarez. According to Suarez, singular substances are singular in and of themselves, requiring no principle of individuation beyond intrinsic constitutive principles.[34] Suarez affirms, in particular, the *per se* individuality and unity of *mens*, rejecting, like Descartes, the argument that a body is required for *mens* to be individuated.[35] Like Descartes, Suarez cites nutrition to prove that the soul's numerical unity is intrinsic, entirely independent of the changing material mass that the soul informs.[36]

Familiar, perhaps, with Suarez's analysis through his teachers at La Flèche,[37] Descartes may have considered the problem of the individu-

---

[33] Aristotle, *Metaphysics*, Bk. V, c. 6, 1015b16–34 and 1016b3–10; and Bk. VII, c. 4, 1029b12–16. For Descartes's (real or contrived) feeling of *continuity* with Aristotle, see the letter to Charlet, AT IV, 141.

[34] See Suarez, Metaphysical Disputation V, Section VI, in *Suarez on Individuation*, trans. Jorge J.E. Gracia (Milwaukee, Wis.: Marquette U. Press, 1982), 121: "Every singular substance is singular in itself, that is, by its entity, and needs no other principle of individuation in addition to its entity, or in addition to the intrinsic principles which constitute its entity."

[35] See Metaphysical Disputation V, Section VI, 5, in *Suarez on Individuation*, 125: "Because the individual difference is intrinsically predicated of the individual thing, it is taken from the intrinsic principle, that is, its entity. This is more obvious in the rational soul, in which, just as being is not caused by itself from matter, so likewise neither is unity or individuality."

[36] See Descartes's letter to Mesland, AT IV, 166–167; and Suarez, *Metaphysical Disputation V*, Section VI, 6, in *Suarez on Individuation*, 126: "It is accidental to nutrition itself that it be made from these or those foods and, nevertheless, from this it comes about that the soul informs this or that matter afterwards; therefore, this is also contingent and accidental to it. Therefore, the soul is not individuated from matter." Geneviève Rodis-Lewis remarks on the similarity of the two positions in *L'individualité selon Descartes*, 33.

[37] In the passage cited above, for example, from Section VI, 5, Suarez makes a point of enlisting Thomas, *Contra Gentiles*, II, ch. 75 and 81.

ation of *mentes* to have been solved and his own task simply to isolate *mentes* from mechanistic causes. Descartes's chief concern seems to have been to establish that *mentes humanas* are "pure substances," unaffected by mechanistic principles but compatible with them. Descartes's *mentes humanas* are not only *entia per se*, intrinsically individual, they are as far removed from physical generation and corruption as Aristotle's celestial intelligences.[38] The main difference between Cartesian *mentes humanas* and the celestial intelligences of Greek antiquity is that Cartesian *mentes humanas* have a finite beginning in time and depend wholly for their being on God's creative will.

9.1. *My existence, my Nothingness*

Meditation IV brings the *ego* face to face with its singularity in a new and more personal sense. Granted that God's creative act is sufficient for *mens* to be *per se* indivisible and incommunicable, what makes *mens mea* properly *mine*?[39] Does the *ego* lay claim to itself only through its shortcomings—when acknowledging its propensity to stray from truth: *gaudet aberrare mens mea*?[40]

A new ground for selfhood is initiated in Meditation III by the second proof of God's existence. Whereas the first proof emphasizes that God exists necessarily, the second proof emphasizes that *I myself* could very well not exist at all.[41] The first proof crowns the *ego*'s effort to withdraw from the senses and the imagination: the *ego* soars above the particularity of what can be sensed or pictured to grasp itself precisely as universal reason (*sum intellectus sive ratio*) and God as the necessity behind all possibility. Emancipated from material moorings, the *ego* discovers truths that are valid for every intelligence.[42] When the *ego* clarifies the proof in a new version, a private spiritual perspective is introduced. Convinced that God exists, the *ego* now puts itself on the

---

[38] See, in this regard, Berman's objection, AT V, 157: "Sed sic angelus et mens nostra erunt idem, cum utraque sit res solum cogitans?"

[39] Paraphrasing G. Lewis, who asks, in *L'individualité selon Descartes*, 103: "L'independance de l'âme par rapport au corps, qui assure la spiritualité de *la* pensée, permettra-t-elle d'affirmer l'individualité de *ma* pensée?"

[40] Meditation II, AT VII, 29.

[41] Meditation III, 47–48: "ulterius quaerere libet an ego ipse habens illam ideam esse possem, si tale ens nullum existeret."

[42] Cf. AT VII, 53: "manifeste concludo Deum etiam existere ut nihil evidentius, nihil certius ab humano ingenio cognosci posse confidam."

line: never mind the idea of the infinite, would "I myself" (*ego ipse*) exist if God did not exist?[43]

The question of God's existence now concerns the *ego* personally. The new path to God's *aseity* springs from the *ego*'s own frailty. Certain of existing but unable to bring itself into being, the *ego* is dispossessed of self-sufficiency in favor of God. To discover God's existence is to discover that I myself am essentially incomplete: *intelligo me esse rem incompletam.*[44] In what sense is the *ego* even entitled to claim existence as *existentia mea?*[45] The *ego* has *no* being at all outside of the divine act that produces it continuously out of nothing. If God were to withdraw not only the infinite power required to sustain the *ego* but the incomprehensible decision to give the *ego* any being at all, the *ego* would instantly return to what it is *a se*: nothing.[46] Powerless to originate myself, bereft of my own *ratio essendi*, I exist *ab alio*, which means that I am wholly the term of a volition that God forms at every moment.[47]

The doctrine of special creation thus implies not only that the soul is *per se* individual and incorruptible but that the *ego*'s identity is defined by the unilateral divine act that gives it a purely relational being: the *ego* is numerically the same *ego* from one instant to the next because its very essence is determined by its dependent relation to God. The *ego*'s dependence on God's creative act is inalienable because the soul can neither undo nor transfer to another *mens humana* the existence that *I myself* receive from God.[48] Since the soul is created immediately by God, the soul's relationship to God is uniquely defined, regardless of how many other divine acts result in other souls or creatures.

The force of Descartes's second proof is that the *ego* is not produced and then abandoned to its own isolated subsistence: for the *ego*, existing and being-related-to-God are inseparable. The binary relation through which the *ego* emerges out of nothingness is not shared—and cannot be shared—by any other *mens*. A first consequence of special creation, in

---

[43] AT VII, 48.

[44] Meditation III, AT VII, 51, and Meditation IV, AT VII, 53.

[45] AT VII, 48: "existentiae meae authorem" and 53: "ab illo singulis momentis totam existentiam meam dependere."

[46] Synopsis, AT VII, 14.

[47] Cf. *Regulae*, XII, AT X, 422: "Notandum est, plurimam propositionum, quae necessariae sunt, conversas esse contingentes: ut quamvis ex eo quod sim, certo concludam Deum esse, non tamen ex eo quod Deus sit, me etiam existere licet affirmare."

[48] Descartes would agree with Locke that suicide is unlawful. See Locke, *Second Treatise of Government*, para. 6, lines 19–22, in *Two Treatises of Government*, ed. Peter Laslett (Cambridge: Cambridge U. Press, 1964), 289.

short, is that each individual *mens humana* is related to God personally, as the indivisible term, as such unique, of God's volition.

Two additional consequences are implied. First, since the *ego* exists only through God's infinite power, the *ego*'s metaphysical debt (at every instant) to God is infinite. Second, since God's creative act is radically unnecessitated, since the *ego* is not brought into being by a prime mover actualizing latent possibilities but produced *ex nihilo* by an infinitely free God, the *ego*'s moral debt (at every instant) to God is infinite. The disproportion between what the *ego* is *a se*, namely nothing at all, and what the *ego* is *ab alio*, namely an incorruptible substance made in "God's image,"[49] reveals God's solicitude (*bonté*),[50] and implies a debt of gratitude on the *ego*'s part. The *ego*'s act of worship at the end of Meditation III is a tribute, born of gratitude: *placet hic aliquandu in ipsius Dei contemplatione immorari.*[51] The *ego* owes itself to God both metaphysically and morally at every second of its incorruptible existence, which is to say infinitely.

The *ego*'s act of gratitude, in turn, provides the foundation for selfhood: whereas the *ego* can hardly claim its existence metaphysically, the *ego* can claim its existence morally as soon as its existence is viewed as the debt that *I myself* owe to God at every instant. The *ego* can thus legitimately speak of *ego ipse*—of *I myself* as distinct from everything else, even from God—by constituting itself as a debtor in response to God's generosity. The *ego*'s paradox is that my existence is mine (*existentia mea*) only if I choose to return it to God at every instant.

The significance of Descartes's second proof comes to light as soon as we compare it to a key Salesian text aimed at preparing the soul for the devotional life. Like Descartes, Francis of Sales was intimately familiar with the Ignatian device of "allowing the creature to work directly with its Creator and God."[52] In the Salesian text, also a meditation, the soul considers the disproportion between its nothingness *a se* and its surpris-

---

[49] Meditation III, AT VII, 51: "Ex hoc uno quod Deus me creavit, valde credibile est me quodammodo ad imaginem et similitudinem ejus factum esse."

[50] In a letter to Elizabeth, 15 September, 1645, Descartes speaks of the importance of "recognizing God's goodness and the immortality of our souls" ("la bonté de Dieu et l'immortalité de nos âmes)." AT IV, 292–293.

[51] AT VII, 52. De Lyunes translates, AT IX, 41: "il me semble très à propos de m'arrêter quelque temps à la contemplation de ce Dieu."

[52] *The Spiritual Exercises of Saint Ignatius*, Annotaciones, 15, trans. Anthony Mottola, 41. See also Pierre Serouet, *Dictionnaire de la Spiritualité* (Paris: Beauchesne, 1964), Tome V, col. 1091: "François faisait presque chaque année sa retraite spirituelle sous la direction d'un jésuite et devait être inité à fond à la méthode des *Exercices*."

ing dignity *ab alio*, and reflects on the special privilege of depending immediately on God (Descartes's doctrine of special creation). Francis of Sales calls attention to three points: (1) the soul (*my* soul) is not coeval with God but has a finite beginning in time; (2) the soul is radically contingent—dependent for its essence on God's free creative act; and (3) despite its finite and contingent essence, the soul is by nature "capable of living eternally and uniting with God," which implies that God and God alone is its author.[53]

A similar scheme is pursued by Descartes in Meditation III. By asking *would I myself exist if God did not*, the *ego* ponders both its existential frailty and spiritual dignity. In the Cartesian meditation, reflection is enhanced by the doctrine of continuous creation. As the second proof unfolds, the *ego* considers (1) its finite origin *at every instant*; (2) its lack of necessity *at every instant*; and (3) its incomprehensible dignity *at every instant*. Both the Salesian and the Cartesian meditations stress that the human soul is powerless to create itself, that the human soul "stands like nothing before God," but also that its dignity rules out a material origin, implying special creation.[54] In both meditations, the soul's dignity consists, not only in metaphysical incorruptibility, but, more importantly, in the capacity to unite with God, starting with contemplation (*intueri, admirari, adorare*), which Descartes explicitly interprets to be a foretaste of beatitude.[55]

Francis of Sales, who, like Descartes, studied jurisprudence (1588–1591) before discovering his true vocation,[56] emphasizes the soul's debt.[57] Since the soul owes its being to God, the soul cannot legitimately dispose of itself against God's will. The soul must, therefore, turn away from the disordered affections through which it has rebelled

---

[53] *Introduction à la vie dévote*, Part I, c. IX, Meditation I, in *Oeuvres Complètes*, I, 47.

[54] *Ibid.*: "O Seigneur, je suis *devant vous comme un vrai rien* (Psalm XXXVIII, 7); O mon âme, *sache que le Seigneur est ton Dieu c'est lui qui t'as faite* et tu ne t'es pas faite toi-même. (Psalm XCIX, 3); O Dieu, je suis *l'ouvrage de vos mains* (Psalm CXXXVII, 8)."

[55] AT VII, 52: "Ut enim in hac sola divinae majestatis contemplatione summam alterius vitae foelicitatem consistere fide credimus, ita etiam jam ex eadem, licet multo minus perfecta, maximam, cujus in hac vita capaces simus, voluptatem percipi posse experimur."

[56] A. Ravier, "Préface et Chronologie," in Saint François de Sales, *Oeuvres*, I, cxvii-cxix.

[57] François de Sales, *Introduction à la vie dévote*, I, c. IX, in *Ouevres*, I, 47: "O mon bon et grand Créateur, combien vous suis-je redevable, puisque vous m'êtes allée prendre dans mon rien, pour me rendre par votre miséricorde ce que je suis." And: "Abaissez-vous devant Dieu. O mon âme, sache que le Seigneur est ton Dieu; c'est lui qui t'a faite, et tu ne t'es pas faite toi-même. O Dieu, je suis l'ouvrage de vos mains."

and separated itself from God and instead "unite with God through love and service."[58] The Salesian meditation culminates with a formal contract to be "signed" by the *ego* "in the presence of God and the whole celestial court."[59]

The contract starts with a detailed acknowledgment of liability: the *ego* ("I, the undersigned") acknowledges receipt of life, care, baptism, clemency—countless treasures received from God without any compensation in return. Significantly, the *ego* acknowledges "having done violence" to its soul by "applying it and using it" against God.[60] The implicit premiss is that the *ego* has a duty to use its spiritual faculties for God's purpose rather than substitute a purpose of its own.[61] Now "self-recovered," the *ego* pleads guilty to the crime of divine *lèse-majesté* and to murder (crucifying Christ by its many sins).[62] Without contesting the justice of a death sentence, the *ego* seeks God's pardon and offers itself up in service, pledging "my soul and all its powers, my mind and all its faculties" to God "now and for all eternity."[63] The key aspect of the contract, for our purposes, is that technical legal terms emphasize the *ego*'s autonomy. The *ego* pledges itself freely to the terms of the contract, without outside coercion: "I desire, propose, choose and resolve." The *ego* is thus free to dispose of itself as long as the terms of self-disposal do not violate God's *lien* on the soul. Moreover, God himself cannot consent to the contract in the *ego*'s place. The *ego* must exercise its *own* right of self-disposal and exercise it freely in order for the contract to be valid: "This is my will, my intention and my unimpeachable and

---

[58] *Ibid.*: "Mais hélas! mon Créateur, au lieu de m'unir à vous par amour et service, je me suis rendue toute rebelle par mes déréglées affections, me séparant et éloignant de vous pour me joindre au péché, n'honorant non plus votre bonté que si vous n'eussiez pas été mon créateur."

[59] *Introduction à la vie dévote*, I, c. XX, in *Oeuvres*, I, 69: "Je soussignée, constituée et établie en la présence de Dieu éternel et de toute la cour céleste…"

[60] *Ibid.*: "J'ai tant et tant de fois violé mon esprit, l'appliquant et l'employant contre la divine Majesté."

[61] A key influence on Francis of Sales was Scupoli's *Spiritual Combat*, which stipulates that seeking perfection requires "The right use of faculties."

[62] *Ibid.*: "Enfin, revenant maintenant à moi-même, prosternée de coeur et d'esprit devant le trône de la justice divine, je me reconnais, avoue et confesse pour légitimement atteinte et convaincue du crime de lèse-majesté divine, et coupable de la Mort et Passion de Jésus-Christ, à raison des péchés que j'ai commis."

[63] *Introduction à la vie dévote*, in *Oeuvres*, I, 70: "Je désire, propose, délibère et me résous irrévocablement de le servir et aimer maintenant et éternellement, lui donnant à ces fins, dédiant et consacrant mon esprit avec toutes ses facultés, mon âme avec toutes ses puissances, mon coeur avec toutes ses affections, mon corps avec tous ses sens."

irrevocable resolution, which I make and confirm without reservation or exception."[64]

The obligation undertaken by the *ego* to serve God "now and forever" is binding because it is undertaken voluntarily, in the presence of witnesses (God, the celestial court and "an officer of the Church Militant") and because God, in turn, accepts it.[65] Moreover, the *ego* is entitled to alienate its "powers and faculties" to God only because God already co-owns them, so that the contract really involves a special case of restitution. Could the *ego* validly give anyone but God dominion over its "powers and faculties"? Since the soul is God's handiwork and "stands before God truly as nothing,"[66] the soul's freedom to dispose of itself is restricted in an absolute sense by God's prior claim. The *ego* cannot alienate itself *from* God without incurring liability. The *ego*'s right to existence, for example, is inalienable precisely because the *ego*'s existence is not the *ego*'s handiwork or property.[67] Aware of his Calvinist opponents' enthusiasm for covenants and contracts[68] and eager to repair the broken Christian communion preemptively, Francis of Sales did not hesitate to frame his revived doctrine of "pure love" in the new contractual language.[69]

What matters for the purpose of analysing Descartes is that the Salesian "contract" rests on a special theory of free consent. By freely acquiescing to God's claim over it, the *ego* not only exercises but actually acquires a *right* of self-disposal that it does not otherwise possess. When

---

[64] *Ibid.*: "Ceci est ma volonté, mon intention et ma résolution inviolable et irrévocable, laquelle j'avoue et confirme sans réserve ni exception."

[65] *Introduction à la vie dévote*, I, c. XXI, in *Oeuvres*, I, 71: "Il ne reste plus sinon que, prenant la plume en main, vous signiez de bon coeur l'acte de votre protestation, et que par après vous alliez à l'autel, où Dieu réciproquement signera."

[66] *Introduction à la vie dévote*, I, c. IX, in *Oeuvres*, I, 47.

[67] Cf. John Locke, Second Treatise of Government, paragraphs 6 and 23, in *Two Treatises of Government*, ed. Peter Laslett, 289 and 302, respectively: "Men being all the Workmanship of one Omnipotent, and infinitely wise Maker; All the servants of one Sovereign Master [...] they are his Property, whose Workmanship they are"; and "For a Man, not having the Power of his own Life, *cannot*, by Compact, or his own Consent, *enslave himself* to any one, nor put himself under the Absolute, Arbitrary Power of another, to take away his Life, when he pleases."

[68] See on this subject Herbert D. Foster, "International Calvinism Through Locke and the Revolution of 1688," *American Historical Review*, XXXII, 475–499; reprinted in John Dunn and Ian Harris, eds., *Locke* (Cheltenham, UK, and Lyme, US: Edward Elgar Publishing Limited, 1997), 1–25.

[69] Against St. Bernard's explicit remark that "true charity is an affection and not a contract" in *De diligendo Deo*, 7, PL, 984c, 985a; cited by Ephrem Boularant in his article on "Désinteressement," *Dictionnaire de Spiritualité* (Paris: Beauchesne, 1957), col. 574.

consenting to affections that draw it away from God, the *ego* acts unlawfully and sins. Conversely, the *ego*'s free consent to serve God "now and forever" is indispensable for redemption: God cannot compel the *ego*'s aquiescence or bring the *ego* to perfection without it.[70]

The doctrine of special creation thus implies a distinctive theory of personal autonomy: the *ego* rules *me* only if God rules *I*—but *I* alone have the power to consent to God's rule.[71] The power of free consent through which the *ego* transfers self-dominion to God cannot be transferred. In order to be autonomous, the *ego* must cooperate with God's rule by freely consenting to it, which means that the *ego*'s consent to right use of its faculty defines the *ego* personally—uniquely and properly: *my* action, *my* intention and *my* resolution. The soul is never pulled to God "like a stone or a convict" but freely cooperates with grace by consenting to it.[72] Even in ecstatic states, the soul is not passive, since the will acquiesces to the divine will.[73] Perfect union with God coincides with perfect freedom since there is nothing left in the soul but a simple act of consent. The question is, how similar to the Salesian doctrine is Descartes's theory of autonomy? Does Descartes, without the benefit of revelation, interpret special creation to hold similar implications?

9.2. *Theodicy*

Meditation IV, the first meditation to be conducted after the discovery that God is *author existentiae meae*, marks a new departure. The *ego* shifts from investigating the nature of *mens* to elucidating what "belongs to

---

[70] Francis of Sales's solution to the Counter-Reformation controversy over freedom and grace (the "de auxiliis" controversy), adopted by Paul V in 1607, is found in *Traité de l'Amour de Dieu*, Book III, chap. V. An immediate source is Scupoli, *Spiritual Combat*, c. XIII, 40: "The will incurs no guilt unless it gives consent to an act, even if the entire force of the lower appetite is exerted towards a guilty end. On the other hand, the will cannot be sanctified and united to God, however strong the grace attracting it, unless it cooperates with that grace by interior acts, and, if requisite, by exterior acts."

[71] Paraphrasing, for the sake of emphasizing the contrast, Joel Feinberg, "The Idea of a Free man," in *Education and the Development of Reason*, ed. R.F. Dearden (London: Routledge and Kegan Paul, 1972), 161: "I am autonomous if I rule me, and no one else rules I."

[72] François de Sales, *Traité de l'Amour de Dieu*, Bk. VII, chap. 2, in *Oeuvres*, I, 671.

[73] François de sales, *Traité de l'Amour de Dieu*, Bk. VI, chap. 11, in *Oeuvres*, 643: "la volonté n'agit que par un très simple acquiescement au bon plaisir divin."

me in a more proper way": *ad me proprius accedens*.[74] The new investigation is framed as a theodicy,[75] implying that knowledge of myself and
knowledge of God are from now on inseparable (*noverim te, noverim me*).
Given that God is infinitely powerful and infinitely perfect, why is the
rational soul, a pure and incorruptible substance, fallible? Illuminated
by the "first truth from which all truths proceed," namely the truth
of God's existence,[76] the *ego* sees itself now first and foremost as God's
handiwork. The new premiss of the investigation, God's infinite perfection, reverses the original question ("how can I know anything?") and
calls for a justification of human fallibility ("why do I ever make mistakes?"). In solving this puzzle, Descartes will radicalize the problem of
individuation.

Fresh from contemplating the true God (*veri dei*), the *ego* makes two
contrasting observations with regard to error. First, no cause of error
or falsity can be found as long as the *ego* keeps its attention fixed
exclusively on God. The *ego*, it seems, is sheltered from error when
it wholly turns itself to the author of its existence: *totusque in eum me
converto*.[77] Second, as soon as the *ego* "reverts to itself" (*ad me reversus*), it
experiences (*experior*) itself falling subject to "innumerable" errors.[78] Two
questions immediately emerge to guide our investigation. First, what is
the role of judgment in rational contemplation and why does the *ego*
become, when wholly turned to God, *as though infallible*? Second, what
is meant by *ad me reversus*? A valid interpretation of the new theory put
forth in Meditation IV must shed light on these two questions.

Unlike Meditations III and V, which elaborate on what is sketched
in Part IV of the *Discours de la Méthode*, Meditation IV unveils an
entirely new doctrine.[79] Whereas Descartes in the *Regulae* endorsed the

---

[74] AT VII, 56.

[75] As explicitly stated to Mesland, May 2, 1644, AT IV, 113: "J'ay tasché d'éclaircir
la difficulté proposée, touchant la cause des erreurs, en supposant que Dieu ait creé le
monde tres-parfait; pour ce que, supposant le contraire, cette difficulté cesse entierement."

[76] See Descartes's letter to Mersenne, 6 May 1630, AT I, 150: "l'existence de Dieu
est la première et la plus eternelle de toutes les veritez qui peuvent estre et la seule d'où
procedent toutes les autres."

[77] AT VII, 54: "Quamdiu de Deo tantum cogito, totusque in eum me converto,
nullam erroris aut falsitatis causam deprehendo."

[78] *Ibid*.: "sed, postmodum ad me reversus, experior me tamen innumeris erroribus
esse obnoxium."

[79] As Rodis-Lewis points out, Meditation III and V form a natural progression,
which Meditation IV interrupts. See Geneviève Rodis-Lewis, "On the Complementarity of Meditations III and V," in A. Rorty, ed., *Essays on Descartes's Meditations*, 275.

standard scholastic view that judgment is an activity of the intellect, Meditation IV argues that judgment is a function of the will. The novelty of the doctrine is generally acknowledged, but its motivation remains puzzling.[80] Why is a new theory of judgment introduced in Meditation IV?

As we shall see, Descartes's new theory of judgment is rooted in a theory of freedom that bears a close affinity to the Salesian theory. The problem of theodicy, of reconciling God's infinite perfection with human fallibility, conveniently allows Descartes to explore human freedom as a dimension of the soul's essential bond to God. Meditation IV does not so much exculpate God for human error as progressively inculpate the *ego* so as to bring the meaning of spiritual freedom to light. With every new step, Meditation IV reveals a new aspect of God's generosity and a new aspect of human dereliction, until the *ego* no longer reverts to itself but uses its freedom to consent to God's will.

The very first attempt at a solution illustrates the double level at which Meditation IV operates. Having called attention to the apparent incompatibility between divine perfection and human fallibility, the *ego* first explains human error as an inevitable consequence of ontological finitude. Since the *ego* participates in God's infinite perfection but also "in some way" in non-being (*quodammodo de nihilo, sive de non ente, participo*), the faculty by which the *ego* judges truth (*facultas verum judicandi*) is simply not infinite. The ontological finitude of *mens humana*, which seems to imply the finitude of its faculties, seems sufficient to account for the human propensity for error: *non adeo mirum esse quod fallar.*

The problem with this first explanation, the *ego* objects, is that it contradicts the infinity of God's power. God has the power to create a *mens humana* that is both finite and infallible. Since God has the power to make the *ego* infallible, the *ego*'s fallibility must be radically reassessed. By refusing to compromise God's infinity, the *ego* discovers a surprising new viewpoint: could it be that is it better for me to be fallible than infallible?[81] The possibility that fallibility is among God's *gifts* implies a new view of selfhood. If the *ego* is as indebted to God for its fallibility as

---

[80] As Anthony Kenny summarizes, in "Descartes on the Will," in J. Cottingham, ed., *Descartes*, 135: "Some time, then, between 1628 and 1640, Descartes changed his mind about the nature of judgment. It is not easy to discover when and why he did so."

[81] AT VII, 55: "Nec dubium est quin potuerit Deus me talem creare, ut nunquam fallerer; nec etiam dubium est quin velit semper id quod est optimum: anne ergo melius est me falli quam non falli?"

it is for its existence, then not only does error not follow inevitably from finitude, error may fruitfully be *mine* in a special sense. What leaves the *ego* dissatisfied with the first explanation?[82] The key is the *ego*'s diagnosis that error is not the same as ignorance. Error deprives the *ego* of truth, like blindness. As a pure substance immediately created by God, the *ego* may lack supreme perfection and have only a finite intelligence, but cannot have a *defective* intelligence that mistakes falsehood for truth. Error cannot, therefore, stem from finitude as such. God immediately causes the *ego* to be the finite *mens humana* that it is, but does not immediately cause the *ego* to err. Does the *ego* then, err precisely *by itself, on its own?*

Before proceeding further, the *ego* confronts the initial presumption of blaming human fallibility on finitude. Since God's ends are impenetrable to a finite intelligence,[83] what appears to the *ego* to be imperfect when viewed in isolation (*singulatim*) may reveal itself to be "most perfect" (*perfectissimum*) when viewed as an integral part of the universe.[84] Far from implying imperfection, the *ego*'s finitude draws it out of isolation in a double sense: (1) finitude enables the *ego* to discover that God exists and (2) finitude enables the *ego* to define itself as a part of God's creation.[85] The argument that fallibility is inevitable because *mens* is finite stems, in effect, from a double presumption: the immensity of God's creative power is denied and God is implicitly reproached and blamed. The error of blaming human error on finitude results from human temerity, which in turn results from the *ego*'s propensity to regard its own self-centered viewpoint as absolute.

A first interpretation of *reversus ad me* thus comes to light: the *ego* falls victim to error when it abandons the premiss of God's infinity and falls back into egocentricity. To the extent that the *ego* now experiences dissatisfaction with any account of the human self that contradicts divine infinity, the *ego* has forestalled the tendency to revert to itself. The chief beneficiary of theodicy is, of course, the *ego*, who doubted the perfection of God's decree and of its own finitude. The question

---

[82] See AT VII, 54: "Verumtamen hoc nondum omnino satisfacit."

[83] AT VII, 55: "scio innumerabilia illum posse quorum causas ignoro. Non absque temeritate me puto posse investigare fines Dei."

[84] AT VII, 55–56: "Occurrit etiam non unam aliquam creaturam separatim, sed omnem rerum universitatem esse spectandam, quoties an opera Dei perfecta sint inquirimus; quod enim forte non immerito, si solum esset, valde imperfectum videretur, ut habens in mundo rationem partis est perfectissimum."

[85] AT VII, 56: "ut ego rationem partis in rerum universitate obtineam."

to be answered is no longer whether God is to blame for human fallibility but: how does human fallibility manifest God's will and infinite solicitude—*bonitas dei*?[86] Wherein lies the benefit of fallibility for the *ego*?

9.3. *My errors, my action*

Ad me proprius accedens: the *ego* is now ready to lay personal claim to errors, which "alone indicate that there is some imperfection in me." Errors are, most properly, *my* errors: *errores mei*.[87] Are my errors (*errores mei*) in some sense more properly mine than my very existence (*existentia mea*)? In Meditation II, as we saw, the *ego* already spoke in the same personal way of *my* mind in the hope of reforming itself: *gaudet aberrare mens mea*.[88] Does the *ego*'s capacity for self-incrimination mark a first affirmation of selfhood—a proper acceding to self that is not a reverting to self? Let us return briefly to this earlier passage, in which the *ego* simultaneously disassociates itself from its own wayward mind and appropriates it as *mens mea*. The *ego*'s diagnosis is that *mens mea* "cannot suffer" to be contained within the limits of truth."[89] How does the indivisible *mens* split into a superior *ego* and a derelict *mens mea*? How does the *ego* take new charge of itself by blaming its mind for delighting in error, then adopting towards it the position of a trainer who hopes gradually to rule over it?[90]

The implicit belief that *mens mea* can be cured of dereliction through the *ego*'s effort raises two key questions: first, what in *mens* balks at being confined within the limits of truth? Second, what power of control, proper to itself and perhaps self-defining, does the *ego* have over *mens mea*?

Meditation IV reiterates the diagnosis that errors are mine (*errores mei*) but places blame squarely on the *ego* itself rather than on *mens mea*. No longer holding itself at a distance, the *ego* identifies itself as the root cause of vagrancy. Neither God nor ontological finitude nor anything but myself can be blamed for an imperfection that is exclusively and

---

[86] Meditation VI, AT VII, 85.

[87] AT VII, 56: "errores mei qui soli imperfectionem aliquam in me arguunt."

[88] AT VII, 29.

[89] *Ibid.*: "gaudet aberrare mens mea, necdum se patitur intra veritatis limites cohiberi."

[90] *Ibid.* and 30: "Adhuc semel laxissimas habenas ei permittamus, ut, illis paulo post opportune reductis, facilius se regi patiatur."

properly mine: *errores mei.* But how is the *ego* capable of wandering away from Truth when its whole being and faculties come immediately from God? What are the grounds that make my dereliction possible, granted that I myself am properly and exclusively responsible for it? The answer is that errors

> "depend on two concurrent causes, namely on the cognitive faculty that is in me and on the elective faculty or freedom of arbitration, which is to say on both the intellect and the will."[91]

Ad me proprius accedens: the *ego* must figure out how a proper self, defined by its very culpability, alone responsible for *errores mei*, arises from the joint activity of intellect and will. On the one hand, both faculties are, as such, indubitably perfect since they are received immediately from God. On the other hand, to the extent that the two faculties are distinct in *mens humana* rather than perfectly indivisible as they are in God, perhaps a chasm is opened for the *ego* to act without knowledge and know without acting.

First, what does the *ego* know of these two faculties? The intellect or *facultas cognoscendi* is the faculty by means of which the *ego* perceives (*percipio*) ideas "about which I am able to judge" (*de quibus judicium ferre possum*).[92] The intellect is a purely receptive power: knowledge is acquired because the intellect "suffers" ideas—in the same way that wax suffers modifications of shape.[93] The intellect increases its cognitive store precisely because it is passively informed by the objective reality of things acting on it.[94] Intellection, in short, is properly "a passion of the mind."[95] The *ego* knows things (including its own volitions and propositional attitudes) precisely to the extent that perception is passive

---

[91] AT VII, 56: "Adverto illos a duabus causis simul concurrentibus dependere, nempe a facultate cognoscendi quae in me est, et a facultate eligendi, sive ab arbitrii libertate, hoc est ab intellectu et simul a voluntate."

[92] AT VII 56: "Nam per solum intellectum percipio tantum ideas de quibus judicium ferre possum."

[93] Letter to Mesland, May 2, 1644, AT IV, 113: "Ie ne mets autre différence entre l'ame et ses idées, que comme un morceau de cire et les diverses figures qu'il peut recevoir."

[94] *Ibid*: "Et comme ce n'est pas proprement une action, mais une passion en la cire, de recevoir diverses figures, il me semble que c'est une passion en l'ame de recevoir telle ou telle idée, et qu'il n'y a que ses volontez qui soient des actions."

[95] Letter to Regius, May 1641, AT III, 372: "Intellectionem proprie mentis passio est." In a similar vein, John Searle warns against speaking of perception as an "activity" of mind, since a key distinction between the Intentionality of perceiving and the Intentionality of acting is thereby offuscated.

and that the intellect perceives only: *percipio tantum*. Let us note that Descartes's position regarding the passivity of cognition conforms with Aristotle's cognitive theory: the mind increases in knowledge by taking on the forms of things.[96]

Based on the passivity of the intellect, Descartes concludes that "no error, properly speaking, is found in the understanding taken in this precise sense."[97] How sound is Descartes's claim in this regard? The objection has been raised that "the product of the understanding can, on its own, be either true or false."[98] Descartes, however, never means to deny that ideas, or combination of ideas, lack a determinate truth value. On the contrary, since the intellect passively perceives "ideas about which I am able to judge," the intellect must perceive, among other things, (1) whether or not the ideas that are perceived combine to make a truth-claim (ideas that combine to form a question, for example, do not) and (2) whether or not the truth-claim that is made is true, false, or undecidable. Descartes's point is not that *truth* is absent until the *ego* passes judgment: rather Descartes's point is that no *error* is made until the *ego* endorses as true, or rejects as false, what the intellect presents. Descartes's distinction is between, on the one hand, the objective falsehood of a proposition, and on the other the error that the *ego* commits if affirming the proposition to be true.

Once again, it matters to Descartes to emphasize that the *ego*'s limited intelligence of things is not the immediate cause of *errores mei*. Since the finitude of the human intellect does not contradict God's infinite power and goodness,[99] the *ego* has no right to complain (*queri*). By distinguishing between error and incomplete knowledge, the *ego* is forced to give up a secret wish for omniscience and becomes reconciled to having only a limited, if open-ended, science. God is under no

---

[96] Cf. *de Anima*, Bk. II, 12, 424a16–24 and Bk. III, 4, 430a3–10.

[97] AT VII, 56: "nec ullus error proprie dictus in eo praecise sic spectato reperitur."

[98] See David Rosenthal's discussion in "Will and the Theory of Judgment," *Essays on Descartes's Meditations*, especially 420: "Descartes denies that the product of the understanding can, on its own, be either true or false." See, further, the authors who interpret Descartes in the same vein, cited by Rosenthal, namely E.M. Curley, "Descartes, Spinoza and the Ethics of Belief," in *Spinoza: Essays in Interpretation*, ed. E. Freeman and M. Mandelbaum (La Salle, Ill.: Open Court, 1975), 159–189; M. Wilson, *Descartes* (London: Routlege and Kegan Paul, 1978), 144; and A. Kenny, "Descartes on the Will," in *Cartesian Studies*, ed. R.J. Butler (Oxford: Basil Blackwell, 1972), 96 and *Descartes* (New York: Random House, 1968), 117.

[99] AT VII, 56: "nempe rationem nullam possum afferre, qua probem Deum mihi majorem quam dederit cognoscendi facultatem dare debuisse."

obligation to put in every creature all of the perfections that he has the power to put in some:[100] rather than nurture resentment, the *ego* must discover the perfection that God has given and continually gives to *mens humana*. Discretely, Descartes implies that rational investigation into human error cures the *ego* of egocentric wishes—helping the soul to prefer God's creative decrees over its own unbridled wishes.

In sharp contrast to the intellect, which receives information by finite increment, the free will is known by immediate experience to exceed every assignable limit.[101] The faculty of volition—*facultas eligendi sive volendi*—is inaugmentable: indeed whereas the *ego* can conceive of an intelligence that is infinitely greater than its own, the *ego* cannot conceive of a free will that is "more ample" than the free will that it finds in itself. God's free will, to be sure, is infinitely more firm and efficacious, extending to infinitely more things than the *ego*'s free will, but the principle itself of free volition, which is indivisibly one,[102] is not greater, as such, in God than in the *ego*.[103] Nothing in *mens humana* is more absolute and perfect than the faculty of free volition—which is why the *ego* understands itself to be made in God's image.[104] Let us note that, since the infinity of free volition is known by immediate inner perception,[105] the *ego* by willing perceives in its freedom three ideas in one: its similitude to God, the idea of infinity and its very self (*ego ipse*).[106] It follows that the *ego* can neither deny nor comprehend its freedom, which exceeds its intellect infinitely and is inseparable from the idea of self: *ego ipse*.

Is Descartes's radical contrast between the two faculties justified? Does the (limitlessly finite) human intellect differ from the (actually infinite) will, or does Descartes overlook their essential symmetry? To Ber-

---

[100] AT VII, 56: "Non tamen ideo puto illum in singulis ex sui operibus omnes perfectiones ponere debuisse, quas in aliquibus ponere potest."

[101] AT VII, 57: "nam sane nullis illam limitibus circumscribi experior."

[102] AT VII, 61: "cum enim voluntas in una tantum re, et tanquam in indivisibili consistat, non videtur ferre ejus natura ut quicquam ab illa demi possit."

[103] AT VII, 57: "non tamen, in se formaliter et praecise spectata, major videtur."

[104] Mediation IV, AT VII, 57: "adeo ut illa praecipue sit, ratione cujus imaginem quandam et similitudinem Dei me referre intelligo."

[105] See Descartes's response to Berman, AT V, 159: "Descendat modo unusquisque in semetipsum et experiatur annon perfectam et absolutam habeta voluntatem, et an possit quicquam concipere quod voluntatis libertate se antecellat. Nemo sane aliter expertus est. In eo igitur major est voluntas intellectu et Deo similior."

[106] Meditation III, AT VII, 51: "illamque similitudinem, in qua Dei idea continetur, a me percipi per eandem facultatem, per quam ego ipse a me percipior."

man's objection that, like willing, intellection, as such, "is intellection—so that our own intellect does not differ from God's",[107] Descartes answers that intellection is inseparable from the object on which it depends.[108] In other words, the intellect, which is passive, is limited by the object that informs it. While the human intellect knows and comprehends finite objects, the infinite totality of infinite truth, God, is known but not comprehended—indeed is known as the very idea of incomprehensibility. God, on the other hand, comprehends himself absolutely: God's intellect, "in which are hidden all of the treasures of science and wisdom,"[109] is actually infinite, infinitely surpassing the human intellect, which is inductive, potentially infinite only.[110] In sharp contrast, the will, which is active, depends on nothing outside of itself. The *facultas volendi* is "perfect and absolute," the same, as such, in the finite human soul as in God. The *ego* perceives its perfect and absolute freedom every time it decides to act or brings about a change simply by willing it.[111] Descartes defines free will as the ability to "do or not to do"—*vel facere vel non facere*—in the absence of external coercion. Specifically, the *ego* experiences itself as acting freely when it acts and at the same time "feels that no external force" determines it to act: *ut a nulla vi externa nos ad id determinari sentiamus*. What defines a force as "external" and what is implied by the *ego*'s very ability to detect outside coercion? First, since the *ego* is immaterial, any bodily force must count as "external" to the *ego*, which implies that the *ego* acts freely—and knows itself to act freely—only to the extent that no bodily appetite or natural force causes the action or determines its content. Brutes, which have no freedom at all, do not actually act but simply undergo changes in behavior caused by stimuli.[112]

Conversely, the experience of resisting/opposing a natural force or bodily appetite, provided it does not result from conditioning or in-

---

[107] Interview with Berman, 16 April 1648, AT V, 158: "sed et sic intelligere est intelligere, et sic nec differt noster intellectus ab Intellectu Dei, etiamsi illius ad plura se extendat."

[108] *Ibid.*: "Intelligere non est intelligere, cum hoc dependeat ab objecto et ab eo separari non possit."

[109] Meditation IV, AT VII, 53: "in quo nempe sunt omnes thesauri scientiarum et sapientiae absconditi."

[110] For Descartes's speculations about the beatific vision *in patria*, see his letter to Newcastle, March or April 1648, AT V, 136–137.

[111] Principes de Philosophy, Part I, Art. 39: "la liberté de notre volonté se connait sans preuve, par la seule experience que nous en avons." (AT IX, 41)

[112] *Regulae*, XII; AT X, 415.

stinct, vividly discloses the *ego*'s autonomy: deliberately resisting anger,
like struggling to hold one's ground against a violent wind,[113] reveals
the soul's power of free volition and, in fact, reveals the *ego* to itsef: *ego
ipse*. Actions that *I myself* cause, as opposed to motions that are caused
in me by external forces are *my* actions in a special and proper sense.
The Ignatian exercise of *agere contra*, designed to purify the exercitant
of worldly attachments and thus "rectify" the will by restoring its indifference, brings the *ego*, as we saw, face to face with its autonomy.[114] A
special case of *agere contra* is the resolve to resist the senses by suspending judgment: the *ego* discovers its agency (and its very existence) by
opposing the natural sway over it of sensory impression. By the same
token, since the *ego* has the power to suspend its judgment—since the
ego is free to refrain from acquiescing to sense impression—judgment
must be an act of the will rather than a perception of the intellect. No
matter how forcefully sensory perception suggests that things identical
to what is perceived exist extramentally, the *ego* remains free to reject
such a conclusion. Judgment *about* what is perceived is causally independent of perception proper. The intellect does not cause the *ego* to
pass judgment deterministically, as though judgment were a necessary
and inevitable effect of the understanding.[115] Rather, the *ego* determines
itself freely to affirm or deny what is proposed to it by the understanding, or to abstain. Moreover, by freely judging that judgment is not
caused by the intellect but by the will, the *ego* at once exercises its free
judgment and perceives the freedom of its arbitration (*arbitrii libertas*).
This brings us back to the genesis of errors (*errores mei*). Since both the
intellect and the free will are received immediately from God and are,
therefore, each perfect in its own right, neither faculty, as such, causes
my errors. The problem is that the will is more ample than the intellect
and

---

[113] See Descartes's dream of 1619, reported by Baillet, AT X, 181: "il fut repoussé
avec violence par le vent qui souffloit contre L'Eglise." For the power of resisting
anger, partly by regarding anger as an external force, see Descartes's letter to Elizabeth,
September 1, 1645, AT IV, 285.

[114] A nice indication of Descartes's familiarity with Ignatian *agere contra* is found in
a letter to Mersenne of January 1630, AT I, 110. Asked how Christian virtues "fit"
with natural virtues, Descartes argues that Christian virtues are designed to oppose
natural impulses "just as, when we have a curved stick, we bend it in the opposite
direction if we want to strengthen it. Since our nature is overly prone to vengeance,
God commands us, not only to forgive our enemies but to love them."

[115] Cf. Fifth Answers, AT VII, 378: "Non vis voluntatem in quicquam ferri ad quod
non determinatur ab intellectu."

"I do not contain it within these limits, but extend it to those things which I do not understand; and since the will is indifferent to these things, it easily deflects from the true and the good, with the result that I fall into error and sin."[116]

Errors, in other words, arise because judgment is a free act of the will rather than the computational result of intellection. The metaphor of *mens mea* as "unbridled" returns, but it is now *I myself*, the moral agent possessed of free will, who fail to exercise my freedom within the limits of truth: *I myself* who force my will to embrace what it neither understands nor loves, *I myself* who cause myself to "fall into error and sin." *Ad me proprius accedens*: the volition that lies behind every other volition, namely judgment, lies in my power alone and, therefore, singularizes me absolutely. Before acting, *I myself* form the decision to act simply by consenting to act. Whether my judgment is explicit or implicit only, I give it, not as *mens sive ratio* with properties that belong universally to all *mentes humanas* but as the absolutely unique free agent that I myself am, *ego ipse*, without precedent and without successor, *hors pair et hors série*.

The judgment that *I myself* make to act or not to act, on Descartes's analysis, is the *ego*'s most basic volition and the ultimate candidate for basic action.[117] By the same token, judgment is the *ego*'s most *personal* act, since God creates and sustains the *ego*'s power to act but puts its exercise in the *ego*'s power: *vis eligendi sive arbitrii libertas*. Moreover, the infinite excess of the *ego*'s power of judgment over its limited intelligence allows the *ego* to fail and, therefore, to discover itself as *personally* culpable. As though empowered to determine myself *without* my own will and *against* my will, I discover a crippling rift between my self-centered exercise of judgment and my will's "better judgment." What is meant by the will's "indifference"? What implicit connection is drawn between the will on the one hand, and the "good and the true?" on the other? By shifting the genesis of error from the intellect to the will, by making error culpable, Descartes's new theory of judgment brings the *ego* face to face with the paradox of freedom.

---

[116] AT VII, 58: "cum latius pateat voluntas quam intellectus, illam non intra eosdem limites contineo, sed etiam ad illa quae non intelligo extendo; ad quae cum sit indifferens, facile vero et boni deflectit, atque ita et fallor et pecco."

[117] For a definition of basic action and the argument that volition best satisfies the criteria, see Hugh McCann, "Volition and Basic Action," *The Philosophical Review* 83 (1974), 451–473.

CHAPTER TEN

BEYOND OBEDIENCE AND INDIFFERENCE

Descartes's initial theory of judgment, as we saw in the *Regulae*, made judgment a function of the intellect. Descartes attributed two faculties to the intellect: a faculty of cognition, through which a thing is intuited and cognized, and a faculty of judgment, through which the intellect judges what is cognized by affirming it or denying it (*affirmando vel negando*).[1] On this first theory, judgment is determined by cognition and follows from cognition by necessity. This uncontroversial intellectualist picture of judgment presented a double advantage for Descartes. First, as the very project of the *Regulae* attests, it meant that reforming the intellect would suffice to reform scientific judgment and launch the project of a new science against both skeptics and dogmatic Aristotelians.[2] Secondly, and more critically, it secured the key Cartesian axiom that simple natures are known perfectly and indubitably, since the same intellect cannot both intuit a simple nature and judge it not to be simple—i.e. judge it to contain something that is not actually intuited.[3]

Descartes's initial attempt to renovate science thus based itself on the widely-held assumption that scientific knowledge is produced exclusively by the intellect, contributing only the restriction that no cognitive means be trusted except for rational intuition and deduction.[4] Since judgment was necessitated by cognition, all that was needed to safeguard scientists from error was to establish rules for the intelligence. If a chief reason to pursue new knowledge lay in presenting the will with improved choices for action,[5] reforming the intellect, as such, was the key to the project.

---

[1] *Regulae*, Rule XII, AT X, 420: "Distinguamus illam facultatem intellectus, per quam res intuetur et cognoscit, ab ea qua judicat affirmando vel negando."

[2] As suggested by *Regulae*, Rule II, AT X, 362: "Ita per hanc propositionem rejicimus illas omnes probabiles tantum cognitiones."

[3] *Ibid.*: "nam si de illa vel minimum quid mente attingamus, quod profecto necessarium est, cum de eadem nos aliquid judicare supponatur, ex hoc ipso concludendum est, nos totam illam cognoscere."

[4] *Regulae*, Rule III, AT X, 370.

[5] *Regulae*, Rule I, 361.

Perhaps advised by Bérulle, Descartes concluded Rule III, as we saw, with a provision aimed at safeguarding religious belief. Descartes's strategy consisted in segregating science from faith by making science depend strictly on the intellect and faith depend just as strictly on the will:

> "[Rational intuition and deduction] are the two secure paths that lead to science: as far as the intellect is concerned, no other paths must be admitted, rather all other paths must be rejected as suspect and liable to error. But this does not prevent us, where what is divinely revealed is concerned, from believing it as more certain than all other knowledge (*omni cognitione certiora credimus*), since faith, which bears always on obscure things, is an act, not of the intellect, but of the will."[6]

Descartes's intellectualist theory of judgment allowed him in effect to propose a sort of double-truth theory. On the one hand, scientific truths are known and affirmed intellectually, on the basis of rational evidence. Error is avoided by preventing faulty intellections from resulting in faulty judgment. On the other hand, revealed truths are embraced voluntarily, without rational evidence. Since the intellect is powerless either to know or to affirm them, religious beliefs cannot be challenged on rational grounds. And since religious beliefs depend on the will alone, avoiding error requires submitting only the will, not the intellect, to the authority of the Church.[7] Moreover, an act of the will suffices to bracket religious beliefs and safeguard them from systematic doubt, since only what is open to intellectual judgment is open to doubt.[8]

By excluding judgment from the realm of religious belief, Descartes felt he could champion scientific innovation without threatening the "obscure things" of faith. What is more, Descartes never denied the possibility of framing rational "preambles of faith": Rather, Rule III specifies that, *if* revealed truths have intelligible foundations, these foundations must be discovered and established by the only two reliable intellectual means to knowledge, namely rational intuition or deduction—"as we will perhaps show one day at more length."[9] Presumably,

---

[6] AT X, 370: "Atque hae duae viae (sc. intuitus et deductio) sunt ad scientiam certissimae, neque plures ex parte ingenii debent admitti, sed aliae omnes ut suspectae erroribusque obnoxiae rejiciendae sunt; quod tamen non impedit quominus illa, quae divinitus revelata sunt, omni cognitione certiora credamus, cum illorum fides, quaecumque est de obscuris, non ingenii actio sit, sed voluntatis."

[7] As Descartes explains in *Discours de la Méthode*, Part VI, AT VI, 60.

[8] See *Discours de la Méthode*, Part III, AT VI, 28.

[9] AT X, 370: "Si quae in intellectu habeat fundamenta, illa omnium maxime per

the intelligible foundations of religious belief would be judged by the intellect to be true, and also embraced by the will as unsurpassably certain. The compatibility of science and faith would be secured. Intellect and will would strengthen the rational basis of religious doctrine by working independently of one another.

When Descartes announced in Rule III that he planned to elaborate new preambles of faith,[10] he assumed that the intelligible foundations of religious doctrine were strictly metaphysical. The project was to establish a rational metaphysics (proving God's existence and the soul's incorruptibility) to serve as the foundation for "theology proper," where the will alone held sway. Descartes had not yet fully elaborated his new mechanistic physics nor encountered areas of religious doctrine that involved *res extensa*. As we know, however, Descartes in 1630 stumbled against a very specific problem: his new theory of colors had to be reconciled with Catholic teaching regarding the eucharist.[11] Forced to explain the whiteness that remains in the host after the substance of the bread has been removed, Descartes spent considerable time framing a new Cartesian theory of transubstantiation, as his detailed answer to Arnauld and later letters to Mesland indicate.[12] In the process, did Descartes rethink, not only the physics of appearances, but how rational perception and judgment are related? If the intellect both perceives (*percipio, intelligo*) and affirms the truth of what is perceived, how is the epistemologic subject able to refrain from affirming that the consecrated host is bread? Must he affirm that the host is bread by a rational judgment but then override his own judgment by an act of will? If, on the other hand, *all* judgments are acts of the will, the problem disappears. Judgment lies consistently within the subject's power and becomes a matter of free choice and moral responsibility. The epistemologic subject is now free to affirm that the host, before consecration, is bread, based on natural evidence (and God's indubitable veracity);

---

alterutram ex viis jam dictis inveniri possint et debeant, ut aliquando fortasse fusum ostendemus."

[10] Presumably, the "beginning of metaphysics" dating from 1629 (See AT I, 350) is the project intimated in *Regulae* Rule III.

[11] See Letter to Mersenne, 25 November, 1630, AT I, 179. Speaking of a "Discourse on Light" to be included in the *Dioptrique*, Descartes writes: "car y voulant décrire les couleurs à ma mode, et par conséquent estant obligé d'y expliquer comment la blancheur du pain demeure au saint Sacrement, je seray bien aise de le faire examiner par mes amis, avant qu'il soit vu de tout le monde."

[12] Fourth Answers, AT VII, 247–256; and Letters CCCLXXIX, AT IV, 215–217, CDXVII, AT IV, 344–348.

and he is equally free to affirm that the consecrated host is the body of Christ, based on supernatural evidence (and God's indubitable veracity). On the earlier theory, the strict segregation of the two spheres, intellectual and voluntary, meant that the epistemologic subject could *believe* that the consecrated host is not bread, but he could not *affirm* it, since affirming and denying was a function of the intellect.

In contrast, on the new theory, the subject both knows and affirms that what he receives is not bread, since judgment is a free act of the will. Descartes may indeed have had good reason to boast that his theory of the eucharist "solved every difficulty."[13] Descartes not only dispensed with scholastic qualities (whiteness) but, in transferring judgment from the intellect to the will, rescued transubstantiation from requiring a double-truth theory. Descartes himself was eager to emphasize the elegantly integrated character of his new theory of judgment. In the Second Answers, he points out that the will is "moved to acquiesce" by two types of light, the natural light of reason and the supernatural light of grace.[14] If the intellect no longer forces judgment, various degrees of voluntary assent are given to various types of evidence. The epistemologic subject is consistently able to guard himself from error at every level, but also to affirm that his religious beliefs are *true*, without contradiction. Writing to Hyperaspistes, Descartes explains that faith means preferring the light of grace to the natural light,[15] which no longer means overriding judgment but simply suspending judgment voluntarily at one level in order to exercise it at a higher level.

The transfer of judgment from the intellect to the will raises, however, a special difficulty. If intellection does not determine judgment, how is "acquiescence" in the will determined? In order to appreciate Descartes's innovation, let us review the main lines of Descartes's mature analysis. The separate soul, *mens*, thinks in two basic ways, namely by perceiving (*percipio, intelligo*), which is a passion of the soul that is made possible by the power of cognition (*vis cognoscendi*); and

---

[13] Fourth Answers, AT VII, 254; "Quae omnes difficultates per meam hujus rei explicationem plane tolluntur." See also 252: "Quae omnia per mea principia explicantur, ut non modo nihil habeam quod verear, ne orthodoxis Theologis offendiculo sit futurum, sed potius magnam me ab ipsis gratiam initurum esse confidam, quod eas in Physica proponam opiniones, quae longe melius quam vulgares cum Theologia consentiant."

[14] Second Answers, AT VII, 148: "Notandum est claritatem, sive perspicuitatem, a qua moveri potest nostra voluntas ad assentiendum, duplicem esse: aliam scilicet a lumine naturali, et aliam a gratia divina."

[15] AT III, 426.

by willing, which is an action of the soul that is made possible by the power of election (*vis eligendi sive voluntas*).[16] The intellect is reduced, in effect, to a single faculty, namely cognition, conceived as a purely receptive aptitude for truth.[17] The will, or faculty of election, is, on the contrary, an active moral power. Meditation IV establishes that, unlike the finite intellect, the free will, as such, is infinite and inaugmentable, which means that the *ego*'s freedom, taken strictly as such, is not less than God's freedom.[18] This absolute infinity of freedom is known by immediate experience and is the chief reason why the *ego* understands itself to bear God's image and semblance.[19] We learn, finally, that the free will, *arbitrii libertas*, is the freedom in us to pass judgment: the free will is the faculty by means of which we "affirm or deny, pursue or shun," or, more exactly, the faculty by means of which we "affirm or deny what is proposed to us by the understanding without experiencing ourselves to be compelled to do so by an outside force."[20]

What is transferred from the intellect to the will is thus precisely the power of affirmation and denial in which judgment consists: no longer determined automatically by the understanding, judgment is now a voluntary act. The *ego* freely acquiesces to what the intellect proposes, or rejects it, by a voluntary determination of the will rather than by an involuntary determination of the intellect. *All* truths are affirmed freely.

Whereas errors in judgment, on the discarded intellectualist theory, could only result from faulty understanding, they now result from rash action. The electivist theory of judgment transforms judgment from a neutral operation occurring in the same way in every *ego* to a moral action that singularizes each *ego* irreducibly. Affirming falsehoods is now a preventable misuse by the *ego* of its free agency rather than an inher-

---

[16] Principes, I, 32; and Passions, I, Art. 17. Note the similarity with John Searle's analysis in *Intentionality*, p. 91.

[17] See Fifth Answers, AT VII, 378: "Plane repugnare mihi persuado, ut intellectus falsum sub ratione veri apprehendat."

[18] AT VII, 57: "sane nullis illam limitibus circumscribi experior" and "sola est voluntas, sive arbitrii libertas, quam tantam in me experior, ut nullius majoris ideam apprehendam."

[19] *Ibid.*: "adeo ut illa praecipue sit, ratione cujus imaginem quandam et similitudinem Dei me referre intelligo."

[20] AT VII, 57: "tantum in eo consistit, quod idem, vel facere vel non facere (hoc est affirmare vel negare, prosequi vel fugere) possimus, vel potius in eo tantum, quod ad id quod nobis ab intellectu proponitur affirmandum vel negandum, sive prosequendum vel fugiendum, ita feramur, ut a nulla vi externa nos ad id determinari sentiamus."

ent infirmity of the understanding: *libertate arbitrii non recte utor*:[21] The new theory of judgment gives sudden primacy to the notions of right and wrong action, along with the notion of culpability, in which the *ego* discovers a personal identity as the agent of its own perfection. Not only does the new electivist theory of judgment exonerate God of blame for human fallibility, it brings to light the spiritual advantage to each *ego* of being fallible. Far from predestining the *ego* to error, the finitude of human intelligence provides the *ego* with a special opportunity to be responsible for itself and indeed improve itself by acting well:

> "I have no right (*jus*) to complain that God wanted me to play a part (*personam sustinere*) in the world that is not of the highest and most preeminent rank in perfection. On the contrary: even though I cannot abstain from errors through the first way, which depends on having a clear and evident perception of everything to be judged, I can abstain from errors through the second way, which depends alone on this: that I remember to abstain from passing judgment every time the truth of a thing lacks clarity."[22]

We have no difficulty in recognizing that the "first way" of avoiding errors is none other than Descartes's abandoned theory of judgment, which put the whole burden on the intellect. By transferring judgment from the intellect to the will, Descartes made a threefold adjustment. First, the *ego* is cured of folly and ingratitude. Instead of a right to complain (*jus conquerendi*) about its middling rank in the scale of creation and, in particular about its finite intelligence and fallibility, the *ego* must be grateful for the infinite freedom that marks it as a moral agent (*debeo gratias ejus datori*).[23]

Secondly, admitting ignorance now testifies to moral perfection rather than cognitive deficiency: the *ego* has a moral incentive to suspend judgment in the face of insufficient evidence and its perfection is enhanced, not diminished, by preferring limited but true science over vanity. Finally, third and most conclusively, the *ego* discovers its proper vocation: unlike more perfect beings (angels), the *ego* is called to be virtuous, not omniscient. The *ego*'s "principal and highest perfection" lies

---

[21] Meditation IV, AT VII, 59.

[22] Meditation IV, AT VII, 61–62: "Et nullum habeo jus conquerendi quod eam me Deus in mundo personam sustinere voluerit, quae non est omnium praecipua et maxime perfecta. Ac praeterea etiam ut non possim ab erroribus abstinere priori illo modo qui pendent ab evidenti eorum omnium perceptione de quibus est deliberandum, possum tamen illo altero qui pendent ab eo tantum, quod recorder, quoties de veritate non liquet, ajudicio ferendo esse, abstinendum."

[23] Meditation IV, AT VII, 60.

in the daily effort of avoiding error, which is to say, in the right use of its free agency, not in noetic brilliance.[24] The *ego*'s good judgments, not its keen intellections, define its personal worth and measure its spiritual stature. What is gained by understanding the genesis of error (*lucratum esse existimo*) is not greater intelligence, as expected, but a new moral identity. By judging that man's "highest and preeminent" perfection lies in avoiding error, the *ego* freely affirms the supremacy of mental actions, no matter how humble, over mental passions, not matter how great. Implicitly, the *ego* acquires more perfection by a single voluntary suspension of judgment than by perceiving myriad truths.

The same premiss, that the *ego* is defined by the actions that it freely initiates rather than by the illuminations that it receives, lies at the heart of Francis of Sales's doctrine. Francis of Sales warns *Philothée* against wishing to receive special graces. The deliberate volitions that lie in *Philothée*'s own power are of greater spiritual benefit, no matter how humble, than illuminations and ecstasies, no matter how divine.[25] The key is that illuminations are not virtues.[26] Virtues are "acquired through work and industry" and alone are necessary to love and serve God.[27] Much like Descartes, Francis of Sales stresses that human perfection lies primarily in acting well, rather than in knowing much: *Philothée* must stop dreaming about receiving angelic insights and confine herself to follow the "more humble but more secure" path of virtue.[28]

Francis of Sales's point is that God has created us with a finite intellect but has left it in our power to conquer a host of small, daily virtues through our own care and effort.[29] Similarly, Descartes's new electivist theory of judgment implies that cautious and deliberate progress in science is preferable to rapid advance based on luck and acci-

---

[24] AT VII, 62: "Qua in re (sc. in habitu non errandi) cum maxima et praecipua hominis perfectio consistat, non parum me hodierna meditatione lucratum esse existimo, quod erroris et falsitatis causam investigarim."

[25] See, e.g., *Introduction à la vie dévote*, Part III, c. II, in *Oeuvres*, 131–132: "Il ne faut pas prétendre à telles grâces, puisqu'elles ne sont nullement nécessaires pour bien servir et aimer Dieu, qui doit être notre unique prétention; aussi, bien souvent ne sont-ce pas des grâces qui puissent être acquises par le travail et industrie, puisque ce sont plutôt des passions que des actions."

[26] *Ibid.*: "Voyez-vous, Philothée, ces perfections ne sont pas des vertus."

[27] *Ibid.*: "Il ne faut pas prétendre à de telles grâces (sc. extases ou ravissements), puisqu'elles ne sont nullement nécessaires pour bien servir et aimer Dieu."

[28] *Introduction à la vie dévote*, Part III, c. 2, in *Oeuvres*, I, 131–132.

[29] *Ibid.*: "Exerçons-nous simplement, humblement et dévotement aux petites vertus, la conquête desquelles Notre-Seigneur a exposée à notre soin et travail."

dents.[30] Science requires conscientious judgments at every step—voluntary affirmations and denials which only a free causal agent made in God's image is able to do. Cartesian science is thus primarily a schooling of the will, not a display of the intelligence—a means to "conquer" the virtue of voluntary self-discipline and "acquire the habit of not erring."[31]

The electivist theory of judgment sheds retrospective light on the *ego*'s initial confusion and leads us to the heart of Descartes's spiritual anthropology. The first question to be answered after the genesis of error is discovered is the following: if the power to avoid error is innate, why does *mens mea* specifically "delight" (*gaudet*) in error? The *ego* is confronted with a double experience of freedom, negative and positive. Negatively, freedom consists in the experience that nothing prevents the *ego* from freely turning its attention in every direction, affirming/denying at face value whatever presents itself. Since the *ego* experiences, on the one hand, a lack of constraint in shifting its attention from object to object but feels each time constrained, on the other hand, by perception, the *ego* equates freedom with the ability to act arbitrarily and judges that judgment, in contrast, follows from information deterministically.

The *ego*'s freedom of judgment, *arbitrii libertas*, in short, veils itself until the *ego* knows itself more properly. Before the *ego* discovers the author of its origin, the *ego*, in effect, puts all of its trust in its own intellect. A new dimension of *reversus ad me* comes to light: greedy for information, the *ego* delights in the very indifference that allows it to roam from intellection to intellection, with the result that the *ego* accumulates "knowledge" uncritically. Aware of its independence from material causes but not yet aware of its dependence on God, the *ego* constitutes itself by default (*privatio*) as its own absolute center and seat of arbitration. Descartes implies, in effect, that the *ego* in this state of partial self-knowledge mistakes itself for God: ignorant of the self-discipline that is required for good judgment, the *ego* endorses every cognition as *per se* indubitable, and thus deceives itself and sins: *ita et fallor et pecco*.

The *ego* is rescued from its confusion by the discovery of God's existence. The key to the emergence of a positive idea of freedom is, as we suggested, the *obligation*—literally *ob-ligatio*—to Another, namely to

---

[30] Meditation IV, AT VII, 61.
[31] AT VII, 62.

God, that the *ego*'s existence *ab alio* defines with absolute necessity (*"sum, ergo deus est"*). Neither a positive theory of freedom nor an electivist theory of judgment is conceivable by the finite *ego* until God's existence is known. Not only is God's existence the "first truth from which all truths proceed and on which all truths depend,"[32] but the judgment that God exists is the first judgment from which a positive theory of freedom proceeds, since the *ego*, by affirming that God alone is necessary *a se*, affirms its own radical contingency and dependence. The judgment that God exists prevents the *ego* from affirming itself as *causa sui* and usurping God's place. A sharp contrast is revealed between the *ego*'s state of volitional indifference, which now must be regarded as the extrinsic upper limit of a purely negative freedom, and God's indifference, which defines the incomprehensible perfection of positive freedom.[33]

The *ego*'s initial delight in straying from the limits of truth—which is to say, in acting arbitrarily—both shows the *ego* its freedom and blinds it to the nature of freedom. Since only an immaterial *res cogitans* has the power to detach itself from stimuli at will, the *ego* concludes that free actions (the experience of being detached from stimuli at will) and intellections (the experience of being determined by stimuli) are antithetical. As long as the *ego* is ignorant of its origin, the *ego* is powerless to detect the voluntary nature of its judgments. More exactly, the *ego* is prevented from considering its judgments to be free as long as *mens mea* delights in acting arbitrarily. The *ego*, wrongly assuming its intellect to be absolute, reasons that, if its judgments were free volitions rather than deterministic intellectual computations, they would, in principle, be unpredictable. Indeed a problem raised by any theory of free agency concerns the unpredictability of voluntary actions. If a causal agent is radically free, if free actions *cannot be determined* by circumstances, or prior events, or states of mind, what prevents free actions from being completely random?[34] In order

---

[32] To Mersenne, May 6, 1630, AT I, 150.

[33] On God's freedom of indifference, see Sixth Answers, AT VII, 431–432: "Repugnat enim Dei voluntatem non fuisse ab aeterno indifferentem ad omnia quae facta sunt aut unquam fient, quia nullum bonum, vel verum, nullumque credendum, vel faciendum, vel omittendum fingi potest, cujus idea in intellectu divino prius fuerit, quam ejus voluntas se determinarit ad efficiendum ut id tale esset."

[34] See Robert Kane, "Two Kinds of Incompatibilism," *Philosophy and Phenomenological Research*, Vol. I, No. 2, December 1989, 227: "Agent cause theorist like Taylor disallow any explanations of agent causation in terms of reasons or causes. But, this leaves them

for the *ego* to abandon an intellectualist theory of judgment, the *ego* must be able to explain how it is possible for voluntray judgments to be appropriate to intellections without being necessitated by intellections.

As we saw, the *ego*'s freedom of judgment, *arbitrii libertas*, is God's image and contains God's idea.[35] Implicitly, only a free agent has the idea of an infinitely free God who willingly creates a free agent *ex nihilo*. Similarly, since the *ego*'s freedom of judgment contains God's idea, it must contain the idea of an incomprehensible infinity of perfection, which means that the *ego* must judge that its freedom of judgment is, ultimately, incomprehensible. God's infinite perfection and the *ego*'s freedom of judgment are both incomprehensible: to affirm them is to affirm the *ego*'s power to affirm what is defined by its very incomprehensibility. But since God is supremely good and true,[36] the *ego* must somehow be tied, precisely as a free agent, to the good and the true in a radical way. How? So far, we know that the will falls away from the good and the true (*a vero et bono deflectit*) when used "indifferently." For the *ego* to deceive itself and sin and for the will to fall away from the good and true are one and the same. Does the will's indifference *precede* the *ego*'s abuse and make it possible? Or does the *ego*, by default, cause the will to be indifferent by failing to present it with what is good and true? Is the will, as such, capable of states other than indifference, or is indifference the will's very essence?

In order for a positive theory of freedom to emerge, three breakthroughs in understanding must occur: first, the *ego* must judge that the power of volition that marks it as made in God's image results from a radically free volition on God's part; second, as a consequence of the first, the *ego* must judge that omniscience is not its most appropriate goal; third, the *ego* must judge that free volition allows it to take personal responsibility for its perfection and thus singularizes it from every other possible *ego*. The first two are realized in Meditation III; the third step is the task of Meditation IV.

---

without any answer to the critical question: 'Why did the agent do A rather than B or B rather than A?'"

[35] Meditation III, AT VII, 51, cited above: "illamque similitudinem, in qua Dei idea continetur."

[36] Second Answers, AT VII, 144: "Cum enim Deus sit summum ens, non potest non esse etiam summum bonum et verum."

10.1. *The Will's Propensity*

Descartes captures the essence of free volition with two closely related statements. First, we learn that indifference is not the essence of human freedom.[37] Free agency is not the capacity to pursue, indifferently, action *a* or action *b*, but rather the capacity to pursue action *a* all the more willingly (i.e. all the less arbitrarily) that action *a* is known to be worthy of pursuit:

> "There is no need for me to be able to will two alternatives equally in order to be free. On the contrary, the more I lean towards one of the two, either because I understand that the good and the true are evidently in it, or because God thus disposes my inner thought, the more freely I elect it. For it is obvious that neither grace, nor natural understanding, ever diminishes freedom: rather, they increase freedom and strengthen it."[38]

The state of indifference is now cast as a state in which the *ego* is inclined neither to act nor to refrain from acting because no good reason presents itself on either side.[39] Since freedom increases with a positive inclination in the will to pursue action *a*, rather than not pursue it, freedom is defined, and even "measured," as a positive inner inclination to act: a *willingness to act*, which is basically a willingness to bring about an inner change, starting with a self-determination to act, without outside coercion. Free agency thus coincides in practice with the experience of an autonomous overcoming of indecision.

How does *willingness to act* arise in the agent and how is it increased? As Descartes explains, natural understanding increases the *ego*'s free-

---

[37] The passage in Meditation IV is reiterated in the Sixth Answers, At VII, 433: "Indifferentia non pertinet ad essentiam humanae libertatis, cum non modo simus liberi, quando ignorantia recti nos reddit indifferentes, sed maxime etiam quando clara perceptio ad aliquid prosequendum impellit."

[38] AT VII, 57–58: "Neque enim opus est me in utramque partem ferri posse, ut sim liber, sed contra, quo magis in una propendeo, sive quia rationem veri et boni in ea evidenter intelligo, sive quia Deus intima cogitationis meae ita disponit, tanto liberius illam eligo; nec sane divina gratia, nec naturalis cognitio unquam imminuunt libertatem, sed potius augent et corroborant."

[39] It is not unlikely that Descartes was familiar with some of the ideas expressed by Buridan in his commentary on Aristotle's *Nicomachean Ethics*, printed in Paris in 1513. Buridan's argument that the will is free to hesitate between two equal alternatives, parodied by later opponents as the dilemma of "Buridan's ass," (the ass starves because it cannot decide between two equal piles of hay), bears a resemblance to Descartes's discussion of indifference. For a good introduction to Buridan and a useful bibliography, see the *Stanford Encyclopedia of Philosophy*, online at http://plato.stanford.edu/entries/buridan/.

dom by providing the *ego* with a good and true reason to act. Grace, in turn, increases the *ego*'s freedom by "disposing" the *ego* to act, presumably by providing a good and true supernatural reason to act. Thus while free agency as a principle is absolutely infinite and inaugmentable, Descartes frames the exercise of free agency as a function correlating the intellect and the will without causal determinism: the greater the light in the *ego*'s understanding, the greater the inclination (*propensio*) that follows in the *ego*'s will.[40]

We know from our previous discussion that one effect of grace is that the will's *propensio* to act is more greatly increased by grace than by natural evidence: the *ego* benefitting from grace *prefers* the light of grace to the natural light,[41] which means that the *ego*'s inner willingness to act when moved by grace supersedes its willingness to act when moved by reason. Implicitly, the highest rational freedom experienced by the *ego* is the freedom to pause and adore God's immense light,[42] while the highest freedom *tout court* is the freedom to affirm the truths of faith and fulfill evangelical precepts.

With characteristic restraint, Descartes points out that "if I always knew clearly what is good and true, I would never hesitate in my judgment and would be entirely free without ever being indifferent."[43] Only when we read the same formulation again in a letter to Mesland, but this time applied to Christ, does the quietly passionate dimension of Descartes's theory become visible.[44]

Conversely, the *ego* is *not free at all* if it acts without inclination, arbitrarily. The danger of a state of indifference is precisely that the *ego* feels *no* propensity to act at all, not even a propensity to refrain deliberately from acting.[45] Once the *ego* knows itself properly and knows

---

[40] Meditation IV, AT VII, 59: *debeo gratias ejus datori.*

[41] Cf. Letter to Hyperaspistes, AT III, 426.

[42] Meditation III, AT VII, 52: "immensi hujus luminis pulchritudinem intueri, admirari, adorare."

[43] Meditation IV, AT VII, 58: "Si semper quid verum et bonum sit clare viderem, nunquam de eo quod esset judicandum vel eligendum deliberarem; atque ita, quamvis plane liber, nunquam tamen indifferens esse possem."

[44] See Letter to Mesland, May 2 1644 (?), AT IV, 117: "On ne laisse pas de meriter, bien que, voyant tres-clairement ce qu'il faut faire, on fasse infalliblement, et sans aucune indifference, *comme a fait Iesus-Christ en cette vie.*" Emphasis added.

[45] See e.g. the *ego*'s indifference with regard to the real distinction between body and soul, Meditation IV, AT VII, 59: "Suppono nullam adhuc intellectui meo rationem occurrere, quae mihi unum magis quam aliud persuadeat. Certe ex hoc ipso sum indifferens ad utrumlibet affirmandum vel negandum, *vel etiam ad nihil de ea re judicandum.*" Emphasis added.

that its perfection lies in acting well rather than in knowing much, the state of indifference is experienced as painful by the *ego* rather than as "delightful." Indifference cripples free agency and condemns the *ego* to inaction. Tormented by indecision, the *ego* cannot act freely, willingly, rationally, until reason persuades it (*ratio persuadet*) that the only *free* action possible in a state of indifference is the self-determination not to act. By suspending judgment, the *ego* avoids acting arbitrarily and exercises a minimal freedom: *infimus gradus libertatis*.[46] Freedom of indifference is thus a test in which the *ego* has a chance to practice self-control for its own sake, in preparation for higher degrees of freedom.

The axiom behind Descartes's correlation of degrees of light in the intellect and magnitudes of propensity in the will is given *more geometrico* in the Second Answers:

> "The will of a *res cogitans* is carried, voluntarily and freely (this indeed belongs to the essence of the will) but nonetheless infallibly to a good that is clearly known."[47]

The axiom implies that *propensio* in the will—what the *ego* experiences as willingness to act—is elicited predictibly, yet not deterministically, by the intellection of a good. The "good and the true" is reduced simply to "good," implying that the will is carried to affirm a truth because a truth is, first and foremost, a good. But the passive form (*fertur*) and the claim of infallibility (*infallibiliter*) seem to contradict the claim of radical autonomy (*voluntarie et libere*). If the will *is carried* infallibly to a good that is known to it, then it seems that its freedom lies in yielding, or submitting, to the good in question, which implies that human freedom is a freedom of obedience, as argued, most notably, by Etienne Gilson.[48] Descartes's own testimony that his theory of freedom agrees with Gibieuf's theory,[49] his explicit remark to Elizabeth that "wisdom consists in submitting to God's will,"[50] and his famous statement to

---

[46] Meditation IV, AT VII, 58.

[47] "Rei cogitantis voluntas fertur, voluntarie quidem et libere (hoc enim est de essentia voluntatis), sed nihilhominus infallibiliter, in bonum sibi clare cognitum." (AT VII, 166).

[48] Cf. E. Gilson, *La liberté chez Descartes et la théologie* (Paris: Alcan, 1913).

[49] See the letter to Mersenne of April 21, 1641, AT III, 360: "Pour ce que j'ai écrit, que l'Indifférence est plustost un défaut qu'une perfection de la liberté en nous [...] je me promets que le Pere Gibieuf deffendra bien ma cause en ce point là; car je n'ai rien écrit qui ne s'accorde avec ce qu'il a mis dans son livre *de Libertate*." On Gibieuf's treatise, see F. Ferrier, *Un Oratorien ami de Descartes. Guillaume Gibieuf et sa philosophie de la liberté* (Paris: Vrin, 1980).

[50] Letter of August 18, 1645, AT IV, 373.

Mersenne that he "never treated of the infinite except to submit to it,"[51] strongly support Gilson's interpretation.

On the other hand, if the will is carried *freely*, of its own accord, it seems that the will's motion is not caused by the good that is perceived, which implies that the will enjoys a freedom of indifference, a "supranoetic" freedom, as a critic of Gilson's interpretation has recently argued.[52] Descartes himself emphasizes that the will is free "to move to one or the other of two alternatives without being determined by the intellect."[53] Is this "supranoetic" freedom true only in the absence of a clearly known good? Descartes in Meditation IV explicates *libere* as *sponte*: the less indifferent I am to what I perceive, the more "spontaneously and freely" I believe it (*sponte et libere*). In the absence of a clearly known good, is the will carried *nowhere* or is it carried *anywhere*, but not spontaneously, not of its own accord? Does the *ego* abuse its freedom when it acts willfully rather than willingly? If the *ego*'s lowest degree freedom consists in self-control for its own sake, does the *ego* deceive itself and sin when it acts licentiously and "does violence" to its own will?

It is helpful at this point to call attention to the similarity between Descartes's axiom and Francis of Sales's definition of the will, which is rooted in scholastic theology:

> "The will has such a great aptitude for the good that, as soon as a good is perceived, the will turns towards it in order to delight in it as in its very congenial object."[54]

On the Salesian picture, the will spontaneously *turns towards* the good that it perceives in order to delight in it. Implicitly, the will cannot delight in falsehood or evil except by mistake—which is also Descartes's

---

[51] Letter to Mersenne, January 28, 1641, AT III, 293: "Je n'ai jamais traité de l'infini que pour me soumettre à lui."

[52] T. Gonthier, *Descartes et la causa Sui* (Paris: Vrin, 2005), 139.

[53] AT VII, 378: "… ansque illa voluntatis libertate, se ipsam sine determinatione intellectus in unam aut alteram partem movendi, quam negabas."

[54] F. de Sales, *Traité de l'Amour de Dieu*, Bk. I, c. 7 ("Description de l'Amour en général"), in *Oeuvres Complètes*, I, 369: "La volonté a une si grande convenance avec le bien, que tout aussitôt qu'elle l'aperçoit elle se tourne de son côté pour se complaire en icelui, comme en son objet très agréable." For scholastic roots, see e.g. Peter Aureoli, *Commentarium in Primum Librum Sententiarum*, Romae, 1596, Distinctio X, Quaestio XXVII (Utrum Spiritus Sanctus procedat ut amor), Articulus tertius: "Quod spiritus in nobis est ipsamet anima, vi amoris egrediens ad amatum."

position, based explicitly on scholastic teaching.[55] To be exact, the will itself never delights in falsehood, rather it is the *ego* that delights in falsehood by mistake, pursuing and affirming false goods without any propensity in the will to do so. It follows that delighting in error—*gaudet aberrare*—separates *mens mea* from the innate capacity for free agency, as though no *ego* were available to determine itself freely to act: deaf to the will's rational propensity to pursue truth as its good, the *ego* unwittingly lets its agency be usurped by alien forces, which means indeed that "my mind" but not *I myself* is in charge of volition. A last interpretation of *reversus ad me* suggests itself: the *ego* falls victim to myriad errors when it falls away from the image of God within and, bereft of genuine free agency, willfully (but not freely) delights in nothingness.[56]

Both Descartes and Francis of Sales admit two different meanings of "natural instinct": a rational instinct that is found in human beings but not in brutes, and a physical instinct to conserve the body and gratify physical appetites, which is shared with brutes.[57] Presumably, the rational instinct is none other than the will's spontaneous *propensio* to turn to the good and the true, while the bio-somatic instinct pushes the *ego* to gratify physical appetites. The *ego* must therefore free itself from the dictatorship of bodily passions—including the cognitive dictatorship of the senses—before it can accede to a minimal degree of freedom by recognizing indifference *as indifference*. A conscious experience of indifference is required before the *ego* is in a position to discover the liberating power of self-control. Like a separatrix, indifference is an ideal limit that separates a realm of increasing freedom above from a realm of increasing subjugation below.

---

[55] Letter to Mersenne, April 27, 1637, AT I, 366: "Il me semble que la doctrine ordinaire de l'école est que *voluntas non fertur in malum, nisi quatenus ei sub aliqua ratione boni repraesentatur ab intellectu*, d'où vient ce mot: *omnis peccans est ignorans*; en sorte que si jamais l'entendement ne representoit rien à la volonté comme bien, qui ne le fust, elle ne pourroit manquer son élection." See also Descartes's Letter to Mesland, 2 May 1644, AT IV, 117: "c'est pourquoy on dit que *omnis peccans est ignorans*."

[56] Cf. Francis of Sales, *Introduction à la vie dévote*, Part I, c. IX, 48: "Je ne veux plus désormais me complaire en moi-même, qui de ma part ne suis rien. De quoi te glorifies-tu, *ô poudre et cendre*, mais plutôt, ô vrai néant?" See also *Traité de l'Amour de Dieu*, Bk. I, c. X, in *Oeuvres*, I, 383: "tandis que la partie intellectuelle de notre âme travaille à l'amour honnête et vertueux, sur quelque objet qui en est digne, il arrive souvent que les sens et facultés de la partie inférieure tendent à l'union qui leur est propre."

[57] See Descartes's letter to Mersenne, Octobre 16, 1639, AT II, 599. For Francis of Sales, see *Traité de l'Amour de Dieu*, Bk. I, c. X, in *Oeuvres*, I, 381–382.

According to Francis of Sales, three distinct stages lead upward to free agency, counteracting mirror stages that lead downward to spiritual death. First, the will is *inspired* by the light of reason or of grace (as opposed to tempted by sin); secondly, the will *delights* in the inspiration (rather than delight in temptation); finally, third, the will *consents* to the rational or divine inspiration, which properly constitutes the *ego*'s virtuous act, rather than consent to sin.[58] Like Descartes, Francis of Sales presents the will precisely as a power of election—*vis eligendi*—and describes the sequence of intentional states involved in free election as follows:

> "The will has a very exclusive affinity for the good; this affinity produces the delight that the will experiences in feeling and perceiving the good; this delight moves and pushes the will towards the good; this motion, in turn, tends to union and, finally, the will, moved and tending to union, seeks out very means to achieve it."[59]

No causal "force of attraction" is exerted on the will.[60] The will's native affinity for the good kindles delight, which, in turn, moves the will to unite with what delights it. Presumably, in Descartes's axiom, the will, similarly, is carried *by its delight*, or inner *propensio*, to the good that it perceives clearly. Descartes repeatedly emphasizes that the intensity of the will's *impetus* or *propensio* varies with the clarity and/or magnitude of the perceived good, yet the will responds of its own accord, all the more forcefully and spontaneously that the perceived good is perceived clearly. Thus when I perceive an evident truth, such as the perfect necessity of God's existence, or the conditional necessity that, if I deliberately doubt (*cogito*), then I exist, I am carried *irresistibly* to affirm it.[61]

---

[58] See *Introduction à la vie dévote*, Part II, c. 18, in *Oeuvres*, I, 110–111.

[59] F. de Sales, *Traité de l'Amour de Dieu*, Bk. I, c. 7, in *Oeuvres*, I, 369: "La volonté donc a une convenance très étroite avec le bien; cette convenance produit la complaisance que la volonté ressent à sentir et apercevoir le bien; cette complaisance émeut et pousse la volonté au bien; ce mouvement tend à l'union, et enfin, la volonté émue et tendante à l'union cherche tous les moyens requis pour y parvenir."

[60] Contrary to Dorottya Kaposi's analysis in "Indifférence et liberté humaine chez Descartes," *Revue de Métaphysique et de Morale* 2004–I, 86. Kaposi interprets the passage of AT VII, 58–59 to imply that "Les raisons proposées par l'entendement inclinent plus ou moins la volonté." Descartes says only that the propensity of the will *follows* the intellection of evidence, not that the intellection of evidence *causes* the will's inclination. The will is radically free, it cannot be inclined, it can only *incline itself*. Much rests on clarifying this subtle point. I thank my anonymous reviewer for directing me to this impressive and important article.

[61] Cf. Meditation III, AT VII, 36; and Meditation IV, AT VII, 58: "non potui quidem non judicare illud quod tam clare intelligebam verum esse."

What initially presented itself as a mystery—why do I affirm truths so spontaneously and irresistibly if I know that God could be deceiving me?[62]—turns out to be the very cornerstone of free volition. Descartes's axiom concludes indeed that, if the will knows a perfection that it lacks, it "instantly" (*statim*) gives this perfection to itself if it lies within its power to do so.[63] Two examples suggest themselves: first, since affirming clear and certain truths is a perfection that lies within the will's power, the will is moved to affirm, for example, that God exists, as soon as the necessity of the proposition is grasped; second, since avoiding error is a perfection that lies within the will's power, the will is moved to affirm the axiom that judgment must be suspended whenever the cognitive grounds to affirm or deny something are insufficient.

This brings us closer to the connection between good judgment and the soul's innate propensity for the good. According to Descartes, volitions, as we know, are actions of the soul rather than passions.[64] A privileged subset of volitions are purely spiritual actions of the soul, since they not only originate in the soul but also terminate in the soul.[65] Descartes cites two examples: (1) willingly loving God (*vouloir aimer Dieu*) and (2) applying one's thought to a purely intelligible object.[66] Descartes's category of purely spiritual actions of the soul, namely volitions that are wholly independent of bodily passions and are aimed at purely intelligible things, is by no means original, but is shared by Francis of Sales, who emphasizes that purely spiritual volitions have greater "force" than volitions that end in physical actions.[67]

Since all volitions are *ipso facto* perceived,[68] part of what the *ego* perceives in willing something intelligible is the degree of *propensio* or

---

[62] Meditation III, AT VII, 36: "Sponte erumpam in has voces."

[63] Second Answers, Axiom 7, AT VII, 166: "ideoque, si norit aliquas perfectiones quibus careat, sibi statim ipsas dabit, si sint in sua potestate."

[64] See *Des Passions de l'âme*, Part I, Art. XVII, AT XI, 342.

[65] *Des Passions de l'âme*, Part I, Art. XVIII, AT XI, 342–343: "Nos volontez sont de deux sortes. Car les unes sont des actions de l'ame, qui se terminent en l'ame mesme."

[66] *Ibid.*: "Car les unes sont des actions de l'ame, qui se terminent en l'ame mesme, comme lors que nous voulons aymer Dieu, ou generalement appliquer nostre pensée à quelque objet qui n'est point materiel."

[67] See e.g., *Traité de l'Amour de Dieu*, Bk. I, c. X, in *Oeuvres*, I, 381: "Puis donc que l'amour est un acte de notre volonté, qui le veut avoir non seulement noble et généreux, mais fort, vigoureux et actif, il en faut retenir la vertu et la force dans les limites des opérations spirituelles; car qui voudrait l'appliquer aux opérations de la partie sensible ou sensitive de notre âme, il affaiblirait d'autant les opérations intellectuelles, esquelles, toutefois, consiste l'amour essentiel."

[68] Passions, I, Art. 19. AT XI, 343.

"willingness" that marks the volition. Descartes speaks of the greater *facility* or *impetus* with which the will is moved when a better or more rational action is willed.[69] When, at the start of Meditation IV, the *ego* remarks that it no longer experiences "any difficulty" in turning away from representational thoughts to what is purely intelligible,[70] we must interpret this to imply that the *ego* has become sufficiently emancipated from the senses that it experiences a very forceful *propensio* when it pursues purely intelligible things. The *ego* pursues intelligible things all the more *freely* that its will is unfettered by material passions or representations: freedom is now defined as the degree of spiritual force, or equivalently, of ease, with which the *ego* pursues spiritual goods.

A fortiori, when the *ego* willingly loves God, which is to say, is freely moved to unite with the unsurpassibly infinite totality of all perfection, the will's *impetus* is invincibly strong. Descartes indeed repeatedly stresses that it is "impossible" to fail to love God if God is known correctly.[71] Hence the key importance of the contemplative pause at the end of Meditation III as a prelude to examining error and the nature of volition. The *ego*'s willingness to interrupt its investigation into itself in order to focus all of its attention on God and "adore the beauty of God's immense light" illustrates the category of spiritual action with special clarity, since the *ego* both applies its intellect to a purely intelligible idea that defies all representation (the idea of an infinite totality of perfection) and also wills itself by a very pure and deliberate volition to love God, at least for the duration of the contemplative pause. As we know, the *ego*, in this privileged state, "finds in itself no cause of error": wholly focused intellectually on God's infinite perfection and wholly mobilized in active adoration, the *ego* neither perceives nor affirms nor loves anything but the indivisible totally of truth.[72]

---

[69] Letter to Mesland (?), February 9, 1645, AT VII, 175: "Certum est voluntatem nostram mairoi tunc facilitate atque impetu se movere."

[70] AT VII, 53: "ut jam absque ulla difficultate cogitationem a rebus imaginabilibus ad intelligibiles tantum, atque ab omni materia secretas, convertam."

[71] See Passions, II, Art. 83, AT XI, 390: "Pour ce qui est de la Devotion, son principal objet est sans doute la souveraine Divinité, à laquelle on ne saurait manquer d'être devot, lorsqu'on la connoist comme il faut." And Sixth Answers, AT VII, 429: "Quisquis Deum, ut par est, novit, non potest ipsum non diligere."

[72] Francis of Sales speaks also of an ecstasy that lifts the *ego* above itself and helps to prevent the *ego* from "returning to itself." See *Traité de l'Amour de Dieu*, Bk. I, c. X, in *Oeuvres*, I, 382: "A mesure que l'extase est plus grande, ou au-dessus de nous ou au-dessous de nous, plus elle empêche notre âme de retourner à soi-même."

We thus have two paradigmatic cases, both of them volitions originating in the soul and terminating in the soul, in which the will's impetus is irresistible: affirming that God exists, and loving God. A question suggests itself: when the *ego* acts alone, independently of sense and the imagination, what difference is there between willing a good freely but infallibly (i.e. being carried freely to a good) and loving a good (i.e. being moved freely to unite with a good)? Descartes defines love generally as an emotion that prompts the soul to "join itself by means of the will" (*se joindre de volonté*) to what appears to suit it.[73] In the more ordinary, psychosomatic case, emotions of love are induced in the will by changes in animal spirits,[74] but when the soul acts alone, i.e. loves God by a pure self-determination of the will, emotions of love are excited in the will by the will's own free judgments.[75] In the case of spiritual love, in short, a free judgment that something is good incites the soul to join itself willingly with it and excites the emotion of love.

Two conclusions follow: first, the irresistible *propensio* with which the *ego* loves God is a paradigmatic case of free agency, since a free judgment that God is infinitely good lies at the source of the *ego*'s irresistible *propensio* to love God; secondly, the free judgment that God is infinitely good is itself a beginning of love, since the *ego* is moved to love God *by judging* that God is infinitely good. Moreover, all sound judgments, strictly speaking, attest to the will's propensity to love perfection and unite itself to perfection, since falsehoods are rejected for the sake of Truth and since judgment is suspended in order to avoid the imperfection of error.

Descartes's doctrine of volition thus argues, in effect, that free agency consists in a natural impetus to love perfection. The key is that the volition that carries the soul to unite with perfection "comes directly from the soul and seems to depend on the soul alone."[76] This means,

---

[73] Passions, II, Art. 79, AT XI, 387: L'amour est une emotion de l'ame [...] qui l'incite à se joindre de volonté aux objets qui paroissent luy estre convenables.

[74] *Ibid.* Descartes gives the general definition of love as the psychosomatic case, after which he distinguishes the psychosomatic case from spiritual love. So, first, the psychosomatic case: "l'amour est une émotion de l'âme *causée par les mouvements des esprits*, qui l'incite à se joindre de volonté aux objets qui paraissent lui être convenables."

[75] *Ibid.* Descartes now distinguishes, second, the case of spiritual love: "Ie dis que ces emotions sont causées par les esprits, affin de distinguer l'Amour et la Haine, qui sont des passions et dependent du corps, tant des jugemens qui portent aussi l'ame a se joindre de volontë avec les choses qu'elle estime bonnes, et à se separer de celles qu'elle estime mauvaises, *que des emotions que ces seuls jugmens excitent en l'ame*. Emphasis added.

[76] *Des Passions de l'âme*, Part I, Art. XVII, AT XI, 342: Celles que je nomme ses

in turn, that the first and most basic of all pure volitions is the sound
and deliberate judgment that Truth (God) must be loved and falsehood
must be shunned. What prompts the root judgment that sets the rule
for all judgments as an imperative? The will *by its nature* loves perfection,[77] which means that free agency is nothing other than the imperative that God (Truth) must be loved above all else, which is to say
that free agency is the inalienable image in the soul of God's absolute
self-love.

Moreover, the judgment that God (Truth) must be loved above all
else moves the *ego* to love Truth more than knowledge (hence the
volition to shun what is doubtful along with what is false) and to love
God more than itself. Descartes's doctrine of judgment and Francis of
Sales's doctrine of pure love coincide because they start from the same
axiom asserting the natural impetus to virtue in the will.[78] Descartes,
like Francis of Sales, asserts that the soul's natural inclination is to
love God for the sake of God's perfection, without thought of personal
reward. Descartes's doctrine of "pure love" is expressed, among other
places, in a letter to Elizabeth:

> "Because the true object of love is perfection, as soon as we raise our
> mind to consider God as he is, we are naturally so inclined to love him,
> that we draw joy even from our afflictions by considering that his will is
> carried out in the fact that we suffer them."[79]

The coherence of the Cartesian doctrine stems from the disproportion
between the finite good that the *ego* finds in itself and the infinite good
that the *ego* finds in God, *and in God's image within*: which is precisely
the infinite freedom to love infinite perfection. Since the *ego* is able
rationally to know that God is an infinite totality of perfection, the *ego*
is able to judge that God exists and thus to move its will freely but
infallibly to love God for God's sake:

---

actions, sont toutes nos volontez, à cause que nous experimentons qu'elles vienent
directement de nostre ame, et semblent ne dependre que d'elle." And Art. XVIII.

[77] Cf. Descartes to Elizabeth, September 15, 1645, AT IV, 292: "Le vray obiet de
l'amour est la perfection."

[78] Cf. Francis of Sales, *Traité de l'Amour de Dieu*, Bk. X, c. X, in *Oeuvres*, I, 842: "La
connaissance naturelle de la Divinité produit infailliblement l'inclination et tendance à
l'aimer plus que nous-mêmes."

[79] AT IV, 292: "Pour ce que le vray obiet de l'amour est la perfection. Lorsque
nous élevons nostre esprit a le (sc. Dieu) considerer tel qu'il est, nous nous trouvons
naturellement si enclins a l'aymer, que nous tirons mesme de la ioye de nos afflictions,
en pensant que sa volonté s'execute en ce que nous les recevons."

"There is so little proportion between the infinite and the finite, that our will, knowing an infinite good, is without doubt set into motion (*ébranlée*), incited and inspired to prefer the bottomless friendship of this infinite goodness to any other sort of love, even of ourselves."[80]

For both Descartes and Francis of Sales, the primacy of the free will is thus really a primacy of spiritual love. Improving on a long line of predecessors,[81] Descartes and Francis of Sales reach beyond the doctrine of the *Reason-Principle* to argue that freedom and virtue stem most fundamentally from the love of God that is inscribed in free agency, and from which love of rational rectitude follows.[82] Spiritual love, the pure volition through which the soul voluntarily unites with God, is the will's very essence. God's image in the soul is the *ego* carried willingly and deliberately to love God by a native impulse for limitless perfection—which is the image of God's "spirated" love for himself.[83]

In order to emphasize the primacy of love, Francis of Sales points out that, even if we were independent of God and without gratitude to God for our existence, we would still be moved to prefer God's infinite goodness over ourselves, provided we were given the power of free will, which is the power to unite with goodness through love.[84] However, if, *per impossibile*, we neither depended on God nor had free will, we would

---

[80] Francis of Sales, *Traité de l'Amour de Dieu*, Bk. X, c. X, in *Oeuvres*, I, 842: "Il y a si peu de proportion entre l'infini et le fini, que notre volonté qui connait un bien infini est sans doute ébranlée, inclinée et incitée de préférer l'amitié de l'abime de cette bonté infinie à toute sorte d'autre amour et à celui-là encore de nous-mêmes."

[81] For a useful review, see Harald Ofstad, *An Inquiry into the Freedom of Decision* (Oslo and London: Norwegian U. Press and George Allen and Unwin Ltd., 1961), Chapter 5 ("Freedom as Rationality or Virtue"), 139–151.

[82] For Plotinus, see Enneads, III, First Tractate, 9: "When our Soul holds to its *Reason-Principle*, to the guide, pure and detached and native to itself, only then can we speak of personal operation, of voluntary act."

[83] To some extent, my position restates, from a new point of view and in new terms, Jean-Luc Marion's position in *Sur la théologie blanche de Descartes*, 421, that the free will is a "primordial good" that makes the higher moral good possible. Both the power of *epoche* (absention) in the face of insufficient knowledge and the power to demonstrate the will's freedom with regard to the intellect by acting intentionally against the evidence of reason represent, not so much a "radicalization of freedom" (except relative to Thomism) but simply the inherent (and very Augustinian) reflexivity of the will's *propensio* (love) for its own dignity, image in itself of God. As we shall see, the temptation to substitute God's *image* for God Himself is faced and overcome in Meditation V.

[84] *Traité de l'Amour de Dieu*, Bk. X, c. XI, in *Oeuvres*, I, 843: "S'il y avait ou pouvait avoir quelque souveraine bonté de laquelle nous fussions indépendants, pourvu que nous pussions nous unir à elle par amour, encore serions-nous incités à l'aimer plus que nous-mêmes."

correctly estimate that God exceeds us in perfection, but we would not
be able to love God.[85] Descartes takes the primacy of love a step further,
since the *ego* stripped of free will would be unable to *judge* that God is
supremely good and thus would be unable to move itself to unite with
God. According to Descartes's new theory, cognition presents the *ego*
with facts, but the will alone is empowered to judge what should be
sought or avoided, since the will alone has a moral propensity to love
the good—which includes a propensity to affirm that truth must be
sought and error avoided.[86]

Descartes's insight is that the intellect by itself cannot avoid error.
In order to avoid error, the epistemological subject must not only be
capable of objective perception, but must *care* about truth. The *ego*'s
judgment that positive infinity marks God as the *ego*'s supreme moral
good means that the *ego* has a free moral propensity to *rank* perfection
in an absolute sense, over and above a cognitive capacity to *compare* any
two magnitudes relative to one another. Since the essence of the will
consists in loving the good, the will, by its inner motions, defines the
moral value of what the intellect perceives. Moreover, the *ego*'s moral
propensity to rank moral perfection absolutely logically precedes the
ego's cognitive capacity to perceive contrast, since the idea of infinity—
absolute and incomparable—precedes and grounds the *ego*'s notion of
itself. Our interpretation of the moral origin of the notion of rank
is indeed confirmed by the *ego*'s self-definition as "a mean between
God and nothingness." The two transcendent extremes that secure the
absolute character of the *ego*'s rank stem from the idea of moral good:
at one extreme of the hierarchy is God, the supremely positive good
than which no good is greater, while at the other extreme is *nihil*—
the unsurpassibly negative case of what lacks perfection infinitely.[87] The

---

[85] *Ibid.*: "Nous l'estimerions certes plus que nous-mêmes; car nous connaitrions
qu'étant infinie, elle serait plus estimable et aimable que nous, mais à proprement
parler, nous ne l'aimerions pas, puisque l'amour regarde l'union."

[86] Citing a key passage from Thomas Aquinas's *Summa Theologiae*, I, Q. 83, Art.
1, Ofstad points out that "it is not quite clear how the connection between 'free'
and 'rational' is to be understood." See *An Inquiry into the Freedom of Decision*, 139–
140. Indeed the Thomist passage both holds judgment to be an act of intellect and
rational deliberation to be characterized by a sort of freedom of indifference: "Man acts
from judgment, because by his apprehensive power he judges that something should be
avoided or sought. But because his judgment, in the case of some particular act, is not
from a natural instinct, but from some act of comparison in the reason, therefore he
acts from free judgment and retains the power of being inclined to various things."

[87] Meditation IV, AT VII, 54: "Animadverto non tantum Dei, sive entis summe

conceptual *scala perfectionis* stretching from infinity to zero reflects the will's moral range, from virtuous union with God through indifference to culpable union with *nihil*.

10.2. *Freedom of consent*

According to Descartes, judgments are thus pure volitions that move the soul to pursue what is good and shun what is evil. It follows that, if volitions are basic actions, judgments are the most basic actions of all, since judgments, implicit or explicit, are volitions that are at the root of other volitions. The description of the free will as the "power to affirm or deny, pursue or shun" may now be clarified: the free will is, most precisely, the power to pursue what is judged to be worthy of pursuit by a free agent, and to shun what is judged to be unworthy. Judgments, in short, move the *ego* either to love or to hate: provided that the will's native propensity to the good and true is the basis for judgment, the *ego* is moved to love what it *ought* to love and to shun what it *ought* to shun, in conformity with God's image.

What does Descartes mean by the sort of rational love to which the *ego* is moved by a true judgment? Love consists in "joining oneself willingly" or "by an act of will" (*se joint de volonté*) to what is judged to be good and true. Conversely, hate consist in "separating oneself willingly" or "by an act of will" from what is judged to be neither good nor true.[88] But what is meant by joining or separating oneself from something willingly (*de volonté*)? Descartes carefully distinguishes the mental action of volition that he calls love and which lies within the *ego*'s power of agency, from both the passive emotion of love that is excited in the soul by a judgment and the passive emotion of desire.[89] Whereas desire is "a passion that concerns the future," love is

> "the *consent* by means of which one considers oneself already to be as though joined with what one loves: so that one imagines a whole, of

---

perfecti, realem et positivam, sed etiam, ut ita loquar, nihili, sive ejus quod ab omni perfectione summe abest, negativam quandam ideam mihi observari, et me tanquam medium inter Deum et nihil."

[88] Combining the definitions given in Meditation IV and Descartes's Second Answers with *Passions de l'âme*, Art. LXXIX, AT XI, 387: "Les jugements portent l'ame à se joindre de volonté avec les choses qu'elle estime bonnes, et à se séparer de celles qu'elle estime mauvaises."

[89] See *Passions de l'âme*, Part II, Art. LXXX, AT XI, 387.

which one is a part and what is loved is another part. Conversely, in hatred, one considers oneself as such to be whole, entirely separate from what is hated."[90]

To love a thing following the judgment that the thing is a good is to *consent* to becoming aggregated, or, more precisely, *con*–gregated, with it. We notice, first, that the *ego*'s consent brings about a sort of *virtual* or conceptual or moral incorporation of the *ego* and the thing loved: the *ego*, in effect, agrees that the good thing and it *ought* to be united and form a new seamless whole, and *by agreeing* to forming a new whole already forms it morally. The *ego*'s consent is thus the critical action that anticipates transforming existing conditions (what *is*) into new, more morally perfect conditions (what *ought* to be). The case of science nicely illustrates the place of consent in Descartes's doctrine. Descartes says that, if the soul perceives that many beautiful things about nature are knowable, the will is "infallibly carried to love" the knowledge of natural things, by which he means that the *ego* considers such knowledge as belonging to it, "not yet in fact, but in right."[91] The motion of love by which the *ego* is carried to the good and true by its own rational judgment, is, in effect, the *ego*'s power freely to perfect itself by entering into a new moral bond with what lies beyond it but suits it and *ought not* to lie beyond it.

The *ego*'s power of election (*facultas eligendi*) and freedom of decision (*arbitrii libertas*) boil down to the power of free consent. The *ego*'s power of free consent gives the *ego* creative control over its own moral perfection, since the *ego* is empowered to increase its perfection simply by acquiescing to merge with the good and true and also to protect its integrity by refusing to merge with what is neither. Presumably, if the *ego*'s consent is not based on sound judgment, the *ego* acts to its moral detriment by consenting to be joined, by mistake, to what is less perfect than itself.

---

[90] *Passions de l'âme*, Part II, Art. LXXX, AT XI, 387: "Par le mot de volonté, je n'entends pas icy parler du desir, qui est une passion à part et se rapporte à l'avenir, mais du *consentement* par lequel on se considere dès à present comme joint avec ce qu'on aime: en sorte qu'on imagine un tout, duquel on pense estre seulement une partie, et que la chose aimée en est une autre. Comme, au contraire, en la Haine on se considere seul comme un tout, entierement separé de la chose pour laquelle on a de l'aversion."

[91] Letter to Chanut, February 1, 1647, AT IV, 602: "Si elle (sc. nostre ame) s'aperce-voit qu'il y a beaucoup de choses à connoistre en la Nature, qui sont fort belles, sa volonté se porteroit infalliblement à aimer la connoissance de ces choses, c'est à dire, à la considerer comme lui appartenant."

Descartes's theory of free consent raises a host of questions. To what extent is the *ego*'s consent given freely if it is given by mistake, out of ignorance? Since Descartes defines indifference as the lowest degree of freedom, and since indifference specifically implies an absence of the positive propensity needed for love, the *ego* that joins itself to what leaves the will indifferent acts *without* love and *without* freedom: the *ego* in this case may be said to yield, or submit, to what lies beyond it, but cannot be said authentically to *consent* to it. Descartes's doctrine implies that consent is by its very nature rational and free. Is submission to an appetite a consent that does not recognize itself as such, or a failure to consent to something better? How deliberate must consent be in order to count as free? Is free consent retractable? As we will see, theological, moral and legal aspects of the *ego*'s power of free consent point to a Cartesian theory of personal responsibility. If we apply Descartes's theory of consent to the highest case of freedom, namely the *ego*'s voluntary love of God, a new coherence emerges. Since it is "impossible" for the *ego* to fail to love God when God is adequately known, the (infallible) judgment that God is unsurpassably perfect and the (irresistible) consent to unite with God are closely connected. The *ego*'s will, in effect, is carried to God twice: first by affirming that God is the sovereign good *simpliciter*, in an absolute sense; then by loving God, which is to say consenting to unite with God personally, which is, in turn, equivalent to affirming that God (Truth) is not just the supreme good taken absolutely but is *my* supreme good. As Descartes's axiom carefully establishes, there is a twofold aspect to the will's innate propensity to the good: the will is carried (freely but infallibly) to a clearly known good *and* the will gives itself whatever good it knows itself to lack, if it lies within its power to do so. The will, in short, is naturally carried to affirm that whatever is good in itself is worthy of love, meaning that it is normatively right for the *ego* and is considered by the *ego* as *my* good. Judgment and love differ only in that judgment values the good for its own sake, while love values the good for the sake of the *ego*. In the paradigmatic case of the *ego*'s love of God, the *ego*'s consent is at once free and irresistible because God is *a se* infinitely good—such that no greater good is possible.

Far from being innovative, Descartes's theory of the soul's rational love of God conforms to Augustinian doctrine.[92] By making the

---

[92] See e.g. *De Trinitate*, 8, 8: "We love ourselves all the more that we love God more

soul's rational love of God (Truth) the keystone of first philosophy, Descartes implies that the soul's consenting to form a whole with the divine perfection is its most rational consent and is presupposed by further acts of consent. Thus no consent that contradicts the soul's irresistible love of God can be rationally given, any more than a judgment can be true that contradicts the truth of God's unsurpassable perfection.

Judgment and consent differ subtly in the effects that are caused in the soul. As we saw, the judgment that God is supremely good excites love in the will—both the volition or consent through which the *ego* considers itself to be already joined to God, and the purely spiritual emotion of delight or reverence, which Descartes distinguishes from the volition. The *ego*'s consent to join itself to God, in turn, triggers a new spiritual emotion, which Descartes describes as contentment, or satisfaction: the *ego*'s spiritual contentment is nothing other than its perception of acting virtuously, which is to say, of using its free agency to increase its own perfection.[93] The *ego*'s rational happiness consists in the consciousness of adhering personally to what is perfect in its own right.[94] Freedom of consent thus implies the experience of moral *conscience*, since the *ego* cannot exercise consent without at the same time experiencing a purely spiritual self-contentment or grief, depending on how conscientiously consent is given.

The *ego*'s contemplative rapture at the end of Meditation III illustrates the structure of Descartes's doctrine. The *ego* affirms God's necessary existence, which kindles reverence and moves the *ego* to love God, which is to say moves the *ego* to consent to unite with God's infinite perfection; the *ego*'s consent, in turn, which mirrors God's own creative consent that the *ego* exist, kindles contentment of a very personal nature, specifically *self*–contentment, indeed "the greatest natural bea-

---

than ourselves." See also Ephrem Boularand's review article, "Désintéressement," in *Dictionnaire de Spiritualité* (Paris: Beauchesne, 1957), III, cols. 551–591.

[93] See Descartes's letter to Elizabeth, September 1, 1645, AT IV, 284: "Nous ne sçaurions iamais pratiquer aucune vertu (c'est a dire faire ce que nostre raison nous persuade que nous devons faire), que nous n'en recevions de la satisfaction et du plaisir. Mais il y a deux sortes de plaisirs: les uns qui apartienent a l'esprit seul, et les autres qui a apartienent a l'homme, c'est a dire a l'esprit en tant qu'il est uni au cors."

[94] Cf. Augustine, *De doctrina christiana*, 1, 4, PL 34, 20: "beatitude consists in adhering though love to a thing for its own sake." See also *De Trinitate*, 8, 8, PL 42, 959: "We love ourselves all the more that we love God more than ourselves."

titude in this lifetime."[95] The *ego* by affirming and loving God loves and affirms itself.[96]

Like Descartes, Francis of Sales emphasizes the importance of free consent, indispensable for virtuous action.[97] In a variation of the contractual metaphor, Francis of Sales invokes the consent that is needed for a marriage suit to come to fruition. As we saw, he outlines three stages, all of which are required, but consent occupies a privileged place: first, the woman who is the object of the suit hears the marriage proposal; then she welcomes it; finally, she consents to it.[98] The outcome hinges on the woman's power of consent, since nothing else but her consent can bring about a resolution. If she consents to the proposal, the two parties become *engaged*, which means, in Cartesian terms, that, by consenting, she considers herself already as though joined to the suitor, forming a new spiritual whole of which she is a part and he is another; if, on the other hand, she withholds her consent, no engagement occurs, which means, in Cartesian terms, that she considers herself to be entirely separate from the suitor. Moreover, her power of consent is normatively effective, rather than mechanistically causal: her consent is both necessary and sufficient for the two parties to become engaged, granted that nothing visible is changed in either. Their status relative to one another and to the rest of society and to God is changed simply by her free volition. The power of free consent allows the *ego*

---

[95] AT VII, 52.

[96] See, further, Descartes's explicit statement that seeking to love God for his own sake and seeking personal beatitude coincide; in his letter to Elizabeth, August 18, 1645, AT IV, 275: "Ie remarque qu'il y a de la différence entre la beatitude, le souverain bien et la dernière fin ou but auquel doivent tendre nos actions: car la beatitude n'est pas le souverain bien; mais elle le presuppose, et elle est le contentement ou la satisfaction d'esprit qui vient de ce qu'on le possede. Mais par la fin de nos actions, on peut entendre l'un et l'autre; car le souverain bien est sans doute la chose que nous nous devons proposer pour but en toutes nos actions, et le contentement d'esprit qui en revient, estant l'attrait qui fait que nous le recherchons, est aussy de bon droit nommé notre fin." In 1645, a controversy had broken out over the doctrine of pure love, viewed by some as overly "quietist." See, e.g., Jean-Pierre Camus, *Défense du pur amour contre les attaques de l'amour propre* (1640) and A. Sirmond, *Défense de la vertu* (1641).

[97] *Introduction à la vie dévote*, Part II, c. XVIII, in *Oeuvres*, I, 111: "C'est le consentement qui fait l'acte vertueux."

[98] *Introduction à la vie dévote*, Part II, c. XVIII, in *Oeuvres*, I, 110: "Pour l'entière résolution d'un mariage, trois actions doivent entrevenir quant à la demoiselle que l'on veut marier: car premièrement, on lui propose le parti; secondement, elle agrée la proposition, et en troisième lieu, elle consent. Ainsi Dieu voulant faire en nous, par nous et avec nous, quelque action de grande charité, premièrement, il nous la propose par son inspiration; secondement, nous l'agréons; tiercement, nous y consentons."

to dispose of itself morally and legally. The *ego* owns itself in a special sense by exercising its power of consent since the power of consent is, equivalently, a power of self-commitment. Free consent empowers the *ego* to transform existing conditions into new moral conditions—better conditions if the *ego* commits itself as it *should*, worse conditions if the *ego* commits itself blindly and to its detriment, which is to say if the *ego* commits itself against the norm of every self-commitment, which is the *ego*'s *rationalissime* self-commitment to God (Truth). Moral autonomy and moral responsibility are tied to the *scala perfectionis* that is inscribed in the free will's very essence.

If the woman gives her consent and becomes engaged, is she no longer free to retract it? The point of Francis of Sales's metaphor is that God seeks neither obedience nor submission but free consent. In God's courtship of the finite human soul (*Philothée*), freedom of consent is no more abrogated than in the ordinary case of a human mariage suit. The woman who consents to a marriage proposal cannot be said to *obey* the suitor, since no commandment is issued to her. Neither does she *submit* to the suitor since no coercion is applied and no compulsion is present. Indeed if she were merely obeying a command or if she were yielding to force, the engagement would be invalid. She would be able to retract her consent on the grounds that she never actually *consented* to the proposal, since her consent was not free. Similarly, the *ego* must hold itself *responsible* for loving God (Truth) above all things because both the (infallible) judgment that God (Truth) is supremely good and the consent to unite with God were and are free volitions. In other words, the only absolutely unretractable consent is the soul's consent to unite with God—as the soul's conscience attests, since any consent that violates the soul's love of God induces the experience of grief and remorse.[99] Moral culpability, like legal liability, depends on distinguishing free consent from obedience and submission; what is more, as Francis of Sales and Descartes imply, moral merit, like the legal enforceability of a contract, also depends on the same distinction. Without freedom of consent, the soul is neither culpable nor meritorious.[100]

---

[99] Cf. Descartes's nightmares of November 11, 1619, as reported by Baillet, AT X, 186: "L'épouvante dont il fut frappé dans le second songe, marquoit, à son sens, sa syndérèse, c'est-a–dire, les remords de sa conscience touchant les péchez qu'il pouvait avoir commis pendant le cours de sa vie jusqu'alors."

[100] See Francis of Sales's mentor, Scupoli, *The Spiritual Combat*, c. 13, 40: "The will incurs no guilt unless it gives consent to an act, even if the entire force of the lower appetite is exerted towards a guilty end. On the other hand, the will cannot be

Bracketing the theological issue of merit, Descartes implies that the natural experience of conscience, which we experience as rewarding consent that is based on good judgment with joy and to punish blind volitions with anxiety, presupposes, and thus proves, freedom of consent.[101] The similarity between Francis of Sales's theory of consent and Descartes's analysis of love helps to clarify the notion of *propensio* in Meditation IV. The varying *propensio* felt in the will is precisely the varying degree of acquiescence given by the will to what the intellect shows it. When the *ego* affirms a truth, the *ego* freely consents to form a new cognitive whole with it, all the more willingly that the truth in question is clearly perceived to be evident. Equivalently, the *ego* witholds its consent from what is false or dubious. With every conscientious judgment, including the judgment that judgment must be suspended when clear evidence is lacking, the *ego* loves God and loves itself for God's sake, increasing its perfection and beatitude.

Cartesian freedom is thus neither a freedom of obedience, nor a freedom of indifference, but, very precisely, a *freedom of consent*. What is the difference? The difference between *consent* and *obedience* is that consent strengthens and exercises the *ego*'s free agency while obedience transfers and submits it to authority without the self-commitment that is love. The *ego*, according to Descartes, does not obey reason: the *ego* loves reason and freely consents to join itself to what reason proposes. Consequently, the *ego* is, and remains, responsible for the consent that it freely gives to reason—or to grace. Generally, from Descartes's point of view, to obey authority through compulsion rather than consent to authority freely can only be a bad, even demonic, impulse: *a malo Spiritu propellebar*.[102] Thus a Turk who, based on faulty arguments, acquiesces to articles of Christian Faith without the light of grace, is at fault for not cooperating with reason: *ratione sua non recte uteretur*.[103] Obviously, the soul

---

sanctified and united to God, however strong the grace attracting it, unless it cooperates with that grace by interior acts, and, if requisite, by exterior acts."

[101] See Letter to Mersenne, April 27, 1637, AT I, 366: "Pour bien faire, il suffit de bien juger."

[102] "Olympica," AT X, 185–186: "Le vent qui le poussoit vers l'église du collège, lorsqu'il avoit mal au côté droit, n'étoit autre chose que le mauvais Génie qui tâchoit de le jetter par force dans un lieu, où son dessein étoit d'aller volontairement. C'est pourquoy Dieu ne permit pas qu'il avançat plus loin."

[103] Second Answers, AT VII, 148: "Dico infidelem qui, omni gratia supernaturali destitutus, et plane ignorans ea quae nos Christiani credimus a Deo esse revelata, ipsa tamen, quamvis sibi obscura, falsis aliquibus ratiociniis adductus amplecteretur, non ideo fore fidelem, sed potius in eo peccaturum, quod ratione sua non recte uteretur."

is free, among other things, to *elect* obedience—to *consent* to comply with authority out of love.[104] Voluntary, or "loving" obedience, as Francis of Sales calls it, is structurally a form of free consent.[105] Descartes's theory of free consent implicitly outlaws forced conversion and any form of contractual slavery.

Consent and indifference, on the other hand, are opposites, as Descartes explains when he contrasts the state of the will before acting and while acting.[106] Before acting, the will is in a state of indifference. While acting, however, the will, by definition, consents to the action that it carries out. While Cartesian free will is "supernoetic" in the sense that it is not determined by the intellect,[107] the will is not by any means "free of all constraints, not only external, but internal"[108] since Cartesian freedom is precisely the freedom *to constrain oneself* by consenting to a determinate course of action. In order to extract itself from causal determinisms (what is) and be able to consent to a creative plan (what ought to be), the will seeks above all to be cured of indifference by turning to the light of reason (or to a higher light). When Descartes speaks of "the things to which the will is indifferent,"[109] he characterizes them as things that are neither true, nor good, nor clear, nor precise.[110] The will is thus indifferent only by default, when it has "nowhere to turn." Gontier's mistake is partly based on misinterpreting God's own "essential" indifference.[111] God's will is indifferent to "all that is made" or "will ever be made" (*omnia quae facta sunt aut unquam fient*),[112] but is not indifferent to Himself. As anyone schooled by the Jesuits knows,

---

[104] Cf. *Discours de la Méthode*, Part VI, AT VI, 60: "des personnes, a qui je defere et dont l'authorité ne peut gueres moins sur mes actions, que ma propre raison sur mes pensées."

[105] François de Sales, *Traité de l'Amour de Dieu*, Livre I, c. 6, in *Oeuvres*, I, 368: "Dieu, ayant créé l'homme à son image et semblance, veut que, comme en lui, tout y soit ordonné par l'amour et pour l'amour." "L'amour n'a point de forçats ni d'esclaves, ains réduit toutes choses à son obéissance avec une force si délicieuse, que, comme rien n'est si fort que l'amour, aussi rien n'est si aimable que sa force."

[106] Letter to Mesland (?), 9 February, 1645, AT IV, 173: "Notandum etiam libertatem considerari posse in actionibus voluntatis, vel antequam eliciantur, vel dum eliciantur. Et quidem spectata in iis, antequam eliciantur, involvit indifferentiam secundo modo sumptam, non autem primo modo."

[107] Citing T. Gontier, *Descartes et la causa sui*, 139.

[108] Citing T. Gonthier, *Descartes et la causa sui*, 135.

[109] Meditation IV, AT VII, 58: "ad quae cum sit indifferens."

[110] Meditation IV, AT VII, 58 and 59.

[111] *Descartes et la causa sui*, 136.

[112] Sixth Answers, AT VII, 431–432.

God loves Himself at once irresistibly and with infinite freedom, His own self-subsisting love being the Third Person of the Trinity. Similarly, human freedom, which is God's image in the soul, consists neither in indifference nor in obedience, but in electing Truth.[113]

Descartes's "horse and rider" metaphor in Meditation II confirms our analysis.[114] The *ego*, freshly emerged from the certainty of the *cogito*, recognizes that *mens mea* wanders aimlessly as long as no truth is available to it. The soul's freedom at this pivotal junction is twofold: in so far as I lack true knowledge, I am free to err (freedom of indifference), but in so far as I myself indubitably exist, I am free to make myself comply with reason (freedom of obedience). The *ego* does not seek, however, to make itself obey reason. Rather, the *ego* renounces an authoritarian stance for the sake of gradually governing *mens mea* "more easily:" *facilius se regi*.[115] The *ego*, in short, seeks to elicit its own power of free consent, thanks to which the unified soul will *acquiesce* to the authority of reason (or of a higher light) and elect Truth of its own accord.[116]

Neither a freedom of obedience nor a freedom of indifference, Descartes's freedom of consent is just the sort of freedom that is needed for the emergence of Contractual Law.[117] What evidence is there that the notion of contract was familiar to Descartes and that the philosophical underpinnings of contractual obligation were of interest to him? As we know, Descartes studied Law at Poitiers in 1615 and received a Law license on November 10, 1616.[118] Descartes's "provisional morality" maxims in the *Discourse on Method* include, as we know, a ban on "all promises through which one's freedom is in some way abrogated."[119] Descartes specifies that he does not mean to reject laws and contracts, which allow "good projects" to be conducted and commerce to pro-

---

[113] Cf. Descartes's letter to Mesland of 2 May, 1644, AT IV, 117: "On ne laisse pas de meriter, bien que, voyant tres clairement ce qu'il faut faire, on le fasse infalliblment et sans aucune indifference, comme a fait Iesus-Christ en cette vie."

[114] AT VII, 29–30: "Gaudet aberrare mens mea, necdum se patitur intra veritates limites cohiberi. Est igitur, et adhuc semel laxissimas habenas ei permittamus, ut, illis paulo post opportune reductis, facilius se regi patiatur."

[115] AT VII, 30.

[116] On the importance of assent and cooperation in the doctrine of grace formulated by the Council of Trent, see Olivier Boulnois, "Le refoulement de la liberté d'indifférence et les polémiques anti-scotistes," *Les Études philosophiques*, 2002/2, 201.

[117] See Charles Fried, *Contract as Promise. A Theory of Contractual Obligation* (Cambridge, MA: Harvard U. Press, 1981).

[118] See Geneviève Rodis-Lewis, *Descartes* (Paris: Calmann Lévy, 1997), 41.

[119] *Discours de la Méthode*, Part III, AT VI, 24: "ie mettois entre les excès toutes les promesses par lesquelles on retranche quelquechose de sa liberté."

ceed securely, on the basis of self-imposed obligations.[120] Rather, his
concern seems to be the difference between simple consent and *irrevocable* consent with regard to scientific knowledge. What Descartes rejects
is being irrevocably pledged to a provisional and evolving theory as
though to an immutable and complete doctrine.[121] The experience of
promising finished manuscripts to Mersenne at fixed dates and then of
pleading for delays "like a creditor," may have alerted Descartes to the
special difficulty of fitting the project of science into emerging contractual frameworks.[122]

[120] *Ibid.*: "Non que je desprouvasse les lois, qui, pour remedier a l'inconstance des
esprits foibles, permettent, lorsqu'on a quelque bon dessein, ou mesme, pour la seureté
du commerce, quelque dessein qui n'est qu'indifferent, qu'on face (sic) des voeux ou des
contrats qui obligent a y perseverer."
[121] *Ibid.*: "i'eusse pensé commettre une grande faute contre le bon sens, si, pour ce
que i'approuvois alors quel chose, ie me fusse obligé de la prendre pour bonne encore
après, lorsqu'elle auroit peutestre cessé de l'estre, ou que i'aurois cessé de l'estimer
telle."
[122] See Descartes's letter to Mersenne of late November 1633, AT I, 270: "Ie voulois
faire comme les mauvais payeurs, qui vont prier leur creanciers e leur donner un peu
de delay, lors qu'ils sentent approcher le temps de leur dette."

CHAPTER ELEVEN

IS FREE AGENCY REQUIRED FOR
THE PERCEPTION OF TRUTH?

Since Hobbes, not Descartes, is typically invoked as *fons et origo* of Contract Law, and, in particular, of the view that a contract is an implicit consent,[1] let us briefly review the exchange between Descartes and Hobbes over freedom and consent in the Third Objections and Answers. Hobbes objects, first, that in Meditation IV human free will "is assumed without proof, against the opinion of Calvinists."[2] In response, Descartes denies that any proof is required since freedom is known by direct acquaintance of the fact, directly experienced by each one of us and known very expressly (*notissimum*) to the natural light.[3] More importantly, Hobbes attacks, second, Descartes's innovative theory that judgment is an act of the will rather than an act of the intellect. Hobbes insists that it no more depends on the will to believe something or acquiesce to it than it depends on the will to know that something is true. We believe what is proved by sound arguments, Hobbes says, "whether we want to or not": *volentes nolentes credimus.*[4] Hobbes grants Descartes that defending or rejecting propositions are voluntary acts, but he insists that the involvement in the public defense of propositions in no ways implies that the mind's *inner consent* depends on the will: *sed non ideo sequitur assenssum internum dependere a voluntate.*[5] At stake is nothing less than the character of "inner consent." If the inner con-

---

[1] Notably by P.S. Atiyah. See "Promises and the Law of Contract," *Mind* 87 (July 1979), 410–418; *The Rise and Fall of Freedom of Contract* (Oxford: Clarendon, 1979); and *Promises, Morals, and the Law* (Oxford: Clarendon, 1981), especially 124–212.

[2] AT VII, 190: "Notandum quoque arbitrii libertatem assumi sine probatione, contra opinionem Calvinistarum."

[3] AT VII, 191: "Nihil autem de libertate hic assumpi, nisi quod omnes experimur in nobis; estque lumine naturali notissimum. Nemo tamen, cum seipsum tantum respicit, non experitur unum et idem esse voluntarium et liberum."

[4] AT VII, 192: "Praeterea non modo scire aliquid verum est, sed et credere vel assensum praebere, aliena sunt a voluntate; nam quae validis argumentis probantur, vel ut credibilia narrantur, volentes nolentes credimus."

[5] *Ibid.*: "verum est, quod affirmare et negare, propugnare et refellere propositiones sunt actus voluntatis; sed non ideo sequitur assensum internum dependere a voluntate."

sent through which the members of a society surrender power to an absolute authority is simply dictated by reason and produced computationally, *nolentes volentes*, then coercion does not invalidate the social contract.[6] Hobbes, as we know, considered all talk of "free will" to be nonsense.[7]

Descartes's answer rests on the axiom that consent is by its very nature free. On the Cartesian view, we cannot give our consent except willingly. We cannot acquiesce to anything *nolentes volentes* since, by definition, we can only give our consent by means of a free volition. Hobbes's claim that we consent to things "willingly or unwillingly" is equivalent to the claim that we consent to things "whether we consent to them or not." Hobbes's claim is, therefore, incoherent—like claiming that we willingly pursue goods "willingly or unwillingly." To Descartes, the "inner" consent through which the *ego* acquiesces to a truth may be irresistible but it cannot be *involuntary*. Thus to consent to a proposition (or to a creed, or to a course of action, or, for that matter, to a contract) is freely to *elect* it. Implicitly, a consent that is extorted by force does not have the same legitimacy as a consent that is given freely.[8]

Hobbes's challenge to Descartes's theory of judgment stipulates that the intellect consents automatically to what is rationally evident. The innovative distinction drawn by Descartes between, on the one hand, the passive perception of a proposition and, on the other, the free volition that judges it to be true, puts the burden on Descartes to account for the experience invoked by Hobbes, namely the experience

---

[6] See *Leviathan*, Part I, c. XIV, sections 2–9, reprinted in Stephen Darwall, ed., *Contractarianism/Contractualism* (Malden, Victoria and Berlin: Blackwell Publishing, 2003), 30–32. especially, 30: "It is a precept, or general rule of reason *that every man ought to endeavour peace, as far as he has hope of obtaining it*." See also P.S. Atiyah, *Promises, Morals, and the Law*, 179: "The view that promising is, in essence, reducible to a form of consent is to be found in *Leviathan*, where Hobbes argues in effect that a promise is an expression of consent not to interfere with others in their enjoyment of their natural rights."

[7] Hobbes, *Leviathan*, Part I, c. VI, section 53 and c. V, section 5; reprinted in Stephen Darwall, ed., *Contractarianism/Contractualism*, 25 and 14: "If a man should talk of a *round triangle*, or of *a free subject, a free will*, or any *free* but free from being hindred by opposition, I should not say he were in an error, but that his words were without meaning, that is to say, absurd."

[8] See, on this subject, John Dunn, "Consent in the Political Theory of John Locke," in *The Historical Journal*, X, 2 (1967), 153–182; reprinted in *Locke*, John Dunn and Ian Harris, eds., (Cheltenham, UK, and Lyme, US: Edward Elgar Publishing, 1997), I, 16.

that we are not free to believe a rational truth or not in our inner-most sanctuary: *volentes nolentes credimus*. Descartes must explain how the *vis cognoscendi* presents information to the *ego*. This requires, in turn, a Cartesian theory of Intentionality. How are the *ego*'s two faculties related? Does the passive *vis cognoscendi* operate independently of the free will? Or does the reflexive perception of its own receptivity pre-suppose the free will? Is free agency required, not only to judge that a theorem is true, but to perceive its truth in the first place?

11.1. *Intentionality and its Objects*

Whereas Meditation II examined a reduced *cogito* in order to affirm the fact of a causal agent based on immediate acquaintance,[9] Meditation V focuses instead on *(ex)cogito* as an Intentional deployment of rational thought towards its objects.[10] The *ego* discovers on the fifth day that it possesses the faculty to think *about* things other than itself, whether such things exist or not. The *ego* discovers, in particular, that it has the power to think about innumerable figures: *Possum innumeras figuras excogitare*.[11] The point of the day's meditation is to bracket myself as an existing agent without extension in order to investigate the inherent Intentionality of the *vis cognoscendi* that puts me in mental contact with things that I am not. How does this contact happen? How does *mens* grasp what most radically differs from itself, namely the essence of body?

---

[9] Second Answers, AT VII, p. 140: "... ex eo quod apud se experiatur, fieri non posse ut cogitet, nisi existat." Cf. Bertrand Russell, *The Problems of Philosophy* (London, Oxford and new York: Oxford U. Press, 1977), 135–136: "When a belief is true, there is a corresponding fact, in which several objects of the belief form a single complex. In regard to any complex fact, there are, theoretically, two ways in which it may be known: (1) by means of a judgment, in which its several parts are judged to be related as they are in fact related; and (2) by means of *acquaintance* with the complex fact itself, which may (in the large sense) be called perception... The second way of knowing a complex fact, the way of acquaintance, is only possible when there is such a fact. We may say that a truth is self-evident, in the first and most absolute case, when we have acquaintance with the fact which corresponds to the truth."

[10] Following John Searle's practice of capitalizing Intentional so as to distinguish it from the ordinary "intentional" as well as his definition of Intentionality. See J. Searle, *Intentionality*, 1: "Intentionality is that property of many mental states and events by which they are directed at or about or of objects and states of affairs in the world."

[11] AT VII, 64.

The mind's capacity to bracket existence when intending geometric objects takes up where Meditation I left off—where it stumbled against hyperbolic doubt after proposing mathematical truths as a possible foothold of certainty precisely because of their indifference to existing *in rerum natura* and their independence from sensory experience.[12] On the fifth day, newly empowered to avoid error through the recovery of volition *qua* free,[13] the *ego* seeks in turn to examine cognition *qua* Intentional. If the will, *vis volendi seu eligendi*, is characterized by its essential and inalienable inclination freely to elect what is good,[14] what analogous inclination marks the pure intelligence? What does the *vis cognoscendi seu intelligendi* record most fundamentally and inalienably about its Intentional objects? A good way for the *ego* to find out is for it to direct its attention to a new class of ideas, namely the ideas of extended things "in so far as they are in my thought" (*quatenus sunt in mea cogitatione*). The mind's cognitive power will best display its essence, not by gazing reflexively at itself (*cogito*), but by turning its gaze away (*excogito*) from the subject who subjectively thinks (and exists) towards objects that are thought but "perhaps exist nowhere outside of thought."[15]

Quite apart from the radical initiative of accounting for the essence of material things geometrically, Descartes focuses on mathematical ideas for two reasons. First, mathematical truths, as we know from Meditation I, sharply reveal the rift between subjective indubitability (*persuasio*) and justified validity (*scientia*).[16] The meditator has so far relied

---

[12] AT VII, 20: "... atqui Arithmeticam, Geometriam, aliasque ejusmodi, quae nonnisi de simplicissimis et maxime generalibus rebus tractant, atque utrum eae sint in rerum natura necne, parum curant, aliquid certi atque indubitati continere."

[13] See Meditation IV, AT VII, 62: "Possum ... quoties de rei veritate non liquet, a judicio ferendo esse abstinendum; [...] atque ita habitum quemdam non errandi acquiram."

[14] See e.g. Second Answers, AT VII, "Axiomata", 166: "Rei cogitantis voluntas fertur, voluntarie quidem et libere (hoc enim est de essentia voluntatis), sed nihilominus infallibiliter, in bonum sibi clare cognitum." A useful introduction to the debate over "freedom of indifference" and in particular to Gibieuf's theory, largely endorsed by Descartes, is found in Jean Orcibal, "Néo-platonisme et jansénisme: du *De libertate* du P. Gibieuf à *L'Augustinus*" (1975), reprinted in *Études d'Histoire et de Littérature religieuses* (Klincksieck, 1997), 303–325.

[15] AT VII, p. 64: "fortasse nullibi gentium extra cogitationem meam existant."

[16] As Harry Frankfurt points out in "Descartes's Validation of Reason," 264, Descartes does not take "indubitable" and "true" to be synonyms. See also 266, where Frankfurt summarizes the problem facing clear and distinct intuitions: "The fact that he is persuaded of their truth to this extent is not the same as their being true; nor is

on the will's spontaneous embrace of what is clear and distinct in order to claim the entailment: "I am certain that *x*, therefore *x*." What prevents a failure of Truth-Functionality in this case as in the kindred case "I believe that *x*"—from which "*x*" hardly follows?[17]

A critical aim of Meditation V is the overcoming of the psychologism that inevitably clings to the doctrine of subjective indubitability.[18]Mathematical ideas play a key role in allowing the meditator to pass from *persuasio* to *scientia*,[19] not only because mathematical ideas are innate, as Rodis-Lewis emphasizes,[20] but also because the *ego* cannot rely on the same sort of immediate existential intuition that secures the *cogito*. I grasp my agency indubitably, but solipsistically, since I alone am immediately aware that I act and, therefore, that I actually exist. Since figures and numbers "perhaps exist nowhere in the world" and are not derived from sensation but are freely "excogitated,"[21] the Intentional activity that thinks them and understands their logical properties is at once radically immanent to my Intentional prospect and radically abstract.

---

his inability at the time to conceive that he could be mistaken the same as his being in fact free of error."

[17] For analysis of the "Failure of Truth-Functionality" and intentionality, see R.M. Chisholm, "Sentences about Believing," *Proceedings of the Aristotelian Society* 56 (1955/56), 125–148.

[18] For a strong statement against psychologism, see e.g. Bertrand Russell, "The Axiom of Infinity," (1904), reprinted in *The Collected Papers of Bertrand Russell*, ed. Alasdair Urquhart (London and New York: Routledge, 1994), vol. IV, 478: "The truth is that, throughout logic and mathematics, the existence of the human or any other mind is totally irrelevant; mental processes are studied by means of logic, but the subject-matter of logic does not presuppose mental processes, and would be equally true if there were no mental processes … a truth and the knowledge of it are as distinct as an apple and the eating of it."

[19] Cf. Janowski, *Cartesian Theodicy*, 76, ftn. 59, who emphasizes the distinction made by Descartes to Regius between *science* and *persuasion*: "… ac proinde, ne tunc quidem, cum illas ex istis principiis deduximus, *scientiam* (sic), sed tantum *persuasionem*, de illis (sc. de conclusionibus ex claris principiis deductis) nos habuisse." (Letter to Regius of 24 May 1640, AT III, 64–65).

[20] "On the Complementarity of Meditation III and V," in *Essays on Descartes's Meditations*, p. 282.

[21] Gassendi will challenge him about this (AT VII, 320–321) as will Berman (AT V, 161–162), but Descartes holds firm against Gassendi (AT VII, 381–382) and explains succinctly to Berman: "Non possem enim concipere imperfectum triangulum, nisi in me esset idea perfecti, quia illud hujus negatio." (AT V, 162). Cf. Mark Olson, "Descartes's First Meditation: Mathematics and the Laws of Logic," *Journal of the History of Philosophy*, 26, 1988, 427. Olson points out that rejecting the Aristotelian/Thomistic theory of abstraction "paves the way for the Ontological argument".

What do we know so far about cognition? In Meditation IV, rather than cite the *cogito* as the exemplary case of cognitive infallibility, Descartes, as we saw, cites the special case of rational *contemplatio Dei*, when thought is wholly and exclusively fixed on God.[22] The intellect in this privileged Intentional state detects no possibility of error or falsity (*nullam erroris aut falsitatis causam deprehendo*).[23] Error appears to be possible only when I turn away from God and "revert *apud me.*" Since focusing on the essence of *res extensa*, which is to say on figures and number, means shifting attention away from God to what is, by definition, divisible and multiple it should entail a similar risk—unless there is something that I perceive about figures and numbers that prevents me from reverting *apud me.* What gives mathematical truths their distinctive character? Why does "the child who correctly sums numbers feel assured that he knows about the sum everything that the human mind can know about it"?[24] Mathematics seems to lift the intellect to a higher realm where it soars above mere opinion in order to "feast on truths."[25] The mathematician seems to be raised to the status of *autarches*, self-sufficient and self-disciplined, far from imitative and blind dependence.[26] To solve the riddle of mathematical knowledge is to discover the very essence of the *vis cognoscendi*. Meditation V is indivisibly Descartes's treatise on intentionality and on the philosophy of mathematics.[27]

---

[22] Meditation IV, AT VII, 54: "Quamdiu de Deo tantum cogito, totusque in eum me converto, nullam erroris aut falsitatis causam deprehendo."

[23] See Meditation IV, AT VII, 54. Cf. Thomas Aquinas, *Summa Theologica*, Part II, Q. 180, Art. 6, Reply Obj. 2: "the soul's gaze (is) fixed on the contemplation of the one simple truth. In this operation of the soul there is no error…" Cf. as well François de Sales, *Traité de l'Amour de Dieu*, I, c. 15, in *Oeuvres Complètes*, I, 395.

[24] *Discours de la Méthode* II, AT VI, p. 21: "un enfant instruit en l'Arithmetique, ayant fait une addition suivant les reigles, se peut assurer d'avoir trouve, touchant la somme qu'il examinoit, tout ce que l'esprit humain sçauroit trouver."

[25] See *Discours de la Méthode*, AT VI, 19: "elles (i.e. les mathématiques) accoustumeroient mon esprit a se repaistre de veritez, et ne se contenter point de fausses raisons." Cf. *Discours de la Méthode*, III, AT VI, 27; also the unpublished *Regulae ad Directionem Ingenii*, AT X, 373.

[26] See Descartes's letter to Hogelande, 8 February 1640, AT III, 722–723, where Descartes specifices that only the authentic discoverer, not the servile imitator, can be called "autarches." As Matthew Jones points out, the term is, most prominently, Stoic. See his discussion, "Descartes's Geometry as Spiritual Exercise," *Critical Inquiry*, Fall 2001, 28, 1, 58. On the use of mathematics as a source of mental cultivation in Clavius and in Jesuit schools, see Geneviève Rodis-Lewis, "Descartes et les mathématiques," in *Le discours et sa méthode*, ed. N. Grimaldi et J.–L. Marion (Paris: PUF, 1978), 187–211.

[27] See in this regard Charles Parsons' statement: "The 'philosophy of mathematics',

Reversing his own initial position that "arithmetic and geometry alone are exempt of all falsehood and uncertainty,"[28] Descartes, as we know, took the initiative to cast over mathematical certainty the "almost imperceptible" (*valde tenuis*) shadow of "metaphysical doubt."[29] The very rule that "whatever is known clearly and distinctly is true" requires, Descartes proclaims in the *Discours*, a higher validation, namely the more fundamental metaphysical axiom that "whatever in us is real and true comes from a perfect and infinite being."[30] The clarity and distinctness of self-evident ideas do not evidently imply their veracity: nothing assures us of their truth except the knowledge that God exists.[31]

When Regius vehemently protested that mathematical truths require no further justification, theological or otherwise,[32] Descartes replied that we cannot indeed "withhold our assent" from clear and distinct axioms that are actually grasped.[33] The problem lies in the fact that we often remember (*saepe recordamur*) conclusions that were drawn from evident premises after these premises are out of sight, allowing doubt to slip in "if we are ignorant of God."[34] Descartes appears to be focusing blame on memory, but as Harry Frankfurt and others have emphasized,

---

when it has not concentrated on specific methodological issues in mathematics, has chiefly sought to explain a single impressive gross feature of mathematics: its combination of clarity and certainty with enormous generality." In *Mathematics in Philosophy* (Ithaca, NY: Cornell U. Press, 1983), 176.

[28] *Regulae*, Regula II, AT X, 364: "Diximus ... solas Arithmeticam et geometriam ab omni falsitatis vel incertudinis vitio puras existere."

[29] Meditation III, AT VII, 36, and *Discours*, AT VI, 38: "Lorsqu'il est question d'une certitude métaphysique, on ne peut nier etc."

[30] AT VI, 39: "Mais si nous ne sçavions point que tout ce qui est en nous de reel et de vray, vient d'un estre parfait et infini, pour claires et distinctes que fussent nos idées, nous n'aurions aucune raison qui nous assurat, qu'elles eussent la perfection d'estre vrayes."

[31] Further analysis of Descartes's argument is found in Harry G. Frankfurt, "Descartes's Validation of Reason," in *René Descartes: Critical Assessments*, ed. Georges J.D. Moyal (London and New York: Routledge, 1991), I, 263–275.

[32] See Descartes's letter to Regius, May 24, 1640, AT III, 64: "In secunda dicitis: *axiomatum clare et distincte intellectorum veritatem per se esse manifestam.*"

[33] *Ibid.*: "quod etiam concedo, quandiu clare et distincte intelliguntur, quia mens nostra est talis natura, ut non possit clare intellectis non assentiri."

[34] *Ibid.*: "quod etiam concedo, quandiu clare et distincte intelliguntur, quia mens nostra est talis natura, ut non possit clare intellectis non assentiri; sed quia saepe recordamur conclusionum ex talibus praemissis deductarum, etiamsi ad ipsas praemissas non attendamus, dico tunc, si Deum ignoremus, fingere nos posse illas esse incertas." For Descartes's warm interest in Regius at the time, see his letter to Mersenne of July 22, 1640, AT III, 95.

this is a matter of formulation rather than substance.[35] Meditation I impugns the truth of immediately grasped axioms, regardless of how indubitably they impose themselves on cognition.[36] Quite apart from the need to frame the problem in a manner consistent with the hypothesis that the meditator is a separate *res cogitans*,[37] Meditation V will aim at validating cognition indivisibly as *percipio, intelligo* and *recorder*.[38] The decision to introduce "hyperbolic doubt" and therefore treat *percipio, intelligo* and *recorder* on a par may have stemmed from failed attempts to secure memory (*recorder*) in isolation,[39] but serves in the end to undermine the mathematician's self-idolatry and correct his pride.[40]

Whatever the precipitating cause of Descartes's new position,[41] we must note that nothing about God's existence *per se* changes or affects the spiritual use of Descartes's geometry as a way to stabilize attention and cultivate self-control. Something more than self-techniques of *honnêteté* must therefore be at stake. The metaphysical demotion of the certainty of mathematical evidence, while it may stem from a specific epistemological impasse, represents, as we saw, an overt *prise de position* on Descartes's part in the Catholic controversy with *libertins* and atheists.[42]

---

[35] See Harry Frankfurt's criticism of Willis Doney, "The Cartesian Circle," *Journal of the History of Ideas*, 16 (1955), 324–338, in "Memory and the Cartesian Circle," *Philosophical Review*, 71 (1962), 504–511.

[36] See Meditation I, AT VII, 21: "Imo etiam, quemadmodum judico interdum alios errare circa ea quae se perfectissime scire arbitrantur, ita ego ut fallar quoties duo et tria simul addo, vel numero quadrati latera, vel si quis aliud facilius fingi potest?"

[37] As Harry Frankfurt argues in "Descartes's Validation of Reason," in *René Descartes*, ed. George Moyal, 267–268.

[38] John Searle's argument that all three intentional states are characterized by the same "mind-to-world direction of fit" and therefore fall under the same unified account sheds an interesting light on Descartes's analysis. See John Searle, *Intentionality*, especially 8 and 53.

[39] In the *Regulae*, Descartes did not yet question the veracity of evident premises, but instead hoped to "conserve" evidence as the mind moves from premises to distant theorems by improving memory and using sign notations. See, especially, Rules VII and XVI, AT X, 387–392 and 454–459.

[40] François de Sales, *Traité de l'Amour de Dieu*, I, c. 4, in *Oeuvres Complètes*, p. 363: "Pour faire vivre et régner l'amour de Dieu en nous, nous amortissons l'amour propre."

[41] Which precedes Galileo's 1633 condemnation, since Descartes's doctrine of the creation of eternal truths, stated to Mersenne as early as April 1630, AT I, p. 145, implies that geometry no longer provides the highest standard of evidence.

[42] As Descartes's "follow-up" letter on the creation of mathematical truths to Mersenne of 6 May 1630 makes explicit, AT I, 150: "Ceux qui n'ont point de plus hautes pensées que cela peuvent aisément devenir Athées." A useful survey by Tullio Gregory is found in *Genèse de la raison classique de Charron à Descartes* (Paris: PUF, 2000), 81–111. Mersenne's efforts to combat atheist scientists in both *Quaestiones celeberrimae in Genesim*,

In a letter of 13 November 1639, Descartes agrees with Mersenne about the difficulty of "curing Analysts" of their "opinions regarding God's existence and the honor that is due him."[43] Presumably, the issue is the tendency among "analysts" (mathematicians) to deny God's existence or to fail sufficiently to honor God by denying that his existence has any relevance to mathematics. Descartes indeed goes on to explain that, although arguments are available to convince these analysts of God's existence, "people of this sort, believing themselves to have exceptionally good minds, are often less capable of reasoning than others."[44]

Mathematicians are impaired in their ability to reason metaphysically precisely because they cultivate "the part of the mind that is most useful for mathematics, which is to say the imagination," which "hinders more than it helps" in the case of metaphysical speculation.[45] Mersenne's atheist or at least insufficiently devout "Analysts" must thus (1) be encouraged to elevate their mathematical activity from the level of imagination to the level of reason, and (2) be weaned of their autarchic pride. The letter, in effect, outlines the agenda of Meditation V.[46]

---

published in Paris in 1623, and *L'impiété des deistes, athees et libertins de ce temps*, published in Paris in 1624, are of special relevance. In the latter, for example, Mersenne emphasizes (118) that scientists should recognize that "all of our faculties" are received from God, "on whom absolutely everything depends." (Cf. Faksimile, Stuttgart-Bad Cannstatt 1975, Friedrich Frommann Verlag).

[43] AT II, 622: "Les opinions de vos Analistes, touchant l'Existence de Dieu et l'honneur qu'on luy doit rendre, sont, *comme vous écrivez*, tres-difficiles à guerir." (Emphasis added).

[44] AT II, 622: "non pas qu'il n'y ait moyen de donner des raisons assez fortes pour les convaincre, mais pource que ces gens-là, pensant avoir bon esprit, sont souvent moins capables de raison que les autres."

[45] AT II, 622: "Car la partie de l'esprit qui aide le plus aux Mathematiques, à scavoir l'imagination, nuit plus qu'elle ne sert pour les Speculations Metaphysiques." Cf. Descartes's earlier and unpublished reproof in the *Regulae* of his contemporaries and predecessors for typically devising only "superficial demonstrations, discovered at random rather than methodically, addressed to the eyes and the imagination rather than to the understanding, to the point of eventually destroying up to the habit of using reason." *Regulae*, IV, AT X, 375, lines 16–20: "... atque superficiariis istis demonstrationibus, quae casu saepius quam arte inveniuntur, et magis ad oculos et imaginationem pertinent quam ad intellectum, sic incumbere, ut quodammodo ipsa ratione uti desuescamus."

[46] Descartes goes on to tell Mersenne that he *now* has in his hands "a Discourse where I try to clarify what I have said earlier on the subject." AT II, 622: "J'ay maintenant entre les mains un Discours, où je tasche d'éclaircir ce que j'ay écrit cy-devant sur ce sujet."

Dynamically engaging the threshold between *imaginor* and *percipio*, Meditation V at once elevates the mind's eye from intentional configurations to "unimaginable" truths and derives the theorem that "unimaginable" truths are veridically grasped because rational intentionality is a gift from God and is therefore trustworthy. In contrast to the *nonnulli* featured in Meditation I, who would rather abrogate God's infinite power than give up the certainty of mathematics,[47] the mathematician who allows himself to be reformed by Meditation V will instead *trust* God's infinite power and affirm it as the source of his inalienable capacity to "tell truth from falsehood."[48] Descartes's limited "foundationalism" does not invoke God to ratify Cartesian physics as such but only to establish that the faculty of reasoning "cannot tend, by its essence, to falsehood."[49] Framed this way, the trust we have in our natural light is neither hegemonic nor vainglorious.

We are now in a better position to appreciate the unfolding of Meditation V. The meditator first distinctly imagines (*imaginor*) a continuous quantity extended in length, breadth and depth, then counts (*numero*) various parts in it, and finally assigns (*assigno*) to these parts various shapes, sizes, positions and motions.[50] Not only is the pure idea of extension imagined first (*nempe*),[51] it is, Descartes says, "distinctly" imagined, implying that the mind's eye first presents itself with an isotropic,

---

[47] See on this subject Georges Moyal, who identifies the *nonnulli* in question as atheist mathematicians, in "Veritas aeterna, Deo volente," in *Les études philosophiques*, no. 4, Avril-septembre 1987, 463–489. See as well Julie Klein, "Descartes's Critique of the Atheist Geometer," *The Southern Journal of Philosophy* (2000), Vol. XXXVIII.

[48] Cf. *Discours*, Part III, AT VI, 27: "Dieu nous ayant donné a chascun quelque lumiere pour discerner le vray d'avec le faux…".

[49] See Second Answers, AT VII, 144: "Cum enim Deus sit summum ens, non potest non esse etiam summum bonum et verum, atque idcirco repugnat, ut quid ab eo fit, quod positive tendat in falsum. Atqui, cum nihil reale in nobis esse possit, quod non ab ipso sit datum (ut simul cum ejus existentia demonstratum est), realem autem habeamus facultatem ad verum agnoscendum, illudque a falso distinguendum (ut patet vel ex hoc solo quod nobis insit ideae falsi et veri), nisi haec facultas in verum tenderet […] merito Deus ejus dator pro deceptore haberetur."

[50] At VII, p. 63: "Nempe distincte imaginor quantitatem…; numero in ea varias partes; quaslibet istis partibus magnitudines, figuras, situs, et motus locales, motibusque istis quaslibet duratione assigno."

[51] See Albert Einstein's remark in *Mein Weltbild* (Amsterdam: Querido Verlag, 1934), English translation by Sonja Bargmann in *Ideas and Opinions* (New York: Laurel, 1976), 2nd. edition, 272: "It is clear that the concept of space as a real thing already existed in the extra-scientific conceptual world. Euclid's mathematics, however, knew nothing of this concept as such; it confined itself to the concepts of the object, and the spatial relations between objects […] Space as a continuum does not figure in the conceptual system at all. This concept was first introduced by Descartes, when he described the

simply-connected spatial manifold characterized only by dimension and divisibility.[52] Distinct (non-overlapping) parts can then be numbered, and various curves imagined to construct figures of various shapes and sizes.[53] Figures moreover display "position" (*situs*) and can be moved imaginatively at various rates and for various lengths of time.[54] The constructivist approach that characterizes Euclidean geometry is initially preserved (*imaginor, numero, assigno,*)[55] but gives way to a pure witnessing by the *ego* (*percipio, intelligo*) of the *per se* logical coherence of the concept of limit, geometric figures being "the terms, so to speak, by which substance is bounded."[56]

As though to wean Analysts of the pleasure of "resting" with the imagination, Descartes imperceptibly leads the *ego* from *imaginor* to *percipio*. The characteristic intentional sequence of first aiming at, then hitting a target, is captured by the expression *attendendo percipio*—"by attending I perceive."[57] Although the distinction between imagination

<hr />

point-in-space by its coordinates. Here for the first time geometrical figures appear, in a way, as parts of infinite space, which is conceived as a three-dimensional continuum."

[52] Cf. Rule XII, *Regulae*, AT X, 416–417: "Si vero intellectus examinandum aliquid sibi proponat, quod referri possit ad corpus, ejus idea, quam distinctisse poterit, in imaginatione est formanda. ... ...illas tantum simplices vocamus, quarum cognitio tam perspicua est et distincta, ut in plures magis distincte cognitas mente dividi non possint: tales sunt figura, extensio..."

[53] See Einstein's further remark in *Ideas and Opinions*, 272–273: "The great superiority of the Cartesian treatment of space is by no means confined to the fact that it applies analysis for the purposes of geometry. [...] In the Cartesian treatment ... all surfaces, for example, appear, in principle, on equal footing, without any arbitrary preference for linear structures in building up geometry." In his 1684 *Entretien sur les Sciences*, the Oratorian priest Bernard Lamy, similarly, remarks: "Des-Cartes dans sa geometrie nous a apris la veritable methode de connoitre toutes sortes de lignes courbes." See Bernard Lamy, *Entretiens sur les Sciences*, eds. F. Girbal et P. Clair (Paris: PUF, 1966), 221.

[54] The meditator, in short, is invited to "emerge from doubt" by embracing Cartesian geometry as the essence of material things. See AT II, p. 268 and *Principes*, II, art. 16, AT 9–2, 71; along with Daniel Garber's classic study, "Descartes's physics," in *The Cambridge Companion to Descartes*, ed. John Cottingham, 286–334.

[55] For the importance of construction in Euclid, see e.g. Paul Bernays's remark in "On platonism in mathematics," translated by Charles Parsons in *Philosophy of Mathematics, Selected Readings*, eds. Paul Benacerraf and Hilary Putnam (Cambridge, New York and Sydney: Cambridge U. Press, 1983), 2nd. edition, 258 (with emphasis added by Parsons); "If we compare Hilbert's axiom system to Euclid's [...], we notice that Euclid speaks of figures to be *constructed*, whereas, for Hilbert, systems of points, straight lines, and planes exist from the outset."

[56] *Quintae Responsiones*, AT VII, 381: "figurae Geometricae non considerantur ut substantiae, sed ut termini sub quibus substantia continetur."

[57] AT VII, 63. The French translation by de Luynes (AT IX, 50) renders: "pour peu que j'y applique mon attention, je conçois..." See Richard Cobb-Stevens' discus-

and pure intellection will not be explicitly clarified until Meditation VI,[58] the *ego* is already invited to exercise its power to *excogitate*
figures that cannot be seen by the fleshly eye. The *ego* is able to think
of "innumerable" figures that could not possibly have fallen under the
senses.[59] Not only is the chiliagon implicitly evoked, the verb that is
used by the *ego* to unlock pure geometric Intentions, *excogitare*, will
conspicuously return to describe the pure Intending of God's incomprehensible essence, precisely what is least accessible to the imagination: *nulla alia res potest a me excogitari, a cujus essentiam existentia per-
tineat.*[60]

The cognitive faculty through which I initially grasped myself reflexively as an immaterial causal agent now explores its essential "aboutness"—its power to "attend and perceive" essences that radically differ
from myself, namely in-existent *quanta* appearing in their irrevocable
foreignness. By bracketing extramental existence and focusing on ideas
that lie *in* myself (*apud me invenio*) but are not *of* myself, I discover my
intelligence precisely as a spiritual exposure to alterity. To think (*cogito*) is to know myself, but to think *of* innumerable figures (*excogito*) is
to discover that my faculty of intellect exposes me to things that are
radically removed from the sphere of my own reflexivity. Spiritual substance, *mens*, is as radically Intentional as it is free.

<hr/>

sion in *Husserl and Analytic Philosophy*, (Dordrecht & Boston: Kluwer Academic Publishers, 1990), 132–133. In analysing Husserl's *Logical Investigations*, Cobb-Stevens writes:
"Husserl approves of Brentano's use of the term 'intentional', on the grounds that its
original Latin sense evokes the metaphor of first aiming at something and subsequently
hitting the mark. These images aptly describe the relationship between meaning and
intuition." Victor Caston, in turn, documents the presence of a similar metaphor
in Plato's *Cratylus* and the *Theaetetus*; see "Connecting Traditions: Augustine and the
Greeks on Intentionality," in *Ancient and Medieval Theories of Intentionality*, 27 and 28.

[58] AT VII, 72: "Cum triangulum imaginor, non tantum intelligo illud esse figuram
tribus lineis comprehensam, sed simul etiam istas tres lineas tanquam praesentes acie
mentis intueor, atque hoc est quod imaginari appello. Si vero de chiliogono velim
cogitare, equidem aeque bene intelligo illud esse figuram constantem mille lateribus,
ac intelligo triangulum esse figuram constantem tribus; sed non eodem modo illa mille
latera imaginor, sive tanquam praesentia intueor."

[59] AT VII, 64: "neque ad rem attinet, si dicam mihi forte a rebus externis per organa
sensuum istam trianguli ideam advenisse ...; possum enim alias innumeras figuras
excogitare, de quibus nulla suspicio esse potest quod mihi unquam per sensus illapsae
sint."

[60] I do not mean to distinguish *cogitare* and *excogitare* in any clear-cut, absolute sense,
beyond what Cicero implies in *Epistolae ad Atticum*, 9, 6, 7: "ad haec cogita, vel potius
excogita". I mean the distinction mainly metaphorically, to emphasize that Med. V
draws the meditator "out of" the self-enclosure of the *cogito*.

11.2. Velim Nolim

What does it mean to say that *mens* is essentially Intentional, directed to alterity more radically than to itself?[61] When the *ego* applies its attention to numbers and figures, the *ego* perceives innumerable particulars (*particularia innumera*)

> "whose truth appears so openly and conforms so well to my nature that it seems to me, as I start to discover them, that I am not learning anything new but rather remembering (*reminisci*) what I already knew."[62]

Descartes's qualified *anamnesis* doctrine[63] calls out sympathetically to Augustinians such as Arnauld and Gibieuf,[64] but also to the very *nonnulli* whom Meditation V is designed to "cure," in so far as naturalists and *esprits forts* typically modelled themselves on Socrates.[65] Descartes, however, avails himself of the first-person meditational narrative to turn *anamnesis* into a pure description of the *ego*'s experience, free of metaphysical commitments:

> "I seem to be remembering what I already knew before, which is to say to be noticing (*advertere*) for the first time things that were in some sense

---

[61] Recall in this regard the speculation advanced in Meditation III, AT VII, 45: "... ac proinde priorem quodammodo in me esse perceptionem infiniti quam finiti."

[62] AT VII, 63–64: "quorum veritas adeo aperta est et naturae meae consentanea, ut, dum illa primum detego, non tam videar aliquid novi addiscere, quam eorum quae jam ante sciebam reminisci."

[63] Cf. Descartes's defense of innate ideas in *Epistola ad G. Voetium*, AT VIII-2, 166–167: "Sed notandum est eas omnes res, quarum cognitio dicitur nobis esse a natura indita, non ideo a nobis expresse cognosci; sed tantum tales esse, ut ipsas, absque ullo sensuum experimento, ex proprii ingenii viribus, cognoscere possimus. Cujus generis sunt omnes geometricae veritates, non tantum maxime obviae, sed etiam reliquae, quantumvis abstrusae videantur. Atque inde Socrates apud Platonem, puerum quemdam de Geometricis elementis interrogando, sicque efficiendo ut ille puer quasdam veritates ex mente propria erueret, quas prius in ea fuisse non notaverat, reminiscentiam suam probare conabatur."

[64] On the Paris Theology Faculty to whom the *Meditationes* are dedicated and from whom Descartes hopes to receive an official endorsement (AT VII, 1 and 6). For Augustinian *anamnesis*, apart from what is found in the *Confessions* Bk. X, see, e.g., Bonaventure's *Itinerarium mentis in deum*, cap. III, 2: "retinet nihilominus *scientiarum principia et dignitates* ... quin ea audita approbet et eis assentiat, non tanquam de novo percipiat, sed tanquam sibi innata et familiaria recognoscat." Cited from Bonaventure, *The Journey of the Mind to God*, translated by Philotheus Boehner, O.F.M., edited, with Introduction and Notes by Stephen F. Brown (Indianapolis and Cambridge: Hackett Publishing Company, 1993). Bonaventure was declared "Doctor of the Church" in 1588, and a new edition of his works appeared in 1588 and 1596.

[65] See Tullio Gregory, *Genèse de la raison classique*, 313–380.

(*quidem*) in me all along, although I had not previously turned my mind's gaze (*obtutum mentis convertissem*) to them."[66]

The first leg of Descartes's description suggests that mathematical truths are already known to me, since I "seem to remember what I already knew before," while the second leg insists on the luminous experience of a first encounter.[67] Intentional "turning to" (*advertere, convertere*) coincides with my becoming aware that I was not aware of what I knew, so that grasping the least particular truth ($2+3 = 5$), is to grasp myself simultaneously as recovered from oblivion—as "reminded." Most significantly, what my Intentional gaze "hits" *in illa* and re-cognizes as familiar, already "known" to me, is precisely the evident truth that they manifest (*aperta veritas*). The truths in question concern extension and therefore what I myself most emphatically am not, yet each one, *qua* true, conspicuously "accords" with my nature (*naturae meae consentanea*).[68] What exactly "accords" with me? What do I know *of* a triangle and *about* it that "re-minds" me of what I had not knowingly lost? What is the crux of my Intentional experience of *aperta veritas*? This is explained when Descartes turns, next, to what he finds to be "most worthy of consideration."[69] Since innate mathematical ideas, unlike sensations, do not impose themselves on consciousness involuntarily, but are summoned through deliberate intentional acts, whatever alterity they display—and they could not "accord" with my nature without being "other" than me in some crucial sense—is a radically different sort of alterity than the alterity "suffered" in sensation, when, for example, we feel cold whether we want it or not.[70] Once innate

---

[66] AT VII, 64: "... eorum quae jam ante sciebam reminisci, sive ad ea primum advertere, quae dudum quidem in me erant, licet non prius in illa obtutum mentis convertissem."

[67] Does Descartes suppose two distinct states of knowledge, one latent and one conscious, in the same way that Augustine draws a distinction between the "more remote" memory where intellectual ideas lie scattered and the conscious commemorative activity of *cogitatio*—a distinction which in turn evokes the Neoplatonic distinction between *nous* and *dianoia*? See Richard Sorabji, "Why The Neoplatonists Did Not Have Intentional Objects Of Intellection," in *Ancient and Medieval Theories of Intentionality*, 106. While O'Meara argues that discursive reason (*dianoia*) has an intentional "aboutness" and "directedness", Sorabji argues that intellect as such (*nous*), does not.

[68] AT VII, 63: "... particularia innumera de figuris, de numero, de motu, et similibus, attendendo percipio, quorum veritas adeo aperta est et naturae meae consentanea."

[69] AT VII, 64: "maxime considerandum puto".

[70] See e.g. Meditation III, AT VII, 51: "nec unquam non expectanti mihi advenit, ut solent rerum sensibilium ideae ..."

mathematical ideas are freely brought before the mind's gaze, the alterity they exhibit alerts me that "they cannot be judged to be nothing
even though they perhaps exist nowhere."[71] In this regard, they differ
notably from fictions of my own making:

> "and although (*quamvis*) they are thought by me, so to speak, at will
> (*quodammodo ad arbitrium cogitentur*), they are nonetheless not feigned by
> me (*finguntur*), but have their own true and immutable natures."[72]

The intentional states that converge in the presentation of a thought
thus allow me to distinguish true ideas (*ideas veras mihi ingenitas*) from
false suppositions (*falsas positiones*) which I myself invent.[73] The intra-
mental alterity that ideal *quanta* manifest attests to a positivity that is
not conceptually tied to extramental existence. We know from Meditation III that the innate idea of God is paradigmatic of the positivity
that marks true ideas since the actual infinite is "a true idea, not a
mere negation of finitude," and also of the alterity that marks true ideas
since I recognize, as soon as I think it, that it is not in my power to
"add or subtract anything."[74] Moreover the content presented to cognition by the innate idea of God, namely absolute incomprehensibility, is
supremely "clear and distinct."[75]

In contrast, in the case of ideas that I "feign," the same initial freedom is experienced that marks the intentional presentation of innate
ideas, but the content that appears, much like the content of sensory
ideas, fails to impose precise constraints on cognition. If I think of a
chimera, a receding horizon of indeterminacy clings to my thought.

---

[71] AT VII, 64: "Etiam si extra me fortasse nullibi existant, non tamen dici possunt
nihil esse."

[72] AT VII, 64: "et quamvis a me quodammodo ad arbitrium cogitentur, non tamen
a me finguntur, sed suas habent veras et immutabiles naturas."

[73] Descartes draws this distinction a little later in Meditation V, AT VII, 68: "Magna
differentia est inter ejusmodi falsas positiones, et ideas veras mihi ingenitas." See on
this subject two articles that clarify the questions raised by this distinction and the
problems involved: Calvin Normore, "Descartes's Possibilities" and Gregory Brown,
"*Vera Entia*: The Nature of Mathematical Objects in Descartes," both reprinted in
Georges J.D. Moyal, ed., *René Descartes: Critical Assessments*, respectively 68–83 and 84–
102.

[74] Meditation III, AT VII 45 and 51, respectively. The phrase is repeated in Meditation V, AT VII, p. 68: "nihil a me detrahi potest nec mutari."

[75] As Descartes explains in *Primae Responsiones*, AT VII, 112: "prudenter vero hic
quaerit, *an clare et distincte cognoscam infinitum*; [...] qua infinitum est, nullo quidem
modo comprehendi, sed nihilominus tamen intelligi, quatenus scilicet clare et distincte
intelligere aliquam rem talem esse, ut nulli plane in ea limites possint reperiri, est clare
intelligere illam esse infinitam."

I myself must continue to invent and determine its properties. Once I think of a triangle, I encounter a *forma determinata* with properties that are fully fixed in advance of my thinking: there is no "last" property beyond which confusion and indistinctness take over. To recognize that the triangle is a *vera res* possessed of "its own true and immutable essence" is equivalent to grasping that its properties comply in advance and *ad infinitum* with the principle of the excluded middle: this is why the idea of the triangle includes, as Descartes clarifies in his answer to Gassendi, the "perfection of possible existence," which a chimera lacks.[76]

This brings us to a special sort of "attending and perceiving," namely demonstration. A *vera res* existing objectively in the mind, unlike a figment of my own invention, possesses properties that can be known demonstratively.[77] Descartes points out that mathematical demonstration is characterized by what Poincaré will call its "ampliative" character:[78] the mathematician demonstrates *more* properties than were explicitly or intentionally attributed to a given figure beforehand.[79] Thus it is possible for me to prove, for example, that the sum of the three angles of a triangle equals two right angles,

> "which I now (*nunc*) clearly acknowledge whether I want to or not (*velim nolim*), even though I had in no way thought about them beforehand (*antea*), when I imagined a triangle."[80]

---

[76] Descartes adopts the classical position that a chimera "cannot be supposed to exist" after affirming that *existentia possibilis* is a perfection of the idea of the triangle. See *Quintae Responsiones*, AT VII, 383.

[77] Cf. Descartes's answer to Berman (AT V, 160), who questioned the difference between a triangle and a goatstag in this regard: "Sed sic nec chimera erit ens fictum, cum etiam de ea varias proprietates demonstrare queam." Descartes uses the term *connexum* to indicate the notion of logical entailment when he discriminates for Burman between *idea vera* and *suppositio* (*ibid.*). See also John Cottingham's remarks in *The Conversation with Burman* (Oxford: Clarendon Press, 1976), 91.

[78] See Henri Poincaré, "On the nature of mathematical reasoning," in *Philosophy of mathematics, Selected Readings*, eds. Paul Benacerraf and Hilary Putnam, 394–402 [reprinted from *Science and Hypothesis* (New York: Dover, 1952), 1–19].

[79] AT VII, 64: "demonstrari possint variae proprietates de isto triangulo ... quas velim nolim clare nunc agnosco, etiamsi de iis nullo modo antea cogitaverim, cum triangulum imaginatus sum." See further Anthony Kenny, *Descartes* (New York: Random House, 1968), 154, together with Gregory Brown's new step in "Vera Entia: The Nature of Mathematical Objects in Descartes," *René Descartes, Critical Assessments*, ed. Moyal, III, 89–90.

[80] AT VII, 64: "demonstrari possint variae proprietates de isto triangulo ... quas velim nolim clare nunc agnosco, etiamsi de iis nullo modo antea cogitaverim, cum triangulum imaginatus sum."

Demonstrative properties are grasped as mind-independent because the *ego* grasps them *velim nolim* and, at the same time, knows that they have not been put there voluntarily. They exist prior to the *ego*'s Intentional steps and the *ego*'s agency.[81] A part of the perceptual content is that the perceptual content is caused by the properties of the triangle, not the other way around.

Demonstration recalls me from myself by revealing to me the positivity of true things that clearly and distinctly determine my thought *velim nolim*—according to their own "proper and determinate nature," "immutable and eternal (*imutabilis et eterna*)."[82] Ordered steps converge to present me with truths that precede the time at which I first become aware of them and therefore appear to me precisely as time-invariant. What I acknowledge *nunc* as necessary (*velim nolim*) belonged as such to the triangle *antea*, without beginning. Thus whereas I initially *imagine* a triangle and freely apply my inner gaze to its three sides, I now step beyond imagination to *witness* truths that I myself never put there or could have put there. When my thoughts are thoughts of true things, I grasp that

> "My thought does not make [the thing be such and such], or impose any necessity to the thing, rather the necessity [that belongs] to the thing itself determines my thought [to be such and such]."[83]

My thought comprehends the (finite) content of the theorem, but submits to its necessity as to a saturated alterity. The necessity that determines my thought *velim nolim* when I grasp a true fact can only be attested by the experience that I have that I myself am not the cause of it.

A first conclusion must be drawn, namely that I must be a free agent and know myself to be a free agent to perceive that my thought is determined *velim nolim*. Were I not a free agent, I could not know that a characteristic mark of a necessary truth is that I cannot change it at will. It follows by necessity that only a free agent is empowered by nature to know a fact as a *true* fact. Only a free agent "suffers" the involuntary

---

[81] For a nice discussion of this aspect of Descartes's theory, characterized as the "passivity criterion for clear and distinct ideas," see Thomas Vinci, *Cartesian Truth* (New York and Oxford: Oxford U. Press, 1998), 29.

[82] *Ibid.*: "Ut cum, exempli causa, triangulum imaginor … est tamen profecto determinata quaedam ejus natura, sive essentia, sive forma, immutabilis et aeterna…"

[83] Meditation V, AT VII, 67: "non quod mea cogitatio hoc efficiat, sive aliquam necessitatem ulli rei imponat, sed contra quia ipsius rei,… necessitas me determinat ad hoc cogitandum."

necessity of rational evidence. Only a free agent consents to necessary truths because only a free agent perceives necessary truths. Even if the hypothetical members of Hobbes's world consent to a rational truth involuntarily—*volentes nolentes*—their understanding that they "have no choice in the matter" implies that they are free agents to begin with. A second conclusion is that logical necessity is an *incomprehensible* necessity to the free agent that perceives it. The "eternal truths" which the *ego* discovers as mind-independent and true *velim nolim* are, as we know, decreed freely by God and imprinted on the mind. They are necessary *quoad nos* but are merely eternal *quoad Deum*, since there is no necessity "besides God" for him to decree them.[84] To grasp the Pythagorean theorem as time-invariant is to grasp its radical independence from my thought and my existence, but also to explain the necessity that it imposes on my thought as part of its Intentional presentation.[85] The Truth-rule is thus critically enriched by the (clear and distinct) perception that I *cannot change* what I clearly and distinctly perceive to be true because the necessity of Truth exceeds me absolutely and is incomprehensible to me as such. I can *witness* it but I cannot *comprehend* it any more than I can change it. I "give myself" over to the alterity that exceeds me and gives me to know what I cannot give myself whenever I am "re-reminded" of even the least mind-independent truth.[86]

A general corollary of rational intentionality can consequently be framed that simply affirms necessity *quoad nos* by acknowledging that the defining characteristics that make up a valid concept ("true and

---

[84] Letter to Mesland, May 2 1644, AT IV, 118: "Et encore que Dieu ait voulu que quelques veritez fussent necessaires, ce n'est pas à dire qu'il les ait necessairement voulues."

[85] Cf. Bertrand Russell, "Necessity and Possibility," (1905), in *Collected Papers*, IV, 508–520, especially 511: "The view of necessity which we have been hitherto considering is the one which connects it with independence of particular times. This is the view which caused necessary propositions to be spoken of as 'eternal truths'." Bonaventure captured the experience of timelessness associated with necessary truths by saying that intellectual memory "has present in itself a changeless light in which it recalls changeless truths." See *Itinerarium*. cap. III, ed. cit., 64: "Ex *tertia* habetur, quod ipsa habet lucem incommutabilem sibi praesentem, in qua meminit invariabilium veritatem."

[86] Thus the whole argument of Jean-Luc Marion's *Étant donné* (Paris: PUF, 1998) applies to Truth exactly to the same extent that it applies to Beauty. The Pythagorean theorem is as saturated with Truth as a Rothko canvas is with Beauty, and both are equally "unobjectifiable." Nor does it serve to say that a mathematical theorem is a "phenomenon poor in intuition" since what is grasped intentionally is a pure positivity/alterity that phenomenalizes truth, i.e. that allows me to experience truth as such.

immutable nature") belong as properties to the (necessarily) possible (constructible) elements that fall under the concept: "whatever we clearly conceive to belong to the nature of a thing can be said or affirmed of that thing with truth."[87]

11.3. *God's (unbracketable) existence*

Rejected by Aristotelians,[88] embraced by a number of Oratorians and Jansenists,[89] Descartes's reformulation of Anselm's proof[90] fails to convert the modern critic,[91] but deserves new scrutiny as the fulcrum that sets Cartesian science into motion. God's existence, not my own, is the "first truth upon which all truths depend."[92]

Descartes conforms to the letter of Thomist doctrine insofar as he presents his "ontological" or *propter quid* proof only after he has first established God's existence by a proof *quia* in Meditation III.[93] Already

---

[87] See *Secundae Responsiones*, AT VII, 149: "quod clare intelligimus pertinere ad alicujus rei naturam, id potest de ea re cum veritate affirmari"; and, also in *Secundae Responsiones*, AT VII, 162, Definitio 9 ("cum quid dicimus in alicujus rei natura, sive conceptu, contineri, idem est ac si diceremus id de ea re verum esse, sive de ipsa posse affirmari") and 163, Postulatum 4 ("Advertantque illa omnia, quae in iis contineri percipimus, vere de ipsis posse affirmari"). Cf. Malebranche, *De la recherche de la vérité*, IV, ix, in *Oeuvres*, Collection Pléiade (Paris: Gallimard, 1979), I, p. 457: "On doit attribuer à une chose ce que l'on conçoit clairement être renfermé dans l'idée qui la représente." Cf. Gottlob Frege's clarification that "By properties which are asserted of the concept I naturally do not mean the characteristics which make up the concept. These latter are properties of the things which fall under the concept, not of the concept." *Foundations of Arithmetic*, English trans. J.L. Austin (Evanston, Ill: Northwestern U. Press, 1980), 64.

[88] See Alan C. Kors, *Atheism in France, 1650–1729* (Princeton: Princeton U. Press, 1990), vol. I, pp. 297–322.

[89] Most notably by the Oratorians Nicolas Joseph Poisson (*Commentaire … sur la Méthode de Mr. Descartes*—1671) and Bernard Lamy (*Entretiens sur les sciences*—1684). See Alan C. Kors, *Atheism in France*, vol. I, 334–336.

[90] Which Mersenne had already cited against atheist scientists in *Impiété des Deistes, Athees et Libertins*, 113–117.

[91] See Frege's rejection in *The Foundations of Arithmetic*, trans. J.L. Austin, 65: "Affirmation of existence is in fact nothing but denial of the number nought. Because existence is a property of concepts, the ontological argument for the existence of God breaks down."

[92] See Letter to Mersenne, May 6, 1630, AT I, 150: *si Deus non esset, nihilominus istae veritates essent verae.*

[93] Granted that the effect invoked, namely that the human mind possesses the idea of an actual infinity of perfection, is not given through sensation but through pure thought. For Thomas's doctrine, see *Summa Theologiae*, I.1, q. 2, art. 1 and *Summa Contra Gentiles* I.1. c. 22. Descartes cites *Summa Theologiae*, I.2, art. 2, in his *Primae*

convinced of God's existence, the *ego* does not set out in Meditation V
to prove it anew *per essentiam* but to bracket extramental existence as
such in order to examine ideal *quanta*. Mathematical *anamnesis* leads
the *ego* away from the self-enclosed *cogito* to the gradual recognition of
extramental necessity, which in turn leads it to the "first and principle
innate idea." The *ego* perceives ("remembers") the evidence of God's
infinite extramental necessity and, therefore, necessary existence *a se*.
The *ego*, acting as its own autonomous guide, is guided all along and
from the start by the inner light of rational freedom—"God the inner
master" illuminating the Intentional experience of the understanding.[94]

   The prelapsarian character of grasping God's infinite positivity and
therefore absolute existence as a pure analytic truth (*per se nota secundum
se*)[95] suggest that the *ego*, detached from sense, is lifted to a new status,
and that *anamnesis* corresponds to a first degree of grace.[96] This explains
why Meditation IV, in which the freedom to cooperate with both reason
and grace is recovered,[97] had to be inserted between Meditation III
and V, after the discovery of the "author of my origin" but before the

---

Responsiones to Caterus, AT VII, 114. For evidence that Descartes consciously ordered
his proofs *quia* and *propter quid* sequentially, see *Primae Responsiones*, AT VII, 120: "Quia
duae tantum sunt viae per quas possit probari Deum esse, una nempe per effectus,
et altera per ipsam ejus essentiam sive naturam, prioremque in Meditatione tertia pro
viribus explanavi, non credidi alteram esse postea praetermittendam." For evidence
that Descartes's Thomist opponents failed to appreciate his conformity with Thomas
in this regard, see Alan Charles Kors, *Atheism in France, 1650–1729* (Princeton: Princeton
U. Press, 1990), vol. 1, 297–307.

[94] Cf. Francis of Sales, *Traité de l'Amour de Dieu*, IV, c. 5, in *Oeuvres*, I, 539: "le sauveur
est une lumière qui éclaire tout homme qui vient au monde" and 541: "la divine loi
naturelle est plantée en l'esprit de tous les mortels," citing Romans I, 20–21. As Robert
Miner points out, Augustinian illumination, as described in *De magistro*, "consists of the
retrieval or recall of something that is already present in the soul, in such a way that it
is intelligibly grasped." I Thank Robert Miner for letting me cite from his unpublished
paper, "Augustinian Recollection," given at Boston College October 17, 2003.

[95] See in this regard Thomas Aquinas, *Summa Contra Gentiles*, I.1., c. 11.

[96] See, for example, what Descartes writes in this regard in the Spring of 1648,
probably to Newcastle, AT V, 137: "... que nostre ame en a desia quelques unes [sc.
illustrations et connoissances directes] de la beneficence de son Createur, *sans lesquelles il
ne seroit pas capable de raisonner?*" (Emphasis added). Note also the preliminary *annotaciones*
of the Ignatian Exercises: "This may happen as a result of his own reasoning or through
the enlightenment of his understanding by Divine grace." Trans. Anthony Mottola, *The
Spiritual Exercises of St. Ignatius*, 37.

[97] AT VII, 58: "... sive quia rationem veri et boni in ea evidenter intelligo, sive quia
Deus intima cogitationis meae ita disponit ... " and "... nec sane divina gratia, nec
naturalis cognitio unquam immunuunt libertatem, sed potius augent et corrobant." Cf.
Francis of Sales, *Traité de l'Amour de Dieu*, IV, c. 6, in *Oeuvres*, I, 542.

transformation from *persuasio* to *scientia* could be completed and the doctrine of innate ideas finalized. The chief benefit of mathematical *anamnesis* is not that it fosters self-reliance but rather that it overcomes self-reliance by revealing to the mind that the natural light it possesses comes from elsewhere and indeed from "God who is Truth."

Nor does the *parity* of innate ideas[98] jeopardize divine incomprehensibility or imply that God "falls" under finite parameters of conceptualization, since on the contrary, truth each time exceeds me in so far as it determines my thought *velim nolim*. I find the idea of God in me *no less* than I find in me the idea of a given figure or number; I understand *no less clearly and distinctly* that it belongs to God's nature to exist than that what I demonstrate to belong to the nature of a given number belongs to it. I must therefore be *no less certain* of the truth of God's existence than of mathematical truths. God's existence *per essentiam* coincides with a saturation of the natural light at its point of origin, where thinking a limit to God's hyperpositivity is unthinkable.[99] Only in paradox does human reason perceive the second-order mind-independence of "God who is Truth," since an excess of light indistinguishable from darkness is needed to deny any admixture of negativity in the case of infinite positivity: "I am not at liberty to think of God without existence."[100]

Descartes of course hopes that God's *per se* existence will "extort" a cry of assent from even the "most stubborn" meditator,[101] just as the *cogito* had earlier elicited a spontaneous "cry" from the *ego* affirming its own existence in Meditation III.[102] The goal is that God's infinite *per se* positivity be acknowledged as the unique case of unconditional necessity, without reference to contingent effects. Like Francis of Sales and other advocates of *l'amour pur*, Descartes wants God to be known and loved for his own sake more fundamentally than for the sake of benefits bestowed to creatures.[103]

---

[98] AT VII, 65: "Certe ejus ideam, nempe entis summe perfecti, non minus apud me invenio, quam ideam cujusvis figurae aut numeri."

[99] See *Primae Responsiones*, AT VII, 119: "quia cogitare *non possumus* ejus existentiam esse possibilem, quin simul etiam, ad immensam ejus potentiam attendentes, agnoscamus illud propria sua vi posse existere, hinc concludemus ipsum revera existere, atque ab aeterno extitisse."

[100] AT VII, 67: "neque enim liberum est Deum absque existentia cogitare."

[101] See *Secundae Responsiones*, AT VII, 156.

[102] AT VII, 36, line 36–37: "ut sponte erumpam in has voces."

[103] See François de Sales, *Traité de l'Amour de Dieu*, Livre 2, ch. 17, in *Oeuvres Complètes* 1969, I, 459; and Jean-Pierre Camus, *La Caritée ou le portrait de la vraie charité* (Paris, 1641), 103.

The "ontological" proof elicits *both* types of love, "true" and "mercenary," in the right order. On the one hand, the truth of God's *per se* existence is the truth without which no truths are possible and is therefore the truth that is prior to myself and independent of myself. On the other, it *explains* the trust that I spontaneously place in my mathematical reasoning and theorems. Once God's (incomprehensible) second-order positivity is grasped as unsurpassably certain (*certissimum videtur*), I remark (*anidmaverto*)

> "that the certainty of all other things depends on this [first certainty] to such an extent that nothing could ever be known perfectly without it."[104]

The *vis intelligendi* beholds itself objectively to be inalienably objective *qua* rational, so that its own rational predilection for veracity is literally mind-independent: *apud me sed non a me effecta*. The mind's rational inclination to truth pre-exists the mind's conscious grasp of it. To "perceive truly" (*vero percepi*) that there is a God, is to understand (*intellexi*) at the very same time (*simul*) that all other things depend on him and that he is not fallacious, and therefore to conclude (*collegi*) "that everything that I perceive (*percipio*) clearly and distinctly must necessarily be true."[105]

The truth-rule, in effect, is grasped as a mind-independent truth about the mind. Introduced in Meditation III as a possibly valid general rule ("jam *videor* pro regula generali"),[106] stated at the end of Meditation IV as a matter of subjective indubitability ("omnis clara et distincta perceptio *proculdubio* est aliquid … ideoque *proculdubio* est vera"),[107] the truth-rule is finally stated as a demonstrated theorem in Meditation V: "collegi illa omnia quae clare et distincte percipio *necessario* esse vera." Once God's *per se* existence is known, the truth-rule, like the Pythagorean theorem, is true "whether I want it or not"—*velim nolim*. Moreover God's existence, once "remembered," is *per se* unforgettable

---

[104] AT VII, 69: "Praeterea etiam animadverto caeterarum rerum certitudinem ab hoc ipso ita pendere, ut absque eo nihil unquam perfecte sciri possit."

[105] AT VII, 70: "Postquam vero percipi Deum esse, quia simul etiam intellexi caetera omnia ab eo pendere, illumque non esse fallacem; atque inde collegi illa omnia, quae clare et distincte percipio, necessario esse vera; etiamsi non attendam amplius ad rationes propter quas istud verum esse judicavi, modo tantum recorder me clare et distincte perspexisse, nulla ratio contraria afferri potest, quae me ad dubitandum impellat, sed veram et certam de hoc habeo scientiam."

[106] AT VII, 35: "ac proinde jam videor pro regula generali posse statuere, illud omne esse verum, quod valde clare et distincte percipio."

[107] AT VII, 62. Note that the French translation at AT IX, 49–50 conveys only the first of these two "proculdubio" ("sans doute").

since rational *anamnesis* has reached its own extrinsic validation in the truth that Truth cannot not be. In contrast, the atheist or agnostic mathematician uses the truth-rule as pragmatically expedient, ignorant (*ignarus*) of what makes it true. If he wants to redeem mathematics from psychologism (or idealism), he must resort to the *pis-aller* argument that "if logic is doubted, then nothing at all can be said." His science is true, but he himself cannot validate its truth as long as he regards reason as self-validating. On the other hand, did reason not just validate itself precisely by renouncing self-validation and deriving itself from the paradox that God cannot be thought as inexistent?

11.4. *Beyond Autarchy*

Although Descartes seems to target atheism as such,[108] his focus is more subtle. The key insight reached in Meditation V is that "all things depend on God": *intellexi omnia ab eo pendere.*[109] This implies that the *res cogitans* who thinks and the quanta that are thought enjoy the same impartial dependence on the divine will. God wants/wills all of these material possibilities *no less* than he wants/wills my existence as a spiritual thing and as a witness of his myriad possibilities.[110] The *ego* acknowledges in particular that everything that it possesses comes from God as a gift: *nihil reale in nobis esse possit, quod non ab ispo datum.*[111] By renouncing itself as center and *autarch* of its own being, the *ego* is cured, not only or even primarily of hyberbolic doubt, but, more importantly, of the originary egoism that marks the *cogito.*[112]

The design of Meditation V is clarified in Descartes's letter to Chanut of February 1, 1647. Outlining the steps that lead human beings to

---

[108] Note that Mersenne had earlier (1623) diagnosed "quod nullas de Deo notitias habeamus" as a chief axiom of atheists, in *Quaestiones celeberrimae in Genesim*, col. 233; and that Descartes in his letter of May 6, 1630, specifically connects his doctrine of the creation of mathematical truths and the infinity of God to forestalling atheism.

[109] Cf. Francis of Sales, *Traité de l'Amour de Dieu*, IV, c. 6, *Oeuvres*, I, 542, cites I Corinthians 4:7 and emphasizes: "Il est vrai que nous avons tout reçu de Dieu".

[110] The call to human being as "witness" of creation is implied, for example, in *Discours de la méthode* Part V, AT VI, 42: "et enfin de l'Homme, a cause qu'il en est le spectateur."

[111] *Secundae Responsiones*, AT VII, 114.

[112] Cf. Jean-Luc Marion, "La solitude de l'*ego*," in *Questions cartésiennes* (Paris: PUF, 1991), 190: "Le *moi* souffre et jouit indissolublement d'un egoisme originel, extra-et-pre-moral, involontaire et constitutif."

love God (the steps that "raise human nature to its highest perfection"),
Descartes says that we must first convince ourselves that the human
soul bears a resemblance to God's own nature, "as though it were
emanated from his sovereign intelligence like a spark."[113] Because our
knowledge, aiming to become infinite like God's own knowledge, seems
to have the power to increase indefinitely, we risk however falling into
"the extravagance of wishing to be gods ourselves."[114] To correct the
pull of this secret extravagance, we must "pay close attention to the
infinity of God's power" and take note that "all things depend on
God."[115] The *res cogitans*, Descartes implies, must recognize its spiritual
dignity but also be reminded of its dependence and finitude.[116]

Once the *ego* recognizes that the power of rational cognition comes
from God, once the *ego* acknowledges, further, the grandeur of a creation to which it belongs as a small part, autarchy is relinquished, the
burden of solitary self-sufficiency is exchanged for trust and gratitude.[117]
Whoever properly understands that all things depend on God is

> "filled with a joy so extreme that, far from being so injurious and un-
> grateful towards God as to wish to take his place, he feels that his life is
> fulfilled already by the fact that God gave him the capacity to reach such
> a level of knowledge; and, joining himself wholly to God through his will,
> he loves God so perfectly that he desires nothing in the world except that
> God's will be accomplished."[118]

---

[113] Letter to Chanut, dated February 1st, 1647, AT IV, 608. Descartes is citing from
Horace, *Sat.*, II, 2, 79. Cf. Francis of Sales, *Traité de l'Amour de Dieu*, I, c. 15, in *Oeuvres
Complètes*, I, 396: "… notre âme est spirituelle, indivisible, immortelle; entend, veut et
veut librement; est capable de juger, discourir, savoir, et avoir des vertus: en quoi elle
ressemble à Dieu."

[114] AT IV, 608: "Nous pouvons venir à l'extravagance de souhaiter d'estre dieux."

[115] AT IV, 608 and 609.

[116] See e.g., Robert Bellarmino, S.J., *Ascensionis in Deum*, Rome, 1615, "Gradus Octa-
vus"; in *Opera Omnia*, ed. Justinus Fèvre (Paris, 1873), Minerva G.M.B.H., (Unverän-
derter Nachdruck—Frankfurt a. M., 1965), 274: "quantum laetari potest anima, quod
sit in genere substantiae spiritualis, ac per hoc coelo et sideribus altior nobilitate naturae, tantum humiliari debet, ac Deo conditori subjici, quod ex nihilo facta sit, et ex se
nihil sit."

[117] Thus Meditation V bursts upon Gibieuf's formulation, namely, in Olivier Boulnois's words, that "Les actions de l'homme étant plus l'oeuvre de Dieu que la sienne
propre, la liberté humaine consiste à consentir à sa cause efficiente et finale." See
O. Boulnois, "Le refoulement de la liberté d'indifférence et les polémiques anti-scotistes," 213. Descartes's point is that logical truths, as well as the human soul, the infinite
freedom of the rational will and the free causal agency through which Truth is loved
and finite truths are pursued are *all* God's works.

[118] AT IV, 609: "la meditation de toutes ces choses remplit un homme qui les entend
bien d'une joye si extreme, que, tant s'en faut qu'il soit injurieux et ingrat envers Dieu

Thus while *scientia mathematica* awakens the mind to its "divine spark" and nurtures its independence and dignity, it incites a secret temptation to autarchic pride. Geneviève Rodis-Lewis calls attention in this regard to Descartes's third dream of 1619, which he himself interpreted as a warning against the "charms of solitude, but devoted to purely human questions."[119] She argues that Descartes was haunted by "*the* supreme original sin, which is to want to rival God."[120] She points out that the dream-element in which Descartes saw a warning against self-enclosed solitude, namely the melon, suggests by its shape the cosmos that is sometimes placed in the hand of God the Father as a monarch's imperial orb.[121] If her insight is not misguided, it suggests that Descartes had personally worried about the secret urge to rival God, the same urge which he explicitly denounces to Chanut in 1647.[122] He tells Chanut indeed that scientists who fail to acknowledge God's infinite power have an inordinate tendency to "roll all things up into a ball" as though God's cosmos were finite and could be treated by human natural reason as a completed totality.[123]

The temptation of autarchy, of a self-reliance so hegemonic and satisfying that it risks hardening into pride, looms large, unless some critical disclosure reveals an unsuspected weakness in the foundation of self-enclosed human activity. If *pura mathesis* requires for its validation the second-order truth that God exists, then reason's most rational insight destitutes itself and cures the mind of (irrational) vainglory. The "view from nowhere" remains God's and God's alone, leaving the crea-

---

isqu'a souhaiter de tenir sa place, il pense deia avoir assez vecu de ce que dieu luy ait fait la grace de parvenir a de telles connoissances; et se ioignant entierement à luy de volonté, il l'aime si parfaitement, qu'il ne desire plus rien au monde, sinon que la volonté de Dieu soit faite." Cf. Francis of Sales, *Traité de l'Amour de Dieu*, II, c. 2, in *Oeuvres*, I, 418: "joindre sa volonté à la Providence"; and V, c. 3, in *Oeuvres*, I, 576: "Il me suffit que Dieu soit Dieu, que sa bonté soit infinie, que sa perfection soit immense; que je meure ou que je vive il importe peu pour moi…"

[119] See Baillet's account, AT X, 185: "Le melon, dont on vouloit lui faire présent dans le premier songe, signifioit, disoit-il, les charmes de la solitude, mais présentez par des sollicitations purement humaines."

[120] See Geneviève Rodis-Lewis, *Descartes*, 65.

[121] Rodis-Lewis, *Descartes*, 65; citing an analysis presented earlier in *Oeuvre de Descartes*, 1971, 52 and 452–453, n. 130–136.

[122] Cf. the intense feeling of contrition and the hypnogogic "terror" attributed by Descartes to his synderesis following the dream with the melon-element. At least as reported by Adrien Baillet, AT X, 186: "L'épouvante dont il fut frappé dans le second songe, marquoit, à son sens, sa syndérèse, c'est-à-dire, les remords de sa conscience touchant les péchez qu'il pouvait avoir commis pendant le course de sa vie jusqu'alors."

[123] See AT IV, 609 and G. Rodis-Lewis's analysis of the same passage in *Descartes*, 66.

ture only with a basic trust in his finite efforts and a new humility. Instead of fostering new increments of self-defeating pride, *pura mathesis*, if acknowledged to require God as its *efficiens et totalis causa*, cultivates devotion instead of self-idolatry.[124] Self-undermining of the kind that is found in the Salesian doctrine of "cooperation," which safeguards human freedom but avoids autarchy, more than any epistemologic consideration, lies at the heart of Descartes's move to introduce hyperbolic doubt and solve it by referring to God the *vis cognoscendi* and its capacity to "attend and perceive" truth by cooperating with the natural light.[125]

Once I renounce myself as the autarchic hegemon of my own enlightenment but instead receive myself and my faculties from God, I am led to give God *l'honneur qui lui est dû*, which is precisely to serve and love God by serving and loving all other beings, possible or actual, for his sake. As Jean-Luc Marion points out, Descartes's definition of charity in the Letter to Voetius implies a passing of the *ego* from self and from self-representation to loving God's infinite alterity and therefore to loving other *egos* for God's sake.[126] This is precisely the transition that is initiated in Meditation V: the *ego* discovers that the essence of cognition is not self-reflexive certainty, but exposure to alterity and above all to the alterity of "God who is Truth" and who shines on all creatures equally and gives *le bon sens*, the inner light, equally to all human beings. The altruistic law invoked in the *Discours* to justify publication but also therefore to recast science from a self-serving trade into a vocation to serve the human community stems directly from the *excogito* of Meditation V and its subordination to God of the initial *cogito*.

In the Sixth Series of Objections, Descartes is challenged by theologians to defend himself against Biblical passages that warn against the vanity of human knowledge.[127] Descartes takes the opportunity to expli-

---

[124] Cf. Francis of Sales's very Ignatian statement: "nous ne devons rien être que pour sa gloire" in *Traité de l'Amour de Dieu*, IV, c. 6, *Oeuvres*, I, 545.

[125] For the Salesian doctrine of "free cooperation," see Francis of Sales, *Traité de l'amour de Dieu*, IV, c. 6, in *Oeuvres*, I, 542–545. In Bk. III, c. 14, *Ouevres*, I, 520, Francis of Sales defines the natural light as "the light whereby we have the power to know God as the author of nature."

[126] Marion cites *Epistola ad G. Voetium*, AT VIII, 2, 112, 21–29: "haec Charitas, hoc est, sancta amicitia, qua Deum prosequimur, et Dei causa etiam omnes homines, quatenus scimus ipsos a Deo amari..." See "La solitude de l'*ego*," *Questions cartésiennes*, 218; and the discussion that follows, 219.

[127] Descartes agrees, this time only, to discuss Scripture, "lest my silence be misinterpreted as a lack on my part of a good answer." See Sixth Answers, AT VII, 429.

cate the philosophy of love that emerges as an integral dimension of his scientific project. When the Apostle, Descartes explains, rejects human science, he rejects only

> "science that is not conjoined to charity, which is to say the science of atheists. For indeed anyone who knows God, as he should, cannot not love Him and not have charity."[128]

The key insight of Meditation V can now be made explicit: since the meditator has truly perceived (*vero percipi*) that God exists and understood (*intellixi*) at the very same time (*simul*) that (a) all things depend on God and (b) that God is not fallacious, he cannot fail to love God and to have charity—by which Descartes means, as we saw, that he cannot fail to love all other beings, and in particular all other human *egos*, for God's sake. Cartesian "foundationalism," it turns out, is less concerned with validating science than with establishing its radical mooring in charity:

> "Thus the Apostle does not mean to deny that any science at all is possible, since he admits that those who love God know him, i.e., have knowledge of him;[129] rather he means only that those who are without charity and therefore do not know God sufficiently, although they may deem themselves to know other things, *nonetheless know not yet what they ought to know and as they ought to know it*. For indeed we must start first with the knowledge of God, then make the knowledge of all other things depend on it alone, which is what I explained in my Meditations."[130]

While the proof *quia* of Meditation III establishes God's existence, it does not give *sufficient knowledge* of God's necessity *nor the right kind* of knowledge of God to transform the meditator from a solitary contemplative to a scientist devoted to public service. Only the proof *per essentiam* allows the meditator to know God as perfectly sovereign and therefore to love God for God's sake, objectively, without thought of self. The personal transformation of the scientist from egoism to altruism is further explained when Descartes turns to *Ecclesiastes* to argue that science

---

[128] AT VII, 429: "... debere tantum intelligi de scientia quae non est cum charitate conjuncta, hoc est, de scientia Atheorum, quia quisquis Deum, ut par est, novit, non potest ipsum non diligere, nec charitatem non habere." The Pauline passage involved is I Corinthians 8:2.

[129] Descartes interprets I Corinthians 8:3, to mean "if someone loves God, he (which is to say God) is known by him." Aware that his reading is controversial (cf. the Revised Standard Version Holy Bible, [San Francisco: Ignatius Press, 1966], NT, 155: "If one loves God, *one* is known by him.") Descartes invokes I John 4, 7: "He who loves is born of God and knows God."

[130] AT VII, 429–430.

"conjoined to charity" satisfies the mind in a new and unanticipated way. Descartes explains that Solomon

> "... repents of his faults and testifies that, as long as he wished to rely exclusively on human knowledge without referring it to God and without regarding it as a gift from God's hand, he was unable to find anything that fully satisfied him or did not appear to him to be full of vanity."[131]

To pursue a science that builds up and does not inflate, that satisfies rather than frustrates, is thus to pursue a science that dignifies the self only by dignifying all human beings as born of God and bearers of God's image. The duty to share fruitful discoveries with all of humanity is a first implication of the charity that derives from "sufficiently" knowing God, since God wills and loves *caetera omnia* no less than he wills and conserves my own existence, which I did not yet "sufficiently" know in Meditation III when I discovered the author of *my* origin, *my* God and *my* Creator.[132]

Before Solomon referred science to God, he lived the well-mannered but secretly empty life of the *honnête homme*, detached from vulgarity but centered on himself. As Descartes explains to Elizabeth, whoever sufficiently knows God and loves him, in contrast, sets aside his own self-interest[133] and finds "incomparably" higher satisfaction in acts that "stem from a pure altruistic affection, without regard for oneself, which is the Christian virtue known as charity."[134]

11.5. *Summary*

Meditation V turns out to be a case of radical dissimulation, but in a very different sense than is usually urged. Under the pretext of combatting atheism by grounding mathematical truth in divine veracity, Descartes cures mathematicians of the temptation of autarchy—and

---

[131] AT VII, 430. Cf. *Ecclesiastes*, 8:17, which is cited against Descartes in the Sixth Objections on 416.

[132] See Meditation III, AT VII, 48–49.

[133] Letter of 15 September, 1645, AT IV, 294: "losqu'on connoist et qu'on ayme Dieu comme il faut ... s'abandonnant du tout a sa volonté, on se despouille de ses propres interests."

[134] *Ibid.* and Letter of 6 October, 1645, AT IV, 308–309: "elle ne scauroit estre si grande qu'est la satisfaction interieure qui accompagne touiours les bonnes actions, et principalement celles qui procedent d'une pure affection pour autruy qu'on ne rapporte point a soy mesme, c'est a dire de la vertu chrestiene qu'on nomme charité."

therefore of constituting themselves as a separate elite of experts, prone to trust rational calculations to the exclusion of other considerations and to offer themselves to the highest bidder without reference to charity. The ethical implications for the social accountability of science are vast, starting with Descartes's own refusal to work on military technology.[135] In place of financial reward and celebrity, Descartes offers the scientist a form of the devout life, marked by "amorous" service and a new indifference for death.[136] Personally convinced that "the light of charity must be preferred to the light of reason,"[137] Descartes also believed that the light of reason cannot by its very nature contradict charity but instead implies and calls for charity, as Meditation V establishes. The fact that the truth of God's existence relieves mathematical truths of "hyperbolic" doubt is a sort of bonus—even a bait: what matters to Descartes is curing the mathematician (*mon semblable, mon frère*) of egoism and preparing him to belong "body and soul" to the cosmos as "just a small part," which is the task of Meditation VI.[138] Once again, the masked philosopher is right to warn: *larvatus prodeo (pro Deo).*[139]

---

[135] See *Discours*, Part VI, AT VI, 78, lines 14–15: "… de ceux qui ne scauroient estre utiles aux uns qu'en nuisant aux autres." See also Part III, AT VI, 31: "les armées qu'on y entretient ne semblent servir qu'a faire qu'on y jouisse des fruits de la paix."

[136] Cf. *Les Passions de l'âme*, art. 83, AT XI, 390: "Lorsqu'on estime l'objet de son amour d'avantage (que soy), la passion qu'on a peut estre nommée Devotion… Pour ce qui est de la Devotion, son principal objet est sans doute la souveraine Divinité, à laquelle on ne sçauroit manquer d'estre devot, lors qu'on la connait comme il faut. […] en la Devotion, l'on prefere telement la chose aimée à soy-mesme, qu'on ne craint pas de mourir pour la conserver."

[137] Letter to Hyperaspistes, August 1641, AT III, section 3, 426: "Quod autem evidentissimum sit … quod lumen gratiae lumini naturae sit praeferendum, nemini fidem catholicam vere habenti dubium vel mirum esse potest."

[138] Cf. Letter to Chanut of June 6, 1647, AT V, 56: "Lorsque nous aimons Dieu, et que par luy nous nous ioignons de volonté avec toutes les choses qu'il a creées, d'autant que nous les concevons plus grandes, plus nobles, plus parfaites, d'autant nous estimons nous aussi d'avantage, à cause que nous sommes des parties d'un tout plus accomply."

[139] Citing, obviously, Jean-Luc Marion's play on "prodeo" in "The Essential Incoherence of Descartes's Definition of Divinity," in A. Rorty, ed., *Essays on Descartes's Meditations*, 330.

CHAPTER TWELVE

AGENCY AND THE ORDER OF NATURE

"J'attends tout de sa force,
et rien de ma faiblesse."

—Corneille

Meditation VI is the journey's *dénouement*, the day of aggregation (*complexio*)—when body and soul are reintegrated on a harmonious new basis and the *ego* is reconciled with the physical cosmos. The key to aggregating body and soul lies with the *ego*'s willingness to embrace the natural order. But what does Descartes mean by the order of nature (*ordo naturae*) and why does he call for the *ego* to stop "perverting" it—*ordinem naturae pervertere*? Does Descartes have a temporal order in mind, as for example when he says that a clear understanding must always *precede* truth-judgments,[1] or does he have a metaphysical order in mind, as for example when he says that the will is *greater* than the intellect and is more similar (*similior*) than it to God?[2] For that matter, what does Descartes really mean by "nature"? Throughout the Meditations, Descartes uses "nature" and "natural" in a variety of contexts, with shifting meanings. *Natura* first appears in Meditation I to emphasize that the human imagination never creates images *ex nihilo* but merely reshuffles and combines memories of existing natures.[3] Similarly, the phrase *rerum natura* refers to the world of actual, existing things, as opposed to logical possibilities like geometric essences.[4] In Meditation II, nature is used in the scholastic sense of a thing's essence

---

[1] Meditation IV: "lumine naturali manifestum est perceptionem intellectus praecedere semper debere voluntatis determinationem." In AT VII, 60.

[2] Meditation IV: "sola est voluntas, sive arbitrii libertas, quam tantam in me experior, ut nullius majoris ideam apprehendam; adeo ut illa praecipue sit, ratione cujus imaginem quandam et similitudinem dei me referre intelligo." (AT VII, 57.) See also the Interview with Burman, AT V, 159: "In eo igitur major est voluntas intellectu et deo similior."

[3] Meditation I, AT VII, 20: "Nam sane pictores ipsi, ne tum quidem, cum Sirenas et Satyriscos maxime inusitatis formis fingere student, naturas omni ex parte novas iis possunt assignare, sed tantummodo diversorum animalium membra permiscent."

[4] AT VII, 20: "atqui Arithmeticam, Geometriam, quae nonnisi de simplicissimis et

or "quiddity."[5] The *ego* investigates the nature of *mens humana* by questioning the bodily identity that is formed "spontaneously and under nature's leadership"—*sponte et a natura duce*.[6] Does nature lead me astray concerning *my* nature?[7] Put more pressingly, *am I so completely tied to body and the senses that I cannot exist without them?*[8] Since body "by nature" is "terminated by a surface, occupies space, can be apprehended by sense and moved," and since none of these properties are implied by the *cogito*, the *ego* concludes that *my* nature as a free agent is distinct from the nature of body.[9] Implicit in the *ego*'s rational self-discovery is the discovery that human nature is not *naturally* known: on the contrary, what I regard myself to be *sponte et natura duce* is full of alien properties—full, in particular, of that undesirable composition of accidents that makes a thing perishable.[10]

After the *cogito* provides the *ego* with a new standard of rational evidence,[11] the "nature" that leads me spontaneously to form a bodily (and mortal) identity is examined critically from the standpoint of the

---

maxime generalibus rebus tractant, atque utrum eae sint in rerum natura necne, parum curant, aliquid certi atque indubitati continere."

[5] See, e.g., the subtitle of Meditation II, namely *De natura mentis humanae: quod ipsa sit notior quam corpus*, following Descartes's instruction to Mersenne that the main goal of each meditation be emphasized. See letter of 28 January 1641; AT III, 297.

[6] Meditation II, AT VII, 25.

[7] Compare with Augustine, *De Trinitate*, X, v, 7 – vii, 9, 136: "Errat autem mens, cum se istis imaginibus tanto amore conjungit, ut etiam se esse aliquid hujusmodi existimet ... Cum itaque se tale aliquid putat, corpus esse se putat."

[8] Meditation II, AT VII, p. 25: "Summe ita corpori sensibusque alligatus, ut sine illis esse non possim?" See also Descartes's Letter to Huygens dated 13 October 1642: "J'ai trouvé (un remède) très puissant, non seulement pour me faire supporter patiemment la mort de ceux que j'aimais, mais aussi pour m'empêcher de craindre la mienne, nonobstant que je sois du nombre de ceux qui aiment le plus la vie." AT III, p. 580.

[9] Cf. Augustine, *De Trinitate*, X, xv, 14 and 15: "Sed quoniam de natura mentis agitur ... si dubitat, cogitat; si dubitat, scit se nescire... Quisquis igitur aliunde dubitat, de his omnibus dubitare non debet... [...] Et cum de se certa est, de substantia sua certa est. nec omnino certa est, utrum aer, an ignis sit, an aliquod corpus, vel aliquid corporis. Non est igitur aliquid eorum." For a study of Descartes's real and/or perceived indebtedness to Augustine, see Henri Gouhier, *Cartésianisme et Augustinisme au XVIIème siècle* (Paris: Vrin, 1978); and Stephen Menn, *Descartes and Augustine*.

[10] Cf. AT VII, 26: "qualis etiam in cadavere cernitur."

[11] On the importance of the *Cogito* as a new standard, see Michelle Beyssade, "The *Cogito*: Privileged Truth or Exemplary Truth?" in *Essays on the Philosophy and Science of René Descartes*, ed. Stephen Voss (New York and Oxford: Oxford U. Press, 1993), 31–39. Cf. Augustine, *De Trinitate*, IX, xi, 16: "cum se mens ipsa novit atque approbat, sic est eadem notitia verbum ejus, ut ei sit per omnino et aequale, atque identidem ... ideoque et imago et verbum est, quia de illa exprimitur, cum cognoscendo eidem coaequatur, et est gigenti aequale quod genitum est."

immaterial (and moral) nature of *res cogitans*, characterized by innate rational freedom. The *ego* now suspects that nature is perhaps only *falsely* a false teacher—that I myself am at fault for falsely conceiving that I receive natural lessons ("*videor doctus a natura*") where none are given:

> "For indeed when I say that this is taught to me by nature, all I mean is that I am carried to believe this by a certain spontaneous impulse (*spontaneo quodam impetu me ferri*)—not that this is shown to me to be true by a natural light (*lumine aliquo naturali*)."[12]

Descartes at this point adds a new dimension by introducing the notion of legitimate trust in order to set the "natural light" against "natural impulses."[13] Whereas there is no faculty (*facultas*) in me that I must trust more than the natural light, my natural impulses (*impetus naturales*) on the other hand have often carried me astray in moral matters and should therefore hardly be trusted in matters of truth.[14]

Descartes's argument differs in a fundamental way from the skeptic argument that sensations deceive us, since the issue that is raised by the notion of trust is the *ego*'s moral self-control: natural impulses *ought* not be trusted because they move us to act "blindly and presumptuously,"[15] while the natural light moves us to act freely and rationally— to embrace precisely what we *ought* to embrace rather than what is embraced automatically—*sponte et a natura duce*. By following its own innate rational instinct rather than natural impulses, the *ego* discovers that its nature is essentially moral, incommensurably higher than bodily nature, which moves and changes deterministically.

Epistemologically, the contrast is nicely illustrated by the example of the sun, of which, Descartes says, we have two representations, one that "advenes" passively from the outside by way of immediate sensation, and a scientific one that results from the *ego*'s deliberate

---

[12] AT VII, p. 38: "Cum hic dico me ita doctum esse a natura, intelligo tantum spontaneo quodam impetu me ferri ad hoc credendum, non lumine aliquo naturali mihi ostendi esse verum."

[13] See also in this regard Descartes's letter to Mersenne of October 16, 1639: "Pour moi, je distingue deux sortes d'instincts: l'un est en nous en tant qu'hommes et est purement intellectuelle; c'est la lumière naturelle ou *intuitus mentis*, auquel seul je tiens qu'on doit se fier; l'autre est en nous en tant qu'animaux, et est une certaine impulsion de la nature..." AT III, p. 599.

[14] Meditation III, AT VII, pp. 38–39.

[15] Meditation III, AT IX, 31: "par une aveugle et téméraire impulsion," which renders, with Descartes's approval, the latin at AT VII, p. 40: "sed tantum ex caeco aliquo impulsu."

rational steps (*idea facta vel factitia*) and is based on innate notions: *ex notionibus quibusdam mihi innatis.*[16] Since by definition nothing is more natural to the *ego* than what belongs to it innately, the implication is that scientific (Copernican) astronomy is more "natural" to the human mind than a spontaneous cosmology *a natura duce*. Conversely, are man's "natural impulses" less natural than innate scientific *rationes*, or are they natural in a very different sense? What is the status of *impetus naturales* and how are they related, if at all, to the innate moral *impetus* that marks the *ego*'s free will?

Meditation VI solves the riddle of *impetus naturales* by framing a comprehensive new theory of nature's teaching. After "walking alone and in darkness" for five symbolic days, the *ego* on the sixth and final day is reintroduced to color and sound, shape and texture, thirst and pain. The sensorial world that was denied in Meditation I—earth, sky, blood, flesh—is not only redeemed but welcomed on a new footing. The *ego* is enfleshed anew, knowingly and by consent. By the end of the meditational journey, the *ego* willingly forms a whole with the flesh "that is mine" and cooperates with the boundless, unfolding flesh of the cosmos.[17] The vastness of material creation is no longer frightening but a source of wonderment, the frailty of the human body is no longer deplored but loved. Meditation VI brings the odyssey of self-discovery to completion by moving the *ego* to wisdom, which consists in uniting with *Natura sive Deus* by a very pure act of will.

12.1. *Natural Wisdom*

From the beginning, Descartes conceived of human being as specially called to become a witness of the visible cosmos. As the content of the suppressed *Le Monde ou Traité de la Lumière* reveals, Descartes meant for his new mechanistic philosophy to culminate in celebrating the human

---

[16] Letter to Mersenne, June 16, 1641, AT III, 383. See also Meditation III, AT VII, 39; and cf. Augustine, *De Trinitate*, XIV, vii: "Hinc admonemur esse nobis in abdito mentis quarumdam rerum quasdam notitias." In this same passage, Augustine discusses the natural light: "Id agunt et litterae, quae de his rebus conscriptae sunt, quas res duce ratione veras esse invenit lector: non quas veras esse credit ei qui scipsit, sicut legitur historia; sed quas veras esse etiam ipse invenit, sive apud se, sive in ipsa mentis luce veritate."

[17] For Descartes's insistence that the physical cosmos is "boundless" (*indéfiny*), see the letter to Chanut, June 6, 1647, AT V, 52, and letter to Henry More, February 5, 1649, AT V, 275.

spectator. Far from stripping the cosmos of beauty, Descartes sought to peer through sensory enchantment to a higher beauty and unveil the solar system to the human gaze. Since light radiating from the sun affects the human retina in a distinctive way, namely by awakening intelligent consciousness, the plan of the *Treatise on Light* called for cosmic phenomena to be divided into four classes, based on their properties relative to light: first came a section on fiery bodies, the sun and stars, "because they emit light;" then came a section on transparent bodies, the heavens, "because they transmit light," then a section on opaque bodies, planets and comets, "because they scatter light;" and finally came a treatise "on Man, because he is the spectator of light."[18] The plan was to integrate Man into the cosmic order by setting him apart, as a star-gazer and lover of wisdom.

The natural light of reason both distinguishes human beings from purely material creatures and relates human beings to *rerum natura* contemplatively, through love and understanding indivisibly joined. Poised at the limit of two realms, the rational agent is *in* the material world, but not *of* it—like Adam before he misused his freedom and subjected his understanding to the senses. Meditation VI recovers the *ego*'s pristine enfleshment and restores human being "body and soul" to contemplation and contemplative happiness. A laborious and continuous vigil, called for at the end of Meditation I, is required for the *ego* to return to the world of existing things (*rerum natura*) with the fullness of human nature—as an effective moral being, empowered, not deceived, by the ordinary revelations of ambient light.

In what does the *ego*'s final and supreme vigilance consist? While the stated goal of Meditation VI is to establish the existence of material things and to confirm the real distinction between soul and body,[19] the deeper goal is to harmonize science and wisdom—which had been Descartes's constant goal from the start, or at least since the nocturnal illuminations of November 11, 1619.[20] Meditation VI brings to fruition

---

[18] *Discours de la Méthode*, Part V, AT VI, 42: "J'entrepris seulement d'y exposer bien amplement ce que je concevais de la Lumiere; puis, a son occasion, d'y adiouster quelque chose du Soleil et des Etoiles fixes, a cause qu'elle en procede presque toute; des Cieux, a cause qu'ils la transmettent; des Planetes, des Cometes, et de la terre, a cause qu'elles la font refleshir; et enfin de L'Homme, a cause qu'il en est le Spectateur."

[19] Cf. the subtitle, AT VII, 71: "De rerum materialium existentia, et reali mentis a corpore distinctione."

[20] See Baillet's account of Descartes's third dream, AT X, 184: "Il (sc. Descartes) jugea que le *Dictionnaire* ne vouloit dire autre chose que toutes les sciences ramassées

Descartes's mission "to acquire wisdom, namely science together with virtue, by joining the functions of the will with those of the understanding."[21] Combining the moral urgency of calling each soul to wisdom individually (*Quod vitae sectabor iter?*)[22] with the speculative universality of the *Traité de l'homme*, Meditation VI includes, but also supersedes, earlier Cartesian sketches of Man as a church organ or as a fountain-complex controlled by the rational soul.[23] The *ego* is led metaphorically to the summit of a high peak, from which Nature and *my* nature are contemplated with irreversible trust.

It is easy to miss the virtuosity of Meditation VI. Poetically vaster than Lucretius's *De rerum natura*, Meditation VI surpasses Aristotle's *Physics* in architectonic solidity. The best introduction to Meditation VI is Descartes's commentary on Seneca's *De vita beata*, written in a series of letters to Elizabeth in 1645. Descartes starts by citing Seneca's maxim that wisdom consists in "acquiescing to the nature of things" (*rerum naturae assentitur*) and criticizes the obscurity of Seneca's statement. How, exactly, is *rerum natura* defined? Surely Seneca did not advocate yielding to natural impulses, which move us for the most part to debauchery.[24]

From Descartes's point of view, the crucial importance of Seneca's doctrine is that it allows us to test the moral scope of unaided reason. Since Seneca was not "enlightened by faith,"[25] his doctrine of the good life is accessible universally to all human beings. How far does natural reason succeed in promoting virtue? If reason suffices for human beings to live virtuously and to find happiness in virtue, then it follows that

---

ensemble; et que le Recueil de Poesies, intitulé *Corpus poetarum*, marquoit en particulier, et d'une manière plus distincte, la Philosophie et la Sagesse jointes ensemble."

[21] See Baillet's account of the abandoned *Studium Bonae Mentis*, written c. 1623, AT X, 191.

[22] AT X, 182–183.

[23] *Traité de L'Homme*, AT XI, 131: "Et enfin quand l'*ame raisonnable* (sic) sera en cette machine, elle y aura son siege principal dans le cerveau, et sera là comme le fontenier."

[24] Letter to Elizabeth, August 18, 1645, AT IV, 273: "Toutes lesquelles explications me semblent fort obscures; car sans doute que, par la nature, il ne veut pas entendre nos inclinations naturelles, vu qu'elles nous portent ordinairement a suivre la volupté, contre laquelle il dispute."

[25] Letter to Elizabeth of August 4, 1645. AT IV, 263: "Ie tascheray icy d'expliquer en quelle sorte il me semble que cete matiere eust deu estre traitée par un Philosophe tel que luy, qui, n'estant point esclairé de la foy, n'avoit que la raison naturelle pour guide." See also Descartes's letter Cristina, on the same subject, November 20, 1647, AT V, 82: "Les Philosophes anciens, qui, n'estant point éclairez de la lumiere de la Foy, ne sçavoient rien de la beatitude surnaturelle, ne consideroient que les biens que nous pouvons posseder en cette vie."

atheists and infidels are fully capable of living morally and are liable for transgressions against the natural law. Conversely, religious coercion cannot be rationally defended, nor, *a fortiori*, any form of theocracy, be it Roman, Reformed, or other. Neither estrangement from the Church nor sectarian commitment, nor even commitment to a religious creed outside of Christianity, exonerates the members of a community from rational virtue. The possibility of a commonwealth that is both secular and just is at stake.[26]

Descartes clarifies that Seneca took *rerum natura* to mean "the order established by God in all of the things that are in the world."[27] Seneca also correctly regarded the order of nature to be "infallible and independent of our will."[28] As long as nature refers to the immutable, mind-independent order established by God, wisdom is safely defined as "acquiescing to the things of nature," or, equivalently, as "conforming to nature's law and example."[29] Consenting to the natural order is now interpreted to mean complying with the natural law, which, Descartes adds, specifically means "doing (*faire*) that for which we believe ourselves to have been born."[30] Wisdom consists precisely in exercising the free agency that brings us to natural perfection. The natural law summons each human being individually to discover by rational reflection what he or she *ought* to do in this lifetime and to resolve to do it.[31]

Revealingly, Descartes next equates Seneca's doctrine of the good life with the Christian doctrine that wisdom consists in "submitting oneself to God's will and following God's will in all of our actions."[32]

---

[26] Did Descartes think that England held a possible promise in this regard? See his confidential statement to Mersenne, April 1, 1640, AT III, 50: "Mais ie vous diray, entre nous, que c'est un pais dont ie prefererois la demeure à beaucoup d'autres; et pour la Religion, on dit que le Roy mesme est Catholique de volonté." The suggestion seems to be that Charles I, married to the Catholic Henrietta Marie, was in a good position to be an irenicist, neither fanatically Calvinist nor subserviant to Rome.

[27] Letter to Elizabeth, August 18, 1645, AT IV, 273: "Mais la suite de son discours fait juger que, par *rerum naturam*, il entend l'ordre establi de Dieu en toutes les choses qui sont au monde."

[28] *Ibid.*: "Considerant cet ordre comme infallible et independant de nostre volonté."

[29] Letter to Elizabeth, August 18, 1645, AT IV, 273: "il dit que: *rerum naturae assentiri et ad illius legem exemplumque formari, sapientia est.*"

[30] *Ibid.*: "c'est a dire que c'est sagesse d'acquiescer a l'ordre des choses et de faire ce pourquoy nous croyons etre nez."

[31] Cf. *Discours de la Méthode*, Part I, AT VI, 10: "Ie pris un jour la resolution d'estudier aussy en moi-même, et d'employer toutes les forces de mon esprit a choisir les chemins que je *devois* suivre." Emphasis added.

[32] AT IV, 273: "Considerant cet ordre comme infallible et independant de nostre volonté, il dit que: *rerum naturae assentiri et ad illius legem exemplumque formari, sapientia est,*

Descartes's use of the word *soumettre* in this context does not contradict our previous analysis of free consent: rather, Descartes means that the free consent that we give to God when we know and love God entails consenting to God's incomprehensibility, which, in turn, entails bearing with equanimity ("*prendre en bonne part*") everything that happens to us.[33] In a first moment, the soul, moved by reason, or faith, or both, knows and loves God—i.e. consents to join itself to God here and now by an act of will. In a second moment, the soul, moved by reason, willingly adheres to the natural order that is established by God (*amor fati*); or, moved by the higher light of faith, submits all of its volitions to God's will (*amor Providentiae*).

By claiming that rational wisdom and Christian submission to God's will are equivalent, Descartes does not deny that Christian submission to God's will (not only living virtuously, but observing the Sabbath, partaking in sacraments, etc.) is uniquely meritorious with regard to the next life.[34] Rather, by distinguishing the rational orthopraxy to which all human beings are called by the natural law from the supernatural orthopraxy to which Christians are called by grace, Descartes makes rational orthopraxy a *prerequisite*, rather than an alternative, to Christian orthopraxy. Since, as the Church teaches, grace is indispensable for Christian orthopraxy, and since grace is independent of the human will, anyone who embraces Christian orthopraxy *without grace* violates God's will. In contrast to rational orthopraxy, which is universally required, Christian orthopraxy is a private matter between the individual soul and God. Coercive conversion and persecution of religious minorities and dissenters violates God's will, in effect, twice.[35]

---

c'est a dire que c'est sagesse d'acquiescer a l'ordre des choses, et de faire ce pourquoy nous croyons estre nez; ou bien, pour parler en Chrestien, que c'est sagesse de se soumettre a la volonté de Dieu, et de la suivre en toutes nos actions."

[33] AT IV, 274: "La beatitude consiste a suivre ainsy l'ordre du monde, et prendre en bonne part toutes les choses qui nous arrivent."

[34] See Letter to Mersenne, March 1642, AT III, 544: "Ie dis qu'on peut connoistre par la raison naturelle que Dieu existe, mais ie ne dis pas pour cela que cette connoissance naturelle merite de soy, et sans la Grace, la Gloire surnaturelle que nous attendons dans le Ciel. Car au contraire, il est evident que, cette Gloire estant surnaturelle, il faut des forces plus que naturelles pour la meriter."

[35] See Second Answers, AT VII, 148: "Nec sane Turcae aliive infideles ex eo peccant, cum non amplectuntur religionem Christianam, quod rebus obscuris, ut obscurae sunt, nolint assentiri. Atque audacter dico infidelem qui, omni gratia supernaturali destitutus, et plane ignorans ea quae nos Chrsitiani credimus a Deo esse revelata, ipsa tamen, quamvis sibi obscura, falsis aliquibus ratiociniis adductus amplecteretur, non ideo fore fidelem, sed potius in eo peccaturum, quod ratione sua non recte uteretur."

Addressed to the Protestant Elizabeth, Descartes's defense of rational wisdom is at once a defense of free agency and a defense of God's
universal election of human beings, at least in this lifetime. Since happiness results from the firm resolve always to act in conformity with
the natural order, there is "a felicity that depends entirely on our free
agency and which all men are capable of acquiring without outside
assistance."[36] Descartes points out that rational wisdom starts with two
basic principles of rational justice. First, by consenting to the natural order, we implicitly embrace our interdependence with other creatures.[37] Secondly, we implicitly agree to suffer illness and natural dis-
asters rationally since "illnesses and misfortunes are no less natural to
man than good health and prosperity."[38] In both cases, adhering to
nature means preferring the good of the whole to narrow, atomistic
self-interest. Rational wisdom forbids (irrational) selfishness and (irrational) superstition. Justice is the very hallmark of rational wisdom and
its logical fruit. Reasoning about wisdom in itself stengthens the habit
of virtue and fills the soul with a sweetness (*douceur*) that exceeds every
bodily pleasure.[39]

What features of the natural order are accessible to human knowledge? Since good judgment is the most basic of virtuous actions, human
felicity starts with the judgment that good judgment requires truth to
be methodically pursued.[40] Urged by Elizabeth to clarify what is essential for good judgment, Descartes summarizes the theory reached in
Meditation IV by emphasizing two requirements:[41] (I) we must know

---

[36] Letter of September 1, 1645, AT IV, 281: "I'ay parlé d'une habitude qui depend
entierement de nostre libre arbitre et que tous les hommes peuvent acquerir sans
aucune assistance d'ailleurs." Elizabeth had pointed out that some human beings are
afflicted with mental illness and thus, it would seem, unjustly deprived of natural felicity.
See Letter of Elizabeth to Descartes, August 16, 1645, AT IV, 269.

[37] Letter to Elizabeth, September 15, 1645, AT IV, 293: "On doit toutefois penser
qu'on ne sçauroit subsister seul, et qu'on est, en effect, l'une des parties de l'univers."
See also Letter to Elizabeth of October 6, 1645, 308.

[38] Letter to Elizabeth, August 4, 1645, AT IV, 266: "Les maladies et les infortunes ne
sont pas moins naturelles a l'homme que les prosperitez et la santé."

[39] Letter to Elizabeth, September 15, AT IV, 296; and Letter to Chanut, February
21, 1648, AT V, 130: "Il me semble avoir trouvé par experience que la consideration de
ces pensées fortifie l'esprit en l'exercice de la vertu."

[40] Letter to Elizabeth, August 4, 1645, AT IV, 267: "Il faut avouer que la plus grande
felicité de l'homme depend de ce droit usage de la raison, et par consequent que
l'estude qui sert a l'acquerir est la plus utile occupation qu'on puisse avoir, comme
elle est aussy sans doute la plus agreable et la plus douce."

[41] See Elizabeth's letter of August 1645, AT IV, 280 and Descartes's letter of Septem-

what is true and (II) we must remember always to affirm it. Descartes stresses that the chief truth to be known (by the intellect) and embraced (by the will) is the truth that "there is a God, upon whom all things depend, whose perfections are infinite, whose power is immense and *whose decrees are infallible*."[42] The last clause, in which we recognize the idea of an infallible and mind-independent natural order, is the subject-matter of Meditation VI. While God's existence and infinite perfections have been established and embraced (Meditations III and V), God's infallible decrees, as such, have not yet been examined. As Descartes tells Elizabeth, the judgment that all things depend infallibly on God is indispensable for wisdom since it "teaches us to receive with equanimity (*recevoir en bonne part*) whatever happens to us, as expressly sent to us by God."[43] Moreover, if we know God correctly, we are "so inclined to love him that we find joy in our afflictions."[44]

At this point we know that physical illness and misfortune are natural events, part of the natural order, but in what sense must they be embraced as expressly sent to us by God and turned into sources of joy? The problem of God's infallible decrees raises a host of questions. The first and most basic is the problem of the existence of material things, to which Meditation VI now turns.

12.2. *Trust and Belief*

Meditation VI never proves by strict demonstration that bodies exist, but instead validates the *ego*'s propensity to believe in their existence: *magna propensio ad credendum*.[45] Logically speaking, the only necessity attaching to material things is the necessity of their possibility, based

---

ber 15, 1645, AT IV, 291: "Il ne peut, ce me semble, y avoir que deux choses qui soyent requises pour estre tousiours disposé a bien juger."

[42] *Ibid*.: "La premiere et la principale est qu'il y a un Dieu, de qui toutes les choses dependent, dont les perfections sont infinies, dont le pouvoir est immense, dont les decrets sont infallibles."

[43] *Ibid*.: "La premiere et la principale est qu'il y a un Dieu, de qui toutes les choses dependent, dont les perfections sont infinies, dont le pouvoir est immense, dont les secrets sont infallibles; car cela nous apprend a recevoir en bonne part toutes les choses qui nous arrivent, comme nous estant expressement envoyées de Dieu."

[44] Letter to Elizabeth, September 15, 1645, AT IV, 292.

[45] Meditation VI, AT VII, 79–80.

on the mind-independent consistency of geometric natures.[46] There is
no necessity that any body actually exist, nor is there any experience
available to the *ego* that proves by conditional necessity that a body
exists.[47] Fortunately, judgment is an election of the will rather than a
perception of the intellect, which means that the *ego* is free to believe by
a rational judgment that there is an external material world, even if the
ego does not in fact know that there is an external material world. The
radical impossibility of proving the existence of the material world (a
fortiori of proving that the sun will rise tomorrow) does not plunge the
Cartesian *ego* into crisis.[48] Instead, the *ego* freely affirms that a material
world exists, based on a number of converging arguments. What are
they?

After discovering what is supremely certain and absolutely necessary
(God's existence) by means of what is certain but contingent (*ego sum, ego
existo*), the *ego* ventures into the nebulous realm that lies below its pure
essence. First, how is imagining possible? Since the pure immaterial
ego cannot imagine anything by applying its intelligence to itself,[49] does
imagining imply that a body is intimately present to the *ego* and, therefore, that a body exists? The conjecture is supported by two closely-
connected arguments. First, the *ego* recognizes by immediate perception
that pure intellection and imagining differ. When imagining a triangle,
the *ego* is aware of making a distinctive mental effort (*animi contentio*) that
is absent in pure intellection.[50] Secondly, unlike pure intellection, the
faculty of imagining is not essential. The *ego* cannot be the substance
that it is without intellect and will, but remains wholly itself without the
imagination. This suggests (*sequi videtur*) that imagining involves some-

---

[46] Meditation VI, AT VII, 71: "Ad minimum scio illas, quatenus sunt purae Mathe-
seos objectum, posse existere, quandoquidem ipsas clare et distincte percipio."

[47] Meditation IV, AT VII, 73: "ullum sumi posse argumentum, quod necessario
concludat aliquod corpus existere."

[48] If we take Hume's basic argument to be that induction cannot be "read off the
phenomena" but requires induction, then Descartes's argument that no proof can
be given of the outside world (a fortiori of causal implication among phenomena)
anticipates Hume.

[49] See Descartes's emphasis in this regard to Mersenne, July 1, 1641, AT III, 394:
"Il est vrai qu'une chose de cette nature ne se sçauroit imaginer, c'est-à-dire, ne se
sçauroit representer par une image corporelle. Mais il ne s'en faut pas estonner; car
nostre imagination n'est propre qu'à se representer des choses qui tombent sous le
sens."

[50] AT VII, 72–73: "Manifeste hic animadverto mihi peculiari quadam animi con-
tentione opus esse ad imaginandum, qua non utor ad intelligendum: quae nova animi
contentio differentiam inter imaginationem et intellectionem puram clare ostendit."

thing outside the mind and other than the mind.[51] Based on these two factors, the *ego* forms the conjecture that a body probably exists: *probabiliter inde conjicio corpus existere*. Does the conjecture hold up to closer examination or is it refuted?

Since imagining includes picturing colors and sounds that are given most vividly in sensation, the *ego* turns to sensation to see if sensory ideas by any chance imply by strict necessity (*necessario concludat*) that material bodies exist.[52] This requires reviewing the history of the *ego*'s cognitive encounter with sensation, which leads to identifying three dialectically-related developmental stages:

> "First, I will recall in myself what things, perceived by sense, I initially thought (*putavi*) to be true and what causes led me to think (*putavi*) that these things were true; then I will examine the causes that later made me revoke them as doubtful; and finally I will consider what I must now believe (*credendum*) about them."[53]

From naive empicirism (all sensations must be trusted as veridical) to skepticism (no sensation must be trusted as veridical) to a new critical synthesis (some aspects of sensation must be given limited trust)—the history of the *ego*'s successive attitudes towards sensation recapitulates human epistemology from Aristotle through Sextus Empiciricus to Descartes. The dialectical path (thesis, antithesis) that leads to the Cartesian resolution (synthesis) means that, while the two earlier stages are superseded, the kernel of truth that each contained is preserved.

As though looking back to a personal infancy as well as to the infancy of humanity, the *ego* narrates the genesis of naive empiricism. Naive empiricism grew spontaneously out of the *ego*'s bodily sensations, which mapped out a bodily identity and placed that same privileged body (*illud corpus*) among other bodies that affected it pleasurably or adversely.[54] Two salient aspects of sensory experience led the *ego* to

---

[51] AT VII, 73: "Ad haec considero istam vim imaginandi quae in me est, prout differt a vi intelligendi, ad mei ipsius, hoc est ad mentis meae essentiam non requiri; unde sequi videtur illam ab aliqua re a me diversa pendere."

[52] AT VII, 74: "videndumque an ex iis quae isto cogitandi modo, quem sensum appello, percipiuntur, certum aliquod argumentum pro rerum corporearum existentia habere possim."

[53] *Ibid.*: "Et primo quidem apud me hic repetam quaenam illa sint quae antehac, ut sensu percepta, vera esse putavi, et quas ob causas id putavi; deinde etiam causas expendam propter quas eadem postea in dubium revocavi; ac denique considerabo quid mihi nunc de iisdem sit credendum."

[54] AT VII, 74: "Primo itaque sensi me habere caput, manus, pedes, et membra caetera ex quibus constat illud corpus, quod tanquam mei partem, vel forte etiam

think that sensory ideas such as blackness, hardness, weight, had real extramental existence. First, sensory ideas were validated pragmatically by the *ego*'s ability to discriminate various bodies from one another.[55] Second, sensory ideas impinged on the mind without the *ego*'s consent: "*experiebar enim illas absque ullo meo consensu mihi advenire.*"[56] The experience of passive reception combined with pragmatic utility seemed to attest to the mind-independence of the "heat" or the "blackness" that were given in sensation.[57]

Descartes's narrative of the genesis of first-order empiricism is the story of the *ego*'s immersion in the flesh—and fall from rational grace. The *ego*, predisposed as a pure intelligence to perceive as true what cannot be changed at will, unaware at birth of its true essence, spontaneously ("naively") errs by embracing sensory ideas that advene to it *velim nolim* as veridical and by conceiving of itself, consequently, as a body. Relying on sense more often than on reason and finding sensory ideas more vivid (*expressas*) than its own deliberate thoughts, the *ego* comes to regard sensory ideas, not only as veridical, but as the very building blocks of knowledge: "I easily persuaded myself that I had nothing in the intellect that I did not first have in the senses."[58]

The moral consequences of Man's spontaneous Aristotelianism are grave. The *ego* feels "all of its appetites and affections" for the body that it informs and cannot feel the pleasure or the pain that other bodies suffer.[59] First-order empiricism, Descartes implies, inevitably breeds injustice and a biased self-love. The *ego*'s innate predisposition to know itself and cherish itself as a separate substance contributes to its moral downfall since it drives the *ego* to yearn for physical, rather than spiritual, immortality. Mistaking itself for a bodily being threatened by bod-

---

tanquam me totum spectabam; sensique hoc corpus inter alia multa corpora versari, a quibus variis commodis vel incommodis affici potest."

[55] AT VII, 75: "reliqua corpora ab invicem distinguebam."

[56] Cf. John Searle's idea that the "direction of causality" is part of a sensory perception, *Intentionality*, 123: "When I see a flower, part of the content of the experience is that this experience is caused by the fact that there is a flower there."

[57] Cf. Searle, *Intentionality*, 91: visual perception is characterized by a "world-to-mind" direction of causation, meaning that the presence of features of the object cause the experience.

[58] AT VII, 75: "Facile mihi persuadebam nullam plane me habere in intellectu, quam non prius habuissem in sensu."

[59] AT VII, 76: "omnes appetitus et affectus in illo et pro illo sentiebam; ac denique dolorem et titillationem voluptatis in ejus partibus, non autem in aliis extra illud positis, advertebam."

ily dangers, innately averse to death, the *ego* distinguishes between *my body* and "what lies outside," prepared to ward off death at the expense of others. At this stage, the *ego* invokes "nature's teaching" to compound its self-love and mask its ignorance, protecting itself from anomalies that might raise doubts and threaten its bodily identity. The *ego* sticks dogmatically to the axiom that sensory ideas imply causes resembling them even though puzzles arise to awaken the intelligence.[60] *Videbar a natura didicisse*: nature's teaching at this stage is a matter of conditioned response rather than rational persuasion.[61]

How was the *ego* ever saved from its dogmatic slumber? The *ego* reports that numerous experiences ruined "all of the faith (*fidem omnem*) that I had in the senses."[62] The betrayal of the senses on key occasions prompted the *ego* to revoke its trust in "nature's teaching" across the board. Nature's teaching is now shunned, not only on the grounds that square towers appear round at a distance, but on the grounds that "nature seems to move me to things from which reason dissuades me."[63]

The skeptical stage is a stage of desolation, but also of heroic self-sufficiency. The *ego* has struggled out from under the dictatorship of the senses but has not yet discovered the radical meaning of its free agency. Involuntarily weaned from the infantile safety of sense, the *ego* estranges itself deliberately from nature's teaching by suspending judgment on a permanent basis (*"Que sais-je?"*). Thus while sensory passivity led to a generally receptive epistemology that culminated in first-order empiricism, the skeptic rebellion, without knowing it, found consolation in the *ego*'s moral prerogative and placed the *ego*'s rational agency above "nature's teaching." By resisting the spontaneous force of sensory ideas and challenging their claim to provide the elements of knowledge, the *ego* stumbled upon its essence and discovered itself to be a free agent, destined to know and love truth.

At the stage of sensory enchantment, human being is receptive, passively at home in a cocoon-like physical cosmos. The existence of mate-

---

[60] AT VII, 76: "Non aliam sane habebam rationem, nisi quia ita doctus sum a natura."

[61] In *Passions of the Soul*, Part II, Art. LXXXIX, AT XI, 394, Descartes speculates that the intense horror that we feel at the contact of a worm, or at the sound of a leaf trembling, comes from the fact that "Horror is instituted by Nature to represent a sudden and unexpected death to the soul."

[62] AT VII, 76: "Postea vero multa paulatim experimenta fidem omnem quam sensibus habueram labefactarunt."

[63] AT VII, 77: "Cum enim viderer ad multa impelli a natura, quae ratio dissuadebat, non multum fidendum esse putabam iis quae a natura docentur."

rial things is taken for granted. In the skeptic reaction, startled out of complacency, human being masters the trauma by actively disavowing a *per se* unknowable world and neither affirms nor denies the existence of material things since no certainty is conceded. How does the *ego* recover from this negativity and advance to a new stage?

The key is to understand that logical necessity is not perceived empirically or known inductively. Independent of *rerum natura*, of every existence except God's, necessity belongs to a purely rational realm of causal structure. Only when the *ego* boldly supposes that no material thing exists does Stoic *epoche* propel the *ego* to discover a purely intelligible realm in which causal consequence holds and implication is indubitable. The rational agent discovers by a purely rational intuition that *I myself* am the cause of the volition that I form and that the conditional necessity that implies the truth of my contingent existence implies the truth of God's perfect necessity. In short, as soon as "I begin better to know myself and the author of my origin," I have an independent standard of causal implication with which to judge that "not everything must be rashly endorsed that seems to be given by sense, but neither must it all be rejected as untrustworhty."[64]

In this last stage, is the existence of bodies affirmed, denied, or left in suspense? The importance of the *ego*'s independent rational standard comes to light with the *ego*'s very first step toward answering the question by framing a new theory of sensation. Before sensory ideas can be critically examined, the *ego* must prove that the distinction between soul and body is real—which is to say that the distinction holds *velim nolim*, independent of the *ego*'s perception, like a mathematical truth. Although the *ego*'s argument belongs to a well-established scholastic tradition of thought-experiments based on reasoning *de Dei potentia absoluta*, in the present context it exemplifies the fact that truth, as such, is independent of phenomena. Since (by God's free decree) *res cogitans* and *res extensa* are ideas that define mutually-exclusive extensions, God has the power (whether it is exercised or not) to create and maintain a *res cogitans* without creating and maintaining a *res extensa* and vice-versa.[65] The distinction between body and soul is a logical fact decreed by God and, therefore, like the Pythagorean theorem, absolutely neces-

---

[64] AT VII, 77–78: "Nunc autem, postquam incipio meipsum meaeque authorem originis melius nosse, non quidem omnia, quae habere videor a sensibus, puto esse temere admittenda; sed neque etiam omnia in dubium revocanda."

[65] AT VII, 78. See also Interview with Burman, AT V, 163: "Cum enim concipias

sary *quoad nos*.[66] Before the *ego* can make rational sense of sensory ideas, the *ego* must recognize that the distinction between body and soul is rationally indubitable and is true independently of the *ego*'s existence or knowledge.

Once the *ego* (freely but infallibily) judges that the distinction between body and soul is real, the *ego* is able to conceptualize the proper order of its faculties. The *ego*'s two essential faculties, will and intellect, are inseparable from its nature (*res cogitans*), which means that the *ego* by its very nature wills (the good) and understands (the true). Moreover, since the *ego* is logically independent of everything but God's immediate creative power, the *ego* is defined as a substance. Thus when we define the *ego* as a substance whose essence consists in "thinking," what we mean is that the nature of the *ego* does not depend on introspection, which means that the *ego* wills (the good) and perceives (truth) as such, and, therefore, in the womb, long before the *ego* grasps itself and becomes conscious of its immaterial nature through meditation.

While will and intellect define the *ego*'s very essence, lower faculties, such as the power of applying the intelligence to extended shapes, namely the faculty of imagination, and, lower still, the ability to receive sensory ideas, do not. The *ego*'s faculties are nested according to metaphysical dependence. Proceeding downwards, a hierarchy of increased contingency emerges. God's infinite power implies ("eminently includes") the possibility of a pure *mens humana*, which in turn implies, *on the condition of embodiment*, the possibility of a (rationally) imaginative, sensitive and locomotive *ego*. Proceeding in the reverse order, from the bottom up, two levels of conditional necessity are defined: human sensation and imagination (if they exist) imply an immaterial substance possessed of intellect and will—which in turn (if it exists) implies God's necessary existence *a se*. Imagination and sense are thus *possible* faculties of the *ego* if and only if the *ego* is created and joined to a created body. These lower faculties are, in turn, *unavoidable* consequences of a divine decision to join an actual *ego* to an actual body.

A first argument in support of the existence of material things emerges. The lower spectrum of logically possible faculties, faculties that could belong to the *ego* on the condition that material things exist,

---

clare substantiam corpoream et clare etiam concipias substantiam cogitantem distinctam a substantia corporea, quaeque illam negat, ut illa negat substantiam cogitantem, ageres certe contra tuam intellectionem."

[66] AT VII, 78: "certum est me a corpore meo revera esse distinctum et absque illo posse existere."

would be *wasted* if no material thing exists. Because of its characteristic passivity, sensation brings the core problem most clearly to light. The *ego*'s faculty of sensing, defined as the capacity to receive and to know (*recipiendi et cognoscendi*) ideas of sensible things, is passive: *passiva quaedam facultas sentiendi*.[67] The faculty would, therefore, be *of no use* if nothing active existed "in me or in something other than myself" to produce these ideas.[68] But no active power in me produces these ideas, since (a) nothing in sensory ideas implies that they must be produced by a rational agent and (b) they are produced in me without my cooperation or even my consent.[69] Therefore, the active power that causes sensory ideas in me must be in a substance other than myself, which necessarily contains all of the reality of the effects formally or eminently.[70]

Descartes's argument combines theory and experience to frame a rational model (*idea facta vel factitia*) of sensation. On the one hand, there is not only the logical possibility that bodies exist but a theoretical *likelihood* that they do, since the full spectrum of human abilities would remain unfulfilled if the *ego* were not embodied and placed in a physical universe. On the other hand, confused and obscure as sensory ideas may be, the *passivity* of sensation is distinctly known to the *ego* now that it knows itself to be a free agent. Two results ensue. First, in contrast to the experience of forming a volition, which attests indubitably and immediately to the *ego*'s causal agency and existence, the experience of the passivity of sensation precludes the possibility that *I myself* am the efficient cause of sensory ideas. The second result is also negative, namely that sensory ideas, unlike the ideas by means of which the *ego* perceives its own volitions, do not imply that their efficient cause must, in principle, be a free agent: sensory ideas do not *rule out* a free agent as their cause, but neither do they *imply* a free cause.

The key importance of free agency in Descartes's metaphysics now comes into full view. At the highest end of the spectrum of mental faculties, the experience of willing a free effect provides the *ego* with the

---

[67] AT VII, 79: "Est quidem in me passiva quaedam facultas sentiendi, sive ideas rerum sensibilium recipiendi et cognoscendi."

[68] AT VII, 79: "Ejus nullum usum habere possem, nisi quaedam activa etiam existeret, sive in me, sive in alio, facultas istas ideas producendi vel efficiendi."

[69] AT VII, 79: "Atque sane in me ipso esse non potest, quia nullam plane intellectionem praesupponit, et me non cooperante, sed saepe etiam invito, ideae istae producuntur."

[70] *Ibid.*: "ergo superest ut sit in aliqua substantia a me diversa, in qua quoniam omnis realitas vel formaliter vel eminenter inesse debet."

indubitable certainty of being a causal agent and, therefore, of actually existing. At the lowest end of the spectrum, the passive reception of sensory ideas yields only negative certainty regarding their cause. Although a number of arguments converge to support the conjecture that sensory ideas are caused by bodies existing outside the *ego*, no proof is possible without the axiom that "the author of my origin" is infinitely good and, therefore, exempt of all malice. Unfounded ("atheist") human reason cannot rule out the possibility that sensory ideas are caused by an immaterial agent directly stimulating the brain. The only basis for affirming that sensory ideas are caused by material things is that God has given the *ego* "a very great propensity to believe" that sensory ideas are caused by material things (*magnam propensionem ad credendum mihi Deus dederit*) and, at the same time, no faculty with which to refute the propensity to believe it. The *ego*'s propensity to believe in the existence of material things is, in short, incorrigible.

Descartes's argument rests on the claim that reason would not be trustworthy if a falsehood could not be disproved. Rather than assume that reason is capable of proving every truth, Descartes assumes that reason is capable of ruling out every falsehood. Perhaps the practice in geometry of ruling out a false hypothesis by a *reductio ad absurdum* convinced Descartes that the chief impediment to axiomatic systems is not that some true theorem remain unproved but that a falsehood not be ruled out. The *ego*'s belief that sensory ideas are caused by an extramental material world cannot be disproved either rationally or empirically. If the belief is true, then material things exist. If the belief is false, then the *ego* is rationally inclined to a non-disprovable falsehood, which implies that God is either not omnipotent or deceitful. Since anything at all follows from a contradiction (God is deceitful), it follows that material things exist. The belief, if false, is true: *Ac proinde rea corporeae existunt.*

12.3. *Doctus a Natura*

Granted that sensations, in themselves, are insufficient to prove the existence of a material world, what information do they yield? Prompted by a new trust in the collective veracity of its faculties and aware that *mens humana* by its very nature inclines to truth, even in the womb, the *ego* now affirms that "everything that I am taught by nature contains some truth": *aliquid habeant veritatis.*[71] The key is that rationally affirming a material world in spite of the insufficiency of sense does not entail a return to naive empiricism. The *ego* now stands above sensation as a free agent called to judge the content of sensory ideas critically. At stake is a new theory of nature and of "nature's teaching."

First, how is nature defined? The *ego*'s autonomy with regard to sense is vividly brought to light by two successive definitions. Nature considered generally (*generaliter spectatam*) is understood by the *ego* to mean

> "nothing other than, either God himself, or the coordination (*coordinatio*) of created things instituted by God."[72]

Analogously, the *ego* takes "my nature in particular" (*naturam meam in particulari*) to mean

> "nothing other than the aggregation (*complexio*) of everything that is given to me by God."[73]

The *ego*'s definitions are not innate ideas but *ideae factae*—working hypotheses that are freely framed on the basis of innate ideas. Nature *generaliter spectata* affords two distinct meanings, comparable to the scholastic distinction between *natura naturans* and *natura naturata.*[74] Nature is first understood to mean "God himself." Since the *ego* no more confuses God and creation than body and mind, nature *generaliter spectata*, in its first sense, must be actually infinite (incomprehensible) and uncreated. One possibility is that nature *generaliter spectata* is the infinite *unity* of all decreed truths. On this interpretation, the coherence of things and of all possible things is, as such, divine. While a universe with different laws is possible absolutely, a universe in which contradictories are simultaneously true is not. This immanentist view, which amounts to positing a "world soul" that is one in essence with God, must be ruled out, since

---

[71] AT VII, 80: "Sane non dubium est quin ea omnia quae doceor a natura aliquid habeant veritatis."

[72] AT VII, 80: "per naturam enim, generaliter spectatam, nihil nunc aliud quam vel Deum ipsum, vel rerum creatarum coordinationem a Deo institutam intelligo."

[73] *Ibid.*: "nec aliud per naturam meam in particulari, quam complexionem eorum omnium quae mihi a Deo sunt tributa."

[74] I thank Jean-Luc Solère for pointing this out and for the reference to Thomas Aquinas, *Summae theologie*, I, Quaestio 85, articulus 6: "natura vero universalis est virtus activa in aliquo universali principio naturae, puta in aliquo caelestium corporum; vel alicuius superioris substantiae, secundum quod etiam Deus a quibusdam dicitur natura naturans." Cf., possibly, Descartes's early *cogitationes privatae*, AT X, 218: "una est in rebus activa vis, amor, charitas, harmonia."

Descartes expressly rejects the view that the law of non-contradiction is a divine necessity. Impossible as it is for us to conceive, the law of non-contradiction depends on God's free decision.[75]

A better candidate for *natura sive Deus*, nature taken in the sense of *natura naturans*, is the uncreated wisdom that moves all things collectively to itself.[76] If the very first meaning of nature is "God himself," then nature taken in this sense must be God's indivisible *velle* and *intelligere*.[77] Since, according to Descartes and to theology, God "made everything for his own sake"—*omnia propter ipsum* (Deum) *facta sunt*—[78] God is both the sole final cause of the universe and its efficient cause.[79] God is *natura naturans* in the sense that all things universally "gravitate" to God. Because the universe is contingent and God is infinite, the creative act that brings the universe into being is at once effective and intentional, aimed at a transcendent purpose that necessarily exists necessarily *a se*. Nature taken in the sense of *natura naturans*, "naturing" or "creating" nature, is not the result of God's decision but is "God himself"—who draws all things out of nothingness by drawing them to itself. Nature *generaliter spectata* must thus be understood, first, to mean God's wisdom, emanated, not made, God from God, true light from true light.[80] How is nature, taken in the second meaning, as the *coordi-*

[75] Letter to Mesland, May 2, 1644, AT IV, 118: "Dieu ne peut avoir esté determiné à faire qu'il fust vray, que les contradictoires ne peuvent estre ensemble, et que, par consequent, il a pu faire le contraire." Descartes concedes that "some contradictions are so obvious that we cannot think of them without judging them to be utterly impossible, such as *Que Dieu auroit pu faire que les creatures ne fussent point dependantes de luy*." See, also, Sixth Answers, AT VII, 435: "Manifestum est nihil omnino esse posse, quod ab ipso non pendeat: non modo nihil subsistens, sed etiam nullum ordinem, nullam legem, nullamve rationem veri et boni."

[76] Cf. Letter to Mersenne, May 27, 1630, AT I, 154: "Dieu mène tout à sa perfection, c'est à dire: tout *collective*, non pas chaque chose en particulier."

[77] See Letter to Mesland, May 2, 1644, AT IV, 119: "L'idée que nous avons de Dieu nous apprend qu'il n'y a en lui qu'une action, toute simple et toute pure; ce que les mots de St. Augustin expriment fort bien: *Quia vides ea, sunt*, etc., parce qu'en Dieu *videre* et *velle* ne sont qu'une même chose."

[78] Letter to Chanut, June 6, 1647, AT V, 53–54: "Ie ne sçache point neantmoins que nous soyons obligez de croire que l'homme soit la fin de la Creation. Mais il est dit que *omnia propter ipsum* (Deum) *facta sunt*."

[79] *Ibid*.: "C'est Dieu seul qui est la cause finale, aussi bien que la cause efficiente de l'Univers."

[80] The *ego*'s first definition of *natura generaliter spectata* explains why Descartes saw no conflict between his doctrine that eternal truths are created—are *not* "emanated from God like rays of the sun"—and the theology of the *Verbum*. See the letter to Mersenne, May 6, 1630, AT I, 150 ("Ce que vous dites de la production du Verbe ne repugne point, ce me semble, à ce que je dis") and the letter to Mersenne of May 27, AT I, 152.

natio that is instituted by God, related to God's wisdom? One possibility is that *natura*, taken as the *coordinatio* of created things, is the same wisdom taken immanently, as divine providence—an unfolding, inductive infinity. Since *natura* in this second sense is "instituted" by God (*a Deo institutam*), we must assume that *natura* in this second sense is not God himself, but God's boundless handiwork.[81] Descartes remarks elsewhere that human reason cannot deny an infinite progression with regard to God's works,[82] and that multiplying inductive steps infinitely reaches actual infinity.[83] Moreover, as we know, the actual infinite is logically prior to the potential infinite, so that induction over an infinite domain presupposes the non-inductive infinite (the idea of God) as an innate idea.[84] On this interpretation, the *coordinatio* of created things, *natura naturata*, is the created image of God's infinity, stamped on the universe in the same way as the idea of God's infinity is stamped as an idea on every *res cogitans*. The universe (*natura naturata*) is a boundless unfolding of perfection, created by, and for the sake of, a transcendent infinite totality of perfection (*natura naturans*). Descartes everywhere insists that God's works are limitless,[85] implying that the universe as a completed totality can be conceived by human reason, but not comprehended.

Thus while God's created truths are accessible to human reason in a piecemeal way, the instituted *coordinatio* of all created truths taken as a

---

[81] In his letter to Mersenne of May 27, 1630, Descartes equates *creavit* with *fecit vel disposuit* (AT I, 152–153). Presumably, the ablative *a Deo* implies that *instituitare* implies God's efficient act as well.

[82] Letter to Clerselier, April 23, 1649, AT V, 355: "Il me semble tres clairement qu'il ne peut y avoir de progrès à l'infiny au regard des idées qui sont en moy, à cause que ie me sens finy. Quand ie n'ose par apres nier le progrés à l'infiny, c'est au regard des oeuvres de Dieu, lequel ie sçay estre infiny, et par consequent que ce n'est pas à moy à prescrire aucune fin à ses ouvrages."

[83] Interview with Berman, AT V, 154: "Cum autem indefinita ita multiplicantur, fiunt infinita, seu potius infinitum, nam tale indefinitum et infinitum idem sunt."

[84] Interview with Berman, AT V, 157: "Cum jam sciam et probaverim esse Deum, et simul animadvertam inter numerandum me non posse pervenire ad numerum maximum, sed semper esse cogitabilem majorem numerum quam a me cogitari possit, sequitur illam vim me non habere a memet ipso, sed eam me accepisse ab aliquo ente me perfectiore, scilicet a Deo."

[85] See the letter to Chanut, June 6, 1647, AT V, 51: "Ie me souviens que le cardinal de Cusa et plusieurs autres Docteurs ont supposé le monde infiny, sans qu'ils ayent iamais esté repris de L'Eglise pour ce sujet; au contrarie, on croit que c'est honorer Dieu, que de faire concevoir ses oeuvres fort grands. Et mon opinion est moins difficile à recevoir que la leur, pour ce que ie ne dis pas que le monde soit *infiny*, mais *indefyni* seulement." See also the Interview with Berman, AT V, 167: "Et sic forsan dicere possumus mundum esse infinitum."

completed infinity is inaccessible to human reason. Descartes, in effect, affirms that divine providence accounts for the cosmic unfolding, but only on the condition of excluding it absolutely from the competence of human science. If nature taken in the first sense (*natura naturans*) is God Himself, the *Verbum* through whom and for whom all things are made,[86] nature taken in the second sense (*natura naturata*) is God's providential plan to bring a boundless creation out of nothing to himself (a plan, thus, with the Incarnation at its center). In both formulations, uncreated and created, nature taken generally is God's providence that "rules the world."[87]

As we saw, wisdom according to Seneca consists in voluntarily consenting to the natural order, which translated into religious terms means, Descartes says, "following God's will in every action."[88] Descartes, as we saw, examined Seneca's doctrine with the hope not only of assimilating it but of improving it.[89] Does the *ego*'s double definition of *natura generaliter spectata* allow rational wisdom to be raised to a higher level of consent/love, closer to the theological level? Since Descartes was convinced that unaided reason suffices, not only to know that felicity is possible in this life, but that a higher felicity is possible in the next life,[90] his doctrine of rational wisdom seems indeed to exceeds Seneca's. But how?

Meditation VI, as we will now see, transforms the Stoic notion of *amor fati* into a subtle new form of rational *amor providentiae*. What is new is not the reframing itself,[91] but the distinctive sort of human initiative that the Cartesian doctrine encourages. First, however, we must examine if and how human nature is specially ruled by divine providence, which is to say, if and how the *ego*'s enfleshment, which seems at first blush to move the *ego* away from reason and from God, in fact moves the *ego* back to God.

---

[86] Cf. Francis of Sales, *Traité de l'Amour de Dieu*, Bk. II, chapters III-VII, in *Oeuvres*, I, 415–430.

[87] Letter to Vatier, February 22, 1638, AT I, 564: "ie me remets du reste à la providence qui regit le monde."

[88] AT IV, 273.

[89] Letter to Elizabeth, July 21, 1645, AT IV, 252: "tascher a rencherir par dessus eux, en adioutant quelque chose a leurs preceptes; car ainsy on peut rendre ces preceptes parfaitement siens, et se disposer a les mettre en pratique."

[90] See the letter to Huygens, October 13, 1642, AT III, 580; and the letter to Elizabeth, September 15, 1645, AT IV, 292.

[91] Cf., most notably, Justus Lipsius, *De constantia* (1584), I.12–19; *Manuductio ad Stoicam philosophiam libre tres* (1604), II.10; and *Physiologia Stoicorum libri tres* (1604), I.12.

Turning to the human microcosm, we find first that *my nature in particular* means the *complexio* of everything that God has alloted to me (*mihi a Deo tributa*). Nature (*natura naturans*) thus decrees that two radically distinct essences, body and soul, be joined to form the human organism that is *my nature*.[92] Descartes, as we know, unambiguously affirms the substantial unity of the human person,[93] and has no quarrel with defining the rational soul as the "form" of the human body.[94] His main concern is that such talk not imply that free agency is a *mode* of the body,[95] precisely because human nature cannot be rationally understood or effectively reformed unless the *ego* is empowered to stand outside of it. The *ego* must know itself to be a *sui generis* causal principle, wholly independent of the body and of material events, in order to consent to the order of nature. Why? Because in the human case, as we will see, the order of nature *does not follow naturally from anything but the ego's autonomous agency.*

What does the *ego*'s "own nature in particular" teach it? Most expressly (*magis expresse*) that "I have a body that must be fed when I feel hungry and must drink when I feel thirsty"—a body with which "I am so narrowly joined and mingled (*conjunctum et quasi permixtum*) that I, who am nothing strictly but a thinking substance, feel pain when it is wounded."[96] In other words, enfleshment teaches the *ego* that it is naked, fragile, dependent. The *ego*, which could have been created in such a way as to inhabit the flesh impassively, like a pilot in a ship, is instead made vulnerable through the body's vulnerability.[97] As

---

[92] The following passage from St. Augustine's *De Trinitate*, XV, vii, 11, may coincide with Descartes's view: "Homo est substantia rationalis constans ex anima et corpore; non est dubium hominem habere animam quae non est corpus, habere corpus quod non est anima. Ac per hoc illa tria non homo sunt, sed hominis sunt, vel in homine sunt."

[93] See his statement to Arnauld, cited previously, in AT VII, p. 228: "In eâdem sexta Meditatione, in quâ egi de distinctione mentis a corpore, simul etiam probavi substantialiter illi esse unitam."

[94] See Letter to Mesland, 1645 or 1646, AT IV, 346: "l'unité numérique du corps de l'homme ne depend pas de sa matiere, mais de sa forme, qui est l'âme."

[95] AT VII, p. 444. Cf. the same concern in Augustine, *De Trinitate*, X, x, 15: "isti autem ipsam mentem in subjecto esse dicunt, corpore scilicet cujus compositio vel temperatio est. Unde consequenter etiam intelligentiam quid aliud quam in eodem subjecto corpore existimant?"

[96] Meditation VI, AT VII, 81.

[97] *Ibid.* Descartes specifically rejects the Platonic model of the soul as "pilot" of the body/ship. "Docet etiam natura, per istos sensus doloris, famis, sitis etc., me non tantum adesse meo corpori ut nauta adest navigio, sed illi arctissime esse conjunctum et quasi permixtum, adeo ut unum quid cum illo componam."

a result of the nature that is alloted to me, *I myself* hunger and thirst.[98]
Thus while the *ego*'s most essential self-revelation is the revelation of
its free agency, the *ego*'s most natural revelation is the revelation of its
insufficiency. Since, as we know, the *ego*'s experience of free agency is a
quasi divine experience of similitude to God, being joined to a body, it
appears, may serve to protect the *ego* from the *hubris* that might result
from the gift of free will.

So far, what "my nature in particular" teaches me most expressly—
and most providentially—is that *I am not God*. Enfleshment teaches
me, moreover, that I am part of the full plenitude of God's creation.
As a result of enfleshment, "I am taught by nature" to thrive in the
lap of God's physical creation—to avoid harmful bodies and pursue
instead those that are beneficial.[99] Insofar as sensations, which are
"confused modes of thinking derived from the union of mind and
body,"[100] help the human organism to survive, sensations are veridical
and trustworthy.[101] Sensations accurately represent the world to me as
harmful or gratifying, hot or cold to touch, sweet or bitter to taste,
distant or close to the ear. But the same sensations that guide me
providentially through a jungle of physical threats and pleasures are
intrinsically perspectival. They impel me, not only to cathect my body,
but to cathect my body over and above every other body, without
regard for justice.[102] Sensations convince me to regard as absolute what
is merely relative. Precisely because I am by nature gifted with will
and intellect, I am lured into presumption. Unlike animals, who simply
react, innocently, to stimuli, I rashly judge that what is sweet *apud me*
is sweet absolutely, or that there is real "blackness" in things that look
black to me, or that distant constellations have the actual form and size

---

[98] In his answers to Arnauld (4th series) Descartes stresses: "Il m'a semblé que j'avais
pris garde assez soigneusement à ce que personne ne pût penser *que l'homme n'est rien
qu'un esprit usant ou se servant du corps.*" AT IX, p. 176.

[99] *Ibid.*: "Doceor a natura varia circa meum corpus alia corpora existere, ex quibus
nonulla mihi prosequenda sunt, alia fugienda." Cf. Augustine, *De Trinitate*, XII, ii, 2:
"Possunt autem et pecora et sentire per corporis sensus extrinsecus corporalia, et ea
memoriae fixa reminisci, atque in eis appetere conducibilia, fugere incommoda."

[100] AT VII, p. 81: "nihil aliud sunt quam confusi quidam cogitandi modi ab unione
et quasi permixione mentis cum corpore exorti."

[101] In a letter to Mersenne dated October 16, 1639, Descartes specifies that the
natural instinct that we have in common with animals is given to us "for the sake of
preserving the body" (*à la conservation de notre corps.*) AT II, p. 599. See also *Principes de la
Philosophie*, III, art. 3 AT VIII, p. 81.

[102] Extrapolating from AT IX, 76: "neque enim ab illo (i.e. corpore meo) poteram
unquam sejungi, ut a reliquis; omnes appetitus et affectus in illo et pro illo sentiebam."

that appear to my eyes.[103] I take human nature to be the measure of all things and theorize that all things revolve around me and for my benefit.[104]

It seems that human nature constitutes an implicit *test* of the soul's justice and provides the *ego* with an opportunity to repent of its presumption and to mature: will the *ego* let itself be ruled for a whole lifetime by fleshly stimuli, or will the *ego* wake up and recover its freedom? Implicitly, naive empiricism corresponds to a stage of latency, when the *ego* is under the tutelage of natural impulses: *natura duce*. Pressed by physical appetites, which make physical gratification disproportionately appealing,[105] eager to manage and control biological impulses, the *ego* posits no higher self, radically distinct from the mortal body that naturally belongs to it.[106] By the same token, the *ego* posits no vaster universe than the bounded geocentric cosmos that presents itself to sight, and which nurtures the belief that "this earth is our principal home and this life is our best."[107]

Does nature, which teaches me to drink when I am thirsty, teach me as well that the heavens revolve around the earth? The answer requires that the *ego* "define more accurately" what is meant in this second case by "nature."[108] Human nature, the "aggregation of all that God has given me" comprises, in effect, three distinct natures: there is a spiritual nature, the pure immaterial *ego*, possessed of *velle* and *intelligere*; there is a bodily nature, a *res extensa*, which is "like a machine that operates uniformly, according to its own proper and universal laws;"[109] and finally, there is a hybrid nature made up of

---

[103] AT VII, p. 82.

[104] See Interview with Berman, AT V, 168: "Et nihilominus haec est usitata consuetudo hominum, qui ipsi putant se Deo carissimos esse, et ideo propter se omnia facta esse; suam habitationem, terram, omnia antecedere, omnia in illa esse et propter illam facta esse. Sed quid nos scimus, quod Deus extra hanc terram in stellis, etc., non produxerit?"

[105] See the letter to Elizabeth, September 1, 1645, AT IV, 284.

[106] Cf. Augustine, *De Trinitate*, X, viii, 11, speaking of *mens*: "Sed aliud secum amando cum eo se confudit et concrevit quodam modo; atque ita dum sicut unum diversa complectitur, unum putavit esse quae diversa sunt."

[107] See Descartes's letter to Elizabeth, dated September 15 1645, AT IV, 292, where Descartes explicates the spiritual harm of geocentrism: "Cela fait qu'on est enclin à penser que cette terre est notre principale demeure, et cette vie notre meilleure."

[108] AT VII, 82: "Accuratius debeo definire quid proprie intelligam, cum dico me aliquid doceri a natura."

[109] Interview with Berman, AT V, 163: "Deus corpus nostrum fabricavit ut machi-

the intimate union of soul and body (*compositio ex mente et corpore.*)[110]
Unlike the pure substance of the soul and the deterministic body, the
soul/body *compositio* is neither possessed of a rational propensity to love
and know truth, nor ruled deterministically by God's physical laws. The
soul/body composite generates its own imperative, its own *telos*, namely,
bodily survival.

When we say that "nature" teaches us that there is real "blackness"
in bodies that surround us, the mistake we make is that we inadver-
tantly take human nature in a more *restricted* sense that the full human
complexio: *hic naturam strictius sumo, quam pro complexione eorum omnium mihi
a Deo tributa sunt.*[111] Specifically, we treat the part in us that is attuned
to bodily survival—the part that perceives "blackness" and treats it as
real—to be the whole of human nature when it is only a subset.[112]

The illusion of nature's deception now unravels. As long as I mistake myself to be the biological organism that I *partly* am, I am spontaneously led (*sponte et a natura duce*) by sensation to endorse perspectival
impressions as true extramental natures. I eat and walk and navigate
through a world of color and sound out of habit, oblivious of my power
of agency and moral freedom.[113] I frame a natural philosophy that for-
malizes and enshrines the inclinations that are given to me for the sake
of my own particular bodily survival. But as soon as I discover my free
agency by refraining from conditioned behaviors, I become mindful of
my actions and judge, in particular, that my natural impulse to avoid
a hot flame does not imply a natural impulse to judge that "heat" is
an extramental essence. By coming out of the world through a volition
that depends on nothing material, I judge that

> "I habitually pervert the order of nature (*ordinem naturae pervertere*). For I
> use sensory perceptions, which have been given by nature only to signify
> to the mind what is beneficial or injurious to the composite of which it

---

nam, et voluit illud agere ut instrumentum universale, quod semper operaretur eodem
modo juxta leges suas."

[110] AT VII, pp. 82–83. One is reminded of the "pneumatic," "psychic" and "somatic"
levels found in, e.g., Clement of Alexandria. See *Le Gnostique de Saint Clément d'Alexandrie:
Opuscule inédit de Fénelon*, published with an introduction and notes by Paul Dudon, S.J.
(Paris: Gabriel Beauchesne, 1930).

[111] AT VII, 82.

[112] *Ibid.*: "In hac enim complexione multa continentur quae ad mentem solam pertinent…"

[113] See the letter to Newcastle, November 23, 1646, AT IV, 573: "Il arrive souvent
que nous marchons et que nous mangeons, sans penser en aucune façon à ce que nous
faisons."

is a part, and which for this purpose are sufficiently clear and distinct, as though they were trustworthy rules for the immediate discernment of the essence of bodies placed outside of us, about which they signify in fact nothing except very obscurely and confusedly."[114]

Until the *ego* exercises its causal efficacy to detach itself from the senses, the *ego* follows, not human nature as such, but a restricted biological nature, which is geared for material survival. As long as body and soul are confused, the *ego* lies dormant, the natural order of human nature is destroyed and human integrity collapses. The *ego*, mistaking itself to be a mode of the body that belongs to it, mistakes what is pragmatically real for what is metaphysically true.

12.4. Ordinem naturae pervertere

What seemed to be a small correction is really a monumental step that goes to the root of man's inability to exercise moral freedom without detachment from the senses and deliberate mental effort. The *ego*, in effect, has framed a rational account of its immersion in the body and postlapsarian loss of autonomy.[115] Joined in the womb to a "machine of flesh and blood," the pure substance of the soul forgets its origin and feels bodily needs as though they were needs "of its very own."[116] Until the *ego* matures sufficiently to resolve "one day" to detach itself from sense and to meditate, the *ego* lies as though bewitched, passively moved to pseudo-agency by a host of *impetus naturales*, shaped by material events.

---

[114] AT VII, 196: "Sed video me in his aliisque permultis ordinem naturae pervertere esse assuetum, quia nempe sensuum perceptionibus, quae proprie tantum a natura datae sunt ad menti significandum quaenam compositio, cujus pars est, commoda sint vel incommoda, et eatenus sunt satis clarae et distinctae, utor tanquam regulis certis ad immediate dignoscendum quaenam sit corporum extra nos positorum essentia, de qua tamen nihil nisi valde obscure et confuse significant."

[115] Augustine's account in *De Trinitate* XII, viii, 13 and 14, is remarkably similar: "Qui (i.e. homo interior) etiam ipse si per illam rationem cui temporalium rerum administratio delegata est, immoderato progressu nimis in exteriora prolabitur, consentiente sibi capite suo, id est, non eam cohibente atque refrenante illa quae in specula consilii praesidet quasi virili portione, inveteratur inter inimicos suos (*Psal.*, vi, 8) virtutis invidos daemones cum suo principe diabolo."

[116] See Letter to Hyperaspistes, August 1641, AT III, 423–424. Descartes speaks of the body's "fetters": *vinculis corporis*. In a letter to Newcastle, March or April 1648, Descartes distinguishes between our earthly body, which "impedes the soul," and a possible glorified body, which "no longer" impedes it (AT V, 137).

In order to adhere to nature, as wisdom requires, the *ego* must act. Only by acting does the *ego* grasp its existence as a causal agent capable of bringing about free effects. By suspending judgment, by adhering to truth before any truth is known except the truth that it lies within a free agent's power to adhere to truth, the *ego* for the first time adheres to the order of nature. The *ego*, in effect, adheres to human nature *only by freely restoring it*. Human nature is not naturally given to human being since human nature is defined by its order and the order collapses if the *ego* abdicates its moral freedom.

Human nature is destroyed if human being acts "mindlessly" rather than willingly and by resolve—which brings us back full circle to orthopraxy. Only by conducting myself deliberately and cautiously, like someone who walks "alone and in darkness," do I adhere to my human nature and conform to the natural law. As long as the hybrid soul/body nature poses successfully as the whole of human nature, human autonomy is perturbed and impeded, if not completely usurped.[117]

How, then, is enfleshment beneficial, providential? Is Descartes a closet Manichean who believes that we are sparks of light trapped in matter by an evil demiurge? Although Descartes, citing Horace, finds it useful to compare the human soul to a "spark of divine light,"[118] and explicitly regards the perishable human body as a "body of clay,"[119] he also emphatically insists that nothing happens or could ever happen that does not depend on God's will.[120] Divine providence governs every detail of individual human actions.[121] Why, then, does the divine wisdom decree the soul's enfleshment?

Descartes suggests two answers. First, enfleshment providentially "joins human beings together in such close society" that mutual charity emerges naturally from self-interest.[122] Secondly and more finda-

---

[117] For "perturbed" (*perturbata*) and "impeded" (*impediri*) see the answers to Arnaud (4th series) AT VII, 228.

[118] Letter to Chanut, February 1, 1647, AT IV, 608: "nous venons à nous persuader qu'elle (sc. nostre ame) est une emanation de sa souveraine intelligence, *et divinae quasi particula aurae.*" (Horace, *Satires*, II, 2).

[119] *Discours de la Méthode*, V, AT VI, 45–46; "Ie me contentay de supposer que Dieu formast le cors d'un homme [...] sans le composer d'autre matiere que celle que i'avois decrite."

[120] Letter to Elizabeth, October 6, 1645, AT IV, 314: "Dieu est tellement la cause universelle de tout, qu'il est en mesme façon la cause totale; et ainsy rien ne peut arriver sans sa volonté."

[121] Letter to Elizabeth, October 6, 1645, AT IV, 315.

[122] Letter to Elizabeth, October 6, 1645, AT IV, 316–317.

mentally, since the exercise of moral freedom is all but lost by the soul's immersion in matter, the *ego* must strive voluntarily to recover it. Human beings cannot take the gift of moral freedom for granted: they must brave obstacles and undergo trials in order to discover their free agency—defend it, value it, cherish it and strengthen it tirelessly against material motions through "laborious vigils."

Enfleshment, in short, provides the *ego* with a chance to pursue moral freedom zealously and place the dignity of consent above the glory of intellect—lest the pure immaterial soul, dazzled by its boundless intelligence, yield to the temptation of autarchy and use its freedom to fall away from God rather than love God.[123] Enfleshment provides the *ego* with a chance to earn back its moral freedom through the effort of self-conduct, step by mindful step, starting with the resolve to embrace the special orthopraxy required for meditation.[124] Since orthopraxy requires that every action be vigilantly directed to the good and the true, the *ego* not only does not fall away from God but joins itself all the more securely to God that it freely cooperates with reason.[125] Orthopraxy is the narrow road that is required for the *ego* to restore the natural order by judging that "it belongs to the mind alone, not to the composite of mind and body, to know the truth of such things (essences)."[126] The fruit of orthopraxy is a mature *ego* that no longer confuses body and soul but instead actively reforms human nature by adhering to God—which is to say, by adhering to *natura generaliter spectata*.[127]

---

[123] Letter to Chanut, February 1, 1647, AT IV, 608: "A cause que nostre connoissance semble se pouvoir accroitre par degrés iusqu'à l'infini, si nous ne considerons rien davantage, nous pouvons venir à l'extravagance d'etre dieux."

[124] See Fourth Answers, AT VII, 228–229: "Verumtamen non inficior arctam illam mentis cum corpore conjunctionem, quam sensibus assidue experimur, in causa esse cur realem ejus ab ipso distinctionem non sine attenta meditatione advertamus."

[125] See the letter to Newcastle, March or April 1648, AT V, 137: "Nostre ame a desia quelques [illustrations et connaissances directes] de la beneficence de son Createur, sans lesquelles il ne seroit pas capable de raisonner."

[126] AT IX, pp. 82–83: "De iis verum scire, ad mentem solam, non autem ad compositum, videtur pertinere." Cf. Augustine, *De Trinitate*, XII, ii, 2: "Sed sublimioris rationis est judicare de istis corporalibus secundum rationes incorporales et sempiternas."

[127] Cf. Augustine, *De Trinitate*, X, v, 7: "Utquid ergo ei praeceptum est, ut se ipsam cognoscat? Credo, ut se ipsam cogitet, et secundum naturam suam vivat, id est, ut secundum naturam suam ordinari appetat, sub eo scilicet cui subdenda est, supra ea quibus praeponenda est; sub illo a quo regi debet, supra ea quae regere debet."

12.5. *Trust and Corrigibility*

If the fruit of orthodoxy is wisdom, a chief result of wisdom, in turn, is that bodily survival is put into proper perspective. Does Cartesian wisdom add anything to Stoic wisdom in this particular regard? As the *ego* now recognizes, man's nature *ut ex mente et corpore compositus* is inevitably liable to error,[128] but the reason for this inescapable vulnerability is not a margin of indeterminacy in the course of natural events.[129] All bodies are rigorously determined by mechanistic principles. Consequently, the human body complies automatically with the natural law. The hiatus between the universalism of the body *qua* body and the particularism of the soul/body composite requires yet another clarification of what is meant by a thing's "nature." According to the *ego*'s new judgment, sensations are trustworthy as long they are interpreted to signify what must be shunned or pursued for the sake of preserving the human organism. But if sense moves a hydropsic to drink, or signals pain in an amputated foot, how is nature trustworthy?[130]

The solution is to recognize that we speak of a thing's nature in two very different ways. When we speak about a thing's nature in a purely nominal sense, we say nothing about the thing's true, extramental nature. If we say that the "nature" of a clock is to keep proper time, the term "nature" is nothing more than a man-made label.[131] The true "nature" of a clock, like the nature of any *res extensa*, is simply to follow mechanistic laws deterministically.[132] The human body, in turn, which is a "machine of bones, nerves, muscles, blood and skin"[133] does not "stray from its nature" (*a natura sua aberrare*) when lesions result in neural signals that prompt the organism to a detrimental behavior which, under ordinary conditions, would be beneficial. A hydropsic

---

[128] AT VII, 88: "Non obstante immensa Dei bonitate, naturam hominis ut ex mente et corpore compositi non posse non aliquando esse fallacem."

[129] Cf. Seneca, Quaest. nat., 7, 27, 5 and 6: "Non ad unam natura formam opus suum praestat, sed ipsa varietate se iactat... ignorat naturae potentiam qui illi non putat aliquando licere nisi quod saepius fecit."

[130] AT VII, 84: "At vero non raro etiam in iis erramus ad quae a natura impellimur: ut cum ii qui aegrotant, potum vel cibum appetunt sibi paulo post nociturum."

[131] AT VII, 85: "Nihil aliud est quam denominatio a cogitatione mea."

[132] AT VII, 85: "per illam vero aliquid intelligo quod revera in rebus reperitur, ac proinde nonnihil habet veritatis."

[133] AT VII, 84: "machinamentum quoddam est ex ossibus, nervis, musculis, venis, sanguine et pellibus ita aptum et compositum."

patient no more acts against nature by drinking water than a broken clock acts against nature when its gears are jammed. In both cases, what is ordinarily expected to occur fails to occur precisely because nature is faithfully followed.[134] The nature of the human body is only nominally teleological: its true nature is to be shaped efficiently by material changes, according to uniform laws.

Sensation, at the interface of body and soul, is characterized by a similar uniformity. Each excited nerve excites the same passion each time in the soul.[135] The uniformity with which material causes result in the same predictable sensations is what allows human being *ut ex mente et corpore compositus* to develop instinctive habits. This means that God's providential constancy of action, governing matter universally, rather than a special design tailored for the human organism, explains the generally successful propagation of the human species. When the human body is normally disposed, the soul is excited by nervous signals to feel thirst to the organism's benefit, but if the body is damaged, it just as naturally excites the same feeling, to the organism's detriment.[136] Sensation, it turns out, is useful to the human organism precisely because sensation *cannot correct itself.* But while sensation cannot

[134] AT VII, 85: "Et quamvis, respiciens ad praeconceptum horologii usum, dicere possim illud, cum horas non recte indicat, a natura sua deflectere; atque eodem modo, considerans machinamentum humani corporis tanquam comparatum ad motus qui in eo fieri solent, putem illud etiam a natura sua aberrare, si ejus fauces sint aridae, cum potus ad ipsius conservationem non prodest; satis tamen animadverto hanc ultimam naturae acceptionem ab altera multum differre: haec enim nihil est quam denominatio a cogitatione mea, hominem aegrotum et horologium male fabricatum cum idea hominis sani et horologii recte facti comparante, dependens, rebusque de quibus dicitur extrinseca; per illam vero aliquid intelligo quod revera in rebus reperitur, ac proinde nonnihil habet veritatis."

[135] See the letter to Newcastle, October 1645, AT IV, 326: "la faim et la soif se sentent de la mesme façon que les couleurs, les sons, les odeurs, et generalement tous les objects des sens exterieurs, à savoir par l'entremise des nerfs, qui sont étendus comme de petits filets depuis le cerveau iusques à toutes les autres parties du corps; en sorte que, lors que quelqu'une de ces parties est mue, l'endroit du cerveau duquel viennent ces nerfs se meut aussi, et son mouvement excite en l'ame le sentiment qu'on attribue à cette partie."

[136] Cf. Interview with Berman, AT V, 163–164: "Et hinc cum bene est dispositum (sc. corpus), dat animae cognitionem rectam; cum male, nihilominus tamen juxta leges suas afficit animam, ut inde resultare debeat talis cognitio a qua illa decipiatur; quam si non suppeditaret corpus, non ageret aequaliter et juxta leges suas universales, essetque in Deo defectus constantiae, quod illud non permitteret aequaliter agere, cum aequales agendi modi et leges adsint."

correct itself, the *ego* is free to refrain from acting,[137] and to impart new instincts in the organism by deliberate design.[138]

Once the *ego* acts, and takes responsibility for employing its faculties in the right order, the *ego* is empowered to correct sensory information by coordinating memory, reason and sense experimentally. Disentangled from biological perspectivism, the *ego* is free to judge that the body *qua* body follows mechanistic laws just as infallibly as the soul *qua* soul embraces every good (truth) that is clearly known to it. Most importantly, the *ego* no longer needs to fear sensory deception.[139] Sensation, like every other aspect of nature, attests to God's infinite power and benevolence.[140] Indeed the *ego* can now joyously dismiss all of its doubts as ridiculous (*ut risu dignae*), especially the doubt that sleep and wakefulness cannot be distinguished. Upholding the natural order of its faculties, the wakeful, vigilant *ego* judges that true extramental creation is marked by a seamless coherence that is conspicuously absent from human dreams.[141] By the same token, human action—free, deliberate, rational—reveals itself to be an integral feature of the natural order and of the coherence of creation. Human orthopraxy is indispensable for nature to be nature.

Consequently, wisdom means, not just bearing natural events with constancy and fortitude, but acting freely to increase human control over natural events.[142] Adhering to nature means becoming "the masters and possessors of nature."[143] The *ego* adheres to God (*natura naturans*), nature (*natura naturata*) and human nature (*natura mea in particulari*) precisely through action—by acting deliberately, responsibly, cautiously, intelligently, but also decisively, innovatively, without paralyzing guilt.

---

[137] See *Des Passions de l'âme*, I, Art. 41, AT XI, 359: "la volonté est tellement libre de sa nature, qu'elle ne peut jamais estre contrainte."

[138] See *Des Passions de l'âme*, I, Art. 44, AT XI, 361: "Que chaque volonté est naturellement jointe à quelque mouvement de la glande; mais que, par industrie ou par habitude, on la peut joindre à d'autres" and Art. 45, AT XI, 62.

[139] AT VII, 39: "Non amplius vereri debeo ne illa, quae mihi quotidie a sensibus exhibentur, sint falsa."

[140] AT VII, 87: "ac proinde nihil plane in iis reperiri, quod non immensam Dei potentiam bonitatemque testetur."

[141] AT VII, 90: "Cum veri eae res occurrunt, quas distincte, unde, ubi, et quando mihi adveniant, adverto, earumque perceptionem absque ulla interruptione cum tota reliqua vita connecto, plane certus sum, non in somnis, sed vigilanti occurere."

[142] See the letter to Newcastle, October 1645, AT IV, 329: "Je ne doute point qu'il n'y ait moyen d'acquérir beaucoup de connaissances, touchant la médecine, qui ont été ignorées jusqu'à présent."

[143] *Discours de la Méthode*, Part VI, AT VI, 62.

As long as it is rooted in orthopraxy, human industry is not "unnatural," rather it restores and fulfills the natural order.

Descartes's theory of action implies, first and foremost, that *it is not a crime to be curious*.[144] Far from transgressing nature, the project of science emerges from the voluntary reform of human nature and exemplifies what it means to be "formed by the natural law" (*illius legem formari*), which commands us to work for the public good.[145] The effort of meditation culminates in wisdom, which in turn culminates in the effort to advance knowledge.[146] With every new experiment, the scientist adheres to nature precisely because his interactions with bodily phenomena and with the cosmos, purged of sensory bias and rooted in immutable truths, strenghtens and augments the "beautiful order within."[147] Unlike passive observation, controlled experiment heals the soul's disorder so that body and soul may stand together in a unified and unifying pursuit of knowledge: *où l'entendement agit avec l'imagination et les sens*.[148] The scientist is rewarded by an inward serenity that does not depend on fortune and is delivered of an exaggerated anguish over biological death. Most importantly, the quest for truth continuously joins the scientist to God and implements the "laborious project" (*laboriosum institutum*) of self-awakening called for at the end of the first Meditation, in the aftermath of the demon's fury: which is to lift the soul from the

---

[144] See the letter to Mersenne of November 13, 1639, AT II, 621: "Ce n'est pas un crime d'être curieux de l'anatomie; et j'ai été un hiver à Amsterdam, que j'allais quasi tous les jours en la maison d'un boucher, pour lui voir tuer des bêtes, et faisais apporter de là en mon logis les parties que je voulais anatomiser plus à loisir."

[145] *Discours*, Part VI, AT VI, 66.

[146] See the letter to Elizabeth, dated 28 June 1643: "je crois qu'il est nécessaire d'avoir bien compris, une fois en sa vie, les principes de la métaphysique, à cause que ce sont eux qui nous donnent la connaissance de Dieu et de notre âme ... mais que le meilleur est de se contenter de retenir en sa mémoire et en sa créance les conclusions qu'on a une fois tirées, puis employer le reste du temps qu'on a pour l'étude, aux pensées où l'entendement agit avec l'imagination et les sens." AT III, p. 695.

[147] Descartes may have been encouraged by direct or indirect knowledge of Augustine's praise of Cicero's picture of the philosophical life, identifying it with Christian wisdom. See *De Trinitate*, XIV, xix, 26: "Hanc contemplativam sapientam ... Cicero commendans in fine dialogi Hortensii: *Quae nobis*, inquit, *dies noctesque considerantibus, acuentibusque intelligentiam, quae est mentis acies, caventibusque ne quando illa hebescat, ide est in philosophia vinetibus magna spes est ... [...] sic existimandum est, quo magis hi fuerint semper in suo cursu, id est, in ratione et investigandi cupiditate, et quo minus se admiscuerint atque implicuerint hominum vitiis et erroribus, hoc his faciliorem ascensum et reditum in coelum fore.*"

[148] "Where the understanding works together with imagination and sensation." See the letter to Elizabeth cited earlier. AT III, 695.

inertia of old habits, to brace it against relapsing into "old opinions," and to replace slumber with the "painstaking vigils" (*laboriosa vigila*) that liberate human initiative from captivity.[149]

12.6. *Trust and Providence*

Why, then, do the Meditations not end with the *ego*'s hard-won new sense of security,[150] but, instead, with the warning to acknowledge the "weakness of our nature"—*naturae nostrae infirmitas est agnoscenda*? After celebrating the coherence of human nature restored by the *ego*'s free agency, after dismissing hyberbolic doubts as laughable, after affirming once again that God's perfection preserves the integrated human *complexio* from deception, the *ego* concludes with what amounts to a limitation theorem. On the threshold of returning to the bustle of life and the adventure of scientific experiment, the *ego*, fully enfleshed but irreversibly awake, offers a last insight and parting injunction. In most of life's circumstances, human action cannot wait for every possible variable to be accurately known and evaluated. Limited by time, the human agent must often determine himself to carry out a course of action without perfect knowledge. It follows that human life is inescapably subject to mistakes at every particular turn—"and the weakness of our nature must be ackowledged."[151] What is the meaning of this pessimistic *coda*?

The *ego*'s final injunction is, first and foremost, a profession of humility. The *ego* understands that *le bon sens* is insufficient to show infallibly what action conforms best to God's will in every particular case.

---

[149] See Meditation I, AT VII, p. 23: "Sed laboriosum est hoc institutum, et desidia quaedam ad consuetudinem vitae me reducit. Nec aliter quam captivus etc." Note that in his sixth series of answers, Descartes, using the same word *consuetudino*, compares the "inveterate inertia" preventing readers who find no fault in his arguments from accepting his novel views to those astronomers who, in spite of conclusive arguments to the contrary, simply cannot imagine that the sun is many times larger than the earth. In AT VII, 446: "Quod conclusiones aegre admittant, id facile tribui potest inveteratae consuetudini aliter de ipsis judicandi; ut jam ante notatum est astronomos non facile imaginari Solem esse majorem terra, quamvis certissimis rationibus id demonstrent."

[150] AT VII, 90: "Ex eo enim quod Deus non sit fallax, sequitur omnino in talibus me non falli."

[151] AT VII, 90: "Sed quia rerum agendarum necessitas non semper tam accurati examinis moram concedit, fatemdum est humanam vitam circa res particulares saepe erroribus esse obnoxiam, et naturae nostrae infirmitas est agnoscenda."

Human life, viewed as the trajectory of a radically autonomous person immersed in worldly vicissitudes and confronted by fortune, is
inevitably marred by partial blindness and subject to stumble after
stumble. What are the options? First and foremost, since the temporal
pressure of public affairs (*rerum agendarum necessitas*) is one of the factors
that aggravates the likelihood of mistakes, one solution, dear to the Stoics, is to live a life of seclusion, "removed from worldly affairs."[152] Like
many of his contemporaries and personal correspondants, Descartes, as
we know, practised intramundane asceticism with hidden zeal, living in
the midst of booming Dutch cities "as isolated as in the most remote
desert."[153] Not even solitude, however, preserves human beings from
"the weakness of our nature"—or so at least little Francine's birth seems
to attest.[154] The concluding paragraph of Meditation VI, as though
forging a last alliance with the theologians to whom the whole work
is dedicated, concedes that human life, no matter how glorious or how
obscure, is always and necessarily no more than a record of moral failings before God. The *ego*'s final insight, however, should not be limited to this obvious interpretation. Preparing to terminate the seclusion
of meditation, the *ego* confronts the problem of how to transfer mental
orthopraxy to physical action. Physical actions are carried out by necessity in half-obscurity, with limited vision in every direction and unexpected challenges everywhere. The project of experimental science, in
particular, is rooted in physical agency, disrupting ancient customs and
revolutionizing practice in a uniquely progressive way. The Stoic *amor
fati* must be metamorphosed into something more personal and more
vital: a distinctly Cartesian cooperation with Providence, based on consenting in advance to unforeseen eventualities for the sake of forging
ahead without crippling inhibition.

An exchange of letters with Elizabeth in 1646 sheds light on the
ego's call for caution, which is really a call for action. Prompted by
a draft of the *Traité des passions*, the exchange addresses the problem
of being "irresolute" and brings closure to Descartes's lifelong struggle
with procrastination. Three steps bring Descartes's mature position to

---

[152] Letter to Elizabeth, May 6, 1646, AT IV, 411–412.

[153] Discours de la Méthode, III, AT VI, 31: "l'ay pu vivre aussy solitaire et retiré que
dans les desers les plus escartez." For the ethos of solitary living in France in the mid-
XVIIth century, see Cristoph Delporte, "La figure de l'ascète au siècle classique," in *La
solitude et les solitaires de Port-Royal*, Actes du colloque organisé par la Société des Amis de
Port-Royal, Septembre 20–21 2001 (Paris: Bibliothèque Mazarine, 2002), 37–68.

[154] See Geneviève Rodis-Lewis, *Descartes*, 195–197.

light. First, in Article 170 of the Treatise on the Passions, Descartes characterizes *irresolution*, lack of resolve in acting, as a type of fear (*Crainte*), which,

> "keeping the soul evenly balanced among the many actions that are possible for it to carry out, causes it to execute none of them and gives the soul time to choose before determining itself to act."[155]

We recognize the predicament invoked at the end of Meditation VI. The *ego* has to decide on a course of action and needs time to determine what course of action is best; if the decision cannot wait, the *ego* must act without evaluating all of its options thoroughly, making it liable to mistakes. In the Treatise on the Passions, Descartes goes on to say that lack of resolve is useful to the extent that it provides time for deliberation, but if it lasts "longer than it must" and if "we spend the time required for action in deliberation," then *irresolution* is very detrimental.[156] In other words, if a temporary lack of resolve turns into chronic procrastination, it is, as the opening paragraph of Meditation I explicitly asserts, culpable.[157] The human agent, Descartes implies, has a duty to act in a timely manner as well as a duty to refrain from acting rashly.

The human agent is thus confronted with two conflicting duties and must figure out how to reconcile them. Descartes emphasizes that excessive *irresolution* is not really a passion but the sign of an overly scrupulous moral conscience—of "too great a desire to act well."[158] The *ego*, in effect, is paralyzed by the fear of acting wrongly. Since the *ego*'s "principal perfection" lies in deliberately suspending action rather than risk acting wrongly,[159] how does the *ego* ever dare to act?

The remedy, Descartes says, is to "develop the habit of forming sound and secure judgments regarding everything that occurs" and to "believe that one has done one's duty when one does what one judges to be the best course of action, even if one's judgment turns

---

[155] AT XI, 459: "L'Irresolution est une espece de Crainte, qui retenant l'ame comme en balance, entre plusieurs actions qu'elle peut faire, est cause qu'elle n'en execute aucune, et ainsi qu'elle a du temps pour choisir avant que de se determiner."

[156] *Ibid.*: "Mais lorsqu'elle dure plus qu'il ne faut, et qu'elle fait employer à deliberer le temps qui est requis pour agir, elle est fort mauvaise."

[157] AT VII, 17: "Quare tamdiu cunctatus sum ut deinceps essem in culpa, si quod temporis superest ad agendum, deliberando consumerem."

[158] AT XI, 460: "C'est un exces d'irresolution, qui vient d'un trop grand desir de bien faire."

[159] AT VII, 58.

out to be wrong."[160] The remedy, in short, is nothing less than the journey of healing offered by *Meditationes*. By "meditating seriously" with Descartes, at least "once in a lifetime," the soul is trained to overcome hesitation and act. Article 170 of *Les Passions de l'âme* confirms that the central concern of Descartes's Meditations is to liberate human action, not only from natural impulses and the limitations of Aristotelian empiricism, but also from the crippling fear that innovation in scientific matters is a transgression.

Descartes understood that the Copernican revolution in science would uproot human beings from the security of custom and launch them into a planetary world in which each person had *per force* to bear personal responsibility for acting—for initiating new ventures, devising new contracts, carrying out new experiments and constructing new technologies. An overly severe conscience, Descartes recognized, is just as detrimental to human advancement as is incontinence and slavery to the passions. In order to act both rationally and resolutely, the *ego* must not only dominate emotions that impel it to act rashly but also protect its conscience from morbid anxiety. The Stoic focus on fortitude, aimed at mobilizing human courage against *shame* must be supplemented by a new focus on the virtue of *taking risks*, aimed at mobilizing human courage against *guilt*. The *ego* must not yield shamefully to lust, greed, fear and anger, but neither must the *ego* become paralysed by guilt. The sage must never act out of anger or lust, but neither can he take refuge in inaction.

After reading the draft of the treatise on passions, Elizabeth protested that Descartes's remedies against various types of excess were impractical and that experience had always served her better than reason in the management of daily business.[161] In response, Descartes clarified that, in the case of the remedy offered in Article 170, while he "wished to flatter a personal shortcoming by depicting procrastination as excusable," he did not mean to undermine decisiveness. Indeed he is the first to value "the diligence of those who always move themselves with zeal to do things that they believe to be their duty, even when they do

---

[160] *Ibid.*: "Le remede contre cet exces, est de s'accoustumer à former des jugements certains et determinez, touchant toutes les choses qui se presentent, et à croire qu'on s'acquite tousjours de son devoir, lors qu'on fait ce qu'on juge etre le meilleur, encore que peut estre on juge tres mal."

[161] Letter to Descartes, April 25, 1646, AT IV, 406: "Ie me suis touiours mieux trouvée de me servir de l'experience que de la raison, aux choses qui la (sc. la vie civile) concernent."

not expect a very fruitful result."[162] In other words, he did not mean to imply that monarchs or princes who act boldly in civil affairs *lack* scruples or a strong moral conscience. On the contrary, they carry out their duty, more concerned, as they should be, with acting dutifully than with a particular given outcome. Descartes, a recluse philosopher, would never presume to instruct Elizabeth on how to conduct her civil affairs. Elizabeth's method of relying on experience is, undoubtedly, the best, since indeed "the best advice is not always the one that succeeds" and dealing with the irrational human multitude forces one has to "take risks" and "to put oneself in the power of Fortune."[163]

Is Descartes arguing that acting rationally ("the best advice") is less effective than boldly gambling when the results of our actions depend on Fortune? Descartes wrote Elizabeth a sort of postscript—an additional clarification, or, rather a correction. He made, he says, a "grevious mistake" in making excuses for procrastination.[164] Although sufficient time must always be devoted to deliberation before an important project, once the project is started, it is best to act promptly and with resolve.[165] Nor should the worry that knowledge is imperfect deter us from acting:

> "There is no cause to fear what is unknown, since the things about which we were most apprehensive before we knew them often turn out better than the things we desired. Therefore the best is to trust divine providence in this regard and to let ourselves be conducted by it."[166]

The clarification is twofold. First, a distinction is drawn between the time of deliberation that precedes acting and the time of implemen-

---

[162] Letter to Elizabeth, May 1646, AT IV, 411: "i'estime neantmoins beaucoup plus la diligence de ceux qui se portent tousiours avec ardeur à faire les choses qu'ils croyent estre en quelque façon de leur devoir, encore qu'ils n'en esperent pas beaucoup de fruit."

[163] AT IV, 412: "C'est pourquoy on est contraint de hazarder, et de se mettre au pouvoir de la Fortune."

[164] Letter to Elizabeth, May 1646, AT IV, 414: "Ie prens la liberté de m'y confesser d'une faute tres-signalée que i'ay commise dans le Traité des passions, en ce que, pour flatter ma negligence, i'y ay mis, au nombre des passions de l'ame qui sont excusables, une ie ne scay quelle langueur qui nous empesche quelquefois de mettre en execution les choses qui ont esté approuvées par nostre iugement."

[165] AT IV, 415: "C'est pourquoy ie me persuade que la resolution et la promptitude sont des vertus tres necessaires pour les affaires déia commencées."

[166] *Ibid.*: "Et l'on n'a pas sujet de craindre ce qu'on ignore; car souvent les choses qu'on a le plus apprehendées, avant que de les connoistre, se trouvent meilleures que celles qu'on a desirées. Ainsi le meilleur est en cela de se fier à la providence divine, et de se laisser conduire par elle."

tation. We recognize in this distinction the distinction that Descartes made to Mesland between the state of the soul before acting, which Descartes is willing to characterize as a state of indifference, and the state of the soul while it acts, which he insists is by definition a state of positive commitment.[167]

Descartes's first clarification to Elizabeth is thus that a strong resolve benefits a project that is already in course. The agent, committed to bringing about a new state of affairs, is all the more effective that his resolve is not hampered by delay—by second thoughts and obsessive worry over the outcome.[168] This is why diligence is valuable in those who "do their duty," even though doubts may persist about the outcome. By the same token, the resolve to *reach* a decision with regard to acting includes the duty to devote sufficient time to deliberation, but also the duty "not to waste in deliberation the time that is left to act." This means that deliberation is not a license to remain irresolute but a duty to overcome hesitation—which means, in turn, that an overly scrupulous conscience that keeps the agent in a state of indifference beyond what is reasonable is a malignant conscience aimed at undermining human initiative. Failing to act out of fear of the unknown is a failure to trust providence. To make excuses for inaction is inexcusable.[169]

The second clarification is that trust in Providence is the beginning and end of virtuous action. Why? Because the essential duty of a free agent is the duty to determine what action duty requires in order to carry it out. As long as the *ego* acts according to its best judgment, the *ego* acts according to the natural order and must, therefore, act confidently, without fear. Why? Because the infallibility of divine providence implies that the finite agent acts rationally when he "abandons himself wholly to God's will and, discarding all personal interests, has no other passion than the passion to please God."[170] The human agent

---

[167] Letter to Mesland (?), February 9, 1645, AT IV, 173: "Notandum etiam libertatem considerari posse in actionibus voluntatis, vel antequam eliciantur, vel dum eliciantur. Et quidem spectata in iis, antequam eliciantur, involvit indifferentiam secundo modo sumptam, non autem primo modo."

[168] Letter to Elizabeth, AT IV, 414–415: "Car si l'affaire reussit, tous les petites avantages qu'on aura peut-etre acquis par ce moyen (sc. en disputant pour les conditions), ne servent pas tant que peut nuire le degoust que causent ordinairement ces delais."

[169] Note that identifying morbid guilt as a demonic attempt to discourage spiritual progress is a central feature of Ignatian doctrine. See *The Spiritual Exercises of St. Ignatius*, "Rules for the Discernment of Spirits," 133.

[170] Letter to Elizabeth, September 15, 1645, AT IV, 294: "S'abandonnant du tout à

who "desires nothing but that God's will be done" acts according to his best judgment without "fearing either death, or suffering, or disgraces," since acting according to his best judgment complies, as such, with God's will.[171]

To act virtuously, to adhere to the order of nature, is to cooperate actively with Providence by trusting that human initiative fulfills, rather than disrupts, the unfolding perfection of the cosmos. Cooperation with Providence is the cornerstone of wisdom,[172] and includes, not just bearing the inevitable—judging that illness and misfortune are part of nature's course—but loving, or willing, the inevitable: if *per impossible* the sage could change God's decrees and avoid bodily death, he would not have the will to do so.[173] Since acting virtuously—trying one's best to determine and implement one's duty—fills the *ego* with a special inner joy, virtuous actions are more likely to succeed.[174] But if they fail, they fail. The need to act here and now, decisively, boldly, providentially tests the *ego*'s willingness to trust its actions to divine Providence, just as exposing human life to moral failures providentially reminds the *ego* to recognize the weakness of human nature—which alone teaches the *ego*, most providentially, to trust in itself by not trusting itself in the least.

---

sa volonté, on se despouille de ses propres interests, et on n'a point d'autre passion que de faire ce qu'on croit luy estre agreable." Thus I disagree with Dorottya Kaposi's statement in "Indifférence et liberté humaine chez Descartes," 80, that: "Ainsi la volonté, faculté par laquelle nous reconnaissons notre similitude à Dieu, ne prétend pas à s'unir avec Dieu, comme chez Gibieuf, mais à être aussi indépendante et aussi libre que celle de son créateur." On the contrary, the free will, *because* it is as independent and free as God's, seeks by its very essence to unite with God through love. In support of her interpretation, Kaposi cites Descartes's letter to Christina of November 20, 1647, but fails to emphasize that he says that our free will *seems* to exempt us from subjection to God. There is a temptation and a trial. What is new in Descartes's theory of human freedom is to emphasize that, through meditation and the progressive recovery of reason, we freely *elect* God (Truth) rather than submit to God heteronomously.

[171] Letter to Chanut, February 1, 1647, 608–609.

[172] See the letter to Elizabeth, September 15, 1645, AT IV, 291: "La premiere et la principale [chose requise pour bien juger] est qu'il y a un Dieu, de qui toutes choses dependent, dont les perfections sont infinies, dont le pouvoir est immense, dont les decrets sont infallibles." See also the letter of October 6, 1645, AT IV, 314: "La seule philosophie suffit pour connoistre qu'il ne sçauroit entrer la moindre pensée en l'esprit d'un homme, que Dieu ne veuille et ait voulu de toute eternité qu'elle y entrast."

[173] Letter to Chanut, February 1, 1647, AT IV, 609: "Il aime tellement ce divin decret, il l'estime si juste et si necessaire, il sçait qu'il en doit si entierement dependre, que, mesme lors qu'il en attend la mort ou quelqu'autre mal, si par impossible il pouvoit le changer, il n'en auroit pas la volonté."

[174] See Letter to Elizabeth, November, 1646, AT IV, 529: "Et mesme aussi i'ose croire que la ioye interieure a quelque secrette force pour se rendre la Fortune plus favorable."

BIBLIOGRAPHY

Ariew, Roger. *Descartes and the Last Scholastics*, Ithaca, N.Y.: Cornell U. Press, 1999.

Atiyah, P.S. *The Rise and Fall of Freedom of Contract*, Oxford: Clarendon, 1979.

Atiyah, P.S. *Promises, Morals, and the Law*, Oxford: Clarendon, 1981.

Audi, Robert. *Action, Intention, and Reason*, Ithaca and London: Cornell U. Press, 1993.

Baillet, Adrien. *La Vie de Monsieur Descartes*, Paris, 1691.

Bérulle, Pierre de. *Discours de l'estat et des Grandeurs de Jésus*, Paris: Edition CERF, 1996.

Biard, Jean, and Rashed, Rashdi, eds. *Descartes et le Moyen Âge*, Paris: Vrin, 1997.

Boulnois, Olivier. *Être et représentation. Une généalogie de la métaphysique moderne à l'époque de Duns Scot (XIII-XIVe siècles)*, Paris: PUF, 1999.

Brémond, Henri. *Histoire Littéraire du sentiment religieux en France*, Paris: Bloud et Gay, 1921.

Burnyeat, Miles. "Idealism and Greek Philosophy: What Descartes Saw and Berkeley Missed," *Philosophical Review* 91, 1982, pp. 3–40.

Chomsky, Noam. *New Horizons in the Study of Language and Mind*, Cambridge, UK: Cambridge U. Press, 2000.

Chomsky, Noam. *Language and Thought*, Wakefield and London: Moyer Bell, 1993.

Cobb-Stevens, Richard. *Husserl and Analytic Philosophy*, Dordrecht and Boston, Kluwer, 1990.

Cottingham, John, ed. *The Cambridge Companion to Descartes*, Cambridge, UK: Cambridge U. Press, 1992.

Dagens, Jean. *Bérulle et les origines de la restauration catholique (1575–1611)*, Desclée de Brouwer, 1952.

Daniels, S.J., Antoine, L. *Les Rapports entre Saint François de Sales et les Pays-Bas, 1550–1700*, Nijmegen: Centrale Drukkerij, 1932.

Darwall, Stephen, ed. *Contractarianism/Contractualism*, Malden, Victoria and Berlin: Blackwell Publishing, 2003.

Descartes, *Oeuvres*, C. Adam and P. Tannery eds., Paris 1891–1912, in 13 volumes.

Ferrier, Francis. *Un oratorien ami de Descartes, Guillaume Gibieuf et sa philosophie de la liberté*, Paris: Vrin, 1979.

Frankfurt, Harry G. "Descartes's Validation of Reason," in *René Descartes: Critical Assessments*, ed. Georges J.D. Moyal, London and New York: Routledge, 1991.

Frankfurt, Harry G. "Memory and the Cartesian Circle," *Philosophical Review* 71 (1962), 504–511.

Frege, Gottlob. *Foundations of Arithmetic*, English trans. J.L. Austin, Evanston, IL: Northwestern U. Press, 1980.

Fried, Charles. *Contract as Promise. A Theory of Contractual Obligation*, Cambridge, MA: Harvard U. Press, 1981.

Gaukroger, Stephen. *Descartes: an Intellectual Biography*, Oxford: Clarendon Press, 1995.

Gilson, Étienne. *Etudes sur le rôle de la pensée médiévale dans la formation du suystème cartésien*, 4th ed., Paris: Vrin, 1975.

Gilson, Étienne. *La liberté chez Descartes*, Paris: Félix Alcan, 1913.

Gleason, S.J., Robert. *The Spiritual Exercises of St. Ignatius*, New York: Doubleday, 1964.

Gonthier, Thierry *Descartes et la Causa Sui*, Paris: Vrin, 2005.

Hatfield, Gary. "Reason, Nature, and God in Descartes," in *Essays on the Philosophy and Science of René Descartes*, ed. Stephen Voss (New York and Oxford: Oxford U. Press, 1993), pp. 259–287.

Jackson, Frank. "Weakness of the Will," *Mind* XCIII (1984).

Kors, A.C. *Atheism in France, 1650–1729*, Princeton: Princeton U. Press, 1990.

Lamy, Bernard. *Entretiens sur les Sciences*, eds. F. Girbal et P. Clair, Paris: PUF, 1966.

Larmore, Charles. "Scepticism," in *The Cambridge History of XVIIth century philosophy*, Cambridge, UK: Cambridge U. Press, 1998.

Macpherson, C.B. *The Political Theory of Possessive Individualism*, Oxford: Oxford U. Press, 1962.

Marion, Jean-Luc. *Étant donné*, Paris: PUF, 1998.

Marion, Jean-Luc. *La théologie blanche de Descartes*, Paris: PUF, 1981.

Markie, Peter. "The Cogito and its Importance," in John Cottingham, ed., *The Cambridge Companion to Descartes*, Cambridge, UK: Cambridge U. Press, 1992.

Meissner, S.J., W.W. "Spiritual Exercises," in *Psyche and Spirit* (Lanham, MD: U. Press of America, 2003), 139–140.

Meyjes, G.H.M. Posthumus, "Hugo Grotius as an irenicist," in *The World of Hugo Grotius*, Proceedings of the International Colloquium organized by the Grotius Committee, Rotterdam, 6–9 April 1983 (Amsterdam and Maarssen: Holland U. Press, 1984), 43–63.

Nédoncelle, Maurice. *Trois Aspects du problème anglo-catholique au XVIIe siècle*, Strasbourg: Bloud et Gay, 1951.

Ofstad, Harold. *An Inquiry into the Freedom of Decision*, Oslo and London: Norwegian U. Press and George Allen and Unwin Ltd., 1961.

Rodis-Lewis, Geneviève. *Descartes*, Paris: Calmann-Lévy, 1995.

Persons, Robert. *First Booke of the Christian Exercise, Appertayning to Resolution*, in *The Christian Directory (1582)*, ed. Victor Houliston, Leiden: Brill, 1998.

Rorty, Amélie Oksenberg, ed. *Essays on Descartes's Meditations*, Berkeley: U. of California Press, 1986.

Sales, François de. *Traité de l'Amour de Dieu*, in *Oeuvres Complètes*, ed. Pléiade.

Scupoli, L. *Spiritual Combat*, revised translation by William Lester and Robert Mohan, New York: Paulist Press, 1978.

Searle, John. *Intentionality*, Cambridge, UK: Cambridge U. Press, 1983.

Sylla, Edith. "Medieval Concepts of the Latitude of forms: the Oxford calculators," *Archives d'histoire doctrinale et littéraire du moyen-age* 40 (1973), 223–283.

Vinci, Thomas. *Cartesian Truth*, Oxford: Oxford U. Press, 1998.

Walker, Arthur. "The Problem of Weakness of Will," *Noûs* 23 (1989).

Weber, Jean-Paul. *La Constitution du texte des Regulae*, Paris: PUF, 1964.

Williams, Bernard. *Descartes: the Project of Pure Enquiry*, Hassock, Sussex: Harvester, 1978.

INDEX

BRILL'S STUDIES
IN
INTELLECTUAL HISTORY

Edited by A.J. Vanderjagt

79. BINKLEY, P. (ed.). *Pre-Modern Encyclopaedic Texts*. 1997. ISBN 90 04 10830 0
80. KLAVER, J.M.I. *Geology and Religious Sentiment*. The Effect of Geological Discoveries on English Society and Literature between 1829 and 1859. 1997. ISBN 90 04 10882 3
81. INGLIS, J. *Spheres of Philosophical Inquiry and the Historiography of Medieval Philosophy*. 1998. ISBN 90 04 10843 2
82. McCALLA, A. *A Romantic Historiosophy*. The Philosophy of History of Pierre-Simon Ballanche. 1998. ISBN 90 04 10967 6
83. VEENSTRA, J.R. *Magic and Divination at the Courts of Burgundy and France*. Text and Context of Laurens Pignon's *Contre les devineurs* (1411). 1998. ISBN 90 04 10925 0
84. WESTERMAN, P.C. *The Disintegration of Natural Law Theory*. Aquinas to Finnis. 1998. ISBN 90 04 10999 4
85. GOUWENS, K. *Remembering the Renaissance*. Humanist Narratives of the Sack of Rome. 1998. ISBN 90 04 10969 2
86. SCHOTT, H. & J. ZINGUER (Hrsg.). *Paracelsus und seine internationale Rezeption in der frühen Neuzeit*. Beiträge zur Geschichte des Paracelsismus. 1998. ISBN 90 04 10974 9
87. ÅKERMAN, S. *Rose Cross over the Baltic*. The Spread of Rosicrucianism in Northern Europe. 1998. ISBN 90 04 11030 5
88. DICKSON, D.R. *The Tessera of Antilia*. Utopian Brotherhoods & Secret Societies in the Early Seventeenth Century. 1998. ISBN 90 04 11032 1
89. NOUHUYS, T. VAN. *The Two-Faced Janus*. The Comets of 1577 and 1618 and the Decline of the Aristotelian World View in the Netherlands. 1998. ISBN 90 04 11204 9
90. MUESSIG, C. (ed.). *Medieval Monastic Preaching*. 1998. ISBN 90 04 10883 1
91. FORCE, J.E. & D.S. KATZ (eds.). *"Everything Connects": In Conference with Richard H. Popkin*. Essays in His Honor. 1999. ISBN 90 04 110984
92. DEKKER, K. *The Origins of Old Germanic Studies in the Low Countries*. 1999. ISBN 90 04 11031 3
93. ROUHI, L. *Mediation and Love*. A Study of the Medieval Go-Between in Key Romance and Near-Eastern Texts. 1999. ISBN 90 04 11268 5
94. AKKERMAN, F., A. VANDERJAGT & A. VAN DER LAAN (eds.). *Northern Humanism between 1469 and 1625*. 1999. ISBN 90 04 11314 2
95. TRUMAN, R.W. *Spanish Treatises on Government, Society and Religion in the Time of Philip II*. The 'de regimine principum' and Associated Traditions. 1999. ISBN 90 04 11379 7
96. NAUTA, L. & A. VANDERJAGT (eds.) *Demonstration and Imagination*. Essays in the History of Science and Philosophy Presented to John D. North. 1999. ISBN 90 04 11468 8
97. BRYSON, D. *Queen Jeanne and the Promised Land*. Dynasty, Homeland, Religion and Violence in Sixteenth-Century France. 1999. ISBN 90 04 11378 9
98. GOUDRIAAN, A. *Philosophische Gotteserkenntnis bei Suárez und Descartes im Zusammenhang mit der niederländischen reformierten Theologie und Philosophie des 17. Jahrhunderts*. 1999. ISBN 90 04 11627 3
99. HEITSCH, D.B. *Practising Reform in Montaigne's Essais*. 2000. ISBN 90 04 11630 3
100. KARDAUN, M. & J. SPRUYT (eds.). *The Winged Chariot*. Collected Essays on Plato and Platonism in Honour of L.M. de Rijk. 2000. ISBN 90 04 11480 7
101. WHITMAN, J. (ed.), *Interpretation and Allegory:* Antiquity to the Modern Period. 2000. ISBN 90 04 11039 9
102. JACQUETTE, D., *David Hume's Critique of Infinity*. 2000. ISBN 90 04 11649 4
103. BUNGE, W. VAN. *From Stevin to Spinoza*. An Essay on Philosophy in the Seventeenth-Century Dutch Republic. 2001. ISBN 90 04 12217 6
104. GIANOTTI, T., *Al-Ghazālī's Unspeakable Doctrine of the Soul*. Unveiling the Esoteric Psychology and Eschatology of the Iḥyā. 2001. ISBN 90 04 12083 1
105. SAYGIN, S., *Humphrey, Duke of Gloucester (1390-1447) and the Italian Humanists*. 2002. ISBN 90 04 12015 7
106. BEJCZY, I., *Erasmus and the Middle Ages*. The Historical Consciousness of a Christian Humanist. 2001. ISBN 90 04 12218 4
107. BRANN, N.L. *The Debate over the Origin of Genius during the Italian Renaissance*. The Theories of Supernatural Frenzy and Natural Melancholy in Accord and in Conflict

on the Threshold of the Scientific Revolution. 2002. ISBN 90 04 12362 8

108. ALLEN, M.J.B. & V. REES with M. DAVIES. (eds.), *Marsilio Ficino: His Theology, His Philosophy, His Legacy*. 2002. ISBN 90 04 11855 1

109. SANDY, G., *The Classical Heritage in France*. 2002. ISBN 90 04 11916 7

110. SCHUCHARD, M.K., *Restoring the Temple of Vision*. Cabalistic Freemasonry and Stuart Culture. 2002. ISBN 90 04 12489 6

111. EIJNATTEN, J. VAN. *Liberty and Concord in the United Provinces*. Religious Toleration and the Public in the Eighteenth-Century Netherlands. 2003. ISBN 90 04 12843 3

112. BOS, A.P. *The Soul and Its Instrumental Body*. A Reinterpretation of Aristotle's Philosophy of Living Nature. 2003. ISBN 90 04 13016 0

113. LAURSEN, J.C. & J. VAN DER ZANDE (eds.). *Early French and German Defenses of Liberty of the Press*. Elie Luzac's *Essay on Freedom of Expression* (1749) and Carl Friedrich Bahrdt's *On Liberty of the Press and its Limits* (1787) *in English Translation*. 2003. ISBN 90 04 13017 9

114. POTT, S., M. MULSOW & L. DANNEBERG (eds.). *The Berlin Refuge 1680-1780*. Learning and Science in European Context. 2003. ISBN 90 04 12561 2

115. GERSH, S. & B. ROEST (eds.). *Medieval and Renaissance Humanism*. Rhetoric, Representation and Reform. 2003. ISBN 90 04 13274 0

116. LENNON, T.M. (ed.). *Cartesian Views*. Papers presented to Richard A. Watson. 2003. ISBN 90 04 13299 6

117. VON MARTELS, Z. & A. VANDERJAGT (eds.). *Pius II – 'El Più Expeditivo Pontefice'*. Selected Studies on Aeneas Silvius Piccolomini (1405-1464). 2003. ISBN 90 04 13190 6

118. GOSMAN, M., A. MACDONALD & A. VANDERJAGT (eds.). *Princes and Princely Culture 1450–1650*. Volume One. 2003. ISBN 90 04 13572 3

119. LEHRICH, C.I. *The Language of Demons and Angels*. Cornelius Agrippa's Occult Philosophy. 2003. ISBN 90 04 13574 X

120. BUNGE, W. VAN (ed.). *The Early Enlightenment in the Dutch Republic, 1650–1750*. Selected Papers of a Conference held at the Herzog August Bibliothek, Wolfenbüttel 22–23 March 2001. 2003. ISBN 90 04 13587 1

121. ROMBURGH, S. VAN, "*For My Worthy Freind Mr Franciscus Junius.*" An Edition of the Correspondence of Francis Junius F.F. (1591-1677). 2004. ISBN 90 04 12880 8

122. MULSOW, M. & R.H. POPKIN (eds.). *Secret Conversions to Judaism in Early Modern Europe*. 2004. ISBN 90 04 12883 2

123. GOUDRIAAN, K., J. VAN MOOLENBROEK & A. TERVOORT (eds.). *Education and Learning in the Netherlands, 1400-1600*. 2004. ISBN 90 04 13644 4

124. PETRINA, A. *Cultural Politics in Fifteenth-Century England: The Case of Humphrey, Duke of Gloucester*. 2004. ISBN 90 04 13713 0

125. SCHUURMAN, P. *Ideas, Mental Faculties and Method*. The Logic of Ideas of Descartes and Locke and Its Reception in the Dutch Republic, 1630–1750. 2004. ISBN 90 04 13716 5

126. BOCKEN, I. *Conflict and Reconciliation: Perspectives on Nicholas of Cusa*. 2004. ISBN 90 04 13826 9

127. OTTEN, W. *From Paradise to Paradigm*. A Study of Twelfth-Century Humanism. 2004. ISBN 90 04 14061 1

128. VISSER, A.S.Q. *Joannes Sambucus and the Learned Image*. The Use of the Emblem in Late-Renaissance Humanism. 2005. ISBN 90 04 13866 8

129. MOOIJ, J.J.A. *Time and Mind*. History of a Philosophical Problem. 2005. ISBN 90 04 14152 9

130. BEJCZY, I.P. & R.G. NEWHAUSER (eds.). *Virtue and Ethics in the Twelfth Century*. 2005. ISBN 90 04 14327 0

131. FISHER, S. *Pierre Gassendi's Philosophy and Science*. Atomism for Empiricists. 2005. ISBN 90 04 11996 5

132. WILSON, S.A. *Virtue Reformed*. Rereading Jonathan Edwards's Ethics. 2005. ISBN 90 04 14300 9

133. KIRCHER, T. *The Poet's Wisdom*. The Humanists, the Church, and the Formation of Philosophy in the Early Renaissance. 2005. ISBN 90 04 14637 7

134. MULSOW, M. & J. ROHLS (eds.). *Socinianism and Arminianism.* Antitrinitarians, Calvinists and Cultural Exchange in Seventeenth-Century Europe. 2005. ISBN 90 04 14715 2

135. RIETBERGEN, P. *Power and Religion in Baroque Rome.* Barberini Cultural Policies. 2006. ISBN 90 04 14893 0

136. CELENZA, C. & K. GOUWENS (eds.). *Humanism and Creativity in the Renaissance.* Essays in Honor of Ronald G. Witt. 2006. ISBN 90 04 14907 4

137. AKKERMAN, F. & P. STEENBAKKERS (eds.). *Spinoza to the Letter.* Studies in Words, Texts and Books. 2005. ISBN 90 04 14946 5

138. FINKELSTEIN, A. *The Grammar of Profit: The Price Revolution in Intellectual Context.* 2006. ISBN 90 04 14958 9

139. ITTERSUM, M.J. VAN. *Profit and Principle.* Hugo Grotius, Natural Rights Theories and the Rise of Dutch Power in the East Indies, 1595-1615. 2006. ISBN 90 04 14979 1

140. KLAVER, J.M.I. *The Apostle of the Flesh: A Critical Life of Charles Kingsley.* 2006. ISBN-13: 978-90-04-15128-4 , ISBN-10: 90-04-15128-1

141. HIRVONEN, V., T.J. HOLOPAINEN & M. TUOMINEN (eds.). *Mind and Modality.* Studies in the History of Philosophy in Honour of Simo Knuuttila. 2006. ISBN-13: 978-90-04-15144-4, ISBN-10: 90-04-15144-3

142. DAVENPORT, A.A. *Descartes's Theory of Action.* 2006. ISBN-13: 978-90-04-15205-2, ISBN-10: 90-04-15205-9